Secrets to Happiness

Uplifting Quotes *for* Everyday Life

Edited by *B. C. Aronson*

GRAMERCY BOOKS

NEW YORK

This 2008 edition is published by Gramercy Books, an imprint of Random House Value Publishing.

Gramercy is a registered trademark and the colophon is a trademark of Random House, Inc.

Random House

New York • Toronto • London • Sydney • Auckland

www.valuebooks.com

A catalog record for this title is available from the Library of Congress.

ISBN: 978-0-517-23088-6

Printed and bound in the United States.

10 9 8 7 6 5 4 3 2 1

Table of Contents

IV. Coping with Life's Little Challenges

V. The Road to Success

VI. Faith, Hope, Charity

VII. Love Ever After

Introduction

I have always tried to maintain a positive outlook and to find the good in each situation, even during the not-so-positive twists and turns my life has taken through the years. That outlook came mainly from my dad, who was one of the "Greatest Generation." Even with a rough start in life, he developed and maintained an upbeat attitude that was hard to miss. He was born in 1920 in northwestern Pennsylvania and, because of the stock market crash of 1929 and the subsequent Great Depression, his family could no longer stay together and he ended up in foster care. He admitted to me that he was not a joy as a foster child, and he was shuttled from family to family. He finally ended up with Schuyler Burch, a single, older gentleman, as his foster parent. Mr. Burch saw through my dad's antics and they got along quite famously; he finally found the happiness that had been eluding him up to that point in his life. Eventually he petitioned to adopt my dad, but back in the 1930s, it was frowned upon for a bachelor to even consider adopting, let alone actually attempt it. However, Schuyler was a pillar of the small community in which he lived, and he was friends with the Orphan's Court judge. He challenged the judge to a game of checkers saying, if he won, he would be allowed to adopt my dad. Needless to say, Schuyler's prowess in checkers won him a son. There was not a tighter father-son bond that could be found anywhere.

World War II soon followed and my dad joined the navy. He served in the Pacific on an Attack Cargo Ship, transporting marines and supplies to battle sites. That is where his positive mental outlook was tested and perfected. He told me of several harrowing times where his ship was attacked by kamikazes and submarines. He also told of terrible weather that they had to steam through while loaded with munitions and he was not sure he would ever see home again. My dad said that he made a vow to himself that if he ever made it through that terrible tour of duty alive, he would never worry again. He had enough fretting to last him a lifetime. And that's what he did. Of course, he had a brief moment or two, especially when his son or daughter acted up, but if major crises arose, he was most even-tempered and able to take on the problem. He was happy with his wife and kids and happy being a respected small businessman, "punching holes in the ground" as a water well driller. He loved to tell jokes, play horseshoes, bowl, and make homemade wine, or "cough syrup" as he called it when he gave a bottle to his minister. We lost him far too early at the age of 61, but, if he has his way, he is right now drilling water wells for the angels and telling them jokes as he works.

What has helped me maintain that outlook was my reading the words of positive thinkers such as Norman Vincent Peale, Dale Carnegie, and Earl Nightingale. Their words of positive encouragement have made such a difference to me as they have to many of you. When you read, "Things are only impossible until they're not," —Jean-Luc Picard, how can you not smile and think "Well, everything is going to be OK after all!" Writer and journalist Norman Cousins is also a favorite of mine. One of his beliefs was that "mind over matter" was very important when it came to illness. That is to say, when someone is suffering from a physical ailment, the mind is very powerful in helping to heal the body. Studies showed in many cases that addressing both mind and body make for quicker and better healing. For example, Mr. Cousins relayed a story about himself in his book, *The Healing Heart*. When he suffered a major heart attack, he felt that he had two options available to him on his way to the hospital in the ambulance. He could either panic or suffer the additional trauma that panic could cause, or he could decide to be as calm as possible, neither giving up nor giving in. How he did that was joking along with the paramedics. If they did not sense panic from him, that assisted them in their taking care of his medical issues. By doing that, Mr. Cousins was sure that he kept a bad situation from getting worse.

Therefore, in keeping with that positive outlook, I am always on the lookout for books, magazine articles, and newspaper items on the subject. Whenever I come across a worthwhile quote, I would cut it out or write it down and keep it in a file folder. Every so often, I thumb through my collection and I am reminded of these words of wisdom. If I really liked an article or quotation, I would share it with friends. This is something that I recommend to everyone who is searching for the secret to happiness. Shared wisdom is the surest way to find the words to inspire you to try harder or to rejoice in the things that you already have in your life.

I have arranged this book by topic so if you are looking for a quote on faith or hope, they will be easy for you to find amongst the thousands that I have included in this volume of quotes. Along with quite a few of my favorite quotes from the folks named above, I have found many others. The list runs the gamut from Socrates and Plato, to Oscar Wilde and Mark Twain, to Elvis Presley, Princess Diana and Ice T. There is a wide range of subjects covered as well; they include life, happiness, success, counting one's blessings, faith, hope, charity and of course, love. While the aim of the book is to be positive and uplifting, there are other passages included with titles such as "Coping with Life's Little Challenges" and "Responding and Reacting." They address the situations that stand in the way of finding happiness and address how one can deal with them and then move on.

I hope you enjoy this collection and I hope you find a quote or two that will brighten your day and guide you along the path to finding the secrets to happiness. In the meantime, keep thinking those positive thoughts!

For my father: Alfred L. Burch

Any man can be a father.
It takes someone special to be a dad.
—AUTHOR UNKNOWN

1. A Harmonious Life

AGE

Old age isn't so bad when you consider the alternative.
—MAURICE CHEVALIER

If youth but knew; if old age could!
—HENRI ESTIENNE

Getting older is an adventure, not a problem.
—ANTONIO PIERRO (110 YRS. OLD)

Youth is a disease from which we all recover.
—DOROTHY FULHEIM

A long life may not be good enough, but a good life is long enough.
—BENJAMIN FRANKLIN

Age demands respect; youth, love.
—MARY WOLLSTONECRAFT

Age is a question of mind over matter. If you
don't mind, it doesn't matter.
—SATCHEL PAIGE

Age cannot wither her, nor custom stale her infinite variety.
—WILLIAM SHAKESPEARE

From Birth to age eighteen, a girl needs good parents. From eighteen
to thirty-five, she needs good looks. From thirty-five to fifty-five, she
needs a good personality. From fifty-five on, she needs good cash.
—SOPHIE TUCKER

In a man's middle years there is scarcely a part of the body
he would hesitate to turn over to the proper authorities.
—E.B. White

When I first went into the movies Lionel Barrymore played my
grandfather. Later he played my father and finally he played my husband.
If he had lived, I'm sure I would have played his mother. That's the way
it is in Hollywood. The men get younger and the women get older.
—Lillian Gish

I think age is a very high price to pay for maturity.
—Tom Stoppard

Longevity is one of the more dubious rewards of virtue.
—Ngaio Marsh

You're never too old to become younger.
—Mae West

Getting old ain't for sissies.
—Bette Davis

How old would you be if you didn't know how old you were?
—Satchel Paige

The older I get, the greater power I seem to have to help the world;
I am like a snowball—the further I am rolled, the more I gain.
—Susan B. Anthony

The years between fifty and seventy are the hardest.
You are always being asked to do things, and yet you
are not decrepit enough to turn them down.
—T.S. Eliot

An old man can't do nothin' for me except to
bring me a message from a young man.
—Jackie "Moms" Mabley

A man is only as old as the woman he feels.
—Groucho Marx

Pleasure is the business of the young, business the pleasure of the old.
—FULKE GREVILLE

You know you're getting old when all the names
in your black book have M.D. after them.
—ARNOLD PALMER

If you resolve to give up smoking, drinking, and loving,
you don't actually live longer; it just seems longer.
—CLEMENT FREUD

Do not regret growing older. It is a privilege denied to many.
—ANON

I'd give all wealth that years have piled, the slow result of life's
decay, to be once more a little child for one bright summer-day.
—LEWIS CARROLL

The older I get, the faster I was.
—CHARLES BARKLEY

It's not how old you are, but how you are old.
—MARIE DRESSLER

To me, old age is always fifteen years older than I am.
—BERNARD M. BARUCH

One of the many things nobody ever tells you about middle
age is that it's such a nice change from being young.
—DOROTHY CANFIELD

At fifty, everyone has the face he deserves.
—GEORGE ORWELL

There's many a good tune played on an old fiddle.
—SAMUEL BUTLER

When I am an old woman I shall wear purple with a red
hat which doesn't go, and doesn't suit me. And I shall

spend my pension on brandy and summer gloves and
satin sandals, and say we've no money for butter.
—Jenny Joseph

We are only young once. That is all society can stand.
—Bob Bowen

The older they get the better they were when they were younger.
—Jim Bouton

It's nice to be here. When you're ninety-nine
years old, it's nice to be anywhere.
—George Burns

As a longtime painter, I carry around snapshots of my favorite
paintings the way other old geezers my age carry around
pictures of their grandkids. Grandchildren are wonderful, but
a good painting can help support you in your old age.
—Red Skelton

I still have a full deck; I just shuffle slower now.
—Anon

Life Begins at Forty.
—Walter B. Pitkin

Though it sounds absurd, it is true to say I felt
younger at sixty than I felt at twenty.
—Ellen Glasgow

The secret of staying young is to live honestly,
eat slowly, and lie about your age.
—Lucille Ball

A new broom sweeps clean, but an old one knows the corners.
—English saying

Age is not a particularly interesting subject. Anyone can
get old. All you have to do is live long enough.
—Groucho Marx

You're in pretty good shape for the shape you are in!
—Dr. Seuss

No matter how old you are, there's always
something good to look forward to.
—Lynn Johnston

Well, you know, it's interesting being fifty, . . . You start to reflect on
your life. And you look back over the years at everything you've ever
done. And, with age, middle age, comes wisdom. But I have to say that
I'm not sure that fifty for me is the same as fifty in people years.
—Kermit the Frog

Millions long for immortality who do not know what to
do with themselves on a rainy Sunday afternoon.
—Susan Ertz

In a dream you are never eighty.
—Anne Sexton

TIME

Time is the wisest counsellor of all.
—Pericles

We are involved in a life that passes understanding:
our highest business is our daily life.
—John Cage

You will never "find" time for anything. If
you want time you must make it.
—Charles Buxton

Seize the Time.
—Bobby Seale

Time is eternity begun.
—James Montgomery

How much time he gains who does not look to see
what his neighbor says or does or thinks.
—Marcus Aurelius

The best way to secure future happiness is to be
as happy as is rightfully possible today.
—Charles W. Eliot

Time is what keeps everything from happening at once.
—Ray Cummings

To fill the hour, that is happiness; to fill the hour, and
leave no crevice for a repentance or an approval.
—Ralph Waldo Emerson

Time and tide wait for no man.
—Robert Greene

When it's three o'clock in New York, it's still 1938 in London.
—Bette Midler

Do you know that disease and death must needs overtake
us, no matter what we are doing? … What do you wish to be
doing when it overtakes you? If you have anything better to
be doing when you are so overtaken, get to work on that.
—Epictetus

The illusion that the times that were are better than
those that are, has probably pervaded all ages.
—Horace Greeley

Time is not a line, but a series of now-points.
—Taisen Deshimaru

Our costliest expenditure is time.
—Theophrastus

One day, with life and heart, is more than time enough to find a world.
—James Russell Lowell

Have patience with all things, but chiefly have patience with yourself.
Do not lose courage in considering your own imperfections, but
instantly set about remedying them—every day begin the task anew.
—Saint Francis de Sales

The secret of my success is that I always
managed to live to fly another day.
—Chuck Yeager

Happiness is produced not so much by great pieces of good fortune
that seldom happen, as by little advantages that occur every day.
—Benjamin Franklin

The past is a foreign country: they do things differently there.
—L.P. Hartley

I expect to pass through life but once. If, therefore, there
can be any kindness I can show, or any good thing I can
do to any fellow human being, let me do it now.
—William Penn

Life, we learn too late, is in the living, in the tissue of every day and hour.
—Stephen Leacock

Be ashamed to die until you have won some victory for humanity.
—Horace Mann

To learn new habits is everything, for it is to reach the
substance of life. Life is but a tissue of habits.
—Henri Frederic Amiel

The most thoroughly wasted of all days is that
on which one has not laughed.
—Nicolas de Chamfort

He who has lived a day has lived an age.
—Jean de La Bruyere

Come what may, time and the hour runs through the roughest day.
—William Shakespeare

The best way to secure future happiness is to be
as happy as is rightfully possible today.
—Charles W. Eliot

At any rate, you can bear it for a quarter of an hour!
—Theodore Haecker

Nothing in business is so valuable as time.
—John H. Patterson

Habits are safer than rules; you don't have to watch them.
And you don't have to keep them, either; they keep you.
—Dr. Frank Crane

If we only knew the real value of a day.
—Joseph Farrell

Many people take no care of their money till they come nearly
to the end of it, and others do just the same with their time.
—Johann von Goethe

In order to be utterly happy the only thing necessary is to
refrain from comparing this moment with other moments
in the past, which I often did not fully enjoy because I was
comparing them with other moments of the future.
—André Gide

To sensible men, every day is a day of reckoning.
—John W. Gardner

Live your life each day as you would climb a mountain. An occasional
glance toward the summit keeps the goal in mind, but many
beautiful scenes are to be observed from each new vantage point.
Climb slowly, steadily, enjoying each passing moment; and the view
from the summit will serve as a fitting climax for the journey.
—Harold B. Melchart

Nothing is ours except time.
—Marcus Annaeus Seneca

I look back on my life like a good day's work; it
is done, and I am satisfied with it.
—Grandma Moses

The longest day is soon ended.
—Pliny, the Younger

They deem me mad because I will not sell my days for gold; and
I deem them mad because they think my days have a price.
—Kahlil Gibran

I have fought a good fight, I have finished my course, I have kept the faith.
—2 Tm. 4:7

Always do one thing less than you think you can do.
—Bernard Baruch

You have not lived a perfect day, even though you have
earned your money, unless you have done something
for someone who will never be able to repay you.
—Ruth Smeltzer

Gather ye rose-buds while ye may,
Old time is still a-flying.
And this same flower that smiles today, Tomorrow will be dying.
—Henry David Thoreau

He who allows his day to pass by without practicing
generosity and enjoying life's pleasures is like a
blacksmith's bellows; he breathes, but does not live.
—Sanskrit proverb

Nothing in business is so valuable as time.
—John H. Patterson

To learn new habits is everything, for it is to reach the
substance of life. Life is but a tissue of habits.
—Henri Frederic Amiel

The moment we pass out of our habits we lose
all sense of permanency and routine.
—GEORGE MOORE

Know the true value of time; snatch, seize, and enjoy every
moment of it. No idleness, no laziness, no procrastination:
never put off till tomorrow what you can do today.
—LORD CHESTERFIELD

A day's work is a day's work, neither more nor less, and the
man who does it needs a day's sustenance, a night's repose
and due leisure, whether he be painter or ploughman.
—GEORGE BERNARD SHAW

Without the aid of prejudice and custom, I should
not be able to find my way across the room.
—WILLIAM HAZLITT

And that was victory. The freedom to sprawl loosely upon
a city street, heat his coffee and eat a can of beans ... with
no enemy bullets forcing him to toss the can aside while
diving behind another wall for momentary survival.
—DAVID DOUGLAS DUNCAN

A day is a miniature eternity.
—RALPH WALDO EMERSON

It is too bad if you have to do everything upon reflection
and can't do anything from early habit.
—GEORG CHRISTOPH LICHTENBERG

An hour of pain is as long as a day of pleasure.
—ANON

Many people take no care of their money till they come nearly
to the end of it, and others do just the same with their time.
—JOHANN VON GOETHE

Time is
Too slow for those who wait,
Too swift for those who fear,

Too long for those who grieve,
Too short for those who rejoice.
But for those who love, time is not.
—HENRY VAN DYKE

Motivation is what gets you started. Habit is what keeps you going.
—JIM RYUN

Without duty, life is soft and boneless.
—JOSEPH JOUBERT

One realizes the full importance of time only when
there is little of it left. Every man's greatest capital
asset is his unexpired years of productive life.
—PAUL W. LITCHFIELD

Time is nothing absolute; its duration depends
on the rate of thought and feeling.
—JOHN DRAPER

Most of life is routine—dull and grubby, but routine is the mountain
that keeps a man going. If you wait for inspiration you'll be standing
on the corner after the parade is a mile down the street.
—BEN NICHOLAS

Those who make the worst use of their time are
the first to complain of its brevity.
—JEAN DE LA BRUYERE

Time flies like an arrow. Fruit flies like a banana.
—GROUCHO MARX

What we love to do we find time to do.
—JOHN LANCASTER SPALDING

Time is a fluid condition which has no existence except
in the momentary avatars of individual people.
—WILLIAM FAULKNER

Riches are chiefly good because they give us time.
—CHARLES LAMB

Good habits, which bring our lower passions and
appetites under automatic control, leave our natures
free to explore the larger experiences of life.
—RALPH W. SOCKMAN, D.D.

Death accompanies us at every step and enables us to use those
moments when life smiles at us to feel more deeply the sweetness
of life. The more certain the end, the more tempting the minute.
—THEODORE FONTANE

Time is the moving image of eternity.
—PLATO

Time is an avid gambler who has no need to cheat to win every time.
—CHARLES BAUDELAIRE

To do the useful thing, to say the courageous thing, to contemplate
the beautiful thing: that is enough for one man's life.
—T.S. ELIOT

Anyone can carry his burden, however hard, until nightfall. Anyone can
do his work, however hard, for one day. Anyone can live sweetly, patiently,
lovingly, purely, till the sun goes down. And this is all life really means.
—ROBERT LOUIS STEVENSON

Let us savour the swift delights of the most beautiful of our days!
—ALPHONSE DE LAMARTINE

The forty-four-hour week has no charm for
me. I'm looking for a forty-hour day.
—NICHOLAS MURRAY BUTLER

It is only possible to live happily-ever-after on a day-to-day basis.
—MARGARET BONNANO

When a man sits with a pretty girl for an hour, it seems like a minute. But let him sit on a hot stove for a minute, and it's longer than any hour. That's relativity.
—ALBERT EINSTEIN

Time stays long enough for anyone who will use it.
—ANON

Happiness is to be found along the way, not at the end of the road, for then the journey is over and it is too late. Today, this hour, this minute is the day, the hour, the minute for each of us to sense the fact that life is good, with all of its trials and troubles, and perhaps more interesting because of them.
—ROBERT R. UPDEGRAFF

You can't measure time in days the way you can money in dollars, because each day is different.
—PHILLIP HEWETT

Sufficient to each day are the duties to be done and the trials to be endured.
—T.L. GAYLER

Time is a fixed income and, as with any income, the real problem facing most of us is how to live successfully within our daily allotment.
—MARGARET B. JOHNSTONE

Time is the most valuable thing a man can spend.
—THEOPHRASTUS

Each day provides its own gifts.
—MARTIAL

Time is a storm in which we are all lost.
—WILLIAM C. WILLIAMS

We shall never have more time. We have, and have always had, all the time there is. No object is served in waiting until next week or even until tomorrow. Keep going.... Concentrate on something useful.
—ARNOLD BENNETT

Happiness is not a state to arrive at, but a manner of traveling.
—Margaret Lee Runback

Guard well your spare moments. They are like uncut diamonds.
Discard them and their value will never be known. Improve them
and they will become the brightest gems in a useful life.
—Ralph Waldo Emerson

We must use time as a tool, not as a crutch.
—John F. Kennedy

Choose always the way that seems the best, however rough it
may be; custom will soon render it easy and agreeable.
—Pythagoras

The butterfly counts not months but moments, and has time enough.
—Rabindranath Tagore

Time is the tyrant of the body.
—Anon

Do your best every day and your life will gradually
expand into satisfying fullness.
—Horatio W. Dresser

Seize the hour.
—Sophocles

And each man stands with his face in the light of his
own drawn sword. Ready to do what a hero can.
—Elizabeth Barrett Browning

My advice to you is not to inquire why or whither, but
just to enjoy your ice cream while it's on your plate.
—Thornton Wilder

Time is the coin of your life. It is the only coin you have,
and only you can determine how it will be spent. Be
careful lest you let other people spend it for you.
—Carl Sandburg

Those who face that which is actually before them, unburdened by the past, undistracted by the future, these are they who live, who make the best use of their lives; these are those who have found the secret of contentment.
—ALBAN GOODIER

Make use of time, let not advantage slip.
—WILLIAM SHAKESPEARE

Taking time to live is taking time to appreciate simple silence as better than any kind of talk, or watching a flower, or watching a guy wash the windows on a skyscraper and wondering what he is thinking.
—GERSI DOUCHAN

The highest value in life is found in the stewardship of time.
—ROBERT M. FINE

Time is the only critic without ambition.
—JOHN STEINBECK

Man goeth forth unto his work and to his labor until the evening.
—PSALM 104:23

There is a time for work. And a time for love. That leaves no other time.
—COCO CHANEL

Don't let the fear of the time it will take to accomplish something stand in the way of your doing it. The time will pass anyway; we might just as well put that passing time to the best possible use.
—EARL NIGHTINGALE

Every day give yourself a good mental shampoo.
—SARA JORDAN, M.D.

When you rise in the morning, form a resolution to make the day a happy one for a fellow creature.
—SYDNEY SMITH

O, for an engine to keep back all clocks!
—BEN JOHNSON

Habit is stronger than reason.
—GEORGE SANTAYANA

That man is happiest who lives from day to day and asks
no more, garnering the simple goodness of life.
—EURIPIDES

I come to the office each morning and stay for long hours doing
what has to be done to the best of my ability. And when you've
done the best you can, you can't do any better. So when I go
to sleep I turn everything over to the Lord and forget it.
—HARRY S TRUMAN

Time is the soul of this world.
—PLUTARCH

The value of life lies not in the length of days, but in the use
we make of them; a man may live long yet live very little.
—MICHEL DE MONTAIGNE

Let me tell thee, time is a very precious gift of God; so
precious that it's only given to us moment by moment.
—AMELIA BARR

Reality is a staircase going neither up nor down, we
don't move; today is today, always is today.
—OCTAVIO PAZ

Time is the one thing that can never be retrieved.
—C.R. LAWTON

All my possessions for a moment of time.
—QUEEN ELIZABETH I

He who would make serious use of his life must always
act as though he had a long time to live and schedule
his time as though he were about to die.
—EMILE LITTRE

It's fun to get together and have something good to eat at least
once a day. That's what human life is all about—enjoying things.
—JULIA CHILD

Time is the product of changing realities, beings, existences.
—NICHOLAS BERDYAEV

Some days you tame the tiger. And some days the tiger has you for lunch.
—TUG MCGRAW

It is not in novelty but in habit that we find the greatest pleasure.
—RAYMOND RADIGUET

It is nonsense to say there is not enough time to be fully informed....
Time given to thought is the greatest timesaver of all.
—NORMAN COUSINS

Come, let us give a little time to folly ... and even in a
melancholy day let us find time for an hour of pleasure.
—SAINT BONAVENTURA

We all find time to do what we really want to do.
—WILLIAM FEATHER

If a person gives you his time, he can give you no more precious gift.
—FRANK TYGER

A sense of the value of time ... is an essential preliminary to
efficient work; it is the only method of avoiding hurry.
—ARNOLD BENNETT

There is time for everything.
—THOMAS A. EDISON

Habit is not mere subjugation, it is a tender tie; when one
remembers habit it seems to have been happiness.
—ELIZABETH BOWEN

Write it on your heart that every day is the best day in the year.
—RALPH WALDO EMERSON

Present joys are more to flesh and blood
Than the dull prospect of a distant good.
—JOHN DRYDEN

There is nothing good in this world which time does not improve.
—ALEXANDER SMITH

You may delay, but time will not.
—BENJAMIN FRANKLIN

As every thread of gold is valuable, so is every moment of time.
—JOHN MASON

The laboring man and the artificer knows what every hour of
his time is worth, and parts not with it but for the full value.
—LORD CLARENDON

Minutes are worth more than money. Spend them wisely.
—THOMAS P. MURPHY

O Time! Arrest your flight, and you, propitious hours, stay your couse.
—ALPHONSE DE LAMARTINE

The highest value in life is found in the stewardship of time.
—ROBERT M. FINE

Time is the devourer of everything.
—OVID

Time isn't a commodity, something you pass around like cake.
Time is the substance of life. When anyone asks you to give
your time, they're really asking for a chunk of your life.
—ANTOINETTE BOSCO

The less one has to do, the less time one finds to do it in. One yawns,
one procrastinates, one can do it when one will, and, therefore, one
seldom does it at all; whereas those who have a great deal of business
must buckle to it; and then they always find time enough to do it.
—LORD CHESTERFIELD

Pick my left pocket of its silver dime, but spare
the right—it holds my golden time!
—OLIVER WENDELL HOLMES

No matter what looms ahead, if you can eat today, enjoy the sunlight
today, mix good cheer with friends today, enjoy it and bless God for it.
—HENRY WARD BEECHER

Love and time—those are the only two things in all the world
and all of life that cannot be bought, but only spent.
—GARY JENNINGS

We work not only to produce, but to give value to time.
—EUGENE DELACROIX

Time is the most valuable thing a man can spend.
—LAERTIUS DIOGENES

There are hundreds of tasks we feel we must accomplish in
the day, but if we do not take them one at a time . . . we are
bound to break our own physical or mental structure.
—TED BENGERMINO

Make the most of today. Translate your good intentions into actual deeds.
—GRENVILLE KLEISER

To look up and not down,
To look forward and not back,
To look out and not in, and
To lend a hand.
—EDWARD EVERETT HALE

The most important thing in our lives is what we are doing now.
—ANON

So get a few laughs and do the best you can.
—WILL ROGERS

You may ask me for anything you like except time.
—NAPOLEON BONAPARTE

What a man accomplishes in a day depends upon the way
in which he approaches his tasks. When we accept tough
jobs as a challenge to our ability and wade into them
with joy and enthusiasm, miracles can happen.
—ARLAND GILBERT

Do all the good you can,
By all the means you can,
In all the ways you can,
In all the places you can,
At all the times you can.
—ANON

Do what you can, with what you have, where you are.
—THEODORE ROOSEVELT

So teach us to number our days, that we may
apply our hearts unto wisdom.
—Ps. 90:12

Time is the arbitrary division of eternity.
—ANON

To accomplish our destiny . . . [w]e must cover before
nightfall the distance assigned to each of us.
—DR. ALEXIS CARREL

The ideal never comes. Today is ideal for him who makes it so.
—HORATIO W. DRESSER

Each day, and the living of it, has to be a conscious creation in which
discipline and order are relieved with some play and pure foolishness.
—MAY SARTON

True wisdom lies in gathering the precious
things out of each day as it goes by.
—E.S. BOUTON

We cannot do everything at once, but we can do something at once.
—CALVIN COOLIDGE

Follow your bliss.
—JOSEPH CAMPBELL

Do each daily task the best we can; act as though the
eye of opportunity were always upon us.
—WILLIAM FEATHER

It is no easy thing for a principle to become a man's own unless
each day he maintains it and works it out in his life.
—EPICTETUS

If you are not happy here and now, you never will be.
—TAISEN DESHIMARU

That man is blest who does his best and leaves the rest.
—CHARLES F. DEEMS

Showing up is eighty percent of life.
—WOODY ALLEN

I like the man who faces what he must,
With steps triumphant and a heart of cheer;
Who fights the daily battle without fear.
—SARAH KNOWLES BOLTON

People who postpone happiness are like children who try chasing
rainbows in an effort to find the pot of gold at the rainbow's end.... Your
life will never be fulfilled until you are happy here and now.
—KEN KEYES, JR.

Any man's life will be filled with constant and unexpected
encouragement if he makes up his mind to do his level best each day.
—BOOKER T. WASHINGTON

You have got to own your days and live them, each
one of them, every one of them, or else the years go
right by and none of them belong to you.
—HERB GARDNER

There is no other solution to man's progress but the
day's honest work, the day's honest decisions, the day's
generous utterances and the day's good deed.
—CLARE BOOTHE LUCE

If you always do what interests you, at least one person is pleased.
—KATHARINE HEPBURN'S MOTHER, KATHARINE HOUGHTON HEPBURN

A man should hear a little music, read a little poetry, and see a fine
picture every day of his life, in order that worldly cares may not obliterate
the sense of the beautiful which God has implanted in the human soul.
—JOHANN VON GOETHE

If we cannot meet our everyday surroundings with equanimity and
pleasure and grow each day in some useful direction, then . . . life
is on the road toward misfortune, misery and destruction.
—LUTHER BURBANK

Resolve to edge in a little reading every day, if it is but
a single sentence. If you gain fifteen minutes a day,
it will make itself felt at the end of the year.
—HORACE MANN

Live mindful of how brief your life is.
—HORACE

I work every day—or at least I force myself into my office or
room. I may get nothing done, but you don't earn bonuses
without putting in time. Nothing may come for three
months, but you don't get the fourth without it.
—MORDECAI RICHLER

Add each day something to fortify you against poverty and death.
—MARCUS ANNAEUS SENECA

Realize life as an end in itself. Functioning is all there is.
—OLIVER WENDELL HOLMES, JR.

Each day can be one of triumph if you keep up your interests.
—GEORGE MATTHEW ADAMS

Gladly accept the gifts of the present hour.
—Horace

Every minute of life carries with it its miraculous
value, and its face of eternal youth.
—Albert Camus

There is time enough for everything in the course of the
day if you do but one thing at once; but there is not time
enough in the year if you will do two things at a time.
—Lord Chesterfield

Each day, each hour, an entire life.
—Juan Ramon Jimenel

When action grows unprofitable, gather information;
when information grows unprofitable, sleep.
—Ursula K. LeGuin

Character is simply habit long enough continued.
—Plutarch

Much may be done in those little shreds and patches of time
which every day produces, and which most men throw away.
—Charles Caleb Colton

Time is the relationship between events.
—Yakima Indian Nation

Learn to use ten minutes intelligently. It will pay you huge dividends.
—William A. Irwin

We work not only to produce, but to give value to time.
—Eugene Delacroix

Nothing is more powerful than habit.
—Ovid

Time cannot be expanded, accumulated,
mortgaged, hastened, or retarded.
—Anon

An earnest purpose finds time, or makes it. It seizes on spare
moments, and turns fragments to golden account.
—WILLIAM ELLERY CHANNING

Have a time and place for everything, and do everything in its
time and place, and you will not only accomplish more, but
have far more leisure than those who are always hurrying.
—TYRON EDWARDS

I recommend you to take care of the minutes, for
the hours will take care of themselves.
—LORD CHESTERFIELD

He who does not get fun and enjoyment out of
every day ... needs to reorganize his life.
—GEORGE MATTHEW ADAMS

Act well at the moment, and you have performed
a good action to all eternity.
—JOHANN KASPAR LAVATER

Seize time by the forelock.
—PITTACUS OF MITYLENE

The real secret of how to use time is to pack it as you would a
portmanteau, filling up the small spaces with small things.
—SIR HENRY HADDOW

We should consider every day lost on which
we have not danced at least once.
—FRIEDRICH NIETZSCHE

Life is now ... this day, this hour ... and is probably
the only experience of the kind one is to have.
—CHARLES MACOMB FLANDRAU

What you are afraid to do is a clear indicator
of the next thing you need to do.
—ANON

The great rule of moral conduct is, next to God, to respect Time.
—JOHANN KASPAR LAVATER

One must learn a different . . . sense of time, one that
depends more on small amounts than big ones.
—Sister Mary Paul

It is the time you have wasted for your rose
that makes your rose so important.
—Antoine de Saint-Exupery

The ability to concentrate and to use time well is everything.
—Lee Iacocca

The organized person . . . makes the most of his time and goes to
his bed for the night perfectly relaxed for rest and renewal.
—George Matthew Adams

He's one of those Christmas Eve guys. There are people
like that . . . every day in their lives is Christmas Eve.
—Joe Garagiola, talking about Yogi Berri

During a very busy life I have often been asked, "How did you manage to
it all?" The answer is very simple: it is because I did everything promptly.
—Sir Richard Tangye

He is only rich who owns the day. There is no king, rich man,
fairy, or demon who possesses such power as that.
—Ralph Waldo Emerson

Time is an equal opportunity employer. Each human being has
exactly the same number of hours and minutes every day. Rich
people can't buy more hours. Scientists can't invent new minutes.
And you can't save time to spend it on another day. Even so, time
is amazingly fair and forgiving. No matter how much time you've
wasted in the past, you still have an entire tomorrow. Success
depends upon using it wisely—by planning and setting priorities.
—Denis Waitely

It is better to do the most trifling thing in the world
than to regard half an hour as trifle.
—Johann von Goethe

If I had my life to live over, I would start barefoot earlier in the spring and stay that way later in the fall. I would go to more dances. I would ride more merry-go-rounds. I would pick more daisies.
—NADINE STAIR

The proper function of man is to live, not to exist. I shall not waste my days in trying to prolong them.
—JACK LONDON

Love, and do what you like.
—SAINT AUGUSTINE

Don't be fooled by the calendar. There are only as many days in the year as you make use of. One man gets only a week's value out of a year while another man gets a full year's value out of a week.
—CHARLES RICHARDS

Timely service, like timely gifts, is doubled in value.
—GEORGE MACDONALD

I must govern the clock, not be governed by it.
—GOLDA MEIR

A day, an hour, of virtuous liberty is worth a whole eternity in bondage.
—JOSEPH ADDISON

Most of us spend our lives as if we had another one in the bank.
—BEN IRWIN

No objects of value . . . are worth risking the priceless experience of waking up one more day.
—JACK SMITH

Nothing determines who we will become so much as those things we choose to ignore.
—SANDOR MINAB

While we live, let us live.
—D.H. LAWRENCE

Our grand business undoubtedly is not to see what lies
dimly at a distance but to do what lies clearly at hand.
—THOMAS CARLYLE

If we only knew the real value of a day.
—JOSEPH FARRELL

Every possession and every happiness is but lent by chance for an
uncertain time, and may therefore be demanded back the next hour.
—ARTHUR SCHOPENHAUER

My formula for living is quite simple. I get up in the morning and
I go to bed at night. In between I occupy myself as best I can.
—CARY GRANT

The days come and go like muffled and veiled figures sent from
a distant friendly party, but they say nothing, and if we do not
use the gifts they bring, they carry them as silently away.
—RALPH WALDO EMERSON

It isn't hard to be good from time to time in sports.
What's tough is being good every day.
—WILLIE MAYS

Take the time to come home to yourself everyday.
—ROBIN CASARJEAN

Time is a part of eternity, and of the same piece with it.
—MOSES MENDELSSOHN

Your daily life is your temple and your religion.
—KAHLIL GIBRAN

The great business of life is to be, to do, to do without, and to depart.
—JOHN, VISCOUNT MORLEY OF BLACKBURN

Every day is a messenger of God.
—RUSSIAN PROVERB

Make it a point to do something every day that you
don't want to do. This is the golden rule for acquiring
the habit of doing your duty without pain.
—MARK TWAIN

Unless each day can be looked back upon by an
individual as one in which he has had some fun, some
joy, some real satisfaction, that day is a loss.
—ANON

Know what you want to do, hold the thought firmly,
and do every day what should be done, and every
sunset will see you that much nearer the goal.
—ELBERT HUBBARD

He who has lived a day has lived an age.
—JEAN DE LA BRUYERE

I've been on a calendar, but never on time.
—MARILYN MONROE

I finally figured out the only reason to be alive is to enjoy it.
—RITA MAE BROWN

Life, we learn too late, is in the living, in the tissue of every day and hour.
—STEPHEN LEACOCK

A little space of time before time expires; a little way of breath.
—ALGERNON SWINBURNE

Time is a sandpile we run our fingers in.
—CARL SANDBURG

Time is a kind friend, he will make us old.
—SARA TEASDALE

He possesses dominion over himself, and is happy, who can every day
say, "I have lived." Tomorrow the heavenly Father may either involve
the world in dark clouds, or cheer it with clear sunshine; he will not,
however, render ineffectual the things which have already taken place.
—HORACE

It's better to be a lion for a day than a sheep all your life.
—Sister Elizabeth Kenny

Each day is a little life; every waking and rising a little birth; every fresh morning a little youth; every going to rest and sleep a little death.
—Arthur Schopenhauer

THIS DAY

So often we rob tomorrow's memories by today's economies.
—John Mason Brown

We can see well into the past; we can guess shrewdly in to the future; but that which is rolled up and muffled in impenetrable folds is today.
—Ralph Waldo Emerson

You had better live your best and act your best and think your best today; for today is the sure preparation for tomorrow and all the other tomorrows that follow.
—Harriet Martineau

And what is so rare as a day in June? Then, if ever, come perfect days.
—James Russell Lowell

With the past, I have nothing to do; nor with the future. I live now.
—Ralph Waldo Emerson

Be satisfied, and pleased with what thou art,
Act cheerfully and well thy allotted part;
Enjoy the present hour, be thankful for the past,
And neither fear, nor wish, the approaches of the last.
—Martial

Go within every day and find the inner strength so that the world will not blow your candle out.
—Katherine Dunham

Happy the man, and happy he alone
He can call today his own.
He who, secure within can say,
"Tomorrow, do thy worst, for I have lived today."
—HENRY FIELDING

The present contains all that there is. It is holy
ground; for it is the past, and it is the future.
—ALFRED NORTH WHITEHEAD

Children have neither a past nor a future. Thus they
enjoy the present, which seldom happens to us.
—JEAN DE LA BRUYERE

Today is a new life. Shut the doors on the past and
the future. Live in day-tight compartments.
—DALE CARNEGIE

The past is a bucket of ashes, so live not in your yesterdays,
nor just for tomorrow, but in the here and now.
—CARL SANDBURG

Forget mistakes. Forget failures. Forget everything except what
you're going to do now and do it. Today is your lucky day.
—WILL DURANT

Life is only this place, this time, and these people right here and now.
—VINCENT COLLINS

The present is an eternal now.
—ABRAHAM COWLEY

No mind is much employed upon the present; recollection
and anticipation fill up almost all our moments.
—SAMUEL JOHNSON

I believe that only one person in a thousand knows
the trick of really living in the present.
—STORM JAMESON

It is difficult to live in the present, ridiculous to live in
the future and impossible to live in the past.
—JIM BISHOP

The more I give myself permission to live in the moment and
enjoy it without feeling guilty or judgmental about any other
time, the better I feel about the quality of my work.
—WAYNE DYER

The present is an edifice which God cannot rebuild.
—RALPH WALDO EMERSON

The challenge is in the moment, the time is always now.
—JAMES BALDWIN

The present is the blocks with which we build.
—HENRY W. LONGFELLOW

The future belongs to those who live intensely in the present.
—ANON

We want to live in the present, and the only history that is
worth a tinker's damn is the history we make today.
—HENRY FORD

Today is the blocks with which we build.
—HENRY WADSWORTH LONGFELLOW

The present is elastic to embrace infinity.
—LOUIS ANSPACHER

The present is the symbol and vehicle of the future.
—JOSEPH MCSORELY

Live now, believe me, wait not till tomorrow, gather the roses of life today.
—PIERRE DE RONSARD

The present is all you have for your certain possession.
—ANON

We are here and it is now. Further than that, all knowledge is moonshine.
—H.L. MENCKEN

If we are ever to enjoy life, now is the time, not tomorrow or next year.... Today should always be our most wonderful day.
—THOMAS DREIER

He who lives in the present lives in eternity.
—LUDWIG WITTGENSTEIN

Take in the ideas of the day, drain off those of yesterday. As to the morrow, time enough to consider it when it becomes today.
—EDWARD BULWER-LYTTON

I have everything I need to enjoy my here and now—unless I am letting my consciousness be dominated by demands and expectations based on the dead past or the imagined future.
—KEN KEYES, JR.

The cares of today are seldom those of tomorrow.
—WILLIAM COWPER

One realm we have never conquered: the pure present.
—D.H. LAWRENCE

Yesterday is a cancelled check; tomorrow is a promissory note; today is the only cash you have—so spend it wisely.
—KAY LYONS

It is not the weight of the future or the past that is pressing upon you, but ever that of the present alone. Even this burden, too, can be lessened if you confine it strictly to its own limits.
—MARCUS AURELIUS

I am in the present. I cannot know what tomorrow will bring forth. I can know only what the truth is for me today. That is what I am called upon to serve.
—IGOR STRAVINSKY

Who cares about great marks left behind? We have one life ... Just one. Our life. We have nothing else.
—UGO BETTI

This—the immediate, everyday, and present experience—is IT, the entire and ultimate point for the existence of a universe.
—ALAN WATTS

Few of us ever live in the present, we are forever anticipating what is to come or remembering what has gone.
—LOUIS L'AMOUR

One of these days is none of these days.
—H.G. BOHN

Having spent the better part of my life trying either to relive the past or experience the future before it arrives, I have come to believe that in between these two extremes is peace.
—ANON

Enjoy yourself, drink, call the life you live today your own—but only that; the rest belongs to chance.
—EURIPIDES

This time, like all times, is a very good one if we but know what to do with it.
—RALPH WALDO EMERSON

The time is always right to do what is right.
—MARTIN LUTHER KING, JR.

To those leaning on the sustaining infinite, today is big with blessings.
—MARY BAKER EDDY

The present is all the ready money Fate can give.
—ABRAHAM COWLEY

The here-and-now is no mere filling of time, but a filling of time with God.
—JOHN FOSTER

If you have one eye on yesterday, and one eye on tomorrow, you're going to be cockeyed today.
—ANON

In the present, every day is a miracle.
—JAMES GOULD COZZENS

Look lovingly upon the present, for it holds the
only things that are forever true.
—*A COURSE IN MIRACLES*

Let us live today.
—J.C.F. VON SCHILLER

Work accomplished means little. It is in the past. What
we all want is the glorious and living present.
—SHERWOOD ANDERSON

I just take one day. Yesterday is gone. Tomorrow has
not come. We have only today to love Jesus.
—MOTHER TERESA

Patterns of the past echo in the present and resound through the future.
—DHYANI YWAHOO

The present offers itself to our touch for only an
instant of time and then eludes the senses.
—PLUTARCH

Do not look back on happiness, or dream of it in the future. You
are only sure of today; do not let yourself be cheated out of it.
—HENRY WARD BEECHER

It is now, and in this world, that we must live.
—ANDRÉ GIDE

Look well to this day, for it is life, the very life of life.
In it lies all the realities and verities of existence: the bliss of growth,
the glory of action, spendor of beauty. For yesterday is but a dream,
and tomorrow only a vision. But today well lived makes
every yesterday a dream of happiness and every tomorrow
a vision of hope. Look well, therefore, to this day, for it and
it alone is life! Such is the salutation of the dawn.
—*THE SANSKRIT*

I am not afraid of tomorrow, for I have seen yesterday and I love today.
—WILLIAM ALLEN WHITE

The past, the present and the future are really one: they are today.
—HARRIET BEECHER STOWE

Yesterday is ashes; tomorrow wood. Only
today does the fire burn brightly.
—OLD ESKIMO PROVERB

We can easily manage if we will only take, each day, the burden
appointed to it. But the load will be too heavy for us if we
carry yesterday's burden over again today, and then add the
burden of the morrow before we are required to bear it.
—JOHN NEWTON

Look not mournfully into the past, it comes not back again.
Wisely improve the present, it is thine. Go forth to meet the
shadowy future without fear and with a manly heart.
—HENRY WADSWORTH LONGFELLOW

Everyman's life lies within the present, for the past is
spent and done with, and the future is uncertain.
—MARCUS AURELIUS

The present is the living sum-total of the whole past.
—THOMAS CARLYLE

The flesh endures the storms of the present alone, the
mind those of the past and future as well.
—EPICURUS

The past cannot be regained, although we can learn
from it; the future is not yet ours even though we must
plan for it.... Time is now. We have only today.
—CHARLES HUMMELL

When we have a world of only now, with no shadows of yesterdays
or clouds of tomorrow, then saying what we can do will work.
—GOLDIE IVENER

I can feel guilty about the past, apprehensive about the future, but only in the present can I act. The ability to be in the present moment is a major component of mental wellness.
—ABRAHAM MASLOW

The present, like a note in music, is nothing but as it appertains to what is past and what is to come.
—WALTER SAVAGE LANDOR

Whether it's the best of times or the worst of times, it's the only time we've got.
—ART BUCHWALD

No longer forward nor behind I look in hope or fear; but grateful, take the good I find, the best of now and here.
—JOHN GREENLEAF WHITTIER

I try to learn from the past, but I plan for the future by focusing exclusively on the present. That's where the fun is.
—DONALD TRUMP

There is no present or future, only the past, happening over and over again, now.
—EUGENE O'NEILL

Yesterday has gone. Tomorrow may never come. There is only the miracle of this moment. Savor it. It is a gift.
—ANON

Don't waste today regretting yesterday instead of making a memory for tomorrow.
—LAURA PALMER

I have realized that the past and the future are real illusions, that they exist only in the present, which is what there is and all that there is.
—ALAN WATTS

Defer not till tomorrow to be wise, tomorrow's sun to thee may never rise.
—WILLIAM CONGREVE

Today, well lived, will prepare me for both the
pleasure and the pain of tomorrow.
—Anon

Today is yesterday's effect and tomorrow's cause.
—Phillip Gribble

Now is all we have. Everything that has ever happened to you, and
anything that is ever going to happen to you, is just a thought.
—Wayne Dyer

The secret of health for both mind and body is not to mourn
for the past, not to worry about the future, nor to anticipate
troubles, but to live the present moment wisely and earnestly.
—Buddha

Very few men, properly speaking, live at present,
but are providing to live another time.
—Jonathan Swift

If we open a quarrel between the past and the
present, we shall find we have lost the future.
—Sir Winston Churchill

Real generosity toward the future lies in giving all to the present.
—Albert Camus

Freedom from worries and surcease from strain are
illusions that always inhabit the distance.
—Edwin Way Teale

The idea of "twenty-four-hour living" applies primarily to
the emotional life of the individual. Emotionally speaking,
we must not live in yesterday, nor in tomorrow.
—As Bill Sees It

The present is the now, the here, through
which all future plunges to the past.
—James Joyce

Through loyalty to the past, our mind refuses to realize that tomorrow's
joy is possible only if today's makes way for it; that each wave owes
the beauty of its line only to the withdrawal of the preceding one.
—ANDRÉ GIDE

The present is the necessary product of all the past,
the necessary cause of all the future.
—ROBERT G. INGERSOLL

Tomorrow's life is too late. Live today.
—MARTIAL

When shall we live if not now?
—M.F.K. FISHER

Never put off until tomorrow what you can do today, because
if you enjoy it today, you can do it again, tomorrow.
—ANON

Seize from every moment its unique novelty,
and do not prepare your joys.
—ANDRÉ GIDE

Seize the day, and put the least possible trust in tomorrow.
—HORACE

We cannot put off living until we are ready. The most salient
characteristic of life is its coerciveness: it is always urgent, "here and
now," without any possible postponement. Life is fired at us point-blank.
—JOSÉ ORTEGA Y GASSET

One today is worth two tomorrows.
—BENJAMIN FRANKLIN

Real generosity toward the future lies in giving all to the present.
—ALBERT CAMUS

Why not seize the pleasure at once? How often is happiness
destroyed by preparation, foolish preparation!
—JANE AUSTEN

Freedom from worries and surcease from strain are
illusions that always inhabit the distance.
—EDWIN WAY TEALE

Study as if you were to live forever. Live as if you were to die tomorrow.
—ISIDORE OF SEVILLE

Let me tell thee, time is a very precious gift of God; so
precious that it's only given to us moment by moment.
—AMELIA BARR

Life wastes itself while we are preparing to live.
—RALPH WALDO EMERSON

It is cheap generosity which promises the future
in compensation for the present.
—J.A. SPENDER

You do well to have visions of a better life than of every day, but it is the
life of every day from which the elements of a better life must come.
—MAURICE MAETERLINCK

Who knows if the gods above will add tomorrow's span to this day's sum?
—HORACE

The most effective way to ensure the value of the future is to
confront the present courageously and constructively.
—ROLLO MAY

The span of life is waning fast;
Beware, unthinking youth, beware!
Thy soul's eternity depends
Upon the record moments bear!
—ELIZA COOK

If you spend your whole life waiting for the
storm, you'll never enjoy the sunshine.
—MORRIS WEST

We steal if we touch tomorrow. It is God's.
—HENRY WARD BEECHER

To live only for some future goal is shallow. It's the sides
of the mountain that sustain life, not the top.
—ROBERT M. PIRSIG

Do today's duty, fight today's temptation; do not weaken
and distract yourself by looking forward to things you
cannot see, and could not understand if you saw them.
—CHARLES KINGSLEY

Some people are making such thorough preparation for
rainy days that they aren't enjoying today's sunshine.
—WILLIAM FEATHER

We know nothing of tomorrow; our business
is to be good and happy today.
—SYDNEY SMITH

Present opportunities are neglected, and attainable good is slighted, by
minds busied in extensive ranges and intent upon future advantages.
—SAMUEL JOHNSON

We are always beginning to live, but are never living.
—MANILIUS

The prospect of being pleased tomorrow will never
console me for the boredom of today.
—FRANCOIS DE LA ROCHEFOUCAULD

Fill the unforgiving minute with sixty seconds worth of distance run.
—RUDYARD KIPLING

The habit of looking into the future and thinking that the whole
meaning of the present lies in what it will bring forth is a pernicious one.
There can be no value in the whole unless there is value in the parts.
—BERTRAND RUSSELL

The best preparation for good work tomorrow is to do good work today.
—ELBERT HUBBARD

Very strange is this quality of our human nature which decrees that
unless we feel a future before us we do not live completely in the present.
—PHILLIPS BROOKS

The sole life which a man can lose is that
which he is living at the moment.
—Marcus Aurelius

Today's egg is better than tomorrow's hen.
—Turkish proverb

I always say to myself, what is the most important thing
we can think about at this extraordinary moment.
—Francois de La Rochefoucauld

T'were too absurd to slight for the hereafter, the day's delight!
—Robert Browning

Just do your best today and tomorrow will come ... tomorrow's
going to be a busy day, a happy day.
—Helen Boehm

This—this was what made life: a moment of quiet, the water falling
in the fountain, the girl's voice ... a moment of captured beauty. He
who is truly wise will never permit such moments to escape.
—Louis L'Amour

The best part of our lives we pass in counting on what is to come.
—William Hazlitt

You don't save a pitcher for tomorrow. Tomorrow it may rain.
—Leo Durocher

To finish the moment, to find the journey's end in every step of
the road, to live the greatest number of good hours, is wisdom.
—Ralph Waldo Emerson

Every second is of infinite value.
—Johann von Goethe

The present moment is creative, creating with an unheard-of intensity.
—Le Corbusier

The only way to live is to accept each minute as an unrepeatable
miracle, which is exactly what it is: a miracle and unrepeatable.
—Storm Jameson

God speaks to all individuals through what
happens to them moment by moment.
—J.P. DeCaussade

Who makes quick use of the moment is a genius of prudence.
—Johann Kaspar Lavater

Sometimes I would almost rather have people take
away years of my life than take away a moment.
—Pearl Bailey

Light tomorrow with today.
—Elizabeth Barrett Browning

A preoccupation with the future not only prevents us from seeing
the present as it is, but often prompts us to rearrange the past.
—Eric Hoffer

We do not remember days, we remember moments.
—Cesare Pavese

But what minutes! Count them by sensation, and
not by calendars, and each moment is a day.
—Benjamin Disraeli

Life is a succession of moments. To live each one is to succeed.
—Corita Kent

I live now and only now, and I will do what I want to do this
moment and not what I decided was best for me yesterday.
—Hugh Prather

It may be life is only worthwhile at moments.
Perhaps that is all we ought to expect.
—Sherwood Anderson

The only courage that matters is the kind that
gets you from one moment to the next.
—MIGNON MCLAUGHLIN

A player's effectiveness is directly related to his ability to be right
there, doing that thing, in the moment. . . . He can't be worrying
about the past or the future or the crowd or some other extraneous
event. He must be able to respond in the here and now.
—JOHN BRODIE

Florence Farr once said to me, "If we could say to ourselves, with
sincerity, 'this passing moment is as good as any I shall ever
know,' we could die upon the instant and be united with God."
—WILLIAM BUTLER YEATS

All of us tend to put off living. We are all dreaming of some
magical rose garden over the horizon instead of enjoying the
roses that are blooming outside our windows today.
—DALE CARNEGIE

The man least dependent upon the morrow goes
to meet the morrow most cheerfully.
—EPICURUS

Once to every man and nation comes the moment to decide . . . .
And the choice goes by forever t'wixt that darkness and that light.
—JAMES RUSSELL LOWELL

Be always resolute with the present hour.
Every moment is of infinite value.
—JOHANN WOLFGANG VON GOETHE

It seems to be the fate of man to seek all his consolations in futurity.
—SAMUEL JOHNSON

Love the moment and the energy of the moment
will spread beyond all boundaries.
—CORITA KENT

The present moment is significant, not as the bridge between
past and future, but by reason of its contents, which can fill our
emptiness and become ours, if we are capable of receiving them.
—Dag Hammarskjold

Today is the first day of the rest of your life.
—Abbie Hoffman

When I feel like exercising, I just lie down until the feeling goes away.
—Paul Terry

We must not wish anything other than what happens from moment
to moment, all the while, however, exercising ourselves in goodness.
—Saint Catherine of Genoa

It's not that "today is the first day of the rest of my
life," but that now is all there is of my life.
—Hugh Prather

DAYBREAK

Have hope. Though clouds environs now,
And gladness hides her face in scorn,
Put thou the shadow from thy brow—
No night but hath its morn.
—J.C.F. von Schiller

Snow endures but for a season, and joy comes with the morning.
—Marcus Aurelius

The morning is wiser than the evening.
—Russian proverb

But look, the morn in russet mantle clad
Walks o'er the dew ofyon high eastward hill.
—William Shakespeare

For the mind disturbed, the still beauty of dawn is nature's finest balm.
—Edwin Way Teale

Hold your head high, stick your chest out. You can make it. It gets
dark sometimes, but morning comes.... Keep hope alive.
—JESSE JACKSON

It is a common experience that a problem difficult at night is resolved
in the morning after the committee of sleep has worked on it.
—JOHN STEINBECK

Each day is a new life. Seize it. Live it.
—DAVID GUY POWERS

Always begin anew with the day, just as nature does.
It is one of the sensible things that nature does.
—GEORGE E. WOODBERRY

With each sunrise, we start anew.
—ANON

I have always been delighted at the prospect of a new
day, a fresh try, one more start, with perhaps a bit of
magic waiting somewhere behind the morning.
—J.B. PRIESTLY

Each day the world is born anew for him who takes it rightly.
—JAMES RUSSELL LOWELL

Relying on God has to begin all over again every
day as if nothing had yet been done.
—C.S. LEWIS

Whether one is twenty, forty, or sixty; whether one has succeeded,
failed or just muddled along; whether yesterday was full of
sun or storm, or one of those dull days with no weather at all,
life begins each morning! ... Each morning is the open door
to a new world—new vistas, new aims, new tryings.
—LEIGH MITCHELL HODGES

To be seeing the world made new every morning, as if it were the
morning of the first day, and then to make the
most of it for the individual soul as if each were the last
day, is the daily curriculum of the mind's desire.
—JOHN H. FINLEY

Do not say, "It is morning," and dismiss it with a name of yesterday.
See it for the first time as a newborn child that has no name.
—RABINDRANATH TAGORE

God had infinite time to give us; but how did He give it? In one
immense tract of a lazy millennium? No, but He cut it up into
a near succession of new mornings, and, with each, therefore,
a new idea, new inventions, and new applications.
—RALPH WALDO EMERSON

No matter how big or soft or warm your bed
is, you still have to get out of it.
—GRACE SLICK

Spill not the morning (the quintessence of the day!) in recreations,
for sleep is a recreation. Add not, therefore, sauce to sauce. . . . Pastime,
like wine, is poison in the morning. It is then good husbandry to sow
the head, which hath lain fallow all night, with some serious work.
—THOMAS FULLER

Let us then be up and doing, with a heart for any fate.
—HENRY WADSWORTH LONGFELLOW

Clay lies still, but blood's a rover
Breath's a ware that will not keep.
Up lad: when the journey's over
There'll be time enough to sleep.
—A.E. HOUSMAN

Even if a farmer intends to loaf, he gets up in time to get an early start.
—EDGAR WATSON HOWE

I thank You God for this most amazing day; for the leaping
greenly spirits of trees and a blue true dream of sky; and for
everything which is natural which is infinite which is yes.
—E.E. CUMMINGS

I get up and I bless the light thin clouds and the first twittering
of birds, and the breathing air and smiling face of the hills.
—GIACOMO LEOPARDI

I'm a most lucky and thankful woman. Lucky and thankful for each morning I wake up. For three wonderful daughters and one son. For an understanding and very loving husband with whom I've shared fifty-two blessed years, all in good health.
—THELMA ELLIOTT

If God adds another day to our life, let us receive it gladly.
—MARCUS ANNAEUS SENECA

Wake at dawn with a winged heart and give thanks for another day of loving.
—KAHLIL GIBRAN

Your morning thoughts may determine your conduct for the day. Optimistic thoughts will make your day bright and productive, while pessimistic thinking will make it dull and wasteful. Face each day cheerfully, smilingly and courageously, and it will naturally follow that your work will be a real pleasure and progress will be a delightful accomplishment.
—WILLIAM M. PECK

The first thing each morning, and the last thing each night, suggest to yourself specific ideas that you wish to embody in your character and personality. Address such suggestions to yourself, silently or aloud, until they are deeply impressed upon your mind.
—GRENVILLE KLEISER

Be pleasant until ten o'clock in the morning and the rest of the day will take care of itself.
—ELBERT HUBBARD

Today is a new day. You will get out of it just what you put into it. ... If you have made mistakes, even serious mistakes, there is always another chance for you. And supposing you have tried and failed again and again, you may have a fresh start any moment you choose, for this thing that we call "failure" is not the falling down, but the staying down.
—MARY PICKFORD

Do not shorten the morning by getting up late; look upon it as the quintessence of life, and to a certain extent sacred.
—ARTHUR SCHOPENHAUER

Full many a glorious morning have I seen.
—WILLIAM SHAKESPEARE

As soon as you open your eyes in the morning, you can square away for a happy and successful day. It's the mood and the purpose at the inception of each day that are the important facts in charting your course for the day. We can always square away for a fresh start, no matter what the past has been.
—GEORGE MATTHEW ADAMS

This is the beginning of a new day. God has given me this day to use as I will. I can waste it or use it for good, but what I do today is important, because I am exchanging a day of my life for it! When tomorrow comes, this day will be gone forever, leaving in its place something that I have traded for it. I want it to be gain, and not loss; good, and not evil; success, and not failure; in order that I shall not regret the price I have paid for it.
—ANON

I think in terms of the day's resolutions, not the year's.
—HENRY MOORE

Every new day begins with possibilities. It's up to us to fill it with the things that move us toward progress and peace.
—RONALD REAGAN

Today a thousand doors of enterprise are open to you, inviting you to useful work. To live at this time is an inestimable privilege, and a sacred obligation devolves upon you to make right use of your opportunities. Today is the day in which to attempt and achieve something worthwhile.
—GRENVILLE KLEISER

He who every morning plans the transactions of the day and follows that plan carries thread that will guide him through the labyrinth of the most busy life.
—VICTOR HUGO

A man without a plan for the day is lost before he starts.
—LEWIS K. BENDELE

My credo is etched on my mirror in my bathroom and I see it when I brush my teeth in the morning. It says, "Don't worry,

Be Happy, Feel Good." When you see that first thing, and you reflect on it, the rest of the day seems to glide by pretty well.
—LARRY HAGMAN

Only that day dawns to which we are awake.
—HENRY DAVID THOREAU

The day returns and brings us the petty round of irritating concerns and duties. Help us to play the man, help us to perform them with laughter and kind faces; let cheerfulness abound with industry. Give us to go blithely on our business all this day, bring us to our resting beds weary and content and undishonored, and grant us in the end the gift of sleep.
—ROBERT LOUIS STEVENSON

Put yourself in competition with yourself each day. Each morning look back upon your work of yesterday and then try to beat it.
—CHARLES M. SHELDON

The morning has gold in its mouth.
—GERMAN PROVERB

Do you know what the greatest test is? Do you still get excited about what you do when you get up in the morning?
—DAVID HALBERSTAM

Oft when the white, still dawn lifted the skies and pushed the hills apart, I have felt it like a glory in my heart.
—EDWIN MARKHAM

Sometimes I have believed as many as six impossible things before breakfast.
—LEWIS CARROLL

The mind is found most acute and most uneasy in the morning. Uneasiness is, indeed, a species of sagacity— a passive sagacity. Fools are never uneasy.
—JOHANN VON GOETHE

Day's sweetest moments are at dawn.
—ELLA WHEELER WILCOX

YET TO COME

After all, tomorrow is another day.
SCARLETT O'HARA, *GONE WITH THE WIND*

I have been nothing ... but there is tomorrow.
—LOUIS L'AMOUR

You learn to build your roads on today, because tomorrow's ground is too
uncertain for plans, and futures have a way of falling down in midflight.
—VERONICA SHOFFSTAL

If a man carefully examines his thoughts he will be surprised to find
how much he lives in the future. His well-being is always ahead.
—RALPH WALDO EMERSON

The days that are still to come are the wisest witnesses.
—PINDAR

The future is a world limited by ourselves—in
it we discover only what concerns us.
—MAURICE MAETERLINCK

Every tomorrow has two handles. We can take hold of it
with the handle of anxiety or the handle of faith.
—HENRY WARD BEECHER

Take therefore no thought of the morrow; for the
morrow shall take thought for the things of itself.
—MT. 6:34

The future is the past in preparation.
—PIERRE DAC

In the future everybody will be world famous for fifteen minutes.
—ANDY WARHOL

The only limit to our realization of tomorrow will be our doubts
of today. Let us move forward with strong and active faith.
—FRANKLIN DELANO ROOSEVELT

The future is only the past again, entered through another gate.
—Arthur Wing Pinero

It is not the cares of today, but the cares of tomorrow, that weigh a man down. For the needs of today we have corresponding strength given. For the morrow we are told to trust. It is not ours yet.
—George MacDonald

Take therefore no thought of the morrow; for the morrow shall take thought for the things of itself.
—Mt. 6:34

The future is made of the same stuff as the present.
—Simone Weil

My interest is in the future because I am going to spend the rest of my life there.
—Charles F. Kettering

When all else is lost, the future still remains.
—Christian Bovee

Tomorrow is the mysterious, unknown guest.
—Henry Wadsworth Longfellow

Tomorrow is the only day in the year that appeals to a lazy man.
—Jimmy Lyons

We grow in time to trust the future for our answers.
—Ruth Benedict

I never think of the future—it comes soon enough.
—Albert Einstein

The future is hope!
—John Fiske

The future is wider than vision, and has no end.
—Donald G. Mitchell

Tomorrow is the day when idlers work, and fools
reform, and mortal men lay hold on heaven.
—EDWARD YOUNG

Culture shock is relatively milde in comparison with a
much more serious malady that might be called "future
shock." Future shock is the dizzying disorientations
brought on by the premature arrival of the future.
—ALVIN TOFFLER

I fear there will be no future for those who do not change.
—LOUIS L'AMOUR

The future is something which everyone reaches at the rate of
sixty minutes an hour, whatever he does, whoever he is.
—C.S. LEWIS

The future is the most expensive luxury in the world.
—THORNTON WILDER

The future is a great land.
—ANON

The future is wider than vision, and has no end.
—DONALD G. MITCHELL

It is never safe to look into the future with eyes of fear.
—EDWARD HENRY HARRIMAN

Put aside the need to know some future design and simply leave
your life open to what is needed of it by the Divine forces.
—EMMANUEL

The Future's So Bright I Gotta Wear Shades.
—PAT MACDONALD

Everyone has it within his power to say, this I
am today, that I shall be tomorrow.
—LOUIS L'AMOUR

Where will I be five years from now? I delight in not knowing. That's one of the greatest things about life—its wonderful surprises.
—Marlo Thomas

I got the blues thinking of the future, so I left off and made some marmalade. It's amazing how it cheers one up to shred oranges and scrub the floor.
—D.H. Lawrence

The future belongs to those who believe in the beauty of their dreams.
—Eleanor Roosevelt

Strike when thou wilt, the hour of rest, but let my last days be my best.
—Robert Browning

When I look at the future, it's so bright, it burns my eyes.
—Oprah Winfrey

For you and me, today is all we have; tomorrow is a mirage that may never become reality.
—Louis L'Amour

The future is like heaven—everyone exalts it, but no one wants to go there now.
—James Baldwin

Grow old along with me! The best is yet to be.
—Robert Browning

The future is much like the present, only longer.
—Dan Quisenberry

They who lose today may win tomorrow.
—Miguel de Cervantes

The bridges you cross before you come to them are over rivers that aren't there.
—Gene Brown

I like the dreams of the future better than the history of the past.
—Thomas Jefferson

It is when tomorrow's burden is added to the burden of
today that the weight is more than a man can bear.
—George MacDonald

Yesterday is not ours to recover, but tomorrow is ours to win or lose.
—Lyndon B. Johnson

Everyone's future is, in reality, uncertain and full of unknown
treasures from which all may draw unguessed prizes.
—Lord Dunsany

When all else is lost, the future still remains.
—Christian Bovee

Be of good cheer. Do not think of today's failures, but of the
success that may come tomorrow. You have set yourselves a
difficult task, but you will succeed if you persevere; and you
will find a joy in overcoming obstacles. Remember, no effort
that we make to attain something beautiful is ever lost.
—Helen Keller

People often overestimate what will happen in the next two
years and underestimate what will happen in ten.
—Bill Gates

To the being of fully alive, the future is not ominous but
a promise; it surrounds the present like a halo.
—John Dewey

Que sera, sera,
Whatever will be will be;
The future's not ours to see.
Que sera, sera.
—Jay Livingston

The future is wider than vision, and has no end.
—Donald G. Mitchell

Telling the future by looking at the past assumes that conditions remain
constant. This is like driving a car by looking in the rear view mirror.
—Herb Brody

Future, n. That period of time in which our affairs prosper,
our friends are true, and our happiness is assured.
—AMBROSE BIERCE

The future has a way of arriving unannounced.
—GEORGE WILL

HUMOR

Through humor, you can soften some of the worst blows
that life delivers. And once you find laughter, no matter how
painful your situation might be, you can survive it.
—BILL COSBY

A sharp sense of the ironic can be the equivalent of the faith
that moves mountains. Far more quickly than reason or
logic, iron can penetrate rage and puncture self-pity.
—MOSS HART

Those who have no sense of humor run the risk
of having jokes made at their expense.
—MICHEL PAUL RICHARD

Better lose a Jest than a Friend.
—THOMAS FULLER

[O]f all the countless fold who have lived before our time on this planet
not one is known in history or in legend as having died of laughter.
—MAX BEERBOHM

There's no such thing as a new joke. All jokes are public
domain. It's not the gag, it's how you deliver it.
—MILTON BERLE

What monstrous absurdities and paradoxes have resisted
whole batteries of serious arguments, and then crumbled
swiftly into dust before the ringing death-knell of a laugh!
—AGNES REPPLIER

Children always know when company is in the living room—
they can hear their mother laughing at their father's jokes.
—ANON

When humor is meant to be taken seriously, it's no joke.
—LIONEL STRACHEY

Impropriety is the soul of wit.
—W. SOMERSET MAUGHAM

There is many a true Word spoken in jest.
—JAMES KELLEY

Our five senses are incomplete without the sixth—a sense of humor.
—ANON

There are only a handful of possible jokes. The chief members of this
joke band may be said to be: the fall of dignity [and] mistaken identity.
—MACK SENNET

Laughter is wine for the soul—laughter soft, or loud
and deep, tinged through with seriousness.
—SEAN O'CASEY

All the world loves a clown.
—COLE PORTER

He who laughs, lasts!
—MARY PETTIBONE POOLE

The teller of a mirthful tale has latitude allowed him.
We are content with less than absolute truth.
—CHARLES LAMB

Humor is reason gone mad.
—GROUCHO MARX

People ask what I am really trying to do with
humor. The answer is, "I'm getting even."
—ART BUCHWALD

Humor is, I think, the subtlest and chanciest of literary forms. It is surely not accidental that there are a thousand novelists, essayists, poets, or journalists for each humorist. It is a long, long time between James Thurbers.
—LEO C. ROSTEN

The aim of a joke is not to degrade the human being, but to remind him that he is already degraded
—GEORGE ORWELL

Bad humor is an evasion of reality; good humor is an acceptance of it.
—MALCOLM MUGGERIDGE

Even the gods love jokes.
—PLATO

Aside from laughing it off, the only real answer to a jest is a better jest.
—ORRIN E. KLAPP

The duty of comedy is to correct men by amusing them.
—MOLIERE

To laugh is proper to man.
—FRANCOIS RABELAIS

There's nothing like a gleam of humor to reassure you that a fellow human being is ticking inside a strange face.
—EVA HOFFMAN

He who cannot shine by tought, seeks to bring himself into notice by a witticism.
—VOLTAIRE

To listen to your own silence is the key to comedy.
—ELAYNE BOOSLER

Common sense and a sense of humor are the same thing, moving at different speeds. A sense of humor is just common sense, dancing.
—WILLIAM JAMES

A man must have a good share of wit himself
to endure a great share in another.
—LORD CHESTERFIELD

I'm learning the difference between humor and comedy, between
the laugh that lasts forever and the one that evaporates as soon as
it hits air. Humor is giving, and comedy is taking away. Humor is
companionable, comedy cold. Humor is character, comedy personality.
—ROGER ROSENBLATT

A jest often decides matters of importance more
effectually and happily than seriousness.
—HORACE

Everything is funny as long as it is happening to somebody else.
—WILL ROGERS

Good humor is a tonic for mind and body. It is the best
antidote for anxiety and depression. It is a business asset.
It attracts and keeps friends. It lightens human burdens.
It is the direct route to serenity and contentment.
—GRENVILLE KLEISER

Humor is a rubber sword—it allows you to
make a point without drawing blood.
—MARY HIRSCH

Comedy is an escape, not from truth but from
despair; a narrow escape into faith.
—CHRISTOPHER FRY

A pun is the lowest form of humor—when you don't think of it, first.
—OSCAR LEVANT

Men will let you abuse them if only you will make them laugh.
—HENRY WARD BEECHER

The comic is the perception of the opposite; humor is the feeling of it.
—UMBERTO ECO

Think of what would happen to us in America if there were no
humorists; life would be one long Congressional Record.
—TOM MASSON

Wit is the salt of conversation, not the food.
—WILLIAM HAZLITT

Men will confess to treason, murder, arson, false teeth or a
wig. How many of them will own up to a lack of humor?
—FRANK MOORE COLBY

All higher humor begins with ceasing to take oneself seriously.
—HERMANN HESSE

Laughter is a problem shrinker.
—MIRA KIRSHENBAUM

Comedy is tragedy that happens to the other people.
—ANGELA CARTER

The quality of wit inspires more admiration than confidence.
—GEORGE SANTAYANA

Humor is emotional chaos remembered in tranquility.
—JAMES THURBER

Comedy is acting out optimism.
—ROBIN WILLIAMS

A sense of humor . . . is needed armor. Joy in one's heart
and some laughter on one's lips is a sign that the person
down deep has a pretty good grasp of life.
—HUGH SIDEY

The sense of disproportion is comedy.
—RALPH WALDO EMERSON

Nothing in man is more serious than his sense of
humor; it is the sign that he wants all the truth.
—MARK VAN DOREN

Humor: The ability to laugh at any mistake you survive.
—Jerry Tucker

Never be afraid to laugh at yourself, after all, you could
be missing out on the joke of the century.
—Dame Edna Everage (Barry Humphries)

Humor is . . . despair refusing to take itself seriously.
—P. Arland Ussher

Wit is the sudden marriage of ideas which before their
union were not perceived to have any relation.
—Mark Twain

You are not angry with people when you laugh
at them. Humour teaches tolerance.
—W. Somerset Maugham

The test of a real comedian is whether you laugh
at him before he opens his mouth.
—George Jean Nathan

My way of joking is to tell the truth. It's the funniest joke in the world.
—George Bernard Shaw

His foe was folly & his weapon wit.
—Anthony Hope (Inscription on W.S. Gilbert's memorial)

Humor is falling downstairs if you do it while in
the act of warning your wife not to.
—Kenneth Bird

God writes a lot of comedy . . . the trouble is, he's stuck with
so many bad actors who don't know how to play funny.
—Garrison Keillor

Against the assault of laughter nothing can stand.
—Mark Twain

The kind of humor I like is the thing that makes me
laugh for five seconds and think for ten minutes.
—WILLIAM DAVIS

There's a helluva distance between wisecracking and wit. Wit has
truth in it; wisecracking is simply calisthenics with words.
—DOROTHY PARKER

Wit makes its own welcome and levels all distinctions.
—RALPH WALDO EMERSON

Humor is always based on a modicum of truth. Have
you ever heard a joke about a father-in-law?
—DICK CLARK

Wouldn't a laugh serve us better than to
battle it out with our mortal souls?
—MAUREEN HOWARD

One man's pointlessness is another's barbed satire.
—FRANKLIN P. ADAMS

A comic says funny things; a comedian says things funny.
—ED WYNN

You're only given one little spark of madness. You mustn't lose it.
—ROBIN WILLIAMS

Nothing seems too high or low for the humorist; he is above honor,
above faith, preserving sense in religion and sanity in life.
—SEAN O'CASEY

April 1. This is the day upon which we are reminded of what
we are on the other three hundred and sixty-four.
—MARK TWAIN

Never laugh at live dragons.
—J.R.R. TOLKIEN

Criticizing a political satirist for being unfair is like
criticizing a nose guard for being physical.
—GARRY TRUDEAU

Satire should, like a polished razor keen,
Wound with a touch that's scarcely felt or seen.
—LADY MARY WORTLEY MONTAGU

If I get big laughs, I'm a comedian. If I get little laughs,
I'm a humorist. If I get no laughs, I'm a singer.
—GEORGE BURNS

Hearty laughter is a good way to jog internally
without having to go outdoors.
—NORMAN COUSINS

This is not an easy time for humorists because the
government is far funnier than we are.
—ART BUCHWALD

Comedy keeps the heart sweet.
—MARK TWAIN

Humor is just another defense against the universe.
—MEL BROOKS

Brevity is the soul of wit.
—WILLIAM SHAKESPEARE

The most wasted day is that in which he have not laughed.
— SÉBASTIEN ROCH NICOLAS CHAMFORT

We are in the world to laugh.
—JULES RENARD

Are we having fun yet?
—BILL GRIFFITH (ZIPPY THE PINHEAD COMIC STRIP)

In modern America, anyone who attempts to write satirically about the events of the day finds it difficult to concoct a situation so bizarre that it may not actually come to pass while his article is still on the presses.
—CALVIN TRILLIN

If it were not for these stories, jokes, jests, I should die; they give vent—are the vents—of my moods and gloom
—ABRAHAM LINCOLN

All I need to make a comedy is a park, a policeman and a pretty girl.
—CHARLIE CHAPLIN

All very serious revolutionary propositions begin as huge jokes. Otherwise they would be stamped out by the lynching of their first exponents.
—GEORGE BERNARD SHAW

Wit, n. The salt with which the American humorist spoils his intellectual cookery by leaving it out.
—AMBROSE BIERCE

By rights, satire is a lonely and introspective occupation, for nobody can describe a fool to the life without much patient self-inspection.
—FRANK MOORE COLBY

One horse-laugh is worth ten thousand syllogisms. It is not only more effective; it is also vastly more intelligent.
—H.L. MENCKEN

Satire is something that closes on Saturday night.
—GEORGE S. KAUFMAN

The difference between a satirist and a humorist is that the satirist shoots to kill while the humorist brings his prey back alive.
—PETER DE VRIES

A good laugh is sunshine in a house.
—WILLIAM MAKEPEACE THACKERAY

Anything awful makes me laugh. I misbehaved once at funeral.
—CHARLES LAMB

There is no credit to being a comedian, when you have the
whole Government working for you. All you have to do
is report the facts. I don't even have to exaggerate.
—Will Rogers

[Replying on his deathbed to George Seaton's remark, *"I guess dying
can be very hard."*:] Yes, but not has hard as playing comedy.
—Edmund Gwenn

KNOWLEDGE/
SELF-KNOWLEDGE

The life which is unexamined is not worth living.
—Plato

I want, by understanding myself, to understand others. I want
to be all that I am capable of becoming....This all sounds very
strenuous and serious. But now that I have wrestled with it,
it's no longer so. I feel happy—deep down. All is well.
—Katherine Mansfield

The precept, "Know yourself," was not solely intended
to obviate the pride of mankind; but likewise that
we might understand our own worth.
—Cicero

The most merciful thing in the world, I think, is the inability
of the human mind to correlate all its contents.
—H.P. Lovecraft

It is the individual who knows how little he knows about himself who
stands a reasonable chance of finding out something about himself.
—S.I. Hayakawa

Conscience: the inner voice which warns us
that someone may be looking.
—H.L. Mencken

The most difficult thing in life is to know yourself.
—THALES

Emancipate yourselves from mental slavery.
None but ourselves can free our minds.
—BOB MARLEY

Self-knowledge is the beginning of self-improvement.
—SPANISH PROVERB

Knowing others is wisdom, knowing yourself is Enlightenment.
—LAO-TZU

If you do not ask yourself what it is you know, you will
go on listening to others and change will not come
because you will not hear your own truth.
—SAINT BARTHOLOMEW

Those who think they know it all are very
annoying to those of us who do.
—ROBERT K. MUELLER

A man who knows he is a fool is not a great fool.
—CHUANG-TSE

A fellow who is always declaring he's no fool, usually has his suspicions.
—WILSON MIZNER

No man remains quite what he was when he recognizes himself.
—THOMAS MANN

The more you use your brain, the more brain you will have to use.
—GEORGE A. DORSEY

Learn what you are, and be such.
—PINDAR

When a man begins to understand himself, he begins to live.
—NORVIN G. MCGRANAHAN

We should know what our convictions are, and stand for them. Upon one's own philosophy, conscious or unconscious, depends one's ultimate interpretation of facts. Therefore it is wise to be as clear as possible about one's subjective principles. As the man is, so will be his ultimate truth.
—CARL JUNG

To understand is to forgive, even oneself.
—ALEXANDER CHASE

I prefer an accommodating vice to an obstinate virtue.
—MOLIERE

It is not only the most difficult thing to know oneself, but the most inconvenient, too.
—JOSH BILLINGS

One may understand the cosmos, but never the ego; the self is more distant than any star.
—G.K. CHESTERTON

He knows the universe and does not know himself.
—JEAN DE LA FONTAINE

To know oneself, one should assert oneself.
—ALBERT CAMUS

Knowledge is the conformity of the object and the intellect.
—AVERROES

Inviting people to laugh with you while you are laughing at yourself is a good thing to do. You may be the fool but you're the fool in charge.
—CARL REINER

It is doubtless a vice to turn one's eyes inward too much, but I am my own comedy and tragedy.
—RALPH WALDO EMERSON

The happy man is he who knows his limitations, yet bows to no false gods.
—ROBERT W. SERVICE

Self-understanding rather than self-condemnation is
the way to inner peace and mature conscience.
—Joshua Loth Liebman

Learn what you are and be such.
—Pindar

Sometimes it is more important to discover what
one cannot do, than what one can.
—Lin Yutang

It is not the eyes of others that I am wary of, but my own.
—Noel Coward

Self-searching is the means by which we bring new vision, action,
and grace to bear upon the dark and negative side of our natures.
With it comes the development of that kind of humility that
makes it possible for us to receive God's hell. . . . We find that bit by
bit we can discard the old life—the one that did not work—for a
new life that can and does work under conditions whatever.
—As Bill Sees It

No man ever understands quite his own artful dodges to
escape from the grim shadow of self-knowledge.
—Joseph Conrad

I'm a salami writer. I try to write good salami, but salami is salami.
—Stephen King

A book must be the ax for the frozen sea within us.
—Franz Kafka

Ninety percent of the world's woe comes from people not
knowing themselves, their abilities, their frailties, and
even their real virtues. Most of us go almost all the way
through life as complete strangers to ourselves.
—Sydney J. Harris

Somehow we learn who we really are and then live with that decision.
—Eleanor Roosevelt

Every human being is intended to have a character of his own:
to be what no others are, and to do what no other can do.
—WILLIAM ELLERY CHANNING

A single event can awaken within us a stranger totally unknown to us.
—ANTOINE DE SAINT-EXUPERY

Many men go fishing all of their lives without
knowing that it is not fish they are after.
—HENRY DAVID THOREAU

I . . . know what I do, and am unmoved by
men's blame, or their praise either.
—ROBERT BROWNING

Resolve to be thyself; and know that he who
finds himself, loses his misery.
—MATTHEW ARNOLD

You can live a lifetime and, at the end of it, know more
about other people than you know about yourself.
—BERYL MARKHAM

Egotism—usually just a case of mistaken nonentity
—BARBARA STANWYCK

You can succeed if nobody else believes it, but you will
never succeed if you don't believe in yourself.
—WILLIAM J.H. BOETCKER

Do not attempt to do a thing unless you are sure of yourself, but do
not relinquish it simply because someone else is not sure of you.
—STEWART E. WHITE

What you think about yourself is much more
important than what others think of you.
—MARCUS ANNAEUS SENECA

No one can make you feel inferior without your consent.
—ELEANOR ROOSEVELT

A man cannot be comfortable without his own approval.
—MARK TWAIN

From self alone expect applause.
—MARION L. BURTON

Every man stamps his value on himself . . . man
is made great or small by his own will.
—J.C.F. VON SCHILLER

A humble knowledge of oneself is a surer road to
God than a deep searching of the sciences.
—THOMAS À KEMPIS

I care not so much what I am to others as what I am to
myself. I will be rich by myself, and not by borrowing.
—MICHEL DE MONTAIGNE

She lacks confidence, she craves admiration insatiably.
She lives on the reflections of herself in the eyes
of others. She does not dare to be herself.
—ANAÏS NIN

Let a man's talents or virtues be what they may, he will
only feel satisfaction as he is satisfied in himself.
—WILLIAM HAZLITT

I was always willing to take a great deal of the burden of
getting along in life on my own shoulders, but I wasn't willing
to give myself a pat on the back. I was always looking to
somebody else to give me that. . . . That was all wrong.
—RAQUEL WELCH

This above all: to thine own self be true,
And it must follow as the night the day
Thou canst not then be false to any man.
—WILLIAM SHAKESPEARE

Do not let your peace depend on the hearts of men;
whatever they say about you, good or bad, you are not
because of it another man, for as you are, you are.
—THOMAS À KEMPIS

Be content with what you are, and wish not change;
nor dread your last day, nor long for it.
—MARTIAL

People remain what they are, even when their faces fall to pieces.
—BERTOLT BRECHT

You can enjoy encouragement coming from outside,
but you cannot need for it to come from outside.
—VLADIMIR ZWORYKIN

Perhaps the most important thing we can undertake
toward the reduction of fear is to make it easier for
people to accept themselves, to like themselves.
—BONARO OVERSTREET

Rebellion against your handicaps gets you nowhere. Self-pity
gets you nowhere. One must have the adventurous daring to
accept oneself as a bundle of possibilities and undertake the most
interesting game in the world—making the most of one's best.
—HARRY EMERSON FOSDICK

It is better to be hated for what you are than loved for what you are not.
—ANDRÉ GIDE

Awakening begins when a man realizes that he is
going nowhere and does not know where to go.
—GEORGES GURDJIEFF

If there are two hundred people in a room and one
of them doesn't like me, I've got to get out.
—MARLON BRANDO

All the discontented people I know are trying to be something
they are not, to do something they cannot do.
—DAVID GRAYSON

What a man thinks of himself, that is what
determines, or rather indicates, his fate.
—HENRY DAVID THOREAU

As soon as you trust yourself, you will know how to live.
—Johann von Goethe

He who seeks for applause only from without has
all his happiness in another's keeping.
—Oliver Goldsmith

Life, I fancy, would very often be insupportable,
but for the luxury of self-compassion.
—George R. Gissing

To accept ourselves as we are means to value our
imperfections as much as our perfections.
—Sandra Bierig

Blessed is he who expects no gratitude, for he shall not be disappointed.
—William Bennett

The search for a new personality is futile; what is fruitful is
the interest the old personality can take in new activities.
—Cesare Pavese

Not in the shouts and plaudits of the throng, but
in ourselves, are triumph and defeat.
—Henry Wadsworth Longfellow

When you know you are doing your very best within the
circumstances of your existence, applaud yourself!
—Rusty Berkus

You have to deal with the fact that your life is your life.
—Alex Hailey

To find the good life you must become yourself.
—Dr. Bill Jackson

I exist as I am, that is enough,
If no other in the world be aware, I sit content,
And if each and all be aware, I sit content.
—Walt Whitman

Our entire life . . . consists ultimately in accepting ourselves as we are.
—Jean Anouilh

The secret of my success is that at an early age I discovered I was not God.
—Oliver Wendell Holmes, Jr.

Contentment, and indeed usefulness, comes as the infallible
result of great acceptances, great humilities—of not trying
to conform to some dramatized version of ourselves.
—David Grayson

I am somebody. I am me. I like being me. And I
need nobody to make me somebody.
—Louis L' Amour

Do not look for approval except for the consciousness of doing your best.
—Bernard M. Baruch

It is the chiefest point of happiness that a man is willing to be what he is.
—Erasmus

Spirituality is . . . the awareness that survival is the
savage fight between you and yourself.
—Anon

I care not what others think of what I do, but I care very
much about what I think of what I do. That is character!
—Theodore Roosevelt

It's not our disadvantages or shortcomings that are
ridiculous, but rather the studious way we try to hide
them, and our desire to act as if they did not exist.
—Giacomo Leopardi

If you must love your neighbor as yourself, it is at
least as fair to love yourself as your neighbor.
—Nicolas de Chamfort

Of all afflictions, the worst is self-contempt.
—Berthold Auerbach

If God had wanted me otherwise, He would have created me otherwise.
—JOHANN VON GOETHE

The courage to be is the courage to accept
oneself, in spite of being unacceptable.
—PAUL TILLICH

You can't make the Duchess of Windsor into Rebecca of
Sunnybrook Farm. The facts of life are very stubborn things.
—CLEVELAND AMORY

Every man must at last accept himself for his portion, and learn to do
his work with the tools and talents with which he has been endowed.
—CHARLES A. HAWLEY

There's a period of life when we swallow a knowledge of
ourselves and it becomes either good or sour inside.
—PEARL BAILEY

Resolve to be thyself . . . he who finds himself loses his misery!
—MATTHEW ARNOLD

A man should not strive to eliminate his complexes but
to get into accord with them, for they are legitimately
what directs his conduct in the world.
—SIGMUND FREUD

We will discover the nature of our particular genius when we
stop trying to conform to our own or to other people's models,
learn to be ourselves, and allow our natural channel to open.
—SHAKTI GAWAIN

There is always a certain peace in being what
one is, in being that completely.
—UGO BETTI

A true man never frets about his place in the world, but just slides into
it by the gravitation of his nature, and swings there as easily as a star.
—EDWIN H. CHAPIN

I'm not OK, you're not OK—and that's OK.
—WILLIAM SLOANE COFFIN

Man has to live with the body and soul which
have fallen to him by chance.
—José Ortega y Gasset

All the discontented people I know are trying to be something
they are not, to do something they cannot do.
—David Grayson

We expect more of ourselves than we have any right to.
—Oliver Wendell Holmes, Jr.

Do not wish to be anything but what you are.
—Saint Francis de Sales

Our entire life ... consists ultimately in accepting ourselves as we are.
—Jean Anouilh

Try as hard as we may for perfection, the net result of our labors
is an amazing variety of imperfectness. We are surprised at our
own versatility in being able to fail in so many different ways.
—Samuel McChord Crothers

Change occurs when one becomes what she is, not
when she tries to become what she is not.
—Ruth P. Freedman

I is who I is.
—Tom Peterson

If you do not conquer self, you will be conquered by self.
—Napoleon Hill

I can't write a book commensurate with
Shakespeare, but I can write a book by me.
—Sir Walter Raleigh

Do not lose courage in considering your own imperfections.
—Saint Francis de Sales

Be content with what you are, and wish not change;
nor dread your last day, nor long for it.
—Martial

One must not hope to be more than one can be.
—Nicolas de Chamfort

A man can stand a lot as long as he can stand himself.
—Axel Munthe

Growth begins when we start to accept our own weakness.
—Jean Vanier

I have done what I could do in life, and if I could not do better, I did
not deserve it. In vain I have tried to step beyond what bound me.
—Maurice Maeterlinck

We cannot all be masters.
—William Shakespeare

The man with insight enough to admit his
limitations comes nearest to perfection.
—Johann von Goethe

To love others, we must first learn to love ourselves.
—Anon

No one is expected to achieve the impossible.
—French proverb

I am what I am, so take me as I am!
—Johann von Goethe

The one important thing I have learned over the years is the
difference between taking one's work seriously and taking one's
self seriously. The first is imperative and the second is disastrous.
—Margaret Fontey

To dream of the person you would like to be
is to waste the person you are.
—Anon

What thou art, that thou art.
—Thomas à Kempis

At thirty a man should know himself like the palm of
his hand, know the exact number of his defects and
qualities. . . . And above all, accept these things.
—Albert Camus

Believing in our hearts that who we are is enough is
the key to a more satisfying and balanced life.
—Ellen Sue Stern

Learn to . . . be what you are, and learn to resign
with a good grace all that you are not.
—Henri Frederic Amiel

We set up harsh and unkind rules against ourselves. No one
is born without faults. That man is best who has fewest.
—Horace

My recipe for life is not being afraid of myself,
afraid of what I think or of my opinions.
—Eartha Kitt

No man can climb out beyond the limitations of his own character.
—John Morley

To wish to act like angels while we are still
in this world is nothing but folly.
—Saint Teresa of Avila

Sometimes it is more important to discover what
one cannot do, than what one can do.
—Lin Yutang

We cannot all be masters.
—William Shakespeare

A hero is a man who does what he can.
—Romain Rolland

To do all that one is able to do is to be a man; to do
all that one would like to do is to be a god.
—Napoleon Bonaparte

It is only fools who keep straining at high C all their lives.
—Charles Dudley Warner

I long to accomplish a great and noble task, but it my chief duty
to accomplish small tasks as if they were great and noble.
—Helen Keller

May God . . . let me strive for attainable things.
—Pindar

Interest in the lives of others, the high evaluation of these
lives, what are they but the overflow of the interest a man
finds in himself, the value he attributes to his own being?
—Sherwood Anderson

A great obstacle to happiness is to expect too much happiness.
—Bernard de Fontenelle

As we advance in life, we learn the limits of our abilities.
—J.A. Froud

I cannot do everything, but still I can do something; and because I
cannot do everything, I will not refuse to do something I can do.
—Edward Everett Hale

Let a man's talents or virtues be what they may, he will only
feel satisfaction in his society as he is satisfied in himself.
—William Hazlitt

Despair is the price one pays for setting himself an impossible aim.
—Graham Greene

I hope to work, support my children and die quietly without pain.
—Sean Connery

It isn't important to come out on top, what matters
is to be the one who comes out alive.
—BERTOLT BRECHT

Striving for excellence motivates you; striving
for perfection is demoralizing.
—DR. HARRIET BRAIKER

There is overwhelming evidence that the higher the level of
self-esteem, the more likely one will treat others with respect,
kindness, and generosity. People who do not experience
self-love have little or no capacity to love others.
—NATHANIEL BRANDEN

There is a proper balance between not asking enough
of oneself and asking or expecting too much.
—MAY SARTON

Friendship with oneself is all-important, because without
it one cannot be friends with anyone else.
—ELEANOR ROOSEVELT

It is enough that I am of value to somebody today.
—HUGH PRATHER

A man needs self-acceptance or he can't live with himself;
he needs self-criticism or others can't live with him.
—JAMES A. PIKE

If you want to be respected by others, the
great thing is to respect yourself.
—FYODOR DOSTOYEVSKY

Self-love is not opposed to the love of other people.
You cannot really love yourself and do yourself a favor
without doing other people a favor, and vice versa.
—DR. KARL MENNINGER

Imagination was given to us to compensate for what we are not;
a sense of humor was provided to console us for what we are.
—MACK MCGINNIS

You grow up the day you have your first real laugh at yourself.
—ETHEL BARRYMORE

If you make friends with yourself you will never be alone.
—MAXWELL MALTZ

If I am not for myself, who is for me? And if I am only
for myself, what am I? And if not now, when?
—HILLEL

Accept the place the divine providence has found for you.
—RALPH WALDO EMERSON

Too many people overvalue what they are not
and undervalue what they are.
—MALCOLM FORBES

Until you make peace with who you are, you'll
never be content with what you have.
—DORIS MORTMAN

Healthy personalities accept themselves not in any self-idolizing
way, but in the sense that they see themselves as persons who are
worth giving to another and worthy to receive from another.
—WILLIAM KLASSEN

If a man does not keep pace with is companions, perhaps it
is because he hears a different drummer. Let him step to the
music which he hears, however measured or far away.
—HENRY DAVID THOREAU

We do not see things as they are, but as we are ourselves.
—HENRY M. TOMLINSON

I needed to find my way to write. I need about six hours of
uninterrupted time in order to produce about two hours of writing,
and when I accepted that and found the way
to do it, then I was able to write.
—ROBERT B. PARKER

Accept your humanness as well as your
divinity, totally and without reserve.
—EMMANUEL

Unless I accept my faults, I will most certainly doubt my virtues.
—HUGH PRATHER

I've always wanted to be somebody. But I see
now I should have been more specific.
—JANE WAGNER

The deepest principle in human nature is the craving to be appreciated.
—WILLIAM JAMES

Every man must be content with that glory which he may have at home.
—BOETHIUS

Do not attempt to do a thing unless you are sure of yourself, but do
not relinquish it simply because someone else is not sure of you.
—STEWART E. WHITE

Ultimately, love is self approval.
—SONDRA RAY

The fundamental problem most patients have is an
inability to love themselves, having been unloved by
others during some crucial part of their lives.
—BERNIE S. SIEGEL, M.D.

It is a sign of strength, not of weakness, to admit
that you don't know all the answers.
—JOHN P. LOUGBRANE

Who you are is a necessary step to being who you will be.
—EMMANUEL

It's OK if you mess up. You should give yourself a break.
—BILLY JOEL

SELF-CONFIDENCE

If one advances confidently in the direction of his dreams,
and endeavors to live the life which he has imagined, he will
meet with a success unexpected in common hours.
—HENRY DAVID THOREAU

Believe in yourself! Have faith in your abilities! Without
a humble but reasonable confidence in your own
powers you cannot be successful or happy.
—NORMAN VINCENT PEALE

As soon as you trust yourself, you will know how to live.
—JOHANN VON GOETHE

It's so important to believe in yourself. Believe that you can
do it, under any circumstances. Because if you believe you
can, then you really will. That belief just keeps you searching
for the answers, and then pretty soon you get it.
—WALLY "FAMOUS" AMOS

Search and you will find that at the base and birth of every great
business organization was an enthusiast, a man consumed
with earnestness of purpose, with confidence in his powers,
with faith in the worthwhileness of his endeavors.
—B.C. FORBES

My mind to me a kingdom is.
—EDWARD DE VERE, EARL OF OXFORD

I've always seen myself as a winner, even as a kid. If I hadn't, I just might
have gone down the drain a couple of times. I've got something inside
of me, peasantlike and stubborn, and I'm in it 'til the end of the race.
—TRUMAN CAPOTE

It is as proper to have pride in oneself as it
is ridiculous to show it to others.
—FRANCOIS DE LA ROCHEFOUCAULD

As is our confidence, so is our capacity.
—WILLIAM HAZLITT

Pride . . . is the direct appreciation of oneself.
—Arthur Schopenhauer

Calm self-confidence is as far from conceit as the desire
to earn a decent living is remote from greed.
—Channing Pollock

Only so far as a man believes strongly, mightily, can
he act cheerfully, or do anything worth doing.
—Frederick W. Robertson

To have that sense of one's intrinsic worth which constitutes
self-respect is potentially to have everything.
—Joan Didion

Experience tells you what to do; confidence allows you to do it.
—Stan Smith

Confidence is that feeling by which the mind embarks on great
and honorable courses with a sure hope and trust in itself.
—Cicero

If a man doesn't delight in himself and the force in him and feel that
he and it are wonders, how is all life to become important to him?
—Sherwood Anderson

Your success depends mainly upon what you think of
yourself and whether you believe in yourself.
—William J.H. Boetcker

Never grow a wishbone, daughter, where your backbone ought to be.
—Clementine Paddleford

They conquer who believe they can.
—John Dryden

I am plus my surroundings, and if I do not preserve
the latter I do not preserve myself.
—Jose Ortega y Gasset

Immense power is acquired by assuring yourself in your
secret reveries that you were born to control affairs.
—Andrew Carnegie

Self-reverence, self-knowledge, self-control. These
three alone lead to sovereign power.
—Alfred, Lord Tennyson

Faith in oneself . . . is the best and safest course.
—Michelangelo

Believe that you can whip the enemy, and you have won half the battle.
—General J.E.B. Stuart

Self-reverence, self-knowledge, self-control. These
three alone lead to sovereign power.
—Alfred, Lord Tennyson

Taste . . . is the only morality . . . Tell me what
you like, and I'll tell you what you are.
—John Ruskin

There's one blessing only, the source and cornerstone
of beatitude: confidence in self.
—Marcus Annaeus Seneca

Self-respect will keep a man from being abject when he is
in the power of enemies, and will enable him to feel that
he may be in the right when the world is against him.
—Bertrand Russell

You are the handicap you must face.
You are the one who must choose your place.
—James Lane Allen

The best and most efficient pharmacy is within your own system.
—Robert C. Peale, M.D.

Self-trust is the first secret of success.
—Ralph Waldo Emerson

It's not enough to be Hungarian, you must have talent, too.
—ALEXANDER KORDA

They are able because they think they are able.
—VIRGIL

I am the master of my fate; I am the captain of my soul.
—WILLIAM ERNEST HENLEY

Champions take responsibility. When the ball is coming
over the net, you can be sure I want the ball.
—BILLIE JEAN KING

Self-confidence is the first requisite to great undertakings.
—SAMUEL JOHNSON

Confidence imparts a wonderful inspiration to its possessor.
—JOHN MILTON

Once you get rid of the idea that you must please other people before
you please yourself, and you begin to follow your own instincts—
only then can you be successful. You become more satisfied, and
when you are other people tend to be satisfied by what you do.
—RAQUEL WELCH

One's self-image is very important because if that's in good
shape, then you can do anything, or practically anything.
—SIR JOHN GIELGUD

There is overwhelming evidence that the higher the level of
self-esteem, the more likely one will treat others with respect,
kindness, and generosity. People who do not experience
self-love have little or no capacity to love others.
—NATHANIEL BRANDEN

Optimism is the faith that leads to achievement. Nothing
can be done without hope and confidence.
—HELEN KELLER

Oftentimes nothing profits more than self-esteem, grounded
on what is just and right and well-managed.
—JOHN MILTON

Great poetry is always written by somebody
straining to go beyond what he can do.
—Stephen Spender

The way to develop self-confidence is to do the thing you fear
and get a record of successful experiences behind you.
—William Jennings Bryan

The confidence which we have in ourselves gives birth
to much of that which we have in others.
—Francois de La Rochefoucauld

Class is an aura of confidence that is being sure without being
cocky. Class has nothing to do with money. Class never runs
scared. It is self-discipline and self-knowledge. It's the sure-
footedness that comes with having proved you can meet life.
—Ann Landers

Be always sure you're right, then go ahead.
—Davy Crockett

A good sweat, with the blood pounding through my body, makes
me feel alive, revitalized. I gain a sense of mastery and assurance.
I feel good about myself. Then I can feel good about others.
—Arthur Dobrin

Confidence . . . is directness and courage in meeting the facts of life.
—John Dewey

Never bend your head. Hold it high. Look the world straight in the eye.
—Helen Keller

The way in which we think of ourselves has
everything to do with how our world sees us.
—Arlene Raven

Measure yourself by your best moments, not by your
worst. We are too prone to judge ourselves by our
moments of despondency and depression.
—Robert Johnson

To be confident is to act in faith.
—BERNARD BYNION

"Glamour" is assurance. It is a kind of knowing that you are all right in every way, mentally and physically and in appearance, and that, whatever the occasion or the situation, you are equal to it.
—MARLENE DIETRICH

In forty hours I shall be in battle, with little information, and on the spur of the moment will have to make the most momentous decisions, but I believe that one's spirit enlarges with responsibility and that, with God's help, I shall make them and make them right.
—GENERAL GEORGE S. PATTON

Perhaps I am stronger than I think.
—THOMAS MERTON

The gain in self-confidence of having accomplished a tiresome labour is immense.
—ARNOLD BENNETT

Nothing splendid has ever been achieved except by those who dared believe that something inside them was superior to circumstances.
—BRUCE BARTON

I always thought I should be treated like a star.
—MADONNA

Real adulthood is the result of two qualities: self-discipline and self-reliance. The process of developing them together in balance is called maturing.
—J.W. JEPSON

Do for yourself or do without.
—GAYLORD PERRY

Skill and confidence are an unconquered army.
—GEORGE HERBERT

He can inspire a group only if he himself is filled with confidence and hope of success.
—FLOYD V. FILSON

Your future depends on many things, but mostly on you.
—FRANK TYGER

Only the person who has faith in himself is able to be faithful to others.
—ERICH FROMM

He who would be well taken care of must take care of himself.
—WILLIAM GRAHAM SUMNER

Don't ask of your friends what you yourself can do.
—QUINTUS ENNIUS

The future is not in the hands of fate, but in ours.
—JULES JUSSERANO

For the great benefits of our being—our life, health,
and reason—we look upon ourselves.
—MARCUS ANNAEUS SENECA

Rogers sees daylight. Campbell makes daylight.
—BUM PHILLIPS

There is no dependence that can be sure but
a dependence upon one's self.
—JOHN GAY

What pulls the strings is the force hidden
within; there lies ... the real man.
—MARCUS AURELIUS

Our remedies oft in ourselves do lie.
—WILLIAM SHAKESPEARE

Men are made stronger on realization that the helping
hand they need is at the end of their own arm.
—SIDNEY J. PHIL

He who is plenteously provided for from within
needs but little from without.
—JOHANN VON GOETHE

The best place to find a helping hand is at the end of your own arm.
—SWEDISH PROVERB

If it is to be, it is up to me.
—ANON

You've got to do your own growing, no matter
how tall your grandfather was.
—IRISH PROVERB

The destiny of man is in his own soul.
—HERODOTUS

Do not rely completely on any other human being, however
dear. We meet all of life's greatest tests alone.
—AGNES MACPHAIL

There are three types of baseball players—those who make it happen,
those who watch it happen, and those who wonder what happened.
—TOMMY LASORDA

Believe that with your feelings and your work you are taking
part in the greatest; the more strongly you cultivate this belief,
the more will reality and the world go forth from it.
—RAINER MARIA RILKE

Only those means of security are good, are certain, are
lasting, that depend on yourself and your own vigor.
—NICCOLO MACHIAVELLI

A man who finds no satisfaction in himself, seeks for it in vain elsewhere.
—FRANCOIS DE LA ROCHEFOUCAULD

There ain't nothing from the outside can lick any of us.
—MARGARET MITCHELL

The wise don't expect to find life worth living; they make it that way.
—ANON

If you would have a faithful servant, and one that you like, serve yourself.
—BENJAMIN FRANKLIN

I am not afraid of storms, for I am learning how to sail my ship.
—LOUISA MAY ALCOTT

If you want a thing done, go; if not, send.
—BENJAMIN FRANKLIN

An axe at home saves hiring a carpenter.
—J.C.F. VON SCHILLER

I have always regarded myself as the pillar of my life.
—MERYL STREEP

Every man paddles his own canoe.
—FREDERICK MARRYAT

A secure individual . . . knows that the responsibility
for anything concerning his life remains with
himself—and he accepts that responsibility.
—HARRY BROWNE

No one can really pull you up very high—you lose your grip on
the rope. But on your own two feet you can climb mountains.
—LOUIS BRANDEIS

The best bet is to bet on yourself.
—ARNOLD GLASOW

My future is one I must make myself.
—LOUIS L'AMOUR

To be a man is, precisely, to be responsible.
—ANTOINE DE SAINT-EXUPERY

No bird soars too high if he soars on his own wings.
—WILLIAM BLAKE

The best things in life must come by effort from
within, not by gifts from the outside.
—FRED CORSON

The only discipline that lasts is self-discipline.
—Bum Phillips

Ruin and recovery are both from within.
—Epictetus

The foundations which we would dig about and find are within us, like the Kingdom of Heaven, rather than without.
—Samuel Butler

We carry with us the wonders we seek without us.
—Sir Thomas Browne

If there is no wind, row.
—Latin proverb

No external advantages can supply self-reliance. The force of one's being ... must come from within.
—R.W. Clark

Faced with crisis, the man of character falls back on himself.
—Charles de Gaulle

God creates the animals, man creates himself.
—Georg Christoph Lichtenberg

The only Zen you find on the tops of mountains is the Zen you bring up there.
—Robert M. Pirsig

Man must be arched and buttressed from within, else the temple wavers to dust.
—Marcus Aurelius

God, why do I storm heaven for answers that are already in my heart? Every grace I need has already been given me. Oh, lead me to the Beyond within.
—Macrina Wieherkehr

There is no reality except the one contained within us.
—Herman Hesse

Knowing that we can be loved exactly as we are gives us all the best opportunity for growing into the healthiest of people.
—FRED ROGERS

There is no man so low down that the cure for his condition does not lie strictly within himself.
—THOMAS L. MASSON

Look well into thyself; there is a source which will always spring up if thou wilt always search there.
—MARCUS AURELIUS

Man cannot remake himself without suffering, for he is both the marble and the sculptor.
—DR. ALEXIS CARREL

I've never met a person, I don't care what his condition, in whom I could not see possibilities. I don't care how much a man may consider himself a failure, I believe in him, for he can change the thing that is wrong in his life anytime he is prepared and ready to do it. Whenever he develops the desire, he can take away from his life the thing that is defeating it. The capacity for reformation and change lies within.
—PRESTON BRADLEY

Every man is his own ancestor, and every man his own heir. He devises his own future, and he inherits his own past.
—H.F. HEDGE

It is what you are inside that matters. You, yourself, are your only real capital.
—VLADIMIR ZWORYKIN

The winds and waves are always on the side of the ablest navigators.
—EDWARD GIBBON

Man is not the creature of circumstances, circumstances are the creature of man. We are free agents, and man is more powerful than matter.
—BENJAMIN DISRAELI

Up to a point a man's life is shaped by environment, heredity, and movements and changes in the world about him; then there comes

a time when it lies within his grasp to shape the clay of his life
into the sort of thing he wishes to be.... Everyone has it within
his power to say, this I am today, that I shall be tomorrow.
—Louis L'Amour

You will not find poetry anywhere unless you bring some of it with you.
—Joseph Joubert

Religious faith, indeed, relates to that which is above us,
but it must arise from that which is within us.
—Josiah Royce

We either make ourselves miserable, or we make
ourselves strong. The amount of work is the same.
—Carlos Castaneda

Every time I start a picture ... I feel the same fear, the
same self-doubts ... and I have only one source on which
I can draw, because it comes from within me.
—Federico Fellini

Circumstances—what are circumstances? I make circumstances.
—Napoleon Bonaparte

Heaven and hell is right now.... You make it heaven
or you make it hell by your actions.
—George Harrison

It is our relation to circumstances that determines
their influence over us. The same wind that carries one
vessel into port may blow another off shore.
—Christian Bovee

There's only one corner of the universe you can be
certain of improving, and that's your own self.
—Aldous Huxley

Parents can only give good advice or put them on the right paths, but
the final forming of a person's character lies in their own hands.
—Anne Frank

Each of us makes his own weather, determines the color of
the skies in the emotional universe which he inhabits.
—FULTON J. SHEEN

A life of reaction is a life of slavery, intellectually and
spiritually. One must fight for a life of action, not reaction.
—RITA MAE BROWN

I would not sit waiting for some value tomorrow, nor for something to
happen. One could wait a lifetime. . . . I would make something happen.
—LOUIS L'AMOUR

Circumstances are the rulers of the weak; they
are but the instruments of the wise.
—SAMUEL LOVER

We will either find a way, or make one.
—HANNIBAL

You have to take it as it happens, but you should try to
make it happen the way you want to take it.
—OLD GERMAN PROVERB

Things don't turn up in this world until somebody turns them up.
—JAMES A. GARFIELD

Choice of attention—to pay attention to this and ignore that—is to
the inner life what choice of action is to the outer. In both cases, a man
is responsible for his choice and must accept the consequences.
—W.H. AUDEN

Life is raw material. We are artisans. We can sculpt our existence into
something beautiful, or debase it into ugliness. It's in our hands.
—CATHY BETTER

Most folks are about as happy as they make up their minds to be.
—ABRAHAM LINCOLN

Happiness is not in our circumstances, but in ourselves.
It is not something we see, like a rainbow, or feel, like
the heat of a fire. Happiness is something we are.
—JOHN B. SHEERIN

Change and growth take place when a person has risked himself and dares to become involved with experimenting with his own life.
—HERBERT OTTO

People are always blaming their circumstances for what they are. The people who get on in this world are they who get up and look for the circumstances they want, and, if they can't find them, make them.
—GEORGE BERNARD SHAW

They have rights who dare defend them.
—ROGER BALDWIN

Make good use of bad rubbish.
—ELIZABETH BERESFORD

A filly who wants to run will always find a rider.
—JACQUES AUDIBERTI

Things alter for the worse spontaneously, if they be not altered for the better designedly.
—FRANCIS BACON

Think wrongly, if you please, but in all cases think for yourself.
—DORIS LESSING

Let me listen to me and not to them.
—GERTRUDE STEIN

Each man must for himself alone decide what is right and what is wrong, which course is patriotic and which isn't. You cannot shirk this and be a man. To decide against your conviction is to be an unqualified and excusable traitor, both to yourself and to your country, let men label you as they may.
—MARK TWAIN

The man who makes everything that leads to happiness depend upon himself, and not upon other men, has adopted the very best plan for living happily.
—PLATO

We are taught you must blame your father, your sisters, your brothers, the school, the teachers—you can blame anyone,

but never blame yourself. It's never your fault. But it's always
your fault, because if you want to change, you're the one
who has got to change. It's as simple as that, isn't it?
—KATHARINE HEPBURN

The essence of philosophy is that a man should so live that his
happiness shall depend as little as possible on external things.
—EPICTETUS

If we live good lives, the times are also good.
As we are, such are the times.
—SAINT AUGUSTINE

How much time he gains who does not look to see
what his neighbor says or does or thinks, but only at
what he does himself, to make it just and holy.
—MARCUS AURELIUS

Be yourself and think for yourself; and while your conclusions may not be
infallible, they will be nearer right than the conclusions forced upon you.
—ELBERT HUBBARD

To wait for someone else, or to expect someone else
to make my life richer, or fuller, or more satisfying,
puts me in a constant state of suspension.
—KATHLEEN TIERNEY ANDRUS

Though reading and conversation may furnish us with many ideas
of men and things, our own meditation must form our judgement.
—ISAAC WATTS

The U.S. Constitution doesn't guarantee happiness, only
the pursuit of it. You have to catch up with it yourself.
—BENJAMIN FRANKLIN

All times are beautiful for those who maintain joy
within them; but there is no happy or favorable time
for those with disconsolate or orphaned souls.
—ROSALIA CASTRO

Be thine own palace, or the world's thy jail.
—JOHN DONNE

The efficient man is the man who thinks for himself.
—Charles W. Eliot

Each of us makes his own weather, determines the color of
the skies in the emotional universe which he inhabits.
—Fulton J. Sheen

I am responsible for my own well-being, my own
happiness. The choices and decisions I make regarding
my life directly influence the quality of my days.
—Kathleen Andrus

Learn to depend upon yourself by doing things in
accordance with your own way of thinking.
—Grenville Kleiser

The opportunities for enjoyment in your life are limitless. If you feel
you are not experiencing enough joy, you have only yourself to blame.
—David E. Bresler

If we are not responsible for the thoughts that pass our doors,
we are at least responsible for those we admit and entertain.
—Charles B. Newcomb

When I have been unhappy, I have heard an opera . . . and it seemed the
shrieking of winds; when I am happy, a sparrow's chirp is delicious to
me. But it is not the chirp that makes me happy, but I that make it sweet.
—John Ruskin

Thinking is like loving and dying. Each of us must do it for himself.
—Josiah Royce

Blame yourself if you have no branches or leaves;
don't accuse the sun of partiality.
—Chinese proverb

Nothing can bring you peace but yourself.
—Ralph Waldo Emerson

It is not easy to find happiness in ourselves, and
it is not possible to find it elsewhere.
—Agnes Repplier

No-one gives joy or sorrow.... We gather the
consequences of our own deeds.
—Garuda Purana

In the long run we shape our lives and we shape ourselves.
The process never ends until we die. And the choices
we make are ultimately our own responsibility.
—Eleanor Roosevelt

Felicity, felicity ... is quaffed out of a golden cup ... the flavour is
with you alone, and you can make it as intoxicating as you please.
—Joseph Conrad

Some pursue happiness—others create it.
—Anon

Even God lends a hand to honest boldness.
—Menander

To be obliged to beg our daily happiness from others bespeaks a more
lamentable poverty than that of him who begs his daily bread.
—Charles Caleb Colton

To know what you prefer, instead of humbly saying Amen to what the
world tells you that you ought to prefer, is to have kept your soul alive.
—Robert Louis Stevenson

Man is the artificer of his own happiness.
—Henry David Thoreau

Happiness is like time and space—we make and measure
it ourselves; it is as fancy, as big, as little, as you please,
just a thing of contrasts and comparisons.
—George du Marier

No human being can really understand another, and
no one can arrange another's happiness.
—Graham Greene

If you do not find peace in yourself you will never find it anywhere else.
—Paula A. Bendry

If, after all, men cannot always make history have a meaning, they can always act so that their own lives have one.
—ALBERT CAMUS

Happiness belongs to those who are sufficient unto themselves. For all external sources of happiness and pleasure are, by their very nature, highly uncertain, precarious, ephemeral, and subject to chance.
—ARTHUR SCHOPENHAUER

Under normal periods, any man's success hinges about 5 percent on what others do for him and 95 percent on what he does.
—JAMES A. WORSHAM

No man will succeed unless he is ready to face and overcome difficulties and prepared to assume responsibilities.
—WILLIAM J.H. BOETCKER

The greatest griefs are those we cause ourselves.
—SOPHOCLES

Destiny is not a matter of chance, it is a matter of choice; it is not a thing to be waited for, it is a thing to be achieved.
—WILLIAM JENNINGS BRYAN

I am my own heaven and hell!
—J.C.F. VON SCHILLER

Every man is the architect of his own fortune.
—SALLUST

A wise man will make more opportunities than he finds.
—FRANCIS BACON

Religious faith, indeed, relates to that which is above us, but it must arise from that which is within us.
—JOSIAH ROYCE

If people are suffering, then they must look within themselves. . . . Happiness is not something readymade [Buddha] can give you. It comes from your own actions.
—THE DALAI LAMA

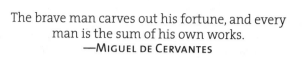

The brave man carves out his fortune, and every
man is the sum of his own works.
—MIGUEL DE CERVANTES

God gives the nuts, but he does not crack them.
—GERMAN PROVERB

If a man wants his dreams to come true, he must wake up.
—ANON

If you want to succeed, you must make your own opportunities as you go.
—JOHN B. GOUGH

God loves to help him who strives to help himself.
—AESCHYLUS

Trust in Allah, but tie your camel first.
—ARABIC PROVERB

Men at some time are masters of their fates.
—WILLIAM SHAKESPEARE

Man is still responsible. . . . His success lies not with the stars, but with
himself. He must carry on the fight of self-correction and discipline.
—FRANK CURTIS WILLIAMS

The people who get on in this world are the people who get up and look
for the circumstances they want, and, if they can't find them, make them.
—GEORGE BERNARD SHAW

Pa, he always said a man had to look spry for himself, because
nobody would do it for him; your opportunities didn't come
knocking around, you had to hunt them down and hog-tie them.
—LOUIS L'AMOUR

No one can help you in holding a good job except Old Man You.
—EDGAR WATSON HOWE

God helps those who help themselves.
—GERMAN PROVERB

To character and success, two things, contradictory as they may seem, must go together—humble dependence and manly independence; humble dependence on God and manly reliance on self.
—WILLIAM WORDSWORTH

If your ship doesn't come in, swim out to it.
—JONATHAN WINTERS

It is vain to ask of the gods what man is capable of supplying for himself.
—EPICURUS

The Ancient Mariner said to Neptune during a great storm, "O God, you will save me if you wish, but I am going to go on holding my tiller straight."
—MICHEL DE MONTAIGNE

He who prays and labours lifts his heart to God with his hands.
—SAINT BERNARD

Ask God's blessing on your work, but don't ask him to do it for you.
—DAME FLORA ROBSON

God has entrusted me with myself.
—EPICTETUS

I think knowing what you cannot do is more important than knowing what you can do.
—LUCILLE BALL

The gods help those who help themselves.
—MARCUS TERENTIUS VARRO

God gives every bird its food, but he does not throw it into the nest.
—JOSIAH HOLLAND

Help yourself and heaven will help you.
—JEAN DE LA FONTAINE

MUSIC

Music, the greatest good that mortals know,
and all of heaven we have below.
—Joseph Addison

Music, in performance, is a type of sculpture. The air
in the performance is sculpted into something.
—Frank Zappa

When I am not too sad to listen, music is my consolation.
—Marcel Proust

Music and silence ... combine strongly because music
is done with silence, and silence is full of music.
—Marcel Marceau

Music is an outburst of the soul
—Frederick Delius

And the night shall be filled with music,
And the cares that infest the day,
Shall fold their tents, like the Arabs,
And as silently steal away.
—Henry Wadsworth Longfellow

Of all noises, I think music is the least disagreeable.
—Samuel Johnson

If you don't live it, it won't come out of your horn.
—Charlie "Bird" Parker

Music is my religion.
—Jimi Hendrix

The aim and final end of all music should be none other
than the glory of God and the refreshment of the soul.
—Johann Sebastian Bach

It may be that when the angels go about their task praising
God, they play only Bach. I am sure, however, that when
they are together en famille, they play Mozart.
—Karl Barth

Music is enough for a lifetime, but a lifetime is not enough for music.
—Sergei Rachmaninov

The truest espression of a people is in its dances and its music,
—Agnes De Mille

A nation creats music—the composer only arranges it.
—Mikhail Glinka

Before I got into rock 'n' roll, I was going to be a dentist
—Greg Allman

All the sounds of the earth are like music.
—Oscar Hammerstein, II

Music's golden tongue flattered to tears this aged man and poor.
—John Keats

When words leave off, music begins.
—Heinrich Heine

I don't know anything about music. In my line you don't have to.
—Elvis Presley

Without music, life would be an error.
—Friedrich Nietzsche

Music washes away from the soul the dust of everyday life.
—Berthold Auerbach

The whole problem can be stated quite simply by asking, 'Is there a
meaning to music?' My answer would be, 'Yes.' And 'Can you state in so
many words what the meaning is?' My answer to that would be, 'No.'
—Aaron Copland

Music is my life, it is a reflection of what I go through.
—LENNY KRAVITZ

If music be the food of love, play on,
Give me excess of it that, surfeiting,
The appetite may sicken and so die
—WILLIAM SHAKESPEARE

After silence that which comes nearest to
expressing the inexpressible is music.
—ALDOUS HUXLEY

Music is well said to be the speech of angels.
—THOMAS CARLYLE

To know whether you are enjoying a piece of music or not
you must see whether you find yourself looking at the
advertisements of Pear's soap at the end of the program.
—SAMUEL BUTLER

Man, if you gotta ask you'll never know.
—LOUIS ARMSTRONG, WHEN ASKED TO DEFINE JAZZ.

Music helps not the toothache.
—GEORGE HERBERT

Music expresses that which cannot be put into
words and cannot remain silent.
—VICTOR HUGO

Heard melodies are sweet, but those unheard are sweeter.
—JOHN KEATS

Who hears music, feels his solitude peopled at once.
—ROBERT BROWNING

To produce music is also in a sense to produce children.
—FRIEDRICH NIETZSCHE

Music is the only language in which you cannot
say a mean or sarcastic thing.
—JOHN ERSKINE

Composers should write tunes that chauffeurs
and errand boys can whistle.
—SIR THOMAS BEECHAM

Without music, life is a journey through a desert.
—PAT CONROY

The best, most beautiful, and most perfect way that we have of
expressing a sweet concord of mind to each other is by music.
—JONATHAN EDWARDS

Music and rhythm find their way into the secret places of the soul.
—PLATO

Music is heard so deeply that is is not heard at all,
but you are the music while the music lasts.
—T.S. ELIOT

The cello is like a beautiful woman who has not grown older, but
younger with time, more slender, more supple, more graceful.
—PABLO CASALS

Is not music the food of love?
—RICHARD SHERIDAN

Music is feeling, then, not sound.
—WALLACE STEVENS

Piano playing, a dance of human fingers
—LUDWIG WITTGENSTEIN

Don't play the saxophone. Let it play you.
—CHARLIE PARKER

Music is edifying, for from time to time it sets the soul in operation.
—JOHN CAGE

Fortissimo at last!
—GUSTAVE MAHLER, ON VISITING NIAGARA FALLS

Blues are the songs of despair, but gospel songs are the songs of hope.
—MAHALIA JACKSON

The music in my heart I bore, long after it was heard no more.
—WILLIAM WORDSWORTH

Music is love in search of a word.
—SIDONIE GABRIELLE

Music is the art of the prophets, the only art that can
calm the agitations of the soul; it is one of the most
magnificent and delightful presents God has given us.
—MARTIN LUTHER

The notes I handle no better than many pianists. But the pauses
between the notes—ah, that is where the art resides!
—ARTUR SCHNABEL

Music is well said to be the speech of angels.
—THOMAS CARLYLE

The trouble with music appreciation in general is
that people are taught to have too much respect for
music; they should be taught to love it instead.
—IGOR STRAVINSKY

All music is folk music. I ain't never heard no horse sing a song.
—LOUIS ARMSTRONG

When I hear music, I fear no danger. I am invulnerable. I see
no foe. I am related to the earliest times, and to the latest.
—HENRY DAVID THOREAU

You were singing? I'm very glad, very well, start dancing now.
—JEAN DE LA FONTAINE

"It Don't Mean a Thing (If It Ain't Got that Swing)"
—DUKE ELLINGTON

The greatest music is made for love, not for money.
—GREG LAKE (EMERSON, LAKE AND PALMER)

[To another musician] Oh, well, you play Bach your way. I'll play him his.
—WANDA LANDOWSKA

Some people tap their feet, some people snap their fingers, and some people sway back and forth. I just sorta do 'em all together, I guess.
—ELVIS PRESLEY

Where there's music there can be no evil.
—MIGUEL CERVANTES

God respects me when I work, but loves me when I sing.
—RABINDRANATH TAGORE

Music is God's gift to man, the only art of Heaven given to earth, the only art of earth we take to Heaven.
—WALTER SAVAGE LANDOR

PEACE

The life of inner peace, being harmonious and without stress, is the easiest type of existence.
—NORMAN VINCENT PEALE

I take it that what all men are really after is some form of, perhaps only some formula of, peace.
—JAMES CONRAD

Nowhere can man find a quieter or more untroubled retreat than in his own soul.
—MARCUS AURELIUS

If there is to be any peace it will come through being, not having.
—HENRY MILLER

The first rule is to keep an untroubled spirit. The second is to look things in the face and know them for what they are.
—Marcus Aurelius

Peace is when time doesn't matter as it passes by.
—Maria Schell

When at night you cannot sleep, talk to the Shepherd and stop counting sheep.
—Anon

The greatest honor history can bestow is the title of peacemaker.
—Richard M. Nixon

As someone pointed out recently, if you can keep your head when all about you are losing theirs, it's just possible you haven't grasped the situation.
—Jean Kerr

When the power of love overcomes the love of power the world will know peace.
—Jimi Hendrix

My aunt once said the world would never find peace until men fell at their women's feet and asked for forgiveness.
—Jack Kerouac

Peace, like charity, beings at home.
—Franklin D. Roosevelt

The mind is never right but when it is at peace within itself.
—Lucius Annaeus Seneca

Peace is not the absence of conflict but the presence of creative alternatives for responding to conflict—alternatives to passive or aggressive responses, alternatives to violence.
—Dorothy Thompson

An insincere peace is better than a sincere war.
—Yiddish Proverb

There may be those on earth who dress better or eat better,
but those who enjoy the peace of God sleep better.
—L. Thomas Holdcroft

When we are unable to find tranquility within
ourselves, it is useless to seek it elsewhere.
—Francois de La Rochefoucauld

If you do not find peace in yourself, you will never find it anywhere else.
—Paula A. Bendry

If there is to be any peace it will come through being, not having.
—Henry Miller

If we have no peace, it is because we have
forgotten that we belong to each other.
—Mother Teresa

I do not want the peace that passeth understanding. I
want the understanding which bringeth peace.
—Helen Keller

In truth, to attain to interior peace, one must be
willing to pass through the contrary to peace.
—Swami Brahmananda

Forgiving those who hurt us is the key to personal peace.
—G. Weatherly

Nothing can bring you peace but yourself.
—Ralph Waldo Emerson

[In] back of tranquility lies always conquered unhappiness.
—David Grayson

Peace is indivisible.
—Maxim Litvinov

In a world filled with causes for worry and anxiety ... we need
the peace of God standing guard over our hearts and minds.
—Jerry W. McCant

Better beans and bacon in peace than cakes and ale in fear.
—AESOP

Peace hath her victories no less renowned than war.
—JOHN MILTON

Peace is much more precious than a piece of land.
—ANWAR AL-SADAT

Peace is not the absence of conflict, but the presence
of God no matter what the conflict.
—ANON

It isn't enough to talk about peace; one must believe in it.
And it isn't enough to believe in it; one must work at it.
—ELEANOR ROOSEVELT

Peace, it's wonderful
—FATHER DIVINE (GEORGE BAKER)

There is no way to peace. Peace is the way.
—A.J. MUSTE

If peace cannot be maintained with honor, it is no longer peace.
—JOHN RUSSELL

It takes two to make peace.
—JOHN F. KENNEDY

SIMPLICITY

Simplicity is the ultimate sophistication.
—LEONARDO DA VINCI

We cannot solve life's problems except by solving them.
—M. SCOTT PECK

Give me neither poverty nor riches; feed me with food convenient for me.
—Proverbs 30:8

Eat when you're hungry. Drink when you're
thirsty. Sleep when you're tired.
—Buddhist proverb

Manifest plainness,
Embrace simplicity,
Reduce selfishness,
Have few desires.
—Lao-tzu

A man must be able to cut a knot, for everything cannot be untied;
he must know how to disengage what is essential from the detail in
which it is enwrapped, for everything cannot be equally considered; in
a word, he must be able to simplify his duties, his business and his life.
—Henri Frederic Amiel

Beauty of style and harmony and grace and
good rhythm depend on simplicity.
—Plato

It is the sweet, simple things of life which are the real ones after all.
—Laura Ingalls Wilder

A little simplification would be the first step
toward rational living, I think.
—Eleanor Roosevelt

Simplicity is an acquired taste. Mankind, left
free, instinctively complicates life.
—Katherine F. Gerould

I take a simple view of living. It is, keep your eyes open and get on with it.
—Sir Laurence Olivier

Simplicity is an exact medium between too little and too much.
—Sir Joshua Reynolds

There are only five things you can do in baseball:
run, throw, catch, hit, and hit with power.
—LEO DUROCHER

Simplicity and naturalness are the truest marks of distinction.
—W. SOMERSET MAUGHAM

You've got a lot of cute stuff. But son, there's only one thing
we're looking for, and that's a pitcher who can tear the catcher's
head off with a fastball. You get one of those, come on back.
—BASEBALL SCOUT, QUOTED BY TOM WOLFE

Start by doing what's necessary, then what's possible
and suddenly you are doing the impossible.
—SAINT FRANCIS OF ASSISI

Simplicity is the key to what I do.
—LIONEL RICHIE

Simplicity is the most difficult thing to secure in this world; it
is the last limit of experience and the last effort of genius.
—GEORGE SAND

Keep breathing.
—SOPHIE TUCKER

It's a round ball and a round bat, and you got to hit it square.
—PETE ROSE

Simplicity is making the journey of this life with just baggage enough.
—ANON

I never thought of myself as a writer, but the simplest thing seemed
to be to put a piece of paper in the roller and start typing.
—CYNTHIA FRIEDMAN

To be simple is to be great.
—RALPH WALDO EMERSON

The niftiest turn of phrase, the most elegant flight of rhetorical fancy, isn't worth beans next to a clear thought clearly expressed.
—JEFF GREENFIELD

There is one art,
No more, no less;
To do all things with art—lessness
—PIET HEIN

All the great things are simple, and many can be expressed in a single word: freedom; justice; honor; duty; mercy; hope.
—SIR WINSTON CHURCHILL

Fishing is much more than fish. It is the great occasion when we may return to the fine simplicity of our forefathers.
—HERBERT HOOVER

The art of art, the glory of expression and the sunshine of the light of letters, is simplicity.
—WALT WHITMAN

Simplicity makes me happy.
—ALICIA KEYS

It is the essence of genius to make use of the simplest ideas.
—CHARLES PEGUY

Reduce the complexity of life by eliminating the needless wants of life, and the labors of life reduce themselves.
—EDWIN WAY TEALE

Genius is the ability to reduce the complicated to the simple.
—C.W. CERAM

It's a simple formula; do your best and somebody might like it.
—DOROTHY BAKER

Success is simple. Do what's right, the right way, at the right time.
—ARNOLD GLASOW

Simplicity, carried to an extreme, becomes elegance.
—JON FRANKLIN

Simplicity is the mean between ostentation and rusticity.
—ALEXANDER POPE

If you can't write your idea on the back of my
calling card, you don't have a clear idea.
—DAVID BELASCO

Simplicity of character is no hindrance to subtlety of intellect.
—JOHN MORLEY

The simplest things give me ideas.
—JOAN MIRO

Simplicity of character is the natural result of profound thought.
—WILLIAM HAZLITT

The obvious is that which is never seen until
someone expresses it simply.
—KAHLIL GIBRAN

The trouble about man is twofold. He cannot learn truths which
are too complicated; he forgets truths which are too simple.
—DAME REBECCA WEST

Is nothing in life ever straight and clear, the way children see it?
—ROSIE THOMAS

I know only that what is moral is what you feel good after
and what is immoral is what you feel bad after.
—ERNEST HEMINGWAY

Art, it seems to me, should simplify.
—WILLA CATHER

If it's working, keep doing it.
If it's not working, stop doing it.
If you don't know what to do, don't do anything.
—DR. MELVIN KONNER

There is no cure for birth or death save to enjoy the interval.
—GEORGE SANTAYANA

I believe that a simple and unassuming manner of life is
best for everyone, best both for the body and the mind.
—ALBERT EINSTEIN

If you don't like something about yourself, change
it. If you can't change it, accept it.
—TED SHACKELFORD

When you are at sea, keep clear of the land.
—PUBLILIUS SYRUS

Many things are lost for want of asking.
—ENGLISH PROVERB

The great business of life is to be, to do, to do without, and to depart.
—JOHN, VISCOUNT MORLEY OF BLACKBURN

Love, and do what you like.
—SAINT AUGUSTINE

My formula for living is quite simple. I get up in the morning and
I go to bed at night. In between I occupy myself as best I can.
—CARY GRANT

If you aren't going all the way, why go at all?
—JOE NAMATH

There is only one meaning of life, the act of living itself.
—ERICH FROMM

The way you get better at playing football is to play football.
—GENE BRODIE

To be simple is the best thing in the world.
—G.K. CHESTERTON

Keep doing what you're doing and you'll
keep getting what you're getting.
—Anon

Teach us Delight in simple things,
And Mirth that has no bitter springs.
—Rudyard Kipling

I have a simple philosophy. Fill what's empty.
Empty what's full. Scratch where it itches.
—Alice Roosevelt Longworth

Everything should be made as simple as possible ... but not simpler.
—Albert Einstein

Simplicity, clarity, singleness: these are the attributes
that give our lives power and vividness and joy.
—Richard Halloway

To keep a lamp burning, we have to keep putting oil in it.
—Mother Teresa

The greatest truths are the simplest, and so are the greatest men.
—Julius Charles Hare

If you walk, just walk. If you sit, just sit. But
whatever you do, don't wobble.
—Anon

The great artist and thinker are the simplifiers.
—Henri Frederic Amiel

First say to yourself what you would be, and then do what you have to do.
—Epictetus

Affected simplicity is an elegant imposture.
—Francois de La Rochefoucauld

You decide what it is you want to accomplish and then you lay out your
plans to get there, and then you just do it. It's pretty straightforward.
—Nancy Ditz

Stay out of jail.
—Alfred Hitchcock's advice to directors

There is a master key to success with which no man can fail. Its name
is simplicity ... reducing to the simplest possible terms every problem.
—Henri Deterding

I searched through rebellion, drugs, diet, mysticism, religion,
intellectualism and much more, only to find that truth
is basically simple and feels good, clear and right.
—Chick Corea

If you would know contentment, let your deeds be few.
—Democritus

If you want to be found, stand where the seeker seeks.
—Sidney Lanier

Do what you can, with what you have, where you are.
—Theodore Roosevelt

What I do, I do very well, and what I don't do well, I don't do at all.
—Anon

Do the duty which lies nearest thee. . . . Thy second
duty will already have become clearer.
—Thomas Carlyle

The ability to simplify means to eliminate the
unnecessary to that the necessary may speak.
—Hans Hofmann

Losers have tons of variety. Champions take pride in
just learning to hit the same old boring winners.
—Vic Braden

There is no greatness where there is not simplicity.
—Leo Tolstoy

The wisdom of life consists in the elimination of nonessentials.
—Lin Yutang

Hitting is timing. Pitching is upsetting timing.
—WARREN SPAHN

All animals except man know that the ultimate of life is to enjoy it.
—SAMUEL BUTLER

An elegant sufficiency, content,
Retirement, rural quiet, friendship, books.
—JAMES THOMSON

If a Plant's Roots Are Too Tight, Repot.
—GARDENING HEADLINE, THE NEW YORK TIMES

The sculptor produces the beautiful statue by chipping away such parts
of the marble block as are not needed—it is a process of elimination.
—ELBERT HUBBARD

The more we reduce the size of our world,
the more we shall be its master.
—JACINTO BENAVENTE

All I had to do was keep turning left.
—GEORGE ROBSON, AFTER WINNING THE INDIANAPOLIS 500

Perfect simplicity is unconsciously audacious.
—GEORGE MEREDITH

My advice about acting? Speak clearly, don't bump into people, and
if you must have motivation, think of your pay packet on Friday.
—NOEL COWARD

Fat hens lay few eggs.
—GERMAN PROVERB

The whole is simpler than the sum of its parts.
—WILLARD GIBBS

Just sit out there and have them go through the moves.
When you see something you don't like, change it.
—JOSHUA LOGAN'S ADVICE TO DIRECTORS

Simplicity, simplicity, simplicity! I say, let your affairs be as two or three, and not a hundred or a thousand.... Simplify, simplify.
—Henry David Thoreau

It is proof of high culture to say the greatest matters in the simplest way.
—Ralph Waldo Emerson

The idea is to get the pencil moving quickly.
—Bernard Malamud

True eloquence consists of saying all that should be said, and that only.
—Francois de La Rochefoucauld

It is proof of high culture to say the greatest matters in the simplest way.
—Ralph Waldo Emerson

I finally figured out the only reason to be alive is to enjoy it.
—Rita Mae Brown

Happiness comes of the capacity to feel deeply, to enjoy simply, to think freely, to risk life, to be needed.
—Storm Jameson

Players have two things to do: Play and keep their mouths shut.
—Sparky Anderson

Give me a look, give me a face,
That makes simplicity a grace;
Robes loosely flowing, hair as free,
Such sweet neglect more taketh me
Than all the adulteries of art:
They strike mine eyes, but not my heart.
—Ben Jonson

Don't let go of the vine.
—Johnny Weissmuller, who played Tarzan, giving advice to acting students

I just take my three swings and go sit on the bench. I don't ever want to mess up my swing.
—Dick Allen

The main obligation is to amuse yourself.
—S.J. Perelman

If you don't throw it, they can't hit it.
—Lefty Gomez

Football is blocking and tackling. Everything else is mythology.
—Vince Lombardi

The rules of soccer are very simple. Basically it's this: If it
moves, kick it; if it doesn't move, kick it until it does.
—Phil Woosnam

Simplicity and repose are qualities that measure
the true value of any work of art.
—Frank Lloyd Wright

Simple style is like white light. It is complex,
but its complexity is not obvious.
—Anatole France

And all the loveliest things there be
Come simply, so, it seems to me.
—Edna St. Vincent Millay

The ordinary arts we practice every day at home are of more
importance to the soul than their simplicity might suggest.
—Sir Thomas More

Just learn your lines and don't bump into the furniture.
—Spencer Tracy

Fear less, hope more; eat less, chew more; whine less, breathe more;
talk less, say more; love more, and all good things will be yours.
—Swedish proverb

Gracias, danke, merci—whatever language is spoken, "thank you"
frequently expressed will cheer your spirit, broaden your friendships,
and lift your lives to a higher pathway as you journey toward perfection.
There is a simplicity—even a sincerity—when "thank you" is spoken.
—Thomas S. Monson

When ideas come, I write them; when they don't come, I don't.
—WILLIAM FAULKNER

Simple truths are a relief from grand speculations.
—VAUVENARGUES

Good friends, good books and a sleepy conscience: this is the ideal life.
—MARK TWAIN

It's a gift to be simple!
It's a gift to be free!
It's a gift to be just who you ought to be!
No, you don't have to struggle now
To live just right.
Just walk with Me,
And you walk in the Light
—SHAKER HYMN

TRUTH

Truth is generally the best vindication against slander.
—ABRAHAM LINCOLN

When in doubt tell the truth.
—MARK TWAIN

Half the Truth is often a great Lie.
—BENJAMIN FRANKLIN

The love of truth has its reward in heaven and even on earth.
—FRIEDRICH NIETZSCHE

A kiss may not be the truth, but it is what we wish were true.
—STEVE MARTIN

If truth is a value it is because it is true and
not because it is brave to speak it.
—W. SOMERSET MAUGHAM

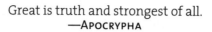

Great is truth and strongest of all.
—APOCRYPHA

Truth exists. Only lies are invented
—GEORGES BRAQUE

Nothing hurts a new truth more than an old error.
—JOHANN WOLFGANG VON GOETHE

Knowing the truth and living it are two things.
—ANON

Truth is what stands the test of experience.
—ALBERT EINSTEIN

Believe those who are seeking the truth; doubt those who find it.
—ANDRE GIDE

The truth may hurt, but lies can kill.
—MORT SAHL

We do not seek for truth in the abstract. . . . Every man sees what
he looks for, and hears what he listenes for, and nothing else.
—GEORGE BERNARD SHAW

Truth is on the march and nothing can stop it.
—EMILE ZOLA

I search after truth, by which man never yet was harmed.
—MARCUS AURELIUS

It takes two to speak the truth—one to speak and another to hear.
—EDWARD R. MURROW

It is always the best policy to speak the truth, unless
of course you are an exceptionally good liar.
—JEROME K. JEROME

The man who finds a truth lights a torch.
—ROBERT G. INGERSOLL

Pretty much all the honest truth telling in the world is done by children.
—Oliver Wendell Holmes

Integrity is telling myself the truth. And honesty
is telling the truth to other people.
—Spencer Johnson

Truth is a torch which gleams in the fog but does not dispel it.
—Claude-Adrien Helvetius

Truth fears no trial.
—Thomas Fuller

Between whom there is hearty truth there is love.
—Henry David Thoreau

The Truth must dazzle gradually
Or every man be blind
—Emily Dickinson

Man passes away; generations are but shadows;
there is nothing stable but truth.
—Josiah Quincy, Jr.

You can bend it and twist it . . . You can misuse and abuse
it . . . But even God cannot change the Truth.
—Michael Levy

Truth can remain silent. Lies must be spoken.
—Mason Cooley

The truth never arrives neatly wrapped.
—Thomas Powers

They who know the truth are not equal to those who love it, and
they who love it are not equal to those who delight in it.
—Confucius

Who speaks the truth stabs Falsehood to the heart.
—James Russell Lowell

Truth angers those whom it does not convince.
—ANON

The truth is out there.
—*X-FILES* CATCHPHRASE

So absolutely good is truth, truth never hurts the teller.
—ROBERT BROWNING

Truth will out.
—JOHN LYDGATE

Every truth has two sides; it is well to look at both,
before we commit ourselves to either.
—AESOP

Truth is a deep kindness that teaches us to be content in our
everyday life and share with the peopl the same happiness.
—KAHLIL GIBRAN

The truth hurts, but only when it ought to.
—ANON

Truth is not a diet but a condiment.
—CHRISTOPHER MORLEY

The stupid believe that to be truthful is easy; only the
artist, the great artist, knows how difficult it is.
—WILLA CATHER

If you tell the truth you don't have to remember anything.
—MARK TWAIN

I would rather the man who presents something for my consideration
subject me to a zephyr of truth and a gentle breeze of responsibility
rather than blow me down with a curtain of hot wind.
—GROVER CLEVELAND

Truth is like the sun. You can shut it out for a time, but it ain't goin' away.
—ELVIS PRESLEY

All necessary truth is its own evidence.
—Ralph Waldo Emerson

Rather than love, than money, than fame, give me truth.
—Henry David Thoreau

The truth will always have a market.
—Jean Shepherd

Fiction is Truth's elder sister. Obviously. No one in the world
knew what truth was till somebody had told a story.
—Rudyard Kipling

There is nothing so powerful as truth; and often nothing so strange.
—Daniel Webster

Opinion is a flitting thing,
But Truth, outlasts the sun—
If then we cannot own them both—
Possess the oldest one—.
—Emily Dickinson

Once in a while there are things the brain simply
refuses to accept as being true because they appear
too improbable, too unlikely, too preposterous.
—Walter Abish

'Tis strange—but true; for truth is always strange;
stranger than fiction: if it could be told.
—Lord Byron

Every step in every proud life is a run from safety to the dark,
and the only thing to trust is what we think is true.
—Richard Bach

Whatever satisfies the soul is truth.
—Walt Whitman

He led a double life. Did that make him a liar? He did
not feel a liar. He was a man of two truths.
—Iris Murdoch

In order that all men may be taught to speak truth, it is necessary that all likewise should learn to hear it.
—Samuel Johnson

There are two kinds of truth: the truth that lights the way and the truth that warms the heart. The first of these is science, and the second is art.
—Raymond Chandler

Ethical truth is as exact and as peremptory as physical truth.
—Herbert Spencer

The truth is rarely pure and never simple.
—Oscar Wilde

How often have I said to you that when you have eliminated the impossible, whatever remains, however improbable, must be the truth?
—John D. Barrow by Arthur Conan Doyle

When money speaks, the truth keeps silent.
—Russian Proverb

WEALTH/MONEY

Ability is a poor man's wealth.
—John Wooden

Being rich is having money; being wealthy is having time.
—Margaret Bonnano

All wealth is relative; and so is its absence.
—Sybille Bedford

A great fortune is a great slavery.
—Seneca

It is wealth to be content.
—Lao-Tzu

I don't care about money. I just want to be wonderful.
—MARILYN MONROE

Riches attract the attention, consideration,
and congratulations of mankind.
—JOHN ADAMS

He is rich who hath enough to be charitable.
—SIR THOMAS BROWNE

I've been rich and I've been poor; rich is better.
—SOPHIE TUCKER

The poor rich man! All he has is what he has bought. What I see is mine.
—HENRY DAVID THOREAU

The value of a dollar is social, as it is created by society.
—RALPH WALDO EMERSON

It is easier for a camel to go through the eye of a needle,
than for a rich man to enter the kingdom of God.
—MATTHEW 19:24

It's no disgrace t' be poor, but it might as well be.
—KIN HUBBARD

Few rich men own their own property. The property owns them.
—ROBERT G. INGERSOLL

The meek shall inherit the earth, but not the mineral rights.
—J. PAUL GETTY

Without a rich heart, wealth is an ugly beggar.
—RALPH WALDO EMERSON

The more wealth, the more worry.
—HILLEL

Empty pockets never held anyone back. Only empty
heads and empty hearts can do that.
—NORMAN VINCENT PEALE

A good wife and health is a man's best wealth.
—ENGLISH SAYING

Nothing that cost only a dollar is worth having.
—ELIZABETH ARDEN

Wealth is not a matter of intelligence it's a matter of inspiration.
—JIM ROHN

Prosperity is the surest breeder of insolence I know.
—MARK TWAIN

Let there be wealth without tears; enough for
the wise man who will ask no further.
—AESCHYLUS

Everything in Rome has its price.
—JUVENAL

Money's the wise man's religion.
—EURIPIDES

I finally know what distinguishes man from
the other beasts: financial worries.
—JULES RENARD

Today the greatest single source of wealth is between your ears.
—BRIAN TRACY

It is better to live rich than to die rich.
—SAMUEL JOHNSON

He does not possess wealth that allows it to possess him.
—BENJAMIN FRANKLIN

Living in the lap of luxury isn't bad, except you never
know when luxury is going to stand up.
—ORSON WELLES

God gave me my money.
—JOHN D. ROCKEFELLER, SR.

There was a time when a fool and his money were
soon parted, but now it happens to everybody.
—Adlai Stevenson

Nature laughs at a miser. He is like the squirrel who buries
his nuts and refrains from digging them up again.
—Henry George

The only foolproof path to wealth is inheritance.
—Tom & David Gardner, *The Motley Fool*

There is no Wealth but Life.
—John Ruskin

Wealth . . . is a relative thing since he that has little and wants less
is richer than he that has much but wants more. . . . A tub was large
enough for Diogenes, but a world was too little for Alexander.
—C.C. Colton

Money is better than poverty, if only for financial reasons.
—Woody Allen

The jingling of the guinea helps the hurt that Honor feels.
—Alfred, Lord Tennyson

No honest hardworking official likes to see good money disappearing
into the hands of the Treasury at the end of the financial year.
—Joyce Cary

He that has a penny in his purse, is worth a
penny: Have and you shall be esteemed.
—Petronius

That man is richest whose pleasures are cheapest.
—Henry David Thoreau

I'd like to live as a poor man with lots of money.
—Pablo Picasso

With his own money a person can live as he likes—a
ruble that's your own is dearer than a brother.
—Maxim Gorky

Knowledge makes one laugh, but wealth makes one dance.
—George Herbert

Money is only useful when you get rid of it. It is like the odd card
in "Old Maid"; the player who is finally left with it has lost.
—Evelyn Waugh

Much work is merely a way to make money; much
leisure is merely a way to spend it.
—C. Wright Mills

The difference between a little money and no money at all
is enormous—and can shatter the world. And the difference
between a little money and an enormous amount of money
is very slight—and that, also, can shatter the world.
—Thornton Wilder

I do want to get rich but I never want to do what there is to do to get rich.
—Gertrude Stein

[The ideal client is] the very wealthy man in very great trouble.
—John W. Sterling, Attorney

When a fellow says, "It hain't the money, but th'
principle o' the thing," it's th' money.
—Kin Hubbard

My problem lies in reconciling my gross habits with my net income.
—Errol Flynn

Even genius is tied to profit.
—Pindar

Ninety percent I'll spend on good times, women, and Irish
whiskey. The other 10 percent I'll probably waste.
—Tug McGraw (on his high baseball salary)

Wealth, properly employed, is a blessing; and a man may
lawfully endeavor to increase it by honest means.
—Muhammad

You know the best way to double your money?
Fold it and put it in your pocket.
—Phyllis Diller

Money cannot buy health, but I'd settle for
a diamond-studded wheelchair.
—Dorothy Parker

Ready money is Aladdin's lamp.
—Lord Byron

That's where the money is.
—Willie Sutton, on why he robbed banks.

The point is to get so much money that money's not the point anymore.
—William Hamilton

Most of us aren't that interested in getting
rich—we just don't want to get poor.
—Andy Rooney

Money couldn't buy friends, but you got a better class of enemy.
—Spike Milligan

Wealth must justify itself in happiness.
—George Santayana

There are some things that money cannot buy.
—The New York Times

There is a gigantic difference between earning
a great deal of money and being rich.
—Marlene Dietrich

If a man has money, it is usually sign, too, that he
knows how to take care of it; don't imagine his money
is easy to get simply because he has plenty of it.
—EDGAR WATSON HOWE

Inherited wealth is a big handicap to happiness. It is as
certain death to ambition as cocaine is to morality.
—WILLIAM K. VANDERBILT

When Gold argues the cause, eloquence is impotant.
—PUBLILIUS SYRUS

Ordinary riches can be stolen, real riches cannot. In your soul
are infinitely precious things that cannot be taken from you
—OSCAR WILDE

Money makes your life easier. If you're lucky to have it, you're lucky.
—ROBERT DE NIRO

I don't like money, actually, but it quiets my nerves.
—JOE LOUIS

One must choose, in life, between making money
and spending it. There's no time to do both.
—EDOUARD BOURDET

A man is rich in proportion to the number of
things which he can afford to let alone.
—HENRY DAVID THOREAU

[A banker is] a man who will lend you money if you
can prove to him that you don't need it.
—JOE E. LEWIS

It is extraordinary how many emotional storms one may
weather in safety if one is ballasted with ever so little gold.
—WILLIAM MCFEE

Wealth is measured not by what you have
but by what you've given away.
—NATIVE AMERICAN SAYING

Salary is no object; I want only enough to keep my body and soul apart.
—Dorothy Parker

Every day I get up and look through the Forbes list of the richest people in America. If I'm not there, I go to work
—Robert Orben

They say it is better to be poor and happy than rich and miserable, but how about a compromise like moderately rich and just moody.
—Princess Diana

When reason rules, money is a blessing.
—Publilius Syrus

You can't be too rich or too thin.
—Wallis Simpson, Duchess of Windsor

Always try to rub up against money, for if you rub up against money long enough, some of it may rub off on you.
—Damon Runyon

Wealth unused might as well not exist.
—Aesop

If women didn't exist, all the money in the world would have no meaning.
—Aristotle Onassis

It's not the money. It's the principle.
—Chicago Daily Tribune

Money is power, freedom, a cushion, the root of all evil, the sum of blessings.
—Carl Sandburg

Money is like a sixth sense without which you cannot make a complete use of the other five.
—W. Somerset Maugham

I finally know what distinguishes man from
the other beasts: financial worries.
—JULES RENARD

Money, n. A blessing that is of no advantage to
us excepting when we part with it.
—AMBROSE BIERCE

Show me the money!
—CAMERON CROWE (*JERRY MAGUIRE*)

Someone stole all my credit cards, but I won't be reporting
it. The thief spends less than my wife did.
—HENNY YOUNGMAN

Cocaine is God's way of telling you you have too much money.
—ROBIN WILLIAMS

A billion here, a billion there, and pretty soon
you're talking about real money.
—EVERETT MCKINLEY DIRKSEN

Money talks.
—APHRA BEHN

With money in your pocket, you are wise and you
are handsome and you sing well too.
—YIDDISH PROVERBS

Another day, another dollar.
—*L.A. TIMES*

WISDOM

Wise men speak because they have something to say;
Fools because they have to say something.
—PLATO

Common sense suits itself to the ways of the world.
Wisdom tries to conform to the ways of Heaven.
—Joseph Joubert

Wisdom is knowing what to do next, skill is knowing
how to do it, and virtue is doing it.
—David Starr Jordan

To see clearly is poetry, prophecy, and religion—all in one.
—John Ruskin

If a man is wise, he gets rich, an' if he gets rich, he gets foolish, or
his wife does. That's what keeps the money movin' around.
—Finley Peter Dunne

Self-reflection is the school of wisdom.
—Baltasar Gracian

Conscience is a mother-in-law whose visit never ends.
—H.L. Mencken

'Tis not knowing much, but what is useful, that makes a wise man.
—Thomas Fuller

Wise Man: One who sees the storm coming before the clouds appear.
—Elbert Hubbard

Serene, I fold my hands and wait,
Nor care for wind, nor tide, nor sea;
I rave no more 'gainst time or fate,
For lo! My own shall come to me.
—John Burroughs

The fool wonders, the wise man asks.
—Benjamin Disraeli

The invariable mark of wisdom is to see the miraculous in the common.
—Ralph Waldo Emerson

Everybody is ignorant, only on different subjects.
—Will Rogers

You can observe a lot by watchin'.
—Yogi Berra

Wisdom is what's left after we've run out of personal opinions.
—Cullen Hightower

Early to bed and hearly to rise makes a man healthy, wealthy, and wise.
—John Clarke

Good judgment comes from experience, and experience—
well, that comes from poor judgment.
—A.A. Milne

Wisdom is knowing what to do next; virtue is doing it.
—David Starr Jordan

As sheer casual reading matter, I still find the English
dictionary the most interesting book in our language.
—Albert Jay Nock

The seat of knowledge is in the head; of wisdom in the heart.
—William Hazlitt

Wisdom remembers. Happiness forgets.
—Mason Cooley

Wisdom is divided into two parts: (a) having a
great deal to say, and (b) not saying it.
—Anon

Anyone who isn't confused doesn't really understand the situation.
—Edward R. Murrow

Wisdom that don't make us happier ain't worth plowing for.
—Josh Billings

It is the province of knowledge to speak, and
it the privilege of wisdom to listen.
—Oliver Wendell Holmes, Sr.

I don't think much of a man who is not wiser
today than he was yesterday.
—Abraham Lincoln

He who knows others is learned; he who knows himself is wise.
—Lao-Tze

A pinch of probably is worth more than a pound of perhaps.
—Fritz Thyssen

The highest form of wisdom is kindness.
—Talmud

Wisdom doesn't automatically come with old age. Nothing
does—except wrinkles. It's true, some wines improve with
age. But only if the grapes were good in the first place.
—Abigail Van Buren

Wisdom cannot be passed on. Wisdom which a wise man tries
to pass on to someone always sounds like foolishness.
—Hermann Hesse

Youth is the time to study wisdom; old age is the time to practice it.
—Henri Rousseau

There is no wisdom in haste.
—Chinese Proverb

Experience is what enables you to recognize
a mistake when you make it again.
—Earl Wilson

The well-bred contradict other people. The wise contradict themselves.
—Oscar Wilde

Science is organized knowledge. Wisdom is organized life.
—Immanuel Kant

Honesty is the first chapter of the book of wisdom.
—Thomas Jefferson

Wisdom at times is found in folly.
—Horace

Sometimes the first duty of intelligent men
is the restatement of the obvious.
—George Orwell

Nine-tenths of wisdom consists in being wise in time.
—Theodore Roosevelt

Wisdom consists of the anticipation of consequences.
—Norman Cousins

There is nothing new under the sun, but there
are lots of old things we don't know.
—Ambrose Bierce

The fear of the Lord is the beginning of wisdom.
—Psalms 111: 10

To acquire knowledge, one must study; but to
acquire wisdom, one must observe.
—Marilyn vos Savant

God, grant me the serenity to accept the things I
cannot change, the courage to change the things I
can, and the wisdom to know the difference.
—Reinhold Niebuhr

The Doors of Wisdom are never shut.
—Benjamin Franklin

He is wise that can make a friend of a foe.
—John Ray

An ounce of Wisdom is worth a Pount of Wit.
—Thomas Fuller

Raphael paints wisdom; Handel sings it, Phidias carves it,
Shakespeare writes it, Wren builds it, Columbus sails it, Luther
preaches it, Washington arms it, Watt mechanizes it.
—Ralph Waldo Emerson

The art of being wise is the art of knowing what to overlook.
—William James

Less is more.
—Ludwig Mies van der Rohe

Knowledge is proud that he has learned so much;
Wisdom is humble that he knows no more.
—William Cowper

Good people are good because they've come to wisdom through failure.
—William Saroyen

An ounce of wisdom is worth more than tons of cleverness.
—Baltasar Gracian

One's prime is elusive. You little girls, when you grow up, must
be on the alert to recognize your prime at whatever time of
your life it may occur. You must then live it to the full.
—Muriel Spark (The Prime of Miss Jean Brodie)

Wisdom is not a product of schooling but of
the lifelong attempt to acquire it.
—Albert Einstein

He is a wise man who does not grieve for the things which
he has not, but rejoices for those which he has.
—Epictetus

Wisdom is ofttimes nearer when we stoop than when we soar.
—William Wordworth

It requires wisdom to understand wisdom; the
music is nothing if the audience is deaf.
—Walter Lippmann

The wise know too well their weakness to assume infallibility;
and he who knows most, knows best how little he knows.
—THOMAS JEFFERSON

Wisdom is knowing when you can't be wise
—PAUL ENGLE

Experience is the same name everyone gives to their mistakes.
—OSCAR WILDE

Besides the noble art of getting things done, there is a
nobler art of leaving things undone.... The wisdom of
life consists in the elimination of nonessentials.
—LIN YUTANG

The awe of God is wisdom.
—ABRAHAM JOSHUA HESCHEL

God is in the Details.
—LUDWIG MIES VAN DER ROHE

To be conscious that you are ignorant is a great step to knowledge.
—BENJAMIN DISRAELI

Wisdom knows the proper limits of things.
—SENECA THE YOUNGER

Wisdom is not knowledge, but lies in the use we make of knowledge.
—N. SRI RAM

The wisest people are the clowns, like Harpo Marx, who would not
speak. If I could have anything I want I would like God to listen to what
Harpo was not saying, and understand why Harpo would not talk.
—PHILIP K. DICK

Expenditure rises to meet income.
—C. NORTHCOTE PARKINSON

Knowledge comes by taking things apart. But
wisdom comes by putting things together.
—JOHN A. MORRISON

I know nothing except the fact of my ignorance.
—Socrates

Be wiser than other people, if you can; but do not tell them so.
—Lord Chesterfield

Common sense is not so common.
—Voltaire

I don't adopt any one's ideas; I have my own.
—Ivan Turgenev

The fool does think he is wise, but the wise
man knows himself to be a fool.
—William Shakespeare

Little is needed to make a wise man happy,
but nothing can content a fool.
—Francois de La Rochefoucauld

I must say I find television very educational. The minute somebody
turns it on, I go into the library and read a good book.
—Groucho Marx

WORK

Nothing worthwhile comes easily. Half effort does not produce
half results, it produces no results. Work, continuous work and
hard work, is the only way to accomplish results that last.
—Hamilton Holt

Hard work never killed anybody, but why take a chance?
—Charlie McCarthy, voiced by Edgar Bergen

If hard work were such a wonderful thing, surely the
rich would have kept it all to themselves.
—Lane Kirkland

Art is man's expression of his joy in labor.
—George Pope Morris

Work is love made visible.
—Kahlil Gibran

I worked my way up from nothing to a state of extreme poverty.
—Groucho Marx

How would you like a job where, every time you make a
mistake, a big red light goes on and 18,000 people boo?
—Jacques Plante

When your work speaks for itself, don't interrupt.
—Henry J. Kaiser

To fulfill a dream, to be allowed to sweat over lonely labor, to be given a
chance to create, is the meat and potatoes of life. The money is the gravy.
—Bette Davis

The happy people are those who are producing something.
—William Ralph Inge

A great many people have come up to me and asked me how
I manage to get so much work done and still keep looking so
dissipated. My answer is "Don't you wish you knew?"
—Robert Benchley

Congenial labor is essence of happiness.
—Arthur Christopher Benson

A specialist is a man who knows more and more about less and less.
—William J. Mayo

Every man's task is his life-preserver.
—Ralph Waldo Emerson

Writing is easy. Just put a sheet of paper in
the typewriter and start bleeding.
—Thomas Wolfe

When I stop [working], the rest of the day is posthumous.
I'm only really alive when I'm working.
—TENNESSEE WILLIAMS

It is only when I am doing my work that I feel
truly alive. It is like having sex.
—FEDERICO FELLINI

She Works Hard for the Money.
—DONNA SUMMER

A woman must have money and a room of
her own if she is to write fiction.
—VIRGINIA WOOLF

After fifty years of living, it occurs to me that the most significant
thing that people do is go to work, whether it is to go to work on
their novel or at the assembly plant or fixing somebody's teeth.
—THOMAS McGUANE

He who labors diligently need never despair, for all
things are accomplished by diligence and labor.
—MENANDER

The fun of being alive is realizing that you have a talent
and you can use it every day, so it grows stronger.... And if
you're in an atmosphere where this talent is appreciated
instead of just tolerated, why, it's just as good as sex.
—LOU CENTLIVRE

There's no labor a man can do that's undignified, if he does it right.
—BILL COSBY

If a man is called to be a streetsweeper, he should sweep
streets even as Michelangelo painted, or Beethoven composed
music or Shakespeare wrote poetry. He should sweep streets
so well that all the hosts of heaven and earth will pause to
say, here lived a great streetsweeper who did his job well.
—MARTIN LUTHER KING, JR.

The days you work are the best days.
—GEORGIA O'KEEFFE

The work praises the man.
—Irish proverb

We put our love where we have put our labor.
—Ralph Waldo Emerson

Originality and the feeling of one's own dignity are
achieved only through work and struggle.
—Fyodor Dostoyevsky

The road to happiness lies in two simple principles: find
what it is that interests you and that you can do well, and
when you find it, put your whole soul into it—every bit of
energy and ambition and natural ability you have.
—John D. Rockefeller III

There is a kind of victory in good work, no matter how humble.
—Jack Kemp

Labor disgraces no man; unfortunately, you
occasionally find men who disgrace labor.
—Ulysses S. Grant

All I've ever wanted was an honest week's pay for an honest day's work.
—Steve Martin

Honest labor bears a lovely face.
—Thomas Dekker

Work is the best method devised for killing time.
—William Feather

I have friends in overalls whose friendship I would not
swap for the favor of the kings of the world.
—Thomas A. Edison

Work and play are words used to describe the
same thing under differing conditions.
—Mark Twain

A professional is someone who can do his best
work when he doesn't feel like it.
—ALISTAIR COOKE

The highest reward for man's toil is not what he
gets for it, but what he becomes by it.
—JOHN RUSKIN

Work expands to fill the time available for its completion.
—C. NORTHCOTE PARKINSON

The test of a vocation is the love of the drudgery it involves.
—LOGAN PEARSALL SMITH

He who considers his work beneath him will be above doing it well.
—ALEXANDER CHASE

Whenever it is possible, a boy should choose some occupation
which he should do even if he did not need the money.
—WILLIAM LYON PHELPS

I love Mickey Mouse more than any woman I've ever known.
—WALT DISNEY

Only he is successful in his business who makes that pursuit
which affords him the highest pleasure sustain him.
—HENRY DAVID THOREAU

Employment is nature's physician, and is essential to human happiness.
—GALEN

Give me a man who sings at his work.
—THOMAS CARLYLE

Until you've lost your reputation, you never realize
what a burden it was or what freedom really is.
—MARGARET MITCHELL

It is difficult to get a man to understand something when
his salary depends upon his not understanding it.
—UPTON SINCLAIR

To love what you do and feel that it matters—
how could anything be more fun?
—Katharine Graham

When men are rightly occupied, their amusement grows out
of their work, as the color-petals out of a fruitful flower.
—John Ruskin

Milton Berle is an inspiration to every young person that
wants to get into show business. Hard work, perseverance, and
discipline: all the things you need ... when you have no talent.
—Dean Martin

Continuity of purpose is one of the most essential
ingredients of happiness in the long run, and for most
men this comes chiefly through their work.
—Bertrand Russell

If work was a good thing the rich would have it all and not let you do it.
—Elmore Leonard

Elbow grease is the best polish.
—English proverb

Work consists of whatever a body is obliged to do, and play
consists of whatever a body is not obliged to do.
—Mark Twain

The more I want to get something done, the less I call it work.
—Richard Bach

If a man wakes up famous, he hasn't been sleeping.
—Wes Izzard

Success is dependent on effort.
—Sophocles

Striving for success without hard work is like trying
to harvest where you haven't planted.
—David Bly

When love and skill work together, expect a masterpiece.
—JOHN RUSKIN

Success comes before work only in the dictionary.
—ANON

Sweat plus sacrifice equals success.
—CHARLES O. FINLEY

Success usually comes to those who are too busy to be looking for it.
—HENRY DAVID THOREAU

In all human affairs there are efforts, there are results, and
the strength of the effort is the measure of the result.
—JAMES LANE ALLEN

There is no more dreadful punishment than futile and hopeless labor.
—ALBERT CAMUS

Any man who has had the job I've had and didn't
have a sense of humor wouldn't still be here.
—HARRY S TRUMAN

Anyone can do any amount of work, provided it isn't the
work he is supposed be doing at that moment.
—ROBERT BENCHLEY

Hang by your thumbs, everybody! Write if you get work!
—RAYMOND H. GOULDING (*BOB AND RAY*)

The heights by great men reached and kept
Were not attained by sudden flight,
But they, while their companions slept,
Were toiling upward in the night.
—HENRY WADSWORTH LONGFELLOW

Opportunity is missed by most people because it
is dressed in overalls, and looks like work.
—THOMAS A. EDISON

Be strong!
We are not here to play, to dream, to drift;
We have hard work to do and loads to lift;
Shun not the struggle—face it; 'tis God's gift.
—Maltbie D. Babcock

If you could once make up your mind never to undertake more
work . . . than you can carry on calmly, quietly, without hurry or
flurry . . . and if the instant you feel yourself growing
nervous and . . . out of breath, you would stop and take a
breath, you would find this simple commonsense rule doing
for you what no prayers or tears could ever accomplish.
—Elizabeth Prentiss

His brow is wet with honest sweat,
He earns whate'er he can,
And looks the whole world in the face,
For he owes not any man.
—Henry Wadsworth Longfellow

It is better to have no emotion when it is work. Do
what needs to be done, and do it coolly.
—Louis L'Amour

Fall in love with what you do for a living. I don't care what it is. It works.
—George Burns

Work is accomplished by those employees who have
not yet reached their level of imcompetence.
—Laurence J. Peter, The Peter Principle

A man's work is from sun to sun, but a mother's work is never done.
—Anon

There are certain natures to whom work is
nothing, the act of work everything.
—Arthur Symons

What a man accomplishes in a day depends upon the way in which he approaches his tasks. When we accept tough jobs as a challenge to our ability and wade into them with joy and enthusiasm, miracles can happen. When we do our work with a dynamic, conquering spirit, we get things done.
—ARLAND GILBERT

He that can work is a born king of something.
—THOMAS CARLYLE

What is the hardest task in the world? To think.
—RALPH WALDO EMERSON

Work keeps at bay three great evils: boredom, vice and need.
—VOLTAIRE

Industry is a better horse to ride than genius.
—WALTER LIPPMAN

Committee: a group of men who individually can do nothing, but as a group decide that nothing can be done.
—FRED ALLEN

He that can work is a born king of something.
—THOMAS CARLYLE

Never despair, but if you do, work on in despair.
—EDMUND BURKE

I'm a great believer in luck. The harder I work, the more of it I seem to have.
—F.L. EMERSON

When two men in a business always agree, one of them is unnecessary.
—WILLIAM WRIGLEY, JR.

Laziness is a secret ingredient that goes into failure. But it's only kept a secret from the person who fails.
—ROBERT HALF

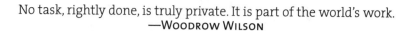

No task, rightly done, is truly private. It is part of the world's work.
—WOODROW WILSON

The one important thing I have learned over the years is the
difference between taking one's work seriously, and taking one's
self seriously. The first is imperative, and the second is disastrous.
—MARGOT FONTEYN

Oh, you hate your job? Why didn't you say so? There's a support
group for that. It's called EVERYBODY, and they meet at the bar.
—DREW CAREY

All work and no play makes Jack a dull boy—and Jill a wealthy widow.
—EVAN ESAR

I like work; it fascinates me. I can sit and look at it for hours. I love to
keep it by me: the idea of getting rid of it nearly breaks my heart.
—JEROME K. JEROME

It is necessary to work, if not from inclination, at least from despair.
Everything considered, work is less boring than amusing oneself.
—CHARLES BAUDELAIRE

Heaven Will Protect the Working Girl.
—EDGAR SMITH

When a man tells you that he got rich through
hard work, ask him: "Whose?"
—DON MARQUIS

They say hard work never hurt anybody, but I figure why take the chance.
—RONALD REAGAN

It is not the prize that can make us happy; it is not even the
winning of the prize. . . . [It is} the struggle, the long hot hour
of the honest fight. . . . There is no human bliss equal to twelve
hours of work with only six hours in which to do it.
—ANTHONY TROLLOPE

PERSEVERANCE

Like ships, men flounder time and time again.
—Henry Miller

Don't leave before the miracle happens!
—Anon

The first need of being is endurance; to endure with
gladness if we can, with fortitude in any event.
—Bliss Carman

Keep on keeping on.
—L.A. Times

The first and final thing you have to do in this world
is to last in it, and not be smashed by it.
—Ernest Hemingway

You may have to fight a battle more than once to win it.
—Margaret Thatcher

I bend, but I do not break.
—Jean de La Fontaine

Fight one more round. When your feet are so tired you have to
shuffle back to the center of the ring, fight one more round.
—James J. Corbett

We can do anything we want to do if we stick to it long enough.
—Helen Keller

For me, at least, there came moments when faith wavered. But there
is the great lesson and the great triumph: keep the fire burning until,
by and by, out of the mass of sordid details there comes some result.
—Oliver Wendell Holmes, Jr.

Diamonds are only lumps of coal that stuck to their jobs.
—B.C. Forbes

To strive, to seek, to find, and not to yield.
—Alfred, Lord Tennyson

To bear is to conquer our fate.
—Thomas Campbell

If you wish success in life, make perseverance your bosom friend.
—Joseph Addison

Men do not fail, they stop trying.
—Elihu Root

Fortune is like the market, where many times, if
you can stay a little, the price will fall.
—Francis Bacon

They who are the most persistent, and work in the true
spirit, will invariably be the most successful.
—Samuel Smiles

With ordinary talent and extraordinary
perseverance, all things are attainable.
—Sir Thomas Foxwell Buxton

He that endureth to the end shall be saved.
—Mt. 10:22

Defeat never comes to any man until he admits it.
—Josephus Daniels

One thing we learned. To make a start and keep plugging.
When I had fights at school, the little while I went, I just
bowed my neck and kept swinging until something hit
the dirt. Sometimes it was me, but I always got up.
—Louis L'Amour

When you get into a tight place and everything goes against you, 'til
it seems as though you could not hold on a minute longer, never give
up then, for that is just the place and time that the tide will turn.
—Harriet Beecher Stowe

Without perseverance talent is a barren bed.
—WELSH PROVERB

If something doesn't come up the way you
want, you have to forge ahead.
—CLINT EASTWOOD

Persistence is the master virtue. Without it, there is no other.
—ANON

If at first you don't succeed, you're running about average.
—M.H. ALDERSON

I'm a slow walker, but I never walk back.
—ABRAHAM LINCOLN

If you stop struggling, then you stop life.
—HUEY NEWTON

The secret of success is constancy of purpose.
—BENJAMIN DISRAELI

Emotional maturity is the ability to stick to a job and to struggle through
until it is finished, to endure unpleasantness, discomfort and frustration.
—EDWARD A. STRECKER

Flaming enthusiasm, backed up by horse sense and persistence,
is the quality that most frequently makes for success.
—DALE CARNEGIE

The only way to the top is by persistent, intelligent, hard work.
—A.T. MERCIER

I am not the smartest or most talented person in the world, but
I succeeded because I keep going, and going, and going.
—SYLVESTER STALLONE

It's the plugging away that will win you the day
So don't be a piker old pard!

Just draw on your grit; it's so easy to quit—
It's the keeping your chin up that's hard.
—Robert W. Service

Flaming enthusiasm, backed up by horse sense and persistence,
is the quality that most frequently makes for success.
—Dale Carnegie

Victory belongs to the most persevering.
—Napoleon Bonaparte

The golden rule is that there are no golden rules.
—George Bernard Shaw

Call the roll in your memory of conspicuously successful [business]
giants and, if you know anything about their careers, you will be
struck by the fact that almost every one of them encountered
inordinate difficulties sufficient to crush all but the gamest of spirits.
Edison went hungry many times before he became famous.
—B.C. Forbes

Make haste slowly.
—Augustus

No one succeeds without effort. . . . Those who succeed
owe their success to their perseverance.
—Ramana Maharshi

Nothing in the world can take place of persistence. Talent will
not; nothing is more common than unsuccessful individuals
with talent. Genius will not; unrewarded genius is almost a
proverb. Education will not; the world is full of educated derelicts.
Persistence and determination alone are omnipotent.
—Calvin Coolidge

Never stop. One always stops as soon as something is about to happen.
—Peter Brook

Tribulation produces perseverance; and perseverance,
character; and character, hope.
—St. Paul

Let me tell you the secret that has led me to my
goal: my strength lies solely in my tenacity.
—Louis Pasteur

You can do what you want to do, accomplish what you want to
accomplish, attain any reasonable objective . . . if you want it, if you will
to do it, if you work to do it, over a sufficiently long period of time.
—William E. Holler

Some men give up their designs when they have almost reached
the goal; while others, on the contrary, obtain a victory by exerting,
at the last moment, more vigorous efforts than before.
—Polybius

There are but two roads that lead to an important goal and to the
doing of great things: strength and perseverance. Strength is the lot
of but a few privileged men; but austere perseverance, harsh and
continuous, may be employed by the smallest of us and rarely fails of
its purpose, for its silent power grows irresistibly greater with time.
—Johann von Goethe

Four steps to achievement: plan purposefully, prepare
prayerfully, proceed positively, pursue persistently.
—William A. Ward

Men who have attained things worth having in this world have
worked while others idled, have persevered when others gave up
in despair, have practiced early in life the valuable habits of self-
denial, industry, and singleness of purpose. As a result, they enjoy in
later life the success so often erroneously attributed to good luck.
—Grenville Kleiser

I know the price of success: dedication, hard work and an
unremitting devotion to the things you want to see happen.
—Frank Lloyd Wright

I realized early on that success was tied to not giving up. Most people in
this business gave up and went on to other things. If you simply didn't
give up, you would outlast the people who came in on the bus with you.
—Harrison Ford

We conquer by continuing.
—George Matheson

In the realm of ideas, everything depends on enthusiasm;
in the real world, all rests on perseverance.
—Johann von Goethe

The way of progress is neither swift nor easy.
—Marie Curie

To persevere, trusting in what hopes he has, is
courage in a man. The coward despairs.
—Euripides

The race is not to the swift, nor the battle to the strong.
—Eccl. 9:11

There's such a thin line between winning and losing.
—John R. Tunis

Perseverance is a great element of success. If you only knock long enough
and loud enough at the gate, you are sure to wake up somebody.
—Henry Wadsworth Longfellow

One thing at a time, all things in succession.
That which grows slowly endures.
—J.G. Holland

By perseverance the snail reached the Ark.
—Charles Haddon Spurgeon

The drops of rain make a hole in the stone
not by violence, but by oft falling.
—Lucretius

Plodding wins the race.
—Aesop

I'm not there yet, but I'm closer than I was yesterday.
—Anon

I've been failing for like, ten or eleven years. When it turns, it'll turn. Right now I'm just tryin' to squeeze through a very tight financial period, get the movie out, and put my things in order.
—FRANCIS FORD COPPOLA

When nothing seems to help, I go and look at a stonecutter hammering away at his rock perhaps a hundred times without as much as a crack showing in it. Yet at the hundred and first blow it will split in two, and I know it was not that blow that did it, but all that had gone before.
—JACOB RIIS

Success generally depends upon knowing how long it takes to succeed.
—CHARLES DE MONTESQUIEU

If we are facing in the right direction, all we have to do is keep on walking.
—ANCIENT BUDDHIST PROVERB

I work every day—or at least I force myself into my office or room. I may get nothing done, but you don't earn bonuses without putting in time. Nothing may come for three months, but you don't earn the fourth without it.
—MORDECAI RICHLER

It's the steady, constant driving to the goal for which you're striving, not the speed with which you travel, that will make your victory sure.
—ANON

Success seems to be largely a matter of hanging on after others have let go.
—WILLIAM FEATHER

Slow and steady wins the race.
—ROBERT LLOYD

One can go a long way after one is tired.
—FRENCH PROVERB

If at first you don't succeed, try, try, try again.
—W.E. HICKSON

The great thing in this world is not so much where
we are, but in what direction we are moving.
—Oliver Wendell Holmes

In our day, when a pitcher got into trouble in a game,
instead of taking him out, our manager would leave him
in and tell him to pitch his way out of trouble.
—Cy Young

It is better to know some of the questions than all of the answers.
—James Thurber

It ain't over 'til it's over.
—Yogi Berra

He conquers who endures.
—Anon

Effort only fully releases its reward after a person refuses to quit.
—Napoleon Hill

Some men give up their designs when they have almost reached
the goal; while others, on the contrary, obtain a victory by exerting,
at the last moment, more vigorous efforts than before.
—Polybius

Never give in! Never give in! Never, never, never, never.... In
nothing great or small, large or petty, never give in
except to convictions or honor and good sense!
—Sir Winston Churchill

No one ever did anything worth doing unless he was prepared
to go on with it long after it became something of a bore.
—Douglas V. Steere

Triumph often is nearest when defeat seems inescapable.
—B.C. Forbes

First there are those who are winners, and know they are winners.
Then there are the losers who know they are losers. Then there

are those who are not winners, but don't know it. They're the ones
for me. They never quit trying. They're the soul of our game.
—Bear Bryant

Don't bother about genius. Don't worry about being clever.
Trust to hard work, perseverance and determination. And the
best motto for a long march is, "Don't grumble. Plug on!"
—Sir Frederick Treves

The great thing, and the hard thing, is to stick to things
when you have outlived the first interest, and not yet got
the second, which comes with a sort of mastery.
—Janet Erskine Stuart

Obstacles cannot crush me, every obstacle yields to stern resolve.
—Leonardo da Vinci

In the clutch of circumstance, I have not winced or cried aloud;
Under the bludgeoning of chance, my head is bloody, but unbowed.
—William E. Henley

And let us not be weary in well doing; for in due
season we shall reap, if we faint not.
—Gal. 6:9

No great thing is created suddenly.
—Epictetus

We shall go on to the end. We shall fight in France, we shall fight with
growing confidence and growing strength in the air, we shall defend
our island, whatever the cost may be. We shall fight on the beaches,
we shall fight on the landing grounds, we shall fight in the fields, and
in the streets, we shall fight in the halls. We shall never surrender.
—Sir Winston Churchill

We shall live to fight again, and to strike another blow.
—Alfred, Lord Tennyson

Endure, and preserve yourselves for better things.
—Virgil

Giving up is the ultimate tragedy.
—ROBERT J. DONOVAN

Man never made any material as resilient as the human spirit.
—BERN WILLIAMS

Character is built into the spiritual fabric of personality
hour by hour, day by day, year by year in much the same
deliberate way that physical health is built into the body.
—E. LAMAR KINCAID

No matter how lonely you get or how many birth
announcements you receive, the trick is not to get
frightened. There's nothing wrong with being alone.
—WENDY WASSERSTEIN

Endurance is one of the most difficult disciplines, but it is
to the one who endures that the final victory comes.
—BUDDHA

Whatever course you decide upon, there is always someone to
tell you that you are wrong. There are always difficulties arising
which tempt you to believe that your critics are right. To map out
a course of action and follow it to an end requires . . . courage.
—RALPH WALDO EMERSON

Be content to grow a little each day. If the improvement
is the sort of thing which is very slow, do not measure
it too often. Do a self-comparison every two weeks,
or every six months, whatever is appropriate.
—LEWIS F. PRESNALL

Every kind of fortune is to be overcome by bearing it.
—VIRGIL

There is no virtue like necessity.
—WILLIAM SHAKESPEARE

Hold on with a bulldog grip, and chew and choke as much as possible.
—ABRAHAM LINCOLN

Big shots are only little shots who keep shooting.
—Christopher Morley

It isn't hard to be good from time to time.... What's
tough is being good every day.
—Willie Mays

There remain times when one can only endure. One lives on, one
doesn't die, and the only thing that one can do is to fill one's mind
and time as far as possible with the concerns of other people. It
doesn't bring immediate peace, but it brings the dawn nearer.
—Arthur Christopher Benson

When we see ourselves in a situation which must be endured and gone
through, it is best to make up our minds to meet it with firmness, and
accommodate everything to it in the best way practical. This lessons the
evil, while fretting and fuming only serve to increase your own torments.
—Thomas Jefferson

The difficulties and struggles of today are but the price we must
pay for the accomplishments and victories of tomorrow.
—William J.H. Boetcker

Slow motion gets you there faster.
—Hoagy Carmichael

The race is not always to the swift, but to those who keep on running.
—Anon

If you want to see the sun shine, you have to weather the storm.
—Frank Lane

Tribulation produces perseverance; and perseverance,
character; and character, hope.
—St. Paul

Be strong!
It matters not how deep entrenched the wrong
How hard the battle goes, the day how long
Faint not—fight on!
Tomorrow comes the song.
—Maltbie D. Babcock

There are no shortcuts to any place worth going.
—BEVERLY SILLS

No furniture so charming as books.
—SYDNEY SMITH

Good people are good because they've come to wisdom through failure.
—WILLIAM SAROYAN

Let me tell you the secret that has led me to my
goal: my strength lies solely in my tenacity.
—LOUIS PASTEUR

He that can't endure the bad will not live to see the good.
—YIDDISH PROVERB

A winner never quits and a quitter never wins.
—ANON

If you want the rainbow, you gotta put up with the rain.
—DOLLY PARTON

Gnaw your own bone; gnaw at it, bury it, unearth it, gnaw it still.
—HENRY DAVID THOREAU

Keep on going, and the chances are that you will stumble on
something, perhaps when you are least expecting it. I never
heard of anyone ever stumbling on something sitting down.
—CHARLES F. KETTERING

Endurance is nobler than strength, and patience than beauty.
—JOHN RUSKIN

This is courage in a man: to bear unflinchingly what heaven sends.
—EURIPIDES

They merit more praise who know how to suffer misery
than those who temper themselves with contentment.
—PIETRO ARETINO

To be unable to bear an ill is itself a great ill.
—BION

Beware of all enterprises that require new clothes.
—HENRY DAVID THOREAU

Continuous efforts—not strength or intelligence—
is the key to unlocking our potential.
—SIR WINSTON CHURCHILL

What cannot be altered must be borne, not blamed.
—THOMAS FULLER

We must dare, and dare again, and go on daring.
—GEORGES JACQUES DANTON

We must endure what fortune sends.
—GREEK PROVERB

"Brave admiral, say but one good word:
What shall we do when hope is gone?"
The words leapt like a leaping sword:
"Sail on! sail on! and on!"
—JOAQUIN MILLER

When it goes wrong, you feel like cutting your throat, but you go on. You
don't let anything get you down so much that it beats you or stops you.
—GEORGE CUKOR

People can bear anything.
—PHILIP SLATER

We must learn from life how to suffer it.
—FRENCH PROVERB

It seems to superficial observers that all Americans are born
busy. It is not so. They are born with a fear of not being busy.
—CHARLES DUDLEY WARNER

Pray that success will not come any faster than you are able to endure it.
—ELBERT HUBBARD

I have accepted fear as a part of life—specifically
the fear of change....I have gone ahead despite the
pounding in the heart that says: turn back....
—ERICA JONG

Wisely and slow. They stumble that run fast.
—WILLIAM SHAKESPEARE

The line between failure and success is so fine that we ... are often
on the line and do not know it. How many a man has thrown up his
hands at a time when a little more effort, a little more patience, would
have achieved success. A little more persistence, a little more effort,
and what seemed hopeless failure may turn to glorious success.
—ELBERT HUBBARD

Grant me the courage not to give up, even though I think it is hopeless.
—ADMIRAL CHESTER W. NIMITZ

The person who makes a success of living is the one who sees his
goal steadily and aims for it unswervingly. That is dedication.
—CECIL B. DE MILLE

Be like a postage stamp—stick to one thing until you get there.
—JOSH BILLINGS

I have often been adrift, but I have always stayed afloat.
—DAVID BERRY

Any man can work when every stroke of his hands brings down the fruit
rattling from the tree ... but to labor in season and out of season, under
every discouragement ... that requires a heroism which is transcendent.
—HENRY WARD BEECHER

God helps those who persevere.
—KORAN

Saints are sinners who kept on going.
—ROBERT LOUIS STEVENSON

To be somebody you must last.
—RUTH GORDON

Great works are performed not by strength, but by perseverance.
—SAMUEL JOHNSON

Perseverance is the most overrated of traits, if it is unaccompanied
by talent; beating your head against a will is more likely to
produce a concussion in the head than a hole in the wall.
—SYDNEY HARRIS

Persistence is the twin sister of excellence. One is
matter of quality; the other, a matter of time.
—MARABEL MORGAN

Whatever necessity lays upon thee, endure; whatever she commands, do.
—JOHANN VON GOETHE

When you get to the end of your rope, tie a knot and hang on.
—FRANKLIN DELANO ROOSEVELT

II. Happiness Is . . .

FAMILY

The family is a haven in a heartless world.
—CHRISTOPHER LASCH

Distant relatives er th' best kind, an' th' further th' better.
—KIN HUBBARD

The family that prays together stays together.
—AL SCALPONE

Having a family is like having a bowling alley installed in your brain.
—MARTIN MULL

Oh, what a tangled web do parents weave / When
they think that their children are naive.
—OGDEN NASH

It is quite easy for me to think of a God of love mainly
because I grew up in a family where love was central
and where lovely relationships were ever present.
—MARTIN LUTHER KING, JR.

In our family, there was no clear line between religion and fly fishing.
—NORMAN MACLEAN, *A RIVER RUNS THROUGH IT*

Many men can make a fortune, but very few can build a Family.
—J.S. BRYAN

[A successful parent is someone] who raises a child who grows
up and is able to pay for his or her own psycholanalysis.
—NORA EPHRON

The only rock I know that stays steady, the only
institution I know that works is the family.
—LEE IACOCCA

When brothers agree, no fortress is so strong as their common life.
—ANTISTHENES

There's a lot of heredity in that family.
—RALPH KINER

Do you know what you call those who use towels and never wash
them, eat meals and never do the dishes, sit in rooms they never
clean, and are entertained till they drop? If you have just answered "A
houseguest," you're wrong because I have just described my kids.
—ERMA BOMBECK

The place of the father in the modern suburban family
is a very small one, particularly if he plays golf.
—BERTRAND RUSSELL

The reason grandparents and grandchildren get along
so well is that they have a common enemy.
—SAM LEVENSON

Cleaning your house while your kids are still growing is
like shoveling the walk before it stops snowing.
—PHYLLIS DILLER

A happy family is but an earlier heaven.
—JOHN BOWRING

Youth is a wonderful thing. What a crime to waste it on children.
—GEORGE BERNARD SHAW

The family is one of nature's masterpieces.
—GEORGE SANTAYANA

The mother's heart is the child's schoolroom.
—HENRY WARD BEECHER

A family is a unit composed not only of children but of men,
women, an occasional animal, and the common cold.
—OGDEN NASH

Happiness is having a large, loving, caring,
close-knit family in another city.
—GEORGE BURNS

The best way to keep children home is to make the home
atmosphere pleasant—and let the air out of the tires.
—DOROTHY PARKER

A boy's best friend is his mother.
—JOSEPH STEFANO (SCREENPLAY FOR *PSYCHO*)

If you don't believe in ghosts, you've never been to a family reunion.
—ASHLEIGH BRILLIANT

How do you like to go up in a swing,
Up in the air so blue?
Oh, I do think it the pleasantest thing
Ever a child can do!
—ROBERT LOUIS STEVENSON

The whole world is my family.
—POPE JOHN XXIII

Boys will be boys.
—PROVERB

Remember that as a teenager you are at the last stage of your
life when you will be happy to hear that the phone is for you.
—FRAN LEBOWITZ

It is a wise father that knows his own child.
—WILLIAM SHAKESPEARE

No matter how many communes anybody
invents, the family always creeps back.
—MARGARET MEAD

When I was a boy of fourteen, my father was so ignorant I could hardly stand to have the old man around. But when I got to be twenty-one, I was astonished at how much he had learned in seven years.
—MARK TWAIN

The old believe everything: the middle-aged suspect everything: the young know everything.
—OSCAR WILDE

There was never a great man who had not a great mother.
—OLIVE SCHREINER

Her voice was ever soft,
Gentle and low, and excellent thing in woman.
—WILLIAM SHAKESPEARE

A family with an old person has a living treasure of gold.
—CHINESE PROVERB

There is little less trouble in governing a private family than a whole kingdom.
—MONTAIGNE

Always be nice to your children because they are the ones who will choose your rest home.
—PHYLLIS DILLER

To understand your parents' love, you must raise children yourself.
—CHINESE PROVERB

Get to know your parents.... Be nice to your siblings. They're the best link to your past and the people most likely to stick with you in the future.
—MARY SCHMICH

My grandfather's a little forgetful, but he likes to give me advice. One day, he took me aside and left me there.
—RON RICHARDS

The family you come from isn't as important as the family you're going to have.
—RING LARDNER

You don't choose your family. They are God's
gift to you, as you are to them.
—Desmond Tutu

They say our mothers really know how to push our
buttons—because they installed them.
—Robin Williams

I have found the best way to give advice to your children is to
find out what they want, and then advise them to do it.
—Harry S Truman

Insanity runs in my family. It practically gallops!
—Joseph Kesselring

There are only two things a child will share willingly;
communicable diseases and its mother's age.
—Benjamin Spock

A baby is God's opinion that the world should go on.
—Carl Sandburg

It's in the kitchen that confidences are exchanged, that family life
takes place; it's among the remains of a meal or when you're elbow-
deep in peelings that you ask yourself what life is all about, rather
than when you're sunk in an armchair in the sitting room.
—Benoite Groult

Give a little love to a child, and you get a great deal back.
—John Ruskin

Happy or unhappy, families are all mysterious.
—Gloria Steinem

When you have to deal with your brother, be pleasant, but get a witness.
—Hesiod

Children aren't happy with nothing to ignore,
And that's what parents were created for.
—Ogden Nash

Big sisters are the crab grass in the lawn of life.
—Charles M. Schulz (Peanuts)

The most remarkable thing about my mother is that
for thirty years she served the family nothing but
leftovers. The original meal has never been found.
—Calvin Trillin

A hundred years from you it will not matter what my bank account
was, the sort of house I lived in, or the kind of car I drove. But the
world may be different, because I was important in the life of a boy.
—Forest E. Witcraft

Sweater. (n.) Garment worn by child when its mother is feeling chilly.
—Ambrose Bierce

The great advantage of living in a large family is that
early lesson of life's essential unfairness.
—Nancy Mitford

In reality, we are still children. We want to find a
playmate for our thoughts and feelings.
—Dr. Wilhelm Stekhel

In search of my mother's garden, I found my own.
—Alice Walker

Being a grownup means assuming responsibility for yourself, for
your children, and—here's the big curve—for your parents.
—Wendy Wasserstein

The most important thing a father can do for
his children is to love their mother.
—Theodore Hesburgh

One touch of nature makes the whole world kin.
—William Shakespeare

FRIENDS/FRIENDSHIP

I keep my friends as misers do their treasure, because, of all the things
granted us by wisdom, none is greater or better than friendship.
—Pietro Aretino

Real friendship is shown in times of trouble; prosperity is full of friends.
—Euripides

If you want to be listened to, you should put in time listening.
—Marge Piercy

"Stay" is a charming word in a friend's vocabulary.
—Louisa May Alcott

We secure our friends not by accepting favors but by doing them.
—Thucydides

I like familiarity. In me it does not breed contempt. Only more familiarity.
—Gertrude Stein

The condition which high friendship demands
is the ability to do without it.
—Ralph Waldo Emerson

When our friends are alive, we see the good qualities they
lack; dead, we remember only those they possessed.
—J. Petit-Senn

The only service a friend can really render is to keep
up your courage by holding up to you a mirror in
which you can see a noble image of yourself.
—George Bernard Shaw

Man is a knot, a web, a mesh into which relationships
are tied. Only those relationships matter.
—Antoine de Saint-Exupery

Good company and good discourse are the very sinews of virtue.
—Izaak Walton

Prosperity makes few friends.
—Vauvenargues

It is not so much our friends' help that helps
us, as the confidence of their help.
—Epicurus

One who knows how to show and to accept kindness
will be a friend better than any possession.
—Sophocles

Friendship requires great communication.
—Saint Francis de Sales

The best preservative to keep the mind in health
is the faithful admonition of a friend.
—Francis Bacon

Friendship is an art, and very few persons
are born with a natural gift for it.
—Kathleen Norris

Friends are an aid to the young, to guard them from error; to the
elderly, to attend to their wants and to supplement their failing power
of action; to those in the prime of life, to assist them to noble deeds.
—Aristotle

Blessed are they who have the gift of making friends, for it is one of God's
best gifts. It involves many things, but above all, the power of getting out
of one's self, and appreciating whatever is noble and loving in another.
—Thomas Hughes

Today a man discovered gold and fame,
Another flew the stormy seas;
Another set an unarmed world aflame,
One found the germ of a disease.
But what high fates my path attend:
For I—today—I found a friend.
—Helen Barker Parker

Good friendships are fragile things and require as much
care as any other fragile and precious thing.
—Randolph Bourne

Good friends, good books and a sleepy conscience: this is the ideal life.
—Mark Twain

The only way to have a friend is to be one.
—Ralph Waldo Emerson

If you think it's difficult to meet new people,
try picking up the wrong golf ball.
—Jack Lemmon

The thicker one gets with some people, the thinner they become.
—Puzant Thomain

My life seems to have become suddenly hollow, and I do
not know what is hanging over me. I cannot even put the
shadow that has fallen on me into words. At least into written
words. I would give a great deal for a friend's voice.
—John Addington Symonds

There is nothing meritorious but virtue and friendship.
—Alexander Pope

The richer your friends, the more they will cost you.
—Elizabeth Marbury

If a man is worth knowing at all, he is worth knowing well.
—Alexander Smith

Loyalty is what we seek in friendship.
—Cicero

[Friends are] God's apology for relations.
—Hugh Kingsmill

The richest man in the world is not the one who still has the first
dollar he ever earned. It's the man who still has his best friend.
—Martha Mason

Greater love hath no man than this, that a man
lay down his life for his friends.
—1 Jn. 15:13

My friends have made the story of my life. In a thousand ways they
have turned my limitations into beautiful privileges, and enabled me
to walk serene and happy in the shadow cast by my deprivation.
—Helen Keller

We have no more right to put our discordant states of mind into the
lives of those around us and rob them of their sunshine and brightness
than we have to enter their houses and steal their silverware.
—Julia Seton

Understand that friends come and go, but with a precious
few you should hold on. Work hard to bridge the gaps in
geography in lifestyle, because the older you get, the more
you need the people you knew when you were young.
—Mary Schmich

There is a magnet in your heart that will attract true friends.
That magnet is unselfishness, thinking of others first . . . when
you learn to live for others, they will live for you.
—Paramahansa Yogananda

We take care of our health, we lay up money, we make our roof
tight and our clothing sufficient, but who provides wisely that
he shall not be wanting in the best property of all—friends?
—Ralph Waldo Emerson

Friendship is the allay of our sorrows, the ease of our passions, the
discharge of our oppression, the sanctuary of our calamities, the
counselor of our doubts, the clarity of our minds, the emission of our
thoughts, the exercise and improvement of what we dedicate.
—Jeremy Taylor

Confidence is the foundation of friendship. If we give it, we will receive it.
—Harry E. Humphreys, Jr.

There is a definite process by which one made people into friends, and
it involved talking to them and listening to them for hours at a time.
—Rebecca West

Do not protect yourself by a fence, but rather by your friends.
—CZECH PROVERB

A quarrel between friends, when made up, adds a new
tie to friendship, as ... the callosity formed 'round a
broken bone makes it stronger than before.
—SAINT FRANCIS DE SALES

You win the victory when you yield to friends.
—SOPHOCLES

It's the friends you can call up at 4 a.m. that matter.
—MARLENE DIETRICH

No greater burden can be born by an individual than
to know none who cares or understands.
—ARTHUR H. STAINBACK

Friendships, like marriages, are dependent on avoiding the unforgivable.
—JOHN D. MACDONALD

The chain of friendship, however bright, does not
stand the attrition of constant close contact.
—SIR WALTER SCOTT

The most called-upon prerequisite of a friend is an accessible ear.
—MAYA ANGELOU

A man with few friends is only half-developed; there are whole
sides of his nature which are locked up and have never been
expressed. He cannot unlock them himself, he cannot even
discover them; friends alone can stimulate him and open him.
—RANDOLPH BOURNE

It is a good thing to be rich, it is a good thing to be strong,
but it is a better thing to be beloved of many friends.
—EURIPIDES

Friendship is the pleasing game of interchanging praise.
—OLIVER WENDELL HOLMES

Friendship multiplies the good of life and divides the evil. 'Tis the sole remedy against misfortune, the very ventilation of the soul.
—BALTASAR GRACIAN

The art of friendship has been little cultivated in our society.
—ROBERT J. HAVIGHURST

It is easier to visit friends than to live with them.
—CHINESE PROVERB

You can always tell a real friend; when you've made a fool of yourself he doesn't feel you've done a permanent job.
—LAURENCE J. PETER

A loyal friend laughs at your jokes when they're not so good, and sympathizes with your problems when they're not so bad.
—ARNOLD H. GLASOW

There is nothing we like to see so much as the gleam of pleasure in a person's eye when he feels that we have sympathized with him, understood him, interested ourself in his welfare. At these moments something fine and spiritual passes between two friends. These moments are the moments worth living.
—DON MARQUIS

Don't ask of your friends what you yourself can do.
—QUINTUS ENNIUS

It is easier to visit friends than to live with them.
—CHINESE PROVERB

He does good to himself who does good to his friend.
—ERASMUS

When a friend is in trouble, don't annoy him by asking if there is anything you can do. Think up something appropriate and do it.
—EDGAR WATSON HOWE

Politeness is an inexpensive way of making friends.
—WILLIAM FEATHER

When my friends lack an eye, I look at them in profile.
—JOSEPH JOUBERT

The worst solitude is to be destitute of sincere friendship.
—FRANCIS BACON

The secret of success in society is a certain heartiness and sympathy.
—RALPH WALDO EMERSON

Sometimes we owe a friend to the lucky circumstance
that we give him no cause for envy.
—FRIEDRICH NIETZSCHE

The chain of friendship, however bright, does not
stand the attrition of constant close contact.
—SIR WALTER SCOTT

We should behave to our friends as we would
wish our friends to behave to us.
—ARISTOTLE

Half the secret of getting along with people is consideration of
their values; the other half is tolerance in one's own views.
—DANIEL FROHMAN

One is taught by experience to put a premium on those
few people who can appreciate you for what you are.
—GAIL GODWIN

A hedge between keeps friendships green.
—ANON

To be social is to be forgiving.
—ROBERT FROST

Friendship is the source of the greatest pleasures, and without
friends even the most agreeable pursuits become tedious.
—SAINT THOMAS AQUINAS

It is well there is no one without fault; for he would not have a friend in the world. He would seem to belong to a different species.
—William Hazlitt

Friends are the sunshine of life.
—John Hay

Friendship is a strong and habitual inclination in two persons to promote the good and happiness of one another.
—Eustace Budgell

Between friends there is no need of justice.
—Aristotle

What I cannot love, I overlook.
—Anaïs Nin

Friendship may sometimes step a few paces in advance of truth.
—Walter Savage Landor

The essence of true friendship is to make allowance for another's little lapses.
—David Storey

Of all the things which wisdom provides to make life entirely happy, much the greatest is the possession of friendship.
—Epicurus

The most beautiful discovery true friends make is that they can grow separately without growing apart.
—Elizabeth Foley

If two friends ask you to judge a dispute, don't accept, because you will lose one friend; on the other hand, if two strangers come with the same request, accept, because you will gain one friend.
—Saint Augustine

Don't flatter yourself that friendship authorizes you to say disagreeable things to your intimates. The nearer you come into relation with a person, the more necessary do tact and courtesy become.
—Oliver Wendell Holmes

There's nothing worth the wear of winning
but laughter, and the love of friends.
—Hilaire Belloc

Keep the other person's well-being in mind when you
feel an attack of soul-purging truth coming on.
—Betty White

I should like to tell you again of my bitter troubles so that mutually,
by recounting our grief, we can lighten each other's sorrow.
—The Kanteletar

A friend should bear his friend's infirmities.
—William Shakespeare

It should be part of our private ritual to devote a quarter of
an hour every day to the enumeration of the good qualities
of our friends. When we are not active we fall back idly
upon defects, even of those whom we most love.
—Mark Rutherford

There are only two people who can tell you the truth about yourself—an
enemy who has lost his temper and a friend who loves you dearly.
—Antisthenes

Each friend represents a world in us, a world possibly not born until
they arrive, and it is only by this meeting that a new world is born.
—Anaïs Nin

A friend is a person with whom I may be sincere.
Before him, I may think aloud.
—Ralph Waldo Emerson

One's friends are that part of the human race
with which one can be human.
—George Santayana

There are moments in life when all that we can bear is the
sense that our friend is near us; our wounds would wince at
consoling words that would reveal the depths of our pain.
—Honore de Balzac

Wear a smile and have friends; wear a scowl and have wrinkles.
—George Eliot

A sympathetic friend can be quite dear as a brother.
—Homer

Those that lack friends to open themselves unto
are cannibals of their own hearts.
—Francis Bacon

I never enter a new company without the hope that I may discover
a friend, perhaps the friend, sitting there with an expectant
smile. That hope survives a thousand disappointments.
—Arthur Christopher Benson

Since there is nothing so well worth having as
friends, never lose a chance to make them.
—Francesco Guicciardini

It is one of the blessings of old friends that you
can afford to be stupid with them.
—Ralph Waldo Emerson

Forget your woes when you see your friend.
—Priscian

In time of great anxiety we can draw power from our friends. We
should at such times, however, avoid friends who sympathize
too deeply, who give us pity rather than strength.
—D. Lupton

Friendship admits of difference of character, as love does that of sex.
—Joseph Roux

Women can form a friendship with a man very well; but to
preserve it, a slight physical antipathy most probably helps.
—Friedrich Nietzsche

It is the weak and confused who worship the
pseudo-simplicities of brutal directness.
—Marshall McLuhan

There are limits to the indulgence which friendship allows.
—CICERO

The bird, a nest; the spider, a web; man, friendship.
—WILLIAM BLAKE

Friends are lost by calling often and calling seldom.
—SCOTTISH PROVERB

Who seeks a faultless friend remains friendless.
—TURKISH PROVERB

I am quite sure that no friendship yields its true pleasure and nobility
of nature without frequent communication, sympathy and service.
—GEORGE E. WOODBERRY

True happiness . . . arises, in the first place, from the
enjoyment of one's self, and in the next from the friendship
and conversation of a few select companions.
—JOSEPH ADDISON

Probably no man ever had a friend he did not dislike a little; we are all so
constituted by nature that no one can possibly entirely approve of us.
—EDGAR WATSON HOWE

Sooner or later you've heard all your best friends have
to say. Then comes the tolerance of real love.
—NED ROREM

Friendship is honey, but don't eat it all.
—MOROCCAN PROVERB

The more we love our friends, the less we flatter them; it
is by excusing nothing that pure love shows itself.
—MOLIERE

Trouble shared is trouble halved.
—DOROTHY SAYERS

What is thine is mine, and all mine is thine.
—PLAUTUS

Give and take makes good friends.
—Scottish proverb

Prosperity is not just scale; adversity is the only balance to weigh friends.
—Plutarch

We shall never have friends if we expect to find them without fault.
—Thomas Fuller

Friends are like a pleasant park where you wish to go; while
you may enjoy the flowers, you may not eat them.
—Edgar Watson Howe

I like a highland friend who will stand by me not only when
I am in the right, but when I am a little in the wrong.
—Sir Walter Scott

A friend who cannot at a pinch remember a thing or two that never
happened is as bad as one who does not know how to forget.
—Samuel Butler

A good friend can tell you what is the matter with you in a
minute. He may not seem such a good friend after telling.
—Arthur Brisbane

Two persons cannot long be friends if they cannot
forgive each other's little failings.
—Jean de La Bruyere

It's important to our friends to believe that we are unreservedly
frank with them, and important to our friendship that we are not.
—Mignon McLaughlin

The first thing to learn in intercourse with others is non-
interference with their own peculiar ways of being happy,
provided those ways do not assume to interfere with ours.
—William James

Prosperity makes friends, adversity tries them.
—Publilius Syrus

True friendship comes when silence between two people is comfortable.
—DAVE TYSON GENTRY

Friendship will not stand the strain of very
much good advice for very long.
—ROBERT LYND

We cannot tell the precise moment when friendship is
formed. As in filling a vessel drop by drop, there is at last a
drop which makes it run over. So in a series of kindnesses
there is, at last, one which makes the heart run over.
—JAMES BOSWELL

Adversity not only draws people together, but brings
forth that beautiful inward friendship.
—SØREN KIERKEGAARD

Nobody who is afraid of laughing, and heartily too, at his friend
can be said to have a true and thorough love for him.
—JULIUS CHARLES HARE

Only friends will tell you the truths you need
to hear to make . . . your life bearable.
—FRANCINE DU PLESSIX GRAY

'Tis the privilege of friendship to talk nonsense,
and have her nonsense respected.
—CHARLES LAMB

The firmest friendships have been formed in mutual adversity,
as iron is most strongly united by the fiercest flame.
—CHARLES CALEB COLTON

A cheerful friend is like a sunny day, which
sheds its brightness on all around.
—JOHN LUBBOCK

I am treating you as my friend, asking you to share my present
minuses in the hope I can ask you to share my future pluses.
—KATHERINE MANSFIELD

Don't believe your friends when they ask you to be honest
with them. All they really want is to be maintained
in the good opinion they have of themselves.
—ALBERT CAMUS

No real friendship is ever made without an initial
clashing which discloses the metal of each to each.
—DAVID GRAYSON

Nothing is ever lost by courtesy. It is the cheapest of pleasures,
costs nothing, and conveys much. It pleases him who gives
and receives and thus, like mercy, is twice blessed.
—ERASTUS WIMAN

A friend in need is a friend indeed.
—RICHARD GRAVES

A true friend unbosoms freely, advises justly, assists
readily, adventures boldly, takes all patiently, defends
courageously, and continues a friend unchangeably.
—WILLIAM PENN

Friendship multiplies the good of life and divides the evil. 'Tis the
sole remedy against misfortune, the very ventilation of the soul.
—BALTASAR GRACIAN

Many a person has held close, throughout their entire lives, two
friends that always remained strange to one another, because one
of them attracted by virtue of similarity, the other by difference.
—EMIL LUDWIG

A friend is never known till a man has need.
—ANON

In times of difficulty friendship is on trial.
—GREEK PROVERB

Do not remove a fly from your friend's forehead with a hatchet.
—CHINESE PROVERB

He who endures penance and hardships for another
delights in that person's company.
—MALIK MUHAMMAD JAYASI

Friendship is a plant which must be often watered.
—ANON

As the yellow gold is tried in fire, so the faith of
friendship must be seen in adversity.
—OVID

Nothing is more limiting than a closed circle of acquaintanceship
where every avenue of conversation has been explored
and social exchanges are fixed in a known routine.
—A.J. CRONIN

Friendship, of itself a holy tie, is made more sacred by adversity.
—JOHN DRYDEN

There is no man that imparteth his joys to his friends,
but he joyeth the more; and no man that imparteth his
griefs to his friends, but he grieveth the less.
—FRANCIS BACON

The proper office of a friend is to side with you when you are in the
wrong. Nearly everybody will side with you when you are in the right.
—MARK TWAIN

We cherish our friends not for their ability to
amuse us, but for ours to amuse them.
—EVELYN WAUGH

No man can be happy without a friend, nor be
sure of his friend till he is unhappy.
—THOMAS FULLER

Never befriend the oppressed unless you are
prepared to take on the oppressor.
—OGDEN NASH

If it's very painful for you to criticize your friends—
you're safe in doing it. But if you take the slightest
pleasure in it, that's the time to hold your tongue.
—ALICE DUER MILLER

Years and years of happiness only make us realize how lucky we are
to have friends that have shared and made that happiness a reality.
—ROBERT E. FREDERICK

Rather throw away that which is dearest to you,
your own life, than turn away a good friend.
—SOPHOCLES

One loyal friend is worth ten thousand relatives.
—EURIPIDES

Friendship is a union of spirits, a marriage of
hearts, and the bond there of virtue.
—SAMUEL JOHNSON

Friendship is the only cement that will ever hold the world together.
—WOODROW WILSON

When one friend washes another, both become clean.
—DUTCH PROVERB

Without wearing any mask we are conscious of,
we have a special face for each friend.
—OLIVER WENDELL HOLMES

Fortify yourself with a flock of friends! You can select them
at random, write to one, dine with one, visit one, or take your
problems to one. There is always at least one who will understand,
inspire, and give you the lift you may need at the time.
—GEORGE MATTHEW ADAMS

The wise man's ... friendship is capable of going to extremes
with many people, evoked as it is by many qualities.
—CHARLES DUDLEY WARNER

Those who cannot give friendship will rarely receive it, and never hold it.
—DAGOBERT D. RUNES

Actions, not words, are the true criterion of the attachment of friends.
—GEORGE WASHINGTON

Friends are relatives you make for yourself.
—EUSTACHE DESCHAMPS

I cannot concentrate all my friendship on any single one of my
friends because no one is complete enough in himself.
—ANAÏS NIN

An old friend never can be found, and nature has
provided that he cannot easily be lost.
—SAMUEL JOHNSON

God gave us our relatives; thank God we can choose our friends.
—ETHEL WATTS MUMFORD

Friendship is almost always the union of a part of one mind
with a part of another; people are friends in spots.
—GEORGE SANTAYANA

It is great to have friends when one is young, but indeed
it is still more so when you are getting old. When we are
young, friends are, like everything else, a matter of course.
In the old days we know what it means to have them.
—EDVARD GRIEG

I keep my friends as misers do their treasure because, of all the things
granted us by wisdom, none is greater or better than friendship.
—PIETRO ARETINO

Always set high value on spontaneous kindness. He whose inclination
prompts him to cultivate your friendship of his own accord will love
you more than one whom you have been at pains to attach to you.
—SAMUEL JOHNSON

We need two kinds of acquaintances, one to
complain to, while we boast to the others.
—LOGAN PEARSALL SMITH

I have learned that to have a good friend is the purest of all
God's gifts, for it is a love that has no exchange of payment.
—FRANCES FARMER

Friendship is only a reciprocal conciliation of interests.
—FRANCOIS DE LA ROCHEFOUCAULD

We die as often as we lose a friend.
—PUBLILIUS SYRUS

A good friend is my nearest relation.
—THOMAS FULLER

Five years from now you will be pretty much the same as you are today
except for two things: the books you read and the people you get close to.
—CHARLES JONES

When you are young and without success, you have
only a few friends. Then, later on, when you are rich and
famous, you still have a few . . . if you are lucky.
—PABLO PICASSO

There is only one thing better than making a new
friend, and that is keeping an old one.
—ELMER G. LETERMAN

Trouble is a sieve through which we sift our acquaintances.
Those too big to pass through are our friends.
—ARLENE FRANCIS

To associate with other like-minded people in small
purposeful groups is for the great majority of men and
women a source of profound psychological satisfaction.
—ALDOUS HUXLEY

To throw away an honest friend is, as it were, to throw your life away.
—SOPHOCLES

In prosperity friends do not leave you unless desired, whereas
in adversity they stay away of their own accord.
—DEMETRIUS

Every man passes his life in the search after friendship.
—RALPH WALDO EMERSON

Acquaintance I would have, but when it depends not
on the number, but the choice of friends.
—ABRAHAM COWLEY

Old friends, we say, are best, when some sudden
disillusionment shakes our faith in a new comrade.
—GELETT BURGESS

We are fonder of visiting our friends in health than in sickness.
We judge less favorably of their characters when any misfortune
happens to them; and a lucky hit, either in business or reputation,
improves even their personal appearance in our eyes.
—WILLIAM HAZLITT

Grief can take care of itself, but to get the full value of
a joy you must have somebody to divide it with.
—MARK TWAIN

You will find yourself refreshed by the presence of cheerful people. Why
not make earnest effort to confer that pleasure on others? . . . Half the
battle is gained if you never allow yourself to say anything gloomy.
—LYDIA M. CHILD

Friends and wine should be old.
—SPANISH PROVERB

Every organism requires an environment of friends, partly to shield
it from violent changes, and partly to supply it with its wants.
—ALFRED NORTH WHITEHEAD

A true friend is the greatest of all blessings, and that
which we take the least care of all to acquire.
—FRANCOIS DE LA ROCHEFOUCAULD

There is a magic in the memory of a schoolboy friendship. It softens the
heart, and even affects the nervous system of those who have no heart.
—BENJAMIN DISRAELI

The best way to keep your friends is not to give them away.
—Wilson Mizner

Old friends are the great blessing of one's later year.... They have a
memory of the same events and have the same mode of thinking.
—Horace Walpole

Friendship without self-interest is one of the
rare and beautiful things of life.
—James Francis Byrnes

A new acquaintance is like a new book. I prefer it, even if bad, to a classic.
—Benjamin Disraeli

Affinities are rare. They come but a few times in a life.
It is awful to risk losing one when it arrives.
—Florence H. Winterburn

The holy passion of Friendship is so sweet and steady
and loyal and enduring a nature that it will last through
a whole lifetime, if not asked to lend money.
—Mark Twain

The shifts of fortune test the reliability of friends.
—Cicero

As in the case of wines that improve with age, the oldest
friendships ought to be the most delightful.
—Cicero

Friendship, like credit, is highest where it is not used.
—Elbert Hubbard

To cement a new friendship, especially between foreigners
or persons of a different social world, a spark with which
both were secretly charged must fly from person to person,
and cut across the accidents of place and time.
—George Santayana

A new friend is like new wine; when it has
aged you will drink it with pleasure.
—Apocrypha

One who's our friend is fond of us; one who's
fond of us isn't necessarily our friend.
—Marcus Annaeus Seneca

That friendship may be at once fond and lasting, there must not only be
equal virtue on each part, but virtue of the same kind; not only the same
end must be proposed, but the same means must be approved by both.
—Samuel Johnson

A real friend helps us think our best thoughts, do
our noblest deeds, be our finest selves.
—Anon

I don't care a damn for your loyal service when you think I am
right; when I really want it most is when you think I am wrong.
—General Sir John Monash

No one person can possibly combine all the elements supposed
to make up what everyone means by friendship.
—Francis Marion Crawford

Be courteous to all, but intimate with few; and let those few
be well tried before you give them your confidence.
—George Washington

He alone has lost the art to live who cannot win new friends.
—S. Weir Mitchell

If a man does not make new acquaintances as he advances
through life, he will soon find himself left alone.
—Samuel Johnson

Wishing to be friends is quick work, but
friendship is a slow-ripening fruit.
—Aristotle

You cannot be friends upon any other terms
than upon the terms of equality.
—Woodrow Wilson

Let him have the key of thy heart, who hath the lock of his own.
—Sir Thomas Browne

Friendship is a single soul dwelling in two bodies.
—Aristotle

Friendship is nothing else than an accord in all things, human
and divine, conjoined with mutual goodwill and affection.
—Cicero

How often we find ourselves turning our backs on our actual
friends, that we may go and meet their ideal cousins.
—Henry David Thoreau

A faithful friend is the medicine of life.
—Apocrypha

I want no men around me who have not the knack of making friends.
—Frank A. Vanderlip

Books and friends should be few but good.
—Anon

The best mirror is an old friend.
—Anon

Be slow to fall into friendship; but when thou
art in, continue firm and constant.
—Socrates

None is so rich as to throw away a friend.
—Turkish proverb

Many a friendship—long, loyal, and self-sacrificing—rested
at first upon no thicker a foundation than a kind word.
—Frederick W. Faber

Those friends thou hast, and their adoption tried,
grapple them to thy soul with hoops of steel.
—William Shakespeare

Sudden friendship, sure repentance.
—Anon

Be slow in choosing a friend, slower in changing.
—BENJAMIN FRANKLIN

Make all good men your well-wishers, and then, in the years'
steady sifting, some of them will turn into friends.
—JOHN HAY

To be capable of steady friendship or lasting love are the two greatest
proofs, not only of goodness of heart, but of strength of mind.
—WILLIAM HAZLITT

Men only become friends by community of pleasures.
—SAMUEL JOHNSON

Seek those who find your road agreeable, your personality
and mind stimulating, your philosophy acceptable, and your
experiences helpful. Let those who do not, seek their own kind.
—JEAN-HENRI FABRE

Accident counts for much in companionship, as in marriage.
—HENRY ADAMS

Friendship that flames goes out in a flash.
—THOMAS FULLER

Forsake not an old friend, for the new is not comparable
to him; a new friend is as new wine.
—ECCLESIASTES

A home-made friend wears longer than one you buy in the market.
—AUSTIN O'MALLEY

The best time to make friends is before you need them.
—ETHEL BARRYMORE

To like and dislike the same things, this is what makes a solid friendship.
—SALLUST

I have always differentiated between two types of friends; those who want proofs of friendship, and those who do not. One kind loves me for myself, and the others for themselves.
—GERARD DE NERVAL

Friends are a second existence.
—BALTASAR GRACIAN

In prosperity our friends know us; in adversity we know our friends.
—JOHN CHURTON COLLINS

Have but few friends, though many acquaintances.
—ANON

Friendship is a furrow in the sand.
—TONGAN PROVERB

True friends ... face in the same direction, toward common projects, interests, goals.
—C.S. LEWIS

It is characteristic of spontaneous friendship to take on, without enquiry and almost at first sight, the unseen doings and unspoken sentiments of our friends; the part known gives us evidence enough that the unknown part cannot be much amiss.
—GEORGE SANTAYANA

One of the signs of passing youth is the birth of a sense of fellowship with other human beings as we take our place among them.
—VIRGINIA WOOLF

Friend: One who knows all about you and loves you just the same.
—ELBERT HUBBARD

He who looks for advantage out of friendship strips it all of its nobility.
—MARCUS ANNAEUS SENECA

Friendship is always a sweet responsibility, never an opportunity.
—KAHLIL GIBRAN

The language of friendship is not words, but meanings.
—Henry David Thoreau

There is no hope or joy except in human relations.
—Antoine de Saint-Exupery

As there are some flowers which you should smell but slightly to
extract all that is pleasant in them ... so there are some men with
whom a slight acquaintance is quite sufficient to draw out all that is
agreeable; a more intimate one would be unsafe and unsatisfactory.
—Walter Savage Landor

Friendship is one mind in two bodies.
—Menclus

The two most important things in life are
good friends and a strong bull pen.
—Bob Lemon

Iron sharpeneth iron; so a man sharpeneth the countenance of his friend.
—Prv. 27:17

Friendship is neither a formality nor a mode: it is rather a life.
—David Grayson

It is good to have friends, even in hell.
—Spanish proverb

A friend is like a poem.
—Persian proverb

I feel the need of relations and friendship, of affection, of friendly
intercourse.... I cannot miss these things without feeling, as
does any other intelligent man, a void and a deep need.
—Vincent van Gogh

A friend is a present you give to yourself.
—Robert Louis Stevenson

We challenge one another to be funnier and smarter.... It's
the way friends make love to one another.
—Annie Gottlieb

Man's best support is a very dear friend.
—Cicero

Friendship needs no words—it is solitude
delivered from the anguish of loneliness.
—Dag Hammarskjold

Friendship is a word the very sight of which
in print makes the heart warm.
—Augustine Birrell

The feeling of friendship is like that of being
comfortably filled with roast beef.
—Samuel Johnson

Friendship marks a life even more deeply than love. Love risks
degenerating into obsession, friendship is never anything but sharing.
—Elie Wiesel

Without friends no one would choose to live,
though he had all other goods.
—Aristotle

A friend is, as it were, a second self.
—Cicero

I have friends in overalls whose friendship I would not
swap for the favor of the kings of the world.
—Thomas A. Edison

Most men's friendships are too inarticulate.
—William James

Love demands infinitely less than friendship.
—George Jean Nathan

If our friends' idealizations of us need the corrective of our own experience, it may be true also that our own sordid view of our lives needs the corrective of our friends' idealizations.
—Oscar W. Firkins

I'm back with my own kind of people here now, the bums and drinkers and no goods and it is a fine thing.
—John Steinbeck

Animals are such agreeable friends—they ask no questions, they pass no criticisms.
—George Eliot

To have a good friend is one of the highest delights of life; to be a good friend is one of the noblest and most difficult undertakings.
—Anon

A friend may well be reckoned the masterpiece of nature.
—Ralph Waldo Emerson

Live so that your friends can defend you, but never have to.
—Arnold Glasow

We call that person who has lost his father, an orphan; and a widower, that man who has lost his wife. But that man who has known that immense unhappiness of losing a friend, by what name do we call him? Here every language holds its peace in impotence.
—Joseph Roux

In poverty and other misfortunes of life, true friends are a sure refuge.
—Aristotle

True friendship is self-love at second hand.
—William Hazlitt

That friendship will not continue to the end which is begun for an end.
—Francis Quarles

Be a friend to thyself, and others will be so too.
—Thomas Fuller

The real friend is he or she who can share all
our sorrow and double our joys.
—B.C. Forbes

Silences make the real conversations between friends.
—Margaret Lee Runbeck

Friendship with oneself is all-important, because without
it one cannot be friends with anyone else.
—Eleanor Roosevelt

The company makes the feast.
—Anon

I am a hoarder of two things: documents and trusted friends.
—Muriel Spark

The reward of friendship is itself. The man who hopes for
anything else does not understand what true friendship is.
—Saint Alfred of Rievaulx

A grateful mind
By owing owes not, but still pays at once
Indebted and discharged.
—John Milton

My best friend is the man who in wishing me well wishes it for my sake.
—Aristotle

Good company upon the road is the shortest cut.
—Anon

GRATITUDE

If the only prayer you said in your whole life
was, "thank you," that would suffice.
—Meister Eckhart

Be thankful for small mercies.
—JAMES JOYCE

God gave you the gift of 86,400 seconds today.
Have you used one to say "thank you"?
—WILLIAM ARTHUR WARD

Gratitude is the sign of noble souls.
—AESOP

[Thanksgiving] as founded be th' Puritans to give thanks
f'r bein' prsarved fr'm th' Indyans, an' we keep it to
give thanks we are presarved fr'm th' Puritans.
—FINLEY PETER DUNNE

Be thankful for small mercies.
—JAMES JOYCE

Gratitude is the most exquisite form of courtesy.
—JACQUES MARITAIN

Some hae meat and canna eat,—
And some wad eat that want it;
But we hae meat, and we can eat,
Sae let the Lord be thankit.
—ROBERT BURNS

We tend to forget that happiness doesn't come as a
result of getting something we don't have, but rather of
recognizing and appreciating what we do have.
—FREDERICK KEONIG

One single grateful thought raised to heaven is the most perfect prayer.
—GOTTHOLD EPHRAIM LESSING

Gratitude is born in hearts that take time to count up past mercies.
—CHARLES E. JEFFERSON

As we express our gratitude, we must never forget that the
highest appreciation is not to utter words, but to live by them.
—JOHN FITZGERALD KENNEDY

Thanksgiving comes to us out of the prehistoric dimness, universal
to all ages and all faiths. At whatever straws we must grasp,
there is always a time for gratitude and new beginnings.
—J. Robert Moskin

HAPPINESS

The only true happiness comes from
squandering ourselves for a purpose.
—William Cowper

Happy is he who learns to bear what he cannot change!
—J.C.F. von Schiller

Happiness is a perfume which you can't pour on
someone without getting some on yourself.
—Ralph Waldo Emerson

The secret of happiness is not in doing what one
likes, but in liking what one has to do.
—Sir James M. Barrie

True happiness, we are told, consists in getting out of one's
self. But the point is not only to get out, you must stay out.
And to stay out, you must have some absorbing errand.
—Henry James

There is no cure for birth and death save to enjoy the interval.
—George Santayana

But what is happiness except the simple harmony
between a man and the life he leads?
—Albert Camus

The world is so full of a number of things,
I'm sure we should all be as happy as kings.
—Robert Louis Stevenson

Happiness is no laughing matter.
—RICHARD WHATELY

Happiness is action.
—DAVID THOMAS

I've had a wonderful evening but this wasn't it.
—GROUCHO MARX

Work and love—these are the basics. Without them there is neurosis.
—THEODOR REIK

If thou workest at that which is before thee ... expecting nothing, fearing
nothing, but satisfied with thy present activity according to Nature,
and with heroic truth in every word and sound which thou utterest,
thou wilt live happy. And there is no man who is able to prevent this.
—MARCUS AURELIUS

All the things I really like to do are either immoral, illegal or fattening.
—ALEXANDER WOOLLCOTT

This is life! It can harden and it can exalt!
—HENRIK IBSEN

Happiness ... leads none of us by the same route.
—CHARLES CALEB COLTON

He works his work, I mine.
—ALFRED, LORD TENNYSON

To be busy is man's only happiness.
—MARK TWAIN

The happiest people are those who are too busy
to notice whether they are or not.
—WILLIAM FEATHER

Happiness depends upon ourselves.
—ARISTOTLE

When I have been unhappy, I have heard an opera ... and it seemed the
shrieking of winds; when I am happy, a sparrow's chirp is delicious to
me. But it is not the chirp that makes me happy, but I that make it sweet.
—JOHN RUSKIN

All happiness depends on a leisurely breakfast.
—JOHN GUNTHER

Living well and beautifully and justly are all one thing.
—SOCRATES

The chief need of the country ... is a really good 5-cent cigar.
—THOMAS R. MARSHALL

The right to happiness is fundamental.
—ANNA PAVLOVA

Happiness ... can exist only in acceptance.
—DENIS DE ROUGEMONT

The happiest excitement in life is to be convinced that one is fighting
for all one is worth on behalf of some clearly seen and deeply felt good.
—RUTH BENEDICT

There is only one way to happiness, and that is to cease worrying
about things which are beyond the power of our will.
—EPICTETUS

Happiness depends on being free, and freedom
depends on being courageous.
—THUCYDIDES

Happiness is the meaning and the purpose of life,
the whole aim and end of human existence.
—ARISTOTLE

There are three ingredients in the good life:
learning, earning and yearning.
—CHRISTOPHER MORLEY

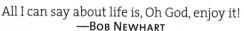

All I can say about life is, Oh God, enjoy it!
—BOB NEWHART

Our greatest happiness does not depend on the condition of life
in which chance has placed us, but is always the result of a good
conscience, good health, occupation and freedom in all just pursuits.
—THOMAS JEFFERSON

A man who limits his interests limits his life.
—VINCENT PRICE

Happiness is experienced when your life gives
you what you are willing to accept.
—KEN KEYES, JR.

To win one's joy through struggle is better than to yield to melancholy.
—ANDRÉ GIDE

Life is a romantic business, but you have to make the romance.
—OLIVER WENDELL HOLMES

Different men seek . . . happiness in different
ways and by different means.
—ARISTOTLE

If a man has important work, and enough leisure and income
to enable him to do it properly, he is in possession of as much
happiness as is good for any of the children of Adam.
—R.H. TAWNEY

It is not the level of prosperity that makes for happiness but
the kinship of heart to heart and the way we look at the world.
Both attitudes are within our power, so that a man is happy so
long as he chooses to be happy, and no one can stop him.
—ALEKSANDR SOLZHENITSYN

Pleasure is the object, duty and the goal of all rational creatures.
—VOLTAIRE

Like swimming, riding, writing or playing golf, happiness can be learned.
—DR. BORIS SOKOLOFF

To complain that life has no joys while there is a single creature whom
we can relieve by our bounty, assist by our counsels or enliven by our
presence, is . . . just as rational as to die of thirst with the cup in our hands.
—THOMAS FITZOSBORNE

There can be no happiness if the things we believe
in are different from the things we do.
—FREYA STARK

Nine requisites for contented living: Health enough to make
work a pleasure. Wealth enough to support your needs. Strength
to battle with difficulties and overcome them. Grace enough to
confess your sins and forsake them. Patience enough to toil until
some good is accomplished. Charity enough to see some good in
your neighbor. Love enough to move you to be useful and helpful
to others. Faith enough to make real the things of God. Hope
enough to remove all anxious fears concerning the future.
—JOHANN VON GOETHE

To live as fully, as completely as possible, to be
happy . . . is the true aim and end to life.
—LLEWELYN POWERS

Our actions are the springs of our happiness or misery.
—PHILIP SKELTON

Happiness, n. An agreeable sensation arising from
contemplating the misery of another.
—AMBROSE BIERCE

The secret of living is to find . . . the pivot of a concept
on which you can make your stand.
—LUIGI PIRANDELLO

Make us happy and you make us good.
—ROBERT BROWNING

Happiness comes of the capacity to feel deeply, to enjoy
simply, to think freely, to risk life, to be needed.
—STORM JAMESON

In about the same degree as you are helpful, you will be happy.
—Karl Reiland

Have a variety of interest.... These interests relax the mind
and lessen tension on the nervous system. People with
many interests live, not only longest, but happiest.
—George Matthew Allen

How unhappy is he who cannot forgive himself.
—Publilius Syrus

There is no happiness except in the realization
that we have accomplished something.
—Henry Ford

All animals except man know that the principle
business of life is to enjoy it.
—Samuel Butler

Men are made for happiness, and anyone who is completely happy
has a right to say to himself: "I am doing God's will on earth."
—Anton Chekhov

It is the chiefest point of happiness that a man is willing to be what he is.
—Erasmus

Happiness is essentially a state of going somewhere, wholeheartedly,
one—directionally, without regret or reservation.
—William H. Sheldon

The secret of happiness ... is to be in harmony with existence,
to be always calm, always lucid, always willing "to be joined to
the universe without being more conscious of it than an idiot,"
to let each wave of life wash us a little farther up the shore.
—Cyril Connolly

One is happy as a result of one's own efforts—once one
knows the necessary ingredients of happiness—simple
tastes, a certain degree of courage, self-denial to a point,
love of work, and, above all, a clear conscience.
—George Sand

Manifest plainness,
Embrace simplicity,
Reduce selfishness,
Have few desires.
—Lao-tzu

Happiness … can exist only in acceptance.
—Denis De Rougemont

To make a man happy, fill his hands with work, his heart with
affection, his mind with purpose, his memory with useful
knowledge, his future with hope, and his stomach with food.
—Frederick E. Crane

If we could learn how to balance rest against effort, calmness
against strain, quiet against turmoil, we would assure
ourselves of joy in living and psychological health for life.
—Josephine Rathbone

Do not worry; eat three square meals a day; say your prayers; be
courteous to your creditors; keep your digestion good; exercise; go slow
and easy. Maybe there are other things your special case requires to
make you happy; but, my friend, these I reckon will give you a good lift.
—Abraham Lincoln

Some pursue happiness, others create it.
—Anon

No man is more cheated than the selfish man.
—Henry Ward Beecher

This is wisdom: to love wine, beauty, and the heavenly
spring. That's sufficient—the rest is worthless.
—Theodore De Banville

Five great enemies to peace inhabit us: avarice, ambition,
envy, anger and pride. If those enemies were to be
banished, we should infallibly enjoy perpetual peace.
—Ralph Waldo Emerson

Happy [is] the man who knows his duties!
—Christian Furchtegott Gellert

Simplicity, clarity, singleness: these are the attributes
that give our lives power and vividness and joy.
—Richard Halloway

Fear less, hope more; eat less, chew more; whine less, breathe more;
talk less, say more; love more, and all good things will be yours.
—Swedish proverb

He who never sacrificed a present to a future good, or a personal to a
general one, can speak of happiness only as the blind speak of color.
—Horace Mann

Happiness is the only sanction in life; where happiness fails,
existence remains a mad and lamentable experiment.
—George Santayana

The man who makes everything that leads to happiness
depend upon himself, and not upon other men, has
adopted the very best plan for living happily.
—Plato

May you have warmth in your igloo, oil in
your lamp, and peace in your heart.
—Eskimo proverb

The pursuit of happiness . . . is the greatest feat man has to accomplish.
—Robert Henri

What can be added to the happiness of man who is in
health, out of debt, and has a clear conscience?
—Adam Smith

Discontent is want of self-reliance; it is infirmity of will.
—Ralph Waldo Emerson

To do the useful thing, to say the courageous thing, to contemplate
the beautiful thing: that is enough for one man's life.
—T.S. Eliot

Happiness is the overcoming of not unknown
obstacles toward a known goal.
—L. Ron Hubbard

The bird of paradise alights only upon the hand that does not grasp.
—JOHN BERRY

Few are they who have never had the chance to achieve
happiness ... and fewer those who have taken that chance.
—ANDRÉ MAUROIS

The grand essentials to happiness in this life are something
to do, something to love and something to hope for.
—JOSEPH ADDISON

Give a man health and a course to steer, and he'll never
stop to trouble about whether he's happy or not.
—GEORGE BERNARD SHAW

Let your boat of life be light, packed only with what you need—a homely
home and simple pleasures, one or two friends worth the name, someone
to love and to love you, a cat, a dog, enough to eat and enough to wear,
and a little more than enough to drink, for thirst is a dangerous thing.
—JEROME K. JEROME

Seek to do good, and you will find that happiness will run after you.
—JAMES FREEMAN CLARKE

Most folks are about as happy as they make up their minds to be.
—ABRAHAM LINCOLN

Practice easing your way along. Don't get het up or in a dither.
Do your best; take it as it comes. You can handle anything if you
think you can. Just keep your cool and your sense of humor.
—SMILEY BLANTON, M.D.

Having a goal is a state of happiness.
—E.J. BARTEK

To live content with small means; to seek elegance rather than
luxury, and refinement rather than fashion; to be worthy, not
respectable, and wealthy, not rich; to study hard, think quietly, talk
gently, act frankly; to listen to the stars and birds, to babes and
sages, with open heart; to bear on cheerfully, do all bravely,

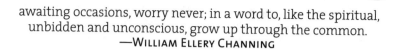

awaiting occasions, worry never; in a word to, like the spiritual,
unbidden and unconscious, grow up through the common.
—WILLIAM ELLERY CHANNING

True happiness ... arises, in the first place, from the
enjoyment of one's self, and in the next, from the friendship
and conversation of a few select companions.
—JOSEPH ADDISON

Everyone chases after happiness, not noticing
that happiness is at their heels.
—BERTOLT BRECHT

The U.S. Constitution doesn't guarantee happiness, only the
pursuit of it. Your have to catch up with it yourself.
—BENJAMIN FRANKLIN

To live and let live, without clamor for distinction or recognition; to
wait on divine Love; to write truth first on the tablet of one's own
heart—this is the sanity and perfection of living, and my human ideal.
—MARY BAKER EDDY

Seek not happiness too greedily, and be not fearful of unhappiness.
—LAO-TZU

Without duty, life is soft and boneless.
—JOSEPH JOUBERT

A multitude of small delights constitute happiness.
—CHARLES BAUDELAIRE

Deliberately to pursue happiness is not the surest way of achieving
it. Seek it for its own sake and I doubt whether you will find it.
—ROBERT J. McCRACKEN

Do all the good you can,
By all the means you can,
In all the ways you can,
In all the places you can,
At all the times you can.
—ANON

The happiest people seem to be those who have no particular
cause for being happy except that they are so.
—WILLIAM RALPH INGE

Enjoyment is not a goal, it is a feeling that
accompanies important ongoing activity.
—PAUL GOODMAN

Happiness lies in the joy of achievement and the thrill of creative effort.
—FRANKLIN DELANO ROOSEVELT

Happiness, happiness . . . the flavor is with you—with you
alone, and you can make it as intoxicating as you please.
—JOSEPH CONRAD

If you pursue happiness you'll never find it.
—C.P. SNOW

All men have happiness as their object: there are no exceptions.
However different the means they employ, they aim at the same end.
—BLAISE PASCAL

We all live with the objective of being happy; our
lives are all different and yet the same.
—ANNE FRANK

One can bear grief, but it takes two to be glad.
—ELBERT HUBBARD

The essence of philosophy is that a man should so live that his
happiness shall depend as little as possible on external things.
—EPICTETUS

We should consider every day lost on which we have not
danced at least once. And we should call every truth false
which was not accompanied by at least one laugh.
—FRIEDRICH NIETZSCHE

Happiness sneaks in through a door you didn't know you left open.
—JOHN BARRYMORE

Pleasure is very seldom found where it is sought. Our brightest
blazes are commonly kindled by unexpected sparks.
—SAMUEL JOHNSON

Happiness, to some, is elation; to others it is mere stagnation.
—AMY LOWELL

The world is so full of a number of things, I'm
sure we should all be as happy as kings.
—ROBERT LOUIS STEVENSON

They seemed to come suddenly upon happiness as if they
had surprised a butterfly in the winter woods.
—EDITH WHARTON

Life is not always what one wants it to be, but to make
the best of it as it is, is the only way of being happy.
—JENNIE JEROME CHURCHILL

When the working day is done
Girls—they want to have fun
Oh girls just want to have fun.
—ROBERT HAZARD

Do you prefer that you be right, or that you be happy?
—A COURSE IN MIRACLES

The happiest people I have known in this world have been
the Saints—and, after these, the men and women who get
immediate and conscious enjoyment from little things.
—HUGH WALPOLE

If only we'd stop trying to be happy we'd have a pretty good time.
—EDITH WHARTON

Happiness is not a goal, it is a by-product.
—ELEANOR ROOSEVELT

Those who seek happiness miss it, and those who discuss it, lack it.
—HOLBROOK JACKSON

One is happy as a result of one's own efforts—once one knows the necessary ingredients of happiness—simple tastes, a certain degree of courage, self-denial to a point, love of work, and, above all, a clear conscience.
—GEORGE SAND

Happiness is like a cat. If you try to coax it or call it, it will avoid you. It will never come. But if you pay no attention to it and go about your business, you'll find it rubbing against your legs and jumping into your lap.
—WILLIAM BENNETT

I know well that happiness is in little things.
—JOHN RUSKIN

Happiness is never stopping to think if you are.
—PALMER SONDREAL

To live happily is an inward power of the soul.
—MARCUS AURELIUS

Action may not always bring happiness, but there is no happiness without action.
—WILLIAM JAMES

Yes, there is a Nirvanah; it is in leading your sheep to a green pasture, and in putting your child to sleep, and in writing the last line of your poem.
—KAHLIL GIBRAN

Knowledge of what is possible is the beginning of happiness.
—GEORGE SANTAYANA

Human happiness and moral duty are inseparably connected.
—GEORGE WASHINGTON

Accept the pain, cherish the joys, resolve the regrets; then can come the best of benedictions—"If I had my life to live over, I'd do it all the same."
—JOAN MCINTOSH

Learn to enjoy every minute of your life. Be happy now. Don't wait for something outside of yourself to make you happy in the future. Think

how really precious is the time you have to spend, whether it's at work or with your family. Every minute should be enjoyed and savored.
—EARL NIGHTINGALE

To attain happiness in another world we need only to believe something; to secure it in this world, we must do something.
—CHARLOTTE PERKINS GILMAN

Enjoy the little things, for one day you may look back and realize they were the big things.
—ROBERT BRAULT

Happiness walks on busy feet.
—KITTE TURMELL

For me it is sufficient to have a corner by my hearth, a book and a friend, and a nap undisturbed by creditors or grief.
—FERNANDEZ DE ANDRADA

The way of a superior man is threefold: Virtuous, he is free from anxieties; wise, he is free from perplexities; bold, he is free from fear.
—CONFUCIUS

The first rule is to keep an untroubled spirit. The second is to look things in the face and know them for what they are.
—MARCUS AURELIUS

Happiness consists more in small conveniences or pleasures that occur every day, than in great pieces of good fortune that happen but seldom.
—BENJAMIN FRANKLIN

Few are they who have never had the chance to achieve happiness . . . and fewer those who have taken that chance.
—ANDRÉ MAUROIS

No one can sincerely try to help another without helping himself.
—CHARLES DUDLEY WARNER

It is not easy to find happiness in ourselves, and it is not possible to find it elsewhere.
—AGNES REPPLIER

Seek happiness for its own sake, and you will not find it; seek for duty,
and happiness will follow as the shadow comes with the sunshine.
—Tyron Edwards

The true way to soften one's troubles is to solace those of others.
—Madame De Maintenon

Happiness hates the timid!
—Eugene O'Neill

The habit of being uniformly considerate toward
others will bring increased happiness to you.
—Grenville Kleiser

Change is an easy panacea. It takes character to
stay in one place and be happy there.
—Elizabeth Clarke Dunn

Pleasure is a reciprocal; no one feels it who does not at the
same time give it. To be pleased, one must please.
—Lord Chesterfield

One must never look for happiness: one meets it by the way.
—Isabelle Eberhardt

Why not learn to enjoy the little things—there are so many of them.
—Anon

The happy people are those who are producing something.
—William Ralph Inge

We cannot hold a torch to light another's path
without brightening our own.
—Ben Sweetland

Happiness . . . consists in giving, and in serving others.
—Henry Drummond

To find out what one is fitted to do, and to secure an
opportunity to do it, is the key to happiness.
—John Dewey

To make a man happy, fill his hands with work.
—FREDERICK E. CRANE

A bit of fragrance always clings to the hand that gives you roses.
—CHINESE PROVERB

It is the very pursuit of happiness that thwarts happiness.
—VIKTOR FRANKEL

The true object of all human life is play.
—G.K. CHESTERTON

Happiness comes only when we push our brains and hearts
to the farthest reaches of which we are capable.
—LEO C. ROSTEN

Make happy those who are near, and those who are far will come.
—CHINESE PROVERB

He that despiseth his neighbor sinneth; but he
that hath mercy on the poor, happy is he.
—PROVERBS 14:21

The older you get, the more you realize that
kindness is synonymous with happiness.
—LIONEL BARRYMORE

Ask yourself whether you are happy, and you cease to be so.
—JOHN STUART MILL

I look at what I have not and think myself unhappy;
others look at what I have and think me happy.
—JOSEPH ROUX

If you have not often felt the joy of doing a kind act, you
have neglected much, and most of all yourself.
—A. NEILEN

The most satisfying thing in life is to have been able
to give a large part of oneself to others.
—PIERRE TEILHARD DE CHARDIN

Instinct teaches us to look for happiness outside ourselves.
—BLAISE PASCAL

Happiness is not a matter of events; it depends
upon the tides of the mind.
—ALICE MEYNELL

One of the things I keep learning is that the secret of
being happy is doing things for other people.
—DICK GREGORY

All who would win joy, must share it; happiness was born a twin.
—LORD BYRON

Most true happiness comes from one's inner life, from the
disposition of the mind and soul. Admittedly, a good inner
life is difficult to achieve, especially in these trying times. It
takes reflection and contemplation and self-discipline.
—W.L. SHIRER

Happiness comes fleetingly now and then to those who
have learned to do without it, and to them only.
—DON MARQUIS

Happiness to a dog is what lies on the other side of the door.
—CHARLTON OGBURN, JR.

A man of gladness seldom falls into madness.
—ANON

If we have not peace within ourselves, it is in
vain to seek it from outward sources.
—FRANCOIS DE LA ROCHEFOUCAULD

The little things are infinitely the most important.
—SIR ARTHUR CONAN DOYLE

The most exquisite pleasure is giving pleasure to others.
—JEAN DE LA BRUYERE

It is better to be happy for a moment and be burned up with
beauty than to live a long time and be bored all the while.
—Don Marquis

Unquestionably, it is possible to do without happiness; it is
done involuntarily by nineteen-twentieths of mankind.
—John Stuart Mill

The supreme happiness of life is the conviction that we are loved.
—Victor Hugo

Suffering is not a prerequisite for happiness.
—Judy Tatelbaum

The happiness of a man in this life does not consist in
the absence, but in the mastery, of his passions.
—Alfred, Lord Tennyson

The happiest person is the person who thinks
the most interesting thoughts.
—William Lyon Phelps

Money, or even power, can never yield happiness unless
it be accompanied by the goodwill of others.
—B.C. Forbes

My life has no purpose, no direction, no aim, no meaning, and
yet I'm happy. I can't figure it out. What am I doing right?
—Charles M. Schulz

The greater part of our happiness or misery depends
on our dispositions, and not our circumstances.
—Martha Washington

Caring about others, running the risk of feeling, and
leaving an impact on people, brings happiness.
—Rabbi Harold Kushner

No man can be merry unless he is serious.
—G.K. Chesterton

It is in his pleasure that a man really lives.
—AGNES REPPLIER

Happiness is not so much in having as sharing. We make a
living by what we get, but we make a life by what we give.
—NORMAN MACEWAN

A joy that's shared is a joy made double.
—ENGLISH PROVERB

Come quickly, I am tasting stars!
—DOM PERIGNON, UPON INVENTING CHAMPAGNE

Happiness grows at our own firesides, and is
not to be picked in strangers' gardens.
—DOUGLAS JERROLD

Happiness is not perfected until it is shared.
—JANE PORTER

We are never so happy or so unhappy as we think.
—FRANCOIS DE LA ROCHEFOUCAULD

If you want to die happily, learn to live; if you
would live happily, learn to die.
—CELIO CALCAGNINI

The road to happiness lies in two simple principles: find
what it is that interests you and that you can do well, and
when you find it put your whole soul into it—every bit of
energy and ambition and natural ability you have.
—JOHN D. ROCKEFELLER III

All happiness depends on courage and work.
—HONORE DE BALZAC

Happiness is: A good martini, a good meal, a good cigar
and a good woman ... or a bad woman, depending
on how much happiness you can stand.
—GEORGE BURNS

It isn't our position, but our disposition, that makes us happy.
—ANON

Joy is the will which labours, which overcomes
obstacles, which knows triumph.
—WILLIAM BUTLER YEATS

The will of man is his happiness.
—J.C.F. VON SCHILLER

The first recipe for happiness is: Avoid too
lengthy meditations on the past.
—ANDRÉ MAUROIS

Happiness lies in the consciousness we have of it.
—GEORGE SAND

Happiness will never be any greater than the idea we have of it.
—MAURICE MAETERLINCK

There are two things to aim at in life: first, to get what you want; and,
after that, to enjoy it. Only the wisest of mankind achieve the second.
—LOGAN PEARSALL SMITH

Five Simple Rules for Happiness:
Free your heart from hatred
Free your mind from worries.
Live simply.
Give more.
Expect less.
—ANON

Man is happy only as he finds a work worth doing—and does it well.
—E. MERRILL ROOT

Happiness is when what you think, what you
say, and what you do are in harmony.
—MAHATMA GANDHI

There's nothing like the power of a smile.
—DREW BARRYMORE

This is true joy of life—being used for a purpose that is recognized by yourself as a mighty one ... instead of being a feverish, selfish little clod of ailments and grievances, complaining that the world will not devote itself to making you happy.
—GEORGE BERNARD SHAW

Continuity of purpose is one of the most essential ingredients of happiness in the long run, and for most men this comes chiefly through their work.
—BERTRAND RUSSELL

Few persons realize how much of their happiness, such as it is, is dependent upon their work.
—JOHN BURROUGHS

The secret of happiness is to admire without desiring.
—F.H. BRADLEY

He is happiest, be he king or peasant, who finds peace in his home.
—JOHANN VON GOETHE

Why not seize the pleasure at once? How often is happiness destroyed by preparation, foolish preparation?
—JANE AUSTEN

Success can also cause misery. The trick is not to be surprised when you discover it doesn't bring you all the happiness and answers you thought it would.
—PRINCE

The happy ending is our national belief.
—MARY MCCARTHY

Happiness seems to require a modicum of external prosperity.
—ARISTOTLE

Happiness is nothing more than good health and a bad memory.
—ALBERT SCHWEITZER

The art of living does not consist in preserving and clinging to a particular mode of happiness, but in allowing happiness to

change its form without being disappointed by the change; happiness, like a child, must be allowed to grow up.
—Charles L. Morgan

A happy life consists in tranquility of mind.
—Cicero

The entire sum of existence is the magic of being needed by just one person.
—Vi Putnam

Man needs, for his happiness, not only the enjoyment of this or that, but hope and enterprise and change.
—Bertrand Russell

Sadness and gladness succeed each other.
—Anon

He who would be happy should stay at home.
—Greek proverb

And may I live the remainder of my life ... for myself; may there be plenty of books and many years' store of the fruits of the earth!
—Horace

In this world there are only two tragedies. One is not getting what one wants, and the other is getting it.
—Oscar Wilde

To be happy means to be free, not from pain or fear, but from care or anxiety.
—W.H. Auden

Wisdom is the most important part of happiness.
—Sophocles

People who postpone happiness are like children who try chasing rainbows in an effort to find the pot of gold at the rainbow's end.... Your life will never be fulfilled until you are happy here and now.
—Ken Keyes, Jr.

Every minute your mouth is turned down you
lose sixty seconds of happiness.
—Tom Walsh

I am happy and content because I think I am.
—Alain-Rene Lesage

Happiness does not depend on outward things,
but on the way we see them.
—Leo Tolstoy

To live we must conquer incessantly, we must
have the courage to be happy.
—Frederic Amiel

It is an aspect of all happiness to suppose that we deserve it.
—Joseph Joubert

What we call happiness is what we do not know.
—Anatole France

Laughter is the best medicine.
—Anon

It is neither wealth nor splendor, but tranquility
and occupation, which give happiness.
—Thomas Jefferson

A reasonable man needs only to practice moderation to find happiness.
—Johann von Goethe

No man is happy unless he believes he is.
—Publilius Syrus

To win one's joy through struggle is better than to yield to melancholy.
—André Gide

We always have enough to be happy if we are enjoying what
we do have—and not worrying about what we don't have.
—Ken Keyes, Jr.

Everyone only goes around the track once in life, and
if you don't enjoy that trip, it's pretty pathetic.
—Gary Rogers

For the happiest life, days should be rigorously
planned, nights left open to chance.
—Mignon McLaughlin

With happiness comes intelligence to the heart.
—Chinese proverb

A happy life must be to a great extent a quiet life, for it is
only in an atmosphere of quiet that true joy can live.
—Bertrand Russell

Who is the happiest of men? He who values the merits of others,
And in their pleasure takes joy, even as though t'were his own.
—Johann von Goethe

Best to live lightly, unthinkingly.
—Sophocles

If you want others to be happy, practice compassion.
If you want to be happy, practice compassion.
—The Dalai Lama

I'm not happy, I'm cheerful. There's a difference. A
happy woman has no cares at all. A cheerful woman
has cares but has learned how to deal with them.
—Beverly Sills

Happiness has many roots, but none more important than security.
—E.R. Stettinius, Jr.

A morning glory at my window satisfies me
more than the metaphysics of books.
—Walt Whitman

What a wonderful life I've had! I only wish I'd realized it sooner.
—Colette

The best way for a person to have happy thoughts
is to count his blessings and not his cash.
—ANON

Happiness is not a station to arrive at, but a manner of traveling.
—MARGARET LEE RUNBECK

Contentment is not happiness. An oyster may be contented.
Happiness is compounded of richer elements.
—CHRISTIAN BOVEE

Those who have easy, cheerful attitudes tend to be
happier than those with less pleasant temperaments
regardless of money, "making it" or success.
—DR. JOYCE BROTHERS

Happy people plan actions, they don't plan results.
—DENNIS WHOLEY

We never enjoy perfect happiness; our most fortunate
successes are mingled with sadness; some anxieties
always perplex the reality of our satisfaction.
—PIERRE CORNEILLE

Happiness is not the end of life; character is.
—HENRY WARD BEECHER

The world is full of people looking for spectacular
happiness while they snub contentment.
—DOUG LARSON

The world of those who are happy is different
from the world of those who are not.
—LUDWIG WITTGENSTEIN

Part of the happiness of life consists not in fighting battles, but
in avoiding them. A masterly retreat is in itself a victory.
—NORMAN VINCENT PEALE

Enjoy yourself. These are the "good old days"
you're going to miss in the years ahead.
—ANON

Happiness is to be found along the way, not at the end of
the road, for then the journey is over and it is too late.
—ROBERT R. UPDEGRAFF

Most people ask for happiness on condition. Happiness
can only be felt if you don't set any condition.
—ARTHUR RUBINSTEIN

O Lord! Unhappy is the man whom man can make unhappy.
—RALPH WALDO EMERSON

A great obstacle to happiness is to expect too much happiness.
—BERNARD DE FONTENELLE

Enjoy your happiness while you have it, and and while you
have it do not too closely scrutinize its foundation.
—JOSEPH FARRALL

Unhappiness is not knowing what we want
and killing ourselves to get it.
—DON HEROLD

The primary cause of unhappiness in the world today is ... lack of faith.
—CARL JUNG

If happiness truly consisted in physical ease and freedom from care,
then the happiest individual ... would be, I think, an American cow.
—WILLIAM LYON PHELPS

First health, then wealth, then pleasure, and
do not owe anything to anybody.
—CATHERINE THE GREAT

Happiness always looks small while you hold it in your hands,
but let it go, and you learn at once how big and precious it is.
—MAXIM GORKY

When unhappy, one doubts everything;
when happy, one doubts nothing.
—JOSEPH ROUX

Happiness is your dentist telling you it won't hurt and
then having him catch his hand in the drill.
—JOHNNY CARSON

It takes great wit and interest and energy to be happy. The
pursuit of happiness is a great activity. One must be open
and alive. It is the greatest feat man has to accomplish.
—ROBERT HENRI

Happy is the man who could search out the causes of things.
—VIRGIL

We act as though comfort and luxury were the chief
requirements of life, when all that we need to make us
really happy is something to be enthusiastic about.
—CHARLES KINGSLEY

The clearest sign of wisdom is continued cheerfulness.
—MICHEL DE MONTAIGNE

Perfect happiness is the absence of striving for happiness.
—CHUANG-TSE

There is a courage of happiness as well as a courage of sorrow.
—MAURICE MAETERLINCK

Man's real life is happy, chiefly because he is
ever expecting that it soon will be so.
—EDGAR ALLAN POE

Those who are the most happy appear to know it the
least; happiness is something that for the most part
seems to mainly consist in not knowing it.
—DR. JOYCE BROTHERS

Life is a romantic business, but you have to make the romance.
—OLIVER WENDELL HOLMES

Happiness comes more from loving than being loved; and often when
our affection seems wounded it is only our vanity bleeding. To love, and
to be hurt often, and to love again—this is the brave and happy life.
—J.E. BUCHROSE

HOME

At home one relies on parents; away from home one relies on friends.
—CHINESE SAYING

Home is where the heart is.
—PLINY THE YOUNGER

So much of what we know of love we learn from home.
—ANON

But every house where Love abides,
And Friendship is a guest,
Is surely home, and home-sweet-home:
For there the heart can rest.
—HENRY VAN DYKE

A man ... is so in the way in the house!
—ELIZABETH GASKELL

Charity begins at home.
—SAYING

It takes a hundred men to make an encampments,
but one woman can make a home.
—ROBERT G. INGERSOLL

Happy is the house that shelters a friend!
—RALPH WALDO EMERSON

I hate housework! You make the beds, you do the dishes—
and six months later you have to start all over again.
—JOAN RIVERS

The dog is a lion in his own house.
—PERSIAN PROVERB

You are a king by your own fireside, as much
as any monarch [on] his throne.
—MIGUEL DE CERVANTES

A man travels the world over in search of what
he needs and returns home to find it.
—GEORGE MOORE

Mid pleasures and palaces though we may roam, be
it ever so humble, there's no place like home.
—JOHN HOWARD PAYNE

It takes a heap o' livin' in a house t' make it home.
—EDGAR A. GUEST

I have six locks on my door all in a row. When I go out, I only
lock every other one. I figure no matter how long somebody
stands there picking the locks, they are always locking three.
—ELAYNE BOOSLER

My home is in whatever town I'm booked.
—POLLY ADLER

I have been very happy with my homes, but homes really
are no more than the people who live in them.
—NANCY REAGAN

The ornament of a house is the friends who frequent it. There is no
event greater in life than the appearance of new persons about our
hearth, except it be the progress of the character which draws them.
—RALPH WALDO EMERSON

East and West, Home is best.
—CHARLES HADDON SPURGEON

The difference between a house and a home is this: A
house may fall down, but a home is broken up.
—ELBERT HUBBARD.

Keep the home fires burning,
While your hearts are yearning,
Though your lads are far away
They dream of home.
There's a silver lining;
Through the dark cloud shining;

Turn the dark cloud inside out,
Till the boys come home.
—Lena Guilbert Ford

What is more agreeable than one's home?
—Marcus Tullius Cicero

Home is the place where, when you have to
go there, they have to take you in.
—Robert Frost

The most important thing a man can know is that, as
he approaches his own door, someone on the other
side is listening for the sound of his footsteps.
—Clark Gable

Home is a place not only of strong affections, but of entire unreserve;
it is life's undress rehearsal, its backroom, its dressing room, from
which we go forth to more careful and guarded intercourse, leaving
behind us much debris of cast-off and everyday clothing.
—Harriet Beecher Stowe

To feel at home, stay at home.
—Clifton Fadiman

Where Thou art—that—is Home.
—Emily Dickinson

Every bird loves its own nest.
—Saying

There's no place like home.
—Hesiod/L. Frank Baum/J.H. Payne

Be it ever so humble, there's no place like
home for wearing what you like.
—George Ade

PETS

Every dog has his day.
—Randle Cotgrave

When I play with my cat, who knows whether she isn't
amusing herself with me more than I am with her?
—Michel Eyquem de Montaigne

Happiness is a warm puppy.
—Charles M. Schulz

Dogs and cats instinctively know the exact moment their owners
will wake up. Then they wake them 10 minutes sooner.
—Anon

No animal should ever jump up on the dining-room furniture unless
absolutely certain that he can hold his own in the conversation.
—Fran Lebowitz

Everyone's pet is the most outstanding. This begets mutual blindness.
—Jean Cocteau

A door is what a dog is perpetually on the wrong side of.
—Ogden Nash

On the Internet, nobody knows you're a dog.
—Peter Steiner

Clouseau: Does yer dewg bite?
Inn Keeper: No.
Clouseau: Nice Doggy (bends down to pet a dachshund—it snarls
and bites him) I thought you said yer dewg did not bite!
Inn Keeper: Zat . . . iz not my dog.
—Peter Sellers

Life with a cat is in certain ways a one-sided proposition. Cats
are not educable; humans are. Moreover, cats know this. If you're
not willing to humor them, you might as well stick to dogs.
—Terry Teachout

Let me assure you that all of our pets, and animals of every
kind will be with us for eternity on the Other Side.
—SYLVIA BROWNE

If you get to thinking you're a person of some influence,
try ordering somebody else's dog around.
—WILL ROGERS

Cats are rather delicate creatures and they are subject to a good many
ailments, but I never heard of one who suffered from insomnia.
—JOSEPH WOOD KRUTCH

Cats are inquisitive, but hate to admit it.
—MASON COOLEY

Pets are humanizing. They remind us we have an obligation and
responsibility to preserve and nurture and care for all life.
—JAMES CROMWELL

Outside of a dog, books are a man's best friend.
Inside of a dog, it's too dark to read.
—GROUCHO MARX

My little dog—a heartbeat at my feet.
—EDITH WHARTON

It is easy to understand why the cat has eclipsed the dog as modern
America's favorite pet. People like pets to possess the same qualities
they do. Cats are irresponsible and recognize no authority, yet are
completely dependent on others for their material needs. Cats
cannot be made to do anything useful. Cats are mean for the fun
of it. In fact, cats possess so many of the same qualities as some
people that it is often hard to tell the people and the cats apart.
—P.J. O'ROURKE

Cats seem to go on the principle that it never does
any harm to ask for what you want.
—JOSEPH WOOD KRUTCH

With my dog I don't get no respect. He keeps barking at the
front door. He don't want to go out. He wants me to leave.
—RODNEY DANGERFIELD

I never married because there was no need. I have three pets
at home which answer the same purpose as a husband. I have
a dog which growls every morning, a parrot which swears
all afternoon, and a cat that comes home late at night.
—Marie Corelli

Ever consider what pets must think of us? I mean, here we come back
from a grocery store with the most amazing haul—chicken, pork,
half a cow. They must think we're the greatest hunters on earth!
—Anne Tyler

Cat: One Hell of a nice animal, frequently mistaken for a meatloaf.
—B. Kliban

There are two means of refuge from the miseries of life: music and cats.
—Albert Schweitzer

A dog is one of the few remaining reasons why some
people can be persuaded to go for a walk.
—O.A. Battista

Horses are sensitive to everything and everyone around them. This
makes them both receptors and messengers for God. Perhaps because
they are prey animals, horses have had to learn how to tune in to the
slightest changes in their inner worlds and outer environments. If you
are ever in doubt about the direction to take in life and you need a
second opinion, you couldn't do better than to listen to a horse's advice.
—Allen and Linda Anderson

A dog teaches a boy fidelity, perseverance, and to
turn around three times before lying down.
—Robert Benchley

Peter Marshall: When you pat a dog on its head he
will usually wag his tail. What will a goose do?
Paul Lynde: Make him bark.
—Hollywood Squares

I am his Highness' dog at Kew;
Pray, tell me sir, whose dog are you?
—Alexander Pope

God is really only another artist. He invented the giraffe, the elephant, and the cat. He has no real style. He just goes on trying other things.
—PABLO PICASSO

The dog was created specially for children. He is the god of frolic.
—HENRY WARD BEECHER

The dog is man's best friend.
—THOMAS HOOD

The best thing about animals is that they don't talk much.
—THORNTON WILDER

III. Counting Your Blessings

BEAUTY

People are like stained-glass windows. They sparkle and shine
when the sun is out, but when the darkness sets in, their true
beauty is revealed only if there is a light from within.
—ELISABETH KÜBLER-ROSS

Beauty is greater than Good, for it includes the Good.
—GOETHE

Why do some people always see beautiful skies and grass and
lovely flowers and incredible human beings, while others are
hard-pressed to find anything or any place that is beautiful?
—LEO BUSCAGLIA

[Dr. Ellie Arroway] Some celestial event. No—no words. No
words to describe it. Poetry! They should've sent a poet [instead
of a scientist]. So beautiful. So beautiful . . . I had no idea.
—CARL SAGAN, *CONTACT, 1997*

In each person I catch the fleeting suggestion of something
beautiful and swear eternal friendship with that.
—GEORGE SANTAYANA

Beauty without grace is the hook without the
bait. Beauty, without expression, tires.
—RALPH WALDO EMERSON

Beauty is not immortal. In a day
Blossom and June and rapture pass away.
—Arthur Stringer

I think the most important thing a woman can have—
next to talent, of course, is—her hairdresser
—Joan Crawford

Not being beautiful was the true blessing.... Not being
beautiful forced me to develop my inner resources.
The pretty girl has a handicap to overcome.
—Golda Meir

Taking joy in living is a woman's best cosmetic.
—Rosalind Russell

Oh! I have slipped the surly bonds of Earth and danced the
skies on laughter-silvered wings. And, while with silent
lifting mind I've trod the high untrespassed sanctity of
space, put out my hand, and touched the face of God.
—John G. Magee, Jr.

Beauty, n. The power by which a woman charms
a lover and terrifies a husband.
—Ambrose Bierce

Life is full of beauty. Notice it. Notice the bumble bee, the small
child, and the smiling faces. Smell the rain, and feel the wind. Live
your life to the fullest potential, and fight for your dreams.
—Ashley Smith

Beauty is an ecstasy; it is as simple as hunger. There is
really nothing to be said about it. It is like the perfume
of a rose: you can smell it and that is all.
—William Somerset Maugham

Love of beauty is Taste. The creation of beauty is Art.
—Ralph Waldo Emerson

When you reach the heart of life you shall find beauty in
all things, even in the eyes that are blind to beauty.
—Kahlil Gibran

Sometimes I do get to places just when God's
ready to have somebody click the shutter.
—ANSEL ADAMS

The world will be saved by beauty.
—FYODOR DOSTOYEVSKI

The purpose of art is the lifelong construction of a state of wonder.
—GLENN GOULD

Beauty is truth, truth beauty,—that is all
Ye know on earth, and all ye need to know.
—JOHN KEATS

I'm tired of all this nonsense about beauty being only skin-deep.
That's deep enough. What do you want—an adorable pancreas?
—JEAN KERR

This Englishwoman is so refined
She has no bosom and no behind.
—STEVIE SMITH

Things are beautiful if you love them.
—JEAN ANOUILH

Beauty is everlasting
And dust is for a time.
—MARIANNE MOORE

Deep down, I'm pretty superficial.
—AVA GARDNER

Beauty is not caused. It is.
—EMILY DICKINSON

Beauty, of whatever kind, invariably excites the human soul to tears.
—EDGAR ALLAN POE

A thing of beauty is a joy forever:
Its loveliness increases; it will never
Pass into nothingness.
—JOHN KEATS

I don't design clothes, I design dreams.
—RALPH LAUREN

She always believed in the old adage, "Leave
them while you're looking good."
—ANITA LOOS (GENTLEMEN PREFER BLONDES)

The future belongs to those who believe in the beauty of their dreams.
—ELEANOR ROOSEVELT

A little beauty is preferable to much wealth.
—SA'DI

A smile is an inexpensive way to improve your looks.
—CHARLES GORDY

GENIUS

Genius . . . an infinite capacity for taking pains.
—JANE ELLICE HOPKINS

Genius is an infinite capacity for giving pains.
—DON HEROLD

Thousands of geniuses live and die undiscovered—
either by themselves or by others.
—MARK TWAIN

Coffee is good for talent, but genius wants prayer.
—RALPH WALDO EMERSON

The definition of genius is that it acts unconsciously; and those who have produced immortal works have done so without knowing how or why.
—WILLIAM HAZLITT

Everyone is a genius at least once a year. The real geniuses simply have their bright ideas closer together.
—GEORG CHRISTOPH LICHTENBERG

I have put my genius into my life; I have put only my talent into my works.
—OSCAR WILDE

When I find the road narrow, and can see no other way of teaching a well established truth except by pleasing one intelligent man and displeasing ten thousand fools—I prefer to address myself to the man.
—MAIMONIDES

Genius prepares with difficulty and executes with ease.
—ANON

Hats off, gentlemen—a genius!
—ROBERT SCHUMANN OF FREDERIC CHOPIN

Towering genius disdains a beaten path. It seeks regions hitherto unexplored.
—ABRAHAM LINCOLN

The world is always ready to receive talent with open arms. Very often it does not know what to do with genius.
—OLIVER WENDELL HOLMES, SR.

Genius without Education is like Silver in the Mine.
—BENJAMIN FRANKLIN

Genius is but a greater aptitude for patience.
—GEORGES BUFFON

Genius is the ability to put into effect what is in your mind.
—F. SCOTT FITZGERALD

Only mediocrity can be trusted to be always at its best. Genius
must always have lapses proportionate to its triumphs.
—Max Beerbohm

Genius can only breathe freely in an atmosphere of freedom.
—John Stuart Mill

Taste is the feminine of genius.
—Edward FitzGerald

Genius is more often found in a cracked pot than in a whole one.
—E.B. White

But the fact that some geniuses were laughed at does not
imply that all who are laughed at are geniuses. They laughed
at Columbus, they laughed at Fulton, they laughed at the
Wright Brothers. But they also laughed at Bozo the Clown.
—Carl Sagan

I am still learning.
—Michelangelo

Genius is 1 percent inspiration and 99 percent perspiration.
—Thomas A. Edison

A person of genius should marry a person of
character. Genius does not herd with genius.
—Oliver Wendell Holmes, Sr.

Discretion is deadly to genius; ruinous to talent.
—E.M. Cioran

Genius defies all anticipation.
—Henri Bergson

Genius is the capacity to see ten things where the ordinary man
sees one, and the man of talent sees two or three, PLUS the ability
to register that multiple perception in the material of his art.
—Ezra Pound

Constant effort and frequent mistakes are the stepping stones of genius.
—ELBERT HUBBARD

There have been only two authentic geniuses in the
world, Willie Mays and Willie Shakespeare.
—TALLULAH BANKHEAD

The first and last thing required of genius is the love of truth.
—JOHANN WOLFGANG VON GOETHE

Mediocrity knows nothing higher than itself,
but talent instantly recognizes genius.
—ARTHUR CONAN DOYLE

An improper mind is a perpetual feast.
—LOGAN PEARSALL SMITH

The public is wonderfully tolerant. It forgives everything except genius.
—OSCAR WILDE

One is not born a genius: one becomes a genius.
—SIMONE DE BEAUVOIR

Genius does what it must, and Talent does what it can.
—EDWARD ROBERT BULWER-LYTTON

Genius sharpens itself on the whetstone of struggle.
—ANON

Genius always finds itself a century too early.
—RALPH WALDO EMERSON

When a true Genius appears in the World, you may know him by
this Sign; that the Dunces are all in Confederacy against him.
—JONATHAN SWIFT

No great genius has ever been without some madness.
—ARISTOTLE

The concept of genius as akin to madness has been carefully
fostered by the inferiority complex of the public.
—Ezra Pound

Talent is that which is in a man's power; genius
is that in whose power a man is.
—James Russell Lowell

You cannot create genius. All you can do it nurture it.
—Ninette De Valois

It takes a lot of time to be a genius, you have to sit around
so much doing nothing, really doing nothing.
—Gertrude Stein

What the world needs is more geniuses with
humility, there are so few of us left.
—Oscar Levant

LIFE

Over a period of time it's been driven home to me that I'm
not going to be the most popular writer in the world, so I'm
always happy when anything in any way is accepted.
—Stephen Sondheim

The advantages of a losing team: (1) There is everything to hope for
and nothing to fear. (2) Defeats do not disturb one's sleep. (3) An
occasional victory is a surprise and a delight. (4) There is no danger
of any club passing you. (5) You are not asked fifty times a day,
"What was the score?"; people take it for granted that you lost.
—Elmer E. Bates

[Life] is demanding of me, "Start again. Begin new
things. Again set to work to build your world."
—Jean Toomer

That which does not kill me makes me stronger.
—Friedrich Nietzsche

One of the most fascinating things about golf is how it reflects the cycle of life. No matter what you shoot, the next day you have to go back to the first tee and begin all over again and make yourself into something.
—Peter Marshall

We look at the dance to impart the sensation of living in an affirmation of life, to energize the spectator into keener awareness of the vigor, the mystery, the humor, the variety, and the wonder of life. This is the function of the American dance.
—Martha Graham

It does not do to dwell on dreams and forget to live, remember that.
—J.K. Rowling

I wanted a perfect ending. Now I've learned, the hard way, that some poems don't rhyme, and some stories don't have a clear beginning, middle, and end. Life is about not knowing, having to change, taking the moment and making the best of it, without knowing what's going to happen next. Delicious ambiguity.
—Gilda Radner

Be glad of life because it gives you the chance to love and to work and to play and to look up at the stars.
—Henry Van Dyke

Everything has its wonders, even darkness and silence, and I learn, whatever state I may be in, therein to be content.
—Helen Keller

All the world's a stage and most of us are desperately unrehearsed.
—Sean O'Casey

Life truly is a boomerang. What you give, you get.
—Dale Carnegie

The basis of optimism is sheer terror.
—Oscar Wilde

The best things in life are free.
—Howard E. Johnson

It isn't important to come out on top. What matters is to come out alive.
—BERTOLT BRECHT

One man's ways may be as good as another's,
but we all like our own best.
—JANE AUSTEN

Until you make peace with who you are, you'll
never be content with what you have.
—DORIS MORTMAN

Sometimes the best deals are the ones you don't make.
—BILL VEECK

The chief danger in life is that you may take too many precautions.
—ALFRED ADLER

Man is born to live, not to prepare for life.
—BORIS PASTERNAK

Fortunately analysis [psycholanalysis] is not the only way to resolve
inner conflicts. Life itself still remains a very effective therapist.
—KAREN HORNEY

A man with ambition and love for his blessings here
on earth is ever so alive. Having been alive, it won't
be so hard in the end to lie down and rest.
—PEARL BAILEY

I had rather be shut up in a very modest cottage, with my
books, my family, and a few old friends, dining on simple
bacon, and letting the world roll on as it liked, than to occupy
the most spendid post, which any human power can give.
—THOMAS JEFFERSON

I have been through a lot and have suffered a great deal. But I have
had lots of happy moments, as well. Every moment one lives is
different from the other. The good, the bad, hardship, the joy, the
tragedy, love, and happiness are all interwoven into one single,
indescribable whole that is called life. You cannot separate the
good from the bad. And perhaps there is no need to do so, either.
—JACQUELYN KENNEDY ONASSIS

If thou wouldst be happy ... have an indifference
for more than what is sufficient.
—William Penn

Contentment is worth more than riches.
—German proverb

A Christian could even give thanks for Hell, because Hell was
a threat and a warning to keep him in the right way.
—Anon

Life itself is always pulling you away from the understanding of life.
—Anne Morrow Lindbergh

Life is like a game of poker: If you don't put any in
the pot, there won't be any to take out.
—Jackie "Moms" Mabley

When something does not insist on being noticed, when we aren't
grabbed by the collar or struck on the skull by a presence or an event,
we take for granted the very things that most deserve our gratitude.
—Cynthia Ozick

Be content with what thou hast received, and
smooth thy frowning forehead.
—Hafez

If thou covetest riches, ask not but for contentment,
which is an immense treasure.
—Sa'di

Try to live the life of the good man who is more
than content with what is allocated to him.
—Marcus Aurelius

In the country of the blind, the one-eyed man is king.
—Michael Apostolius

The measure of life is not its duration, but its donation.
—Peter Marshall

The world is full of people looking for spectacular
happiness while they snub contentment.
—Doug Larson

Who is content with nothing possesses all things.
—Nicolas Boileau

You will live wisely if you are happy in your lot.
—Horace

Talk happiness. The world is sad enough without
your woe. No path is wholly rough.
—Ella Wheeler Wilcox

No one is satisfied with his fortune, or dissatisfied with his intellect.
—Antoinette Deshouliere

When I first open my eyes upon the morning meadows and
look out upon the beautiful world, I thank God I am alive.
—Ralph Waldo Emerson

Luckily, I never feel at one time more than half my pains.
—Joseph Joubert

I think that, as life is action and passion, it is required
of a man that he should share the passion and action of
his time at peril of being judged not to have lived.
—Oliver Wendell Holmes, Jr.

Give thanks for sorrow that teaches you pity; for pain that teaches
you courage—and give exceeding thanks for the mystery which
remains a mystery still—the veil that hides you from the infinite,
which makes it possible for you to believe in what you cannot see.
—Robert Nathan

Adversity has the same effect on a man that severe training
has on the pugilist: it reduces him to his fighting weight.
—Josh Billings

Most of my major disappointments have turned out to be blessings
in disguise. So whenever anything bad does happen to me, I
kind of sit back and feel, well, if I give this enough time, it'll turn
out that this was good, so I shan't worry about it too much.
—WILLIAM GAINES

I have gout, asthma, and seven other maladies,
but am otherwise very well.
—SYDNEY SMITH

You will never be the person you can be if pressure,
tension and discipline are taken out of your life.
—DR. JAMES G. BILKEY

Some troubles, like a protested note of a solvent debtor, bear interest.
—HONORE DE BALZAC

True contentment depends not upon what we have; a tub was large
enough for Diogenes, but a world was too little for Alexander.
—CHARLES CALEB COLTON

My country ... gave me schooling, independence of
action and opportunity for service. ... I am indebted to
my country beyond any human power to repay.
—HERBERT HOOVER

Take full account of the excellencies which you possess, and in gratitude
remember how you would hanker after them, if you had them not.
—MARCUS AURELIUS

To live is the rarest thing in the world. Most people exist, that is all.
—OSCAR WILDE

Each day comes bearing its own gifts. Untie the ribbons.
—RUTH ANN SCHABACKER

We can be thankful to a friend for a few acres or a little money;
and yet for the freedom and command of the whole earth,
and for the great benefits of our being, our life, health, and
reason, we look upon ourselves as under no obligation.
—MARCUS ANNAEUS SENECA

Health is the vital principle of bliss.
—JAMES THOMSON

It ain't so much trouble to get rich as it is to tell when we have got rich.
—JOSH BILLINGS

To every disadvantage there is a corresponding advantage.
—W. CLEMENT STONE

Too many people miss the silver lining because they're expecting gold.
—MAURICE SETTER

Life is the first gift, love is the second, and understanding the third.
—MARGE PIERCY

Many a man curses the rain that falls upon his head, and
knows not that it brings abundance to drive away hunger.
—SAINT BASIL

Failure changes for the better, success for the worse.
—MARCUS ANNAEUS SENECA

He who limps still walks.
—STANISLAW LEC

This is another day! Are its eyes blurred
With maudlin grief for any wasted past?
A thousand thousand failures shall not daunt!
Let dust clasp dust, death, death; I am alive!
—DON MARQUIS

How can they say my life is not a success? Have I not for more than
sixty years gotten enough to eat and escaped being eaten?
—LOGAN PEARSALL SMITH

The difficulties, hardships and trials of life, the obstacles ... are positive
blessings. They knit the muscles more firmly, and teach self-reliance.
—WILLIAM MATTHEWS

Most human beings have an almost infinite
capacity for taking things for granted.
—Aldous Huxley

A wise man cares not for what he cannot have.
—Anon

Trouble is only opportunity in work clothes.
—Henry J. Kaiser

Sunshine is delicious, rain is refreshing, wind braces us
up, snow is exhilarating; there is really no such thing as
bad weather, only different kinds of good weather.
—John Ruskin

A man can refrain from wanting what he has not, and
cheerfully make the best of a bird in the hand.
—Marcus Annaeus Seneca

Long only for what you have.
—André Gide

The superiority of the distant over the present is only due to
the mass and variety of the pleasures that can be suggested,
compared with the poverty of those that can at any time be felt.
—George Santayana

Dwell upon the brightest parts in every prospect . . . and
strive to be pleased with the present circumstances.
—Abraham Tucker

We are never either so wretched or so happy as we say we are.
—Honore de Balzac

Is it so small a thing to have enjoyed the sun, to have lived light
in the spring, to have loved, to have thought, to have done?
—Matthew Arnold

'Tis better to have loved and lost than never to have loved at all.
—Alfred, Lord Tennyson

When the reviews are bad I tell my staff that they
can join me as I cry all the way to the bank.
—LIBERACE

Our real blessings often appear to us in the shape
of pains, losses and disappointments.
—JOSEPH ADDISON

You say grace before meals. All right. But I say grace before
the concert and the opera, and grace before the play and
pantomime, and grace before I open a book, and grace before
sketching, painting, swimming, fencing, boxing, walking,
playing, dancing and grace before I dip the pen in the ink.
—G.K. CHESTERTON

Welcome everything that comes to you, but do not long for anything else.
—ANDRÉ GIDE

No man can be satisfied with his attainment, although
he may be satisfied with his circumstances.
—FRANK SWINNERTON

I seek the utmost pleasure and the least pain.
—PLAUTUS

Thank God for dirty dishes; they have a tale to tell.
While other folks go hungry, we're eating pretty well.
With home, and health, and happiness, we shouldn't want to fuss;
For by this stack of evidence, God's very good to us.
—ANON

Happiness lies, first of all, in health.
—GEORGE WILLIAM CURTIS

We don't understand life any better at forty than
at twenty, but we know it and admit it.
—JULES RENARD

The mere sense of living is joy enough.
—EMILY DICKINSON

To have a full stomach and fixed income are no small things.
—Elbert Hubbard

If you can't be thankful for what you receive,
be thankful for what you escape.
—Anon

Even though we can't have all we want, we ought
to be thankful we don't get all we deserve.
—Anon

Some troubles, like a protested note of a solvent debtor, bear interest.
—Honore de Balzac

The end of pain we take as happiness.
—Giacomo Leopardi

However mean your life is, meet it and live it; do not shun it and call it
hard names. It is not so bad as you are. It looks poorest when you are
richest. The fault-finder will find faults even in Paradise. Love your life.
—Henry David Thoreau

The great business of life it to be, to do, to do without, and to depart.
—John, Viscount Morley of Blackburn

Happy the man who can count his sufferings.
—Ovid

Life may be hard, but it's also wonderful.
—Small Change

Thanksgiving is a sure index of spiritual health.
—Maurice Dametz

Happiness is composed of misfortunes avoided.
—Alphonse Karr

I thank Thee first because I was never robbed before; second,
because although they took my purse they did not take my life;

third, because although they took my all, it was not much; and
fourth because it was I who was robbed, and not I who robbed.
—MATTHEW HENRY

If we go down into ourselves, we find that we
possess exactly what we desire.
—SIMONE WEIL

Who does not thank for little will not thank for much.
—ESTONIAN PROVERB

The greatest saint in the world is not he who prays most or fasts
most; it is not he who gives alms, or is most eminent for temperance,
chastity or justice. It is he who is most thankful to God.
—WILLIAM LAW

Happiness is not being pained in body, or troubled in mind.
—THOMAS JEFFERSON

Be grateful for yourself . . . be thankful.
—WILLIAM SAROYAN

A thankful heart is not only the greatest virtue,
but the parent of all other virtues.
—CICERO

Only a stomach that rarely feels hungry scorns common things.
—HORACE

What is the proper limit for wealth? It is, first, to have what
is necessary; and, second, to have what is enough.
—MARCUS ANNAEUS SENECA

I like living. I have sometimes been wildly, despairingly, acutely
miserable, racked with sorrow, but through it all I still know
quite certainly that just to be alive is a grand thing.
—AGATHA CHRISTIE

You can be happy indeed if you have breathing space from pain.
—GIACOMO LEOPARDI

For everything you have missed, you have gained something else.
—RALPH WALDO EMERSON

To be alive, to be able to see, to walk … it's all a miracle. I have
adapted the technique of living life from miracle to miracle.
—ARTHUR RUBINSTEIN

Better a little fire to warm us than a great one to burn us.
—THOMAS FULLER

Much unhappiness results from our inability to
remember the nice things that happen to us.
—W.N. RIEGER

You can't appreciate home until you've left it, money till it's spent,
your wife till she's joined a woman's club, nor Old Glory till you see it
hanging on a broomstick on the shanty of a consul in a foreign town.
—O. HENRY

Not what we have, but what we enjoy, constitutes our abundance.
—J. PETIT-SENN

The summit of pleasure is the elimination of all that gives pain.
—EPICURUS

A prudent man will think more important what fate
has conceded to him, than what it has denied.
—BALTASAR GRACIAN

If there is a sin against life, it consists perhaps not so
much in despairing of life as in hoping for another, and
in eluding the implacable grandeur of this life.
—ALBERT CAMUS

There is no wealth but life.
—JOHN RUSKIN

Guns aren't lawful;
Nooses give;
Gas smells awful;
You might as well live.
—DOROTHY PARKER

Just to be is a blessing. Just to live is holy.
—Abraham Heschel

He is a man of sense who does not grieve for what
he has not, but rejoices in what he has.
—Epictetus

The talent for being happy is appreciating and liking
what you have, instead of what you don't have.
—Woody Allen

May we never let the things we can't have, or don't have, spoil
our enjoyment of the things we do have and can have.
—Richard L. Evans

Slight not what is near though aiming at what is far.
—Euripides

Happy thou art not; for what thou hast not, still thou
striv'est to get; and what thou hast, forget'est.
—William Shakespeare

There must be more to life than having everything.
—Maurice Sendak

The best things in life are appreciated most after they have been lost.
—Roy L. Smith

Think of the ills from which you are exempt.
—Joseph Joubert

I may not amount to much, but at least I am unique.
—Jean-Jacques Rousseau

Ambition has its disappointments to sour us, but
never the good fortune to satisfy us.
—Benjamin Franklin

Eden is that old-fashioned house we dwell in every day
Without suspecting our abode, until we drive away.
—Emily Dickinson

A man should always consider ... how much
more unhappy he might be than he is.
—Joseph Addison

To be upset over what you don't have is to waste what you do have.
—Ken Keyes, Jr.

If there's no bread, cakes are very good.
—Spanish proverb

Too happy would you be, did ye but know your own advantages!
—Virgil

True contentment ... is the power of getting out of any
situation all that there is in it. It is arduous, and it is rare.
—G.K. Chesterton

Poor and content is rich, and rich enough.
—William Shakespeare

So long as we can lose any happiness, we possess some.
—Booth Tarkington

If we get everything that we want, we will
soon want nothing that we get.
—Vernon Luchies

One cultivated talent, deepened and enlarged, is
worth one hundred shallow faculties.
—William Matthews

He who curbs his desires will always be rich enough.
—French proverb

Reality is a crutch for people who can't cope with drugs.
—Jane Wagner

It matters very little whether a man is discontented in the
name of pessimism or progress, if his discontent does in fact
paralyse his power of appreciating what he has got.
—G.K. Chesterton

How many things there are which I do not want.
—SOCRATES

What you really value is what you miss, not what you have.
—JORGE LUIS BORGES

The unthankful heart . . . discovers no mercies; but let the thankful
heart sweep through the day and, as the magnet finds the iron,
so it will find, in every hour, some heavenly blessings!
—HENRY WARD BEECHER

Happiness is a way station between too much and too little.
—CHANNING POLLOCK

The average man is rich enough when he
has a little more than he has got.
—WILLIAM RALPH INGE

Happy is the man who can do only one thing:
in doing it, he fulfills his destiny.
—JOSEPH JOUBERT

He is not rich that possesses much, but he
that is content with what he has.
—ANON

That daily life is really good one appreciates when one
wakes from a horrible dream, or when one takes the first
outing after a sickness. Why not realize it now?
—WILLIAM LYON PHELPS

He is poor who does not feel content.
—JAPANESE PROVERB

Moderate desires constitute a character fitted to acquire all
the good which the world can yield. He who has this character
is prepared, in whatever situation he is, therewith to be
content and has learned the science of being happy.
—TIMOTHY DWIGHT

Birds sing after a storm; why shouldn't people feel as
free to delight in whatever remains to them?
—Rose Fitzgerald Kennedy

Man never has what he wants, because what he wants is everything.
—C.F. Ramuz

Gratitude is the memory of the heart.
—Massieu

Not what we say about our blessings, but how we use
them, is the true measure of our thanksgiving.
—W.T. Purkiser

People call me an optimist, but I'm really an appreciator ... years ago,
I was cured of a badly infected finger with antibiotics when once my
doctor could have recommended only a hot water soak or, eventually,
surgery.... When I was six years old and had scarlet fever, the first
of the miracle drugs, sulfanilamide, saved my life. I'm grateful for
computers and photocopiers ... I appreciate where we've come from.
—Julian Simon

Freedom is not procured by a full enjoyment of what
is desired, but by controlling the desire.
—Epictetus

Were a man to order his life by the rules of true reason, a frugal
substance joined to a contented mind is for him great riches.
—Lucretius

The way to love anything is to realize that it may be lost.
—G.K. Chesterton

The unthankful heart ... discovers no mercies; but the thankful
heart ... will find, in every hour, some heavenly blessings.
—Henry Ward Beecher

The knowledge that something remains yet unenjoyed
impairs our enjoyment of the good before us.
—Samuel Johnson

Nothing is enough to the man for whom enough is too little.
—EPICURUS

One is never fortunate or as unfortunate as one imagines.
—FRANCOIS DE LA ROCHEFOUCAULD

Health is ... a blessing that money cannot buy.
—IZAAK WALTON

Too much is unwholesome.
—GEORG CHRISTOPH LICHTENBERG

So long as we can lose any happiness, we possess some.
—BOOTH TARKINGTON

If only the people who worry about their liabilities would think about the riches they do possess, they would stop worrying. Would you sell both your eyes for a million dollars ... or your two legs ... or your hands ... or your hearing? Add up what you do have, and you'll find that you won't sell them for all the gold in the world. The best things in life are yours, if you can appreciate yourself.
—DALE CARNEGIE

It is strange what a contempt men have for the
joys that are offered them freely.
—GEORGES DUHAMEL

If you desire many things, many things will seem but a few.
—BENJAMIN FRANKLIN

Content may dwell in all stations. To be low, but above
contempt, may be high enough to be happy.
—SIR THOMAS BROWNE

Happiness always looks small while you hold it in your hands,
but let it go, and you learn at once how big and precious it is.
—MAXIM GORKY

Sufficiency's enough for men of sense.
—EURIPIDES

If you would but exchange places with the other fellow, how much more you could appreciate your own position.
—Victor E. Gardner

This only grant me, that my means may lie too low for envy, for contempt too high.
—Abraham Cowley

Reflect upon your present blessings, of which every man has many; not on your past misfortunes, of which all men have some.
—Charles Dickens

It is possible to own too much. A man with one watch knows what time it is; a man with two watches is never quite sure.
—Lee Segall

We should learn, by reflection on the misfortunes of others, that there is nothing singular in those which befall ourselves.
—Thomas Fitzosborne

You never know what is enough unless you know what is more than enough.
—William Blake

To be able to dispense with good things is tantamount to possessing them.
—Jean Francois Regnard

I have learned to seek my happiness by limiting my desires, rather than in attempting to satisfy them.
—John Stuart Mill

Double—no, triple—our troubles and we'd still be better off than any other people on earth.
—Ronald Reagan

How few are our real wants, and how easy is it to satisfy them! Our imaginary ones are boundless and insatiable.
—Julius Charles Hare

The best things in life are appreciated most after they have been lost.
—Roy L. Smith

The hardest thing is to take less when you can get more.
—KIN HUBBARD

There is satiety in all things, in sleep, and love-making, in
the loveliness of singing and the innocent dance.
—HOMER

Of all the people in the world, those who want
the most are those who have the most.
—DAVID GRAYSON

The man who thinks his wife, his baby, his house, his horse, his dog, and
himself severely unequalled, is almost sure to be a good-humored person.
—OLIVER WENDELL HOLMES

He is not rich that possesses much, but he that covets no more; and
he is not poor that enjoys little, but he that wants too much.
—BEAUMONT

He is not poor that hath not much, but he that craves much.
—THOMAS FULLER

We don't need to increase our goods nearly as much as we need to scale
down our wants. Not wanting something is as good as possessing it.
—DONALD HORBAN

While you fear missing a meal, you aren't fully
aware of the meals you do eat.
—DAN MILLMAN

The private and personal blessings we enjoy—the
blessings of immunity, safeguard, liberty and integrity—
deserve the thanksgiving of a whole life.
—JEREMY TAYLOR

Thank God every morning when you get up that you have
something to do which must be done, whether you like it or not.
—CHARLES KINGSLEY

Independence may be found in comparative as well as
in absolute abundance; I mean where a person contracts
his desires within the limits of his fortune.
—WILLIAM SHENSTONE

When life's problems seem overwhelming, look around and see what
other people are coping with. You may consider yourself fortunate.
—ANN LANDERS

I thank You God for this most amazing day; for the leaping
greenly spirits of trees and a blue true dream of sky; and for
everything which is natural which is infinite which is yes.
—E.E. CUMMINGS

We are no longer happy so soon as we wish to be happier.
—WALTER SAVAGE LANDOR

Greediness of getting more, deprives . . . the enjoyment of what it had got.
—THOMAS SPRAT

Good heavens, of what uncostly material is our earthly happiness
composed . . . if we only knew it. What incomes have we not had
from a flower, and how unfailing are the dividends of the seasons.
—JAMES RUSSELL LOWELL

One of life's gifts is that each of us, no matter how tired
and downtrodden, finds reasons for thankfulness.
—J. ROBERT MASKIN

Joy is the simplest form of gratitude.
—KARL BARTH

Do not spoil what you have by desiring what you have not; remember
that what you now have was once among the things only hoped for.
—EPICURUS

A sound mind in a sound body is a short but full
description of a happy state in this world.
—JOHN LOCKE

Anyone is to be pitied who has just sense
enough to perceive his deficiencies.
—William Hazlitt

He is well paid that is well satisfied.
—William Shakespeare

If all misfortunes were laid in one common heap whence
everyone must take an equal portion, most people would
be contented to take their own and depart.
—Socrates

Moderation is the key to lasting enjoyment.
—Hosea Ballou

True affluence is not needing anything.
—Gary Snyder

And be content with such things as ye have.
—Heb. 13:5

To be without some of the things you want is
an indispensable part of happiness.
—Bertrand Russell

Life is hard. Next to what?
—Anon

Some people think football is a matter of life and death. . . . I
can assure them it is much more serious than that.
—Bill Shankly

The use we make of our fortune determines as to its sufficiency. A little is
enough if used wisely, and too much is not enough if expended foolishly.
—Christian Bovee

The private and personal blessings we enjoy—the
blessings of immunity, safeguard, liberty and integrity—
deserve the thanksgiving of a whole life.
—Jeremy Taylor

Man is fond of counting his troubles, but he does not count his joys. If he counted them up as he ought to, he would see that every lot has enough happiness provided for it.
—FYODOR DOSTOYEVSKY

He is rich that is satisfied.
—THOMAS FULLER

If only every man would make proper use of his strength and do his utmost, he need never regret his limited ability.
—CICERO

The real tragedy of life is not being limited to one talent, but in failing to use that one talent.
—EDGAR WATSON HOWE

To be satisfied with what one has; that is wealth. As long as one sorely needs a certain additional amount, that man isn't rich.
—MARK TWAIN

Happiness is a result of the relative strengths of positive and negative feelings, rather than an absolute amount of one or the other.
—NORMAN BRADBURN

There are men who are happy without knowing it.
—VAUVENARGUES

My crown is called content, a crown that seldom kings enjoy.
—WILLIAM SHAKESPEARE

Thank you, God, for this good life and forgive us is we do not love it enough.
—GARRISON KEILLOR

When we cannot get what we love, we must love what is within our reach.
—FRENCH PROVERB

Nothing will content him who is not content with a little.
—GREEK PROVERB

I am happy and content because I think I am.
—Alain-Rene Lesage

Unhappy is the man, though he rule the world, who
doesn't consider himself supremely blessed.
—Marcus Annaeus Seneca

Normal day, let me be aware of the treasure you are. Let me learn from
you, love you, bless you before you depart. Let me not pass you by
in quest of some rare and perfect tomorrow. Let me hold you while I
may, for it may not always be so. One day I shall dig my nails into the
earth, or bury my face in the pillow, or stretch myself taut, or raise my
hands to the sky and want, more than all the world, your return.
—Mary Jean Iron

Men … always think that something they are going
to get is better than what they have got.
—John Oliver Hobbes

Life is made up of sobs, sniffles, and smiles, with sniffles predominating.
—O. Henry

Service to others is the rent you pay for your room here on earth
—Muhammad Ali

Too many people overvalue what they are not
and undervalue what they are.
—Malcolm Forbes

Left-handers have more enthusiasm for life. They sleep on the wrong
side of the bed and their head gets more stagnant on that side.
—Casey Stengel

We have two lives … the life we learn with
and the life we live with after that.
—Bernard Malamud

Life is what happens to us while we are making other plans.
—Allen Saunders

Poor and content is rich, and rich enough.
—William Shakespeare

Love your life, as it is. You may perhaps have some
pleasant, thrilling, glorious hours, even in a poorhouse.
The setting sun is reflected as brightly from the windows
of the almshouse as from the rich man's abode.
—Henry David Thoreau

Be on the lookout for mercies. The more we look for them, the more
of them we will see.... Better to lose count while naming your
blessings than to lose your blessings to counting your troubles.
—Maltbie D. Babcock

It is more fitting for a man to laugh at life than to lament over it.
—Seneca

Solitude is the profoundest fact of the human condition. Man is the only
being who knows he is alone, and the only one who seeks out another.
—Octavio Paz

I am little concerned with beauty or perfection. I don't
care for the great centuries. All I care about is life,
struggle, intensity. I am at ease in my generation.
—Emile Zola

There are many wonderful things, and nothing
is more wonderful than man.
—Sophocles

Since Life is but a Dream, why toil to no avail?
—Li Po

Making a living and making a life that's worthwhile are not the same
thing. Living the good life and living a good life are not the same thing.
—Robert Fulghum

The art of living is more like wrestling than dancing.
—Marcus Aurelius

Life is fleeting—and therefore endurable.
—Alexander Chase

All fortune belongs to him
who has a contented mind.
—THE PANCHATANTRA

Life is a moderately good play with a badly written third act.
—TRUMAN CAPOTE

Get a checkup. Talk someone you like into getting a checkup. Nag
someone you love into getting a checkup. And while you're at it,
send a check to the American Cancer Society. It's great to be alive.
—JOHN WAYNE

Life is not having been told that the man has just waxed the floor.
—OGDEN NASH

LUCK

Fortune is ever seen accompanying industry.
—OLIVER GOLDSMITH

No man ever wetted clay and then left it, as if there
would be bricks by chance and fortune.
—PLUTARCH

Luck is the residue of design.
—BRANCH RICKEY

Luck is what you have left over after you give 100 percent.
—LANGSTON COLEMAN

One never hugs one's good luck so affectionately as when listening to
the relation of some horrible misfortunes which has overtaken others.
—ALEXANDER SMITH

Luck is largely a matter of paying attention.
—SUSAN M. DODD

The champion makes his own luck.
—Red Blaik

There is in the worst of fortune the best of chances for a happy change.
—Euripides

Luck is a matter of preparation meeting opportunity.
—Oprah Winfrey

Go and wake up your luck.
—Persian proverb

Luck is good planning, carefully executed.
—Anon

It's funny, but ... you're sort of a moving target for fortune,
and you never know when it will befall you.
—Thomas McGuane

I would rather have a lucky general than a smart
general.... They win battles, and they make me lucky.
—Dwight D. Eisenhower

No writer should minimize the factor
that affects everyone, but is beyond control: luck.
—John Jakes

Luck is the by-product of busting your fanny.
—Don Sutton

I think that one can have luck if one tries to
create an atmosphere of spontaneity.
—Federico Fellini

Chance favors those in motion.
—Dr. James H. Austin

There are so many people with all kinds of lucky things
happening to them, and they don't know how to use it.
—Rocky Aoki

People make their own luck.
—David Liederman

Good luck needs no explanation.
—Shirley Temple Black

I find I'm luckier when I work harder.
—Dr. Denton Cooley

We create our fate every day . . . most of the ills we suffer
from are directly traceable to our own behavior.
—Henry Miller

Of course, fortune has its part in human affairs, but
conduct is really much more important.
—Jeanne Detourbey

The lucky fellow is the plucky fellow who has been burning
midnight oil and taking defeat after defeat with a smile.
—James B. Hill

When you work seven days a week, fourteen hours a day, you get lucky.
—Armand Hammer

It's hard to detect good luck—it looks so much
like something you've earned.
—Frank A. Clark

In the queer mess of human destiny, the determining factor is luck.
—William E. Woodward

When something bad happens to me, I think I'm able to deal
with it in a pretty good way. That makes me lucky. Some
people fall apart at the first little thing that happens.
—Christie Brinkley

Work and acquire, and thou hast chained the wheel of Chance.
—Ralph Waldo Emerson

Men who have attained things worth having in this world have worked while others idled, have persevered when others gave up in despair, have practiced early in life the valuable habits of self-denial, industry, and singleness of purpose. As a result, they enjoy in later life the success so often erroneously attributed to good luck.
—GRENVILLE KLEISER

A wise man turns chance into good fortune.
—THOMAS FULLER

Though men pride themselves on their great actions, often they are not the result of any great design, but of chance.
—FRANCOIS DE LA ROCHEFOUCAULD

Luck affects everything. Let your hook be always cast. In the stream where you least expect it, there will be a fish.
—OVID

Luck is everything.... My good luck in life was to be a really frightened person. I'm fortunate to be a coward, to have a low threshold of fear, because a hero couldn't make a good suspense film.
—ALFRED HITCHCOCK

I'm a great believer in luck, and I find the harder I work, the more I have of it.
—THOMAS JEFFERSON

I was thinking of my patients, and how the worst moment for them was when they discovered they were masters of bad or good luck. When they could no longer blame fate, they were in despair.
—ANAÏS NIN

Luck ... taps, once in a lifetime, at everybody's door, but if industry does not open it, luck goes away.
—CHARLES HADDON SPURGEON

I am persuaded that luck and timing have, in my case, been very important.
—MIKE WALLACE

I'm hardnosed about luck.... Yeah, if you spend seven years looking for a job as a copywriter, and then one day somebody

gives you a job, you can say, "Gee, I was lucky I happened to go up there today." But dammit, I was going to go up there sooner or later in the next seventy year.... If you're persistent in trying and doing and working, you almost make your own fortune.
—Jerry Della Femina

What helps luck is a habit of watching for opportunities, of having a patient, but restless mind, of sacrificing one's ease or vanity, of uniting a love of detail to foresight, and of passing through hard times bravely and cheerfully.
—Charles Victor Cherbuliez

Your luck is how you treat people.
—Bridget O'Donnell

I wish I could tell you that the Children's Television Workshop and Sesame Street were thanks to my genius, but it really was a lucky break.
—Joan Ganz Cooney

Superiority to fate is difficult to gain, 'tis not conferred of any, but possible to earn.
—Emily Dickinson

Luck is believing you're lucky.
—Tennessee Williams

Good luck is a lazy man's estimate of a worker's success.
—Anon

I have been extraordinarily lucky. Anyone who pretends that some kind of luck isn't involved in his success is deluding himself.
—Arthur Hailey

You don't just luck into things.... You build step by step, whether it's friendships or opportunities.
—Barbara Bush

Luck is a combination of confidence and getting the breaks.
—Christy Mathewson

Motivation triggers luck.
—Mike Wallace

Luck means the hardships and privations which you have
not hesitated to endure, the long nights you have devoted to
work. Luck means the appointments you have never failed
to keep, the trains you have never failed to catch.
—Max O'Relling

You must always be open to your luck. You cannot
force it, but you can recognize it.
—Henry Moore

Chance never helps those who do not help themselves.
—Sophocles

Failure and success seem to have been allotted to men by
their stars. But they retain the power of wriggling, of fighting
with their star or against it, and in the whole universe the
only really interesting movement is this wriggle.
—E.M. Forster

Luck is a very good word if you put a P before it.
—Anon

Everything that happened to me happened by mistake. I
don't believe in fate. It's luck, timing and accident.
—Merv Griffin

It is a great piece of skill to know how to guide
your luck, even while waiting for it.
—Baltasar Gracian

If fate means you to lose, give him a good fight anyhow.
—William McFee

It's a funny old world—a man's lucky if he gets out of it alive.
—W.C. Fields

Chance works for us when we are good captains.
—George Meredith

Good and bad luck is a synonym, in the great majority
of instances, for good and bad judgment.
—John Chatfield

Some folk want their luck buttered.
—THOMAS HARDY

Fortune favors the brave.
—TERENCE

Nothing is a obnoxious as other people's luck.
—F. SCOTT FITZGERALD

Diligence is the mother of good luck, and God gives all things to industry.
—BENJAMIN FRANKLIN

Probably any successful career has "X" number of breaks in it, and
maybe the difference between successful people and those who
aren't superachievers is taking advantage of those breaks.
—JOAN GANZ COONEY

I was born lucky, and I have lived lucky. What I had
was used. What I still have is being used. Lucky.
—KATHARINE HEPBURN

We must master our good fortune, or it will master us.
—PUBLILIUS SYRUS

PEACE OF MIND

Inner peace creates outer peace.
—REMEZ SASSON

Do not confuse peace of mind with spaced-out insensitivity.
A truly peaceful mind is very sensitive, very aware.
—DALAI LAMA

There are some days when I think I am going to
die from an overdose of satisfaction.
—SALVADOR DALI

For peace of mind, resign as general manager of the universe.
—LARRY EISENBERG

Peace is not something you wish for; it's something you make,
something you do, something you are, something you give away.
—ROBERT FULGHUM

Inner peace is beyond victory or defeat.
—BHAGAVAD GITA

Peace of mind is not the absence of conflict from
life, but the ability to cope with it.
—ANON

Work and live to serve others, to leave the world a little
better than you found it and garner for yourself as much
peace of mind as you can. This is happiness.
—DAVID SARNOFF

Set peace of mind as your highest goal, and organize your life around it.
— BRIAN TRACY

If you want peace, stop fighting. If you want peace
of mind, stop fighting with your thoughts.
—PETER MCWILLIAMS

A man's village is his peace of mind.
—ANWAR AL-SADAT

Peace of mind is that mental condition in
which you have accepted the worst.
—LIN YUTANG

Give up what appears to be doubtful for what is certain.
Truth brings peace of mind, and deception doubt.
—MUHAMMAD ALI

Nothing is more conducive to peace of mind
than not having any opinion at all.
—GEORG CHRISTOPH LICHTENBERG

Poor wandering one!
If such poor love as mine
Can help thee find
True peace of mine—
Why, take it, it is thine!
—W. S. GILBERT

Nothing can bring you peace but yourself. Nothing can
bring you peace but the triumph of principles.
—RALPH WALDO EMERSON

IV. Coping with Life's Little Challenges

REALITY

The past exists only in our memories, the future only
in our plans. The present is our only reality.
—ROBERT M. PIRSIG

A fact is like a sack which won't stand up when it is empty.
In order that it may stand up, one has to put into it the
reason and sentiment which have caused it to exist.
—LUIGI PIRANDELLO

The very greatest mystery is in unsheathed reality itself.
—EUDORA WELTY

Reality is that which, when you stop believing in it, doesn't go away.
—PHILIP K. DICK

If a man will kick a fact out of the window, when he
comes back he finds it again in the chimney corner.
—RALPH WALDO EMERSON

To mention a loved object, a person, or a place to
someone else is to invest that object with reality.
—ANNE MORROW LINDBERGH

Our safety is not in blindness, but in facing our dangers.
—JOHANN CHRISTOPH FRIEDRICH VON SCHILLER

Let us replace sentimentalism by realism, and dare
to uncover those simple and terrible laws which, be
they seen or unseen, pervade and govern.
—Ralph Waldo Emerson

A wise man recognizes the convenience of a general statement,
but he bows to the authority of a particular fact.
—Oliver Wendell Holmes, Sr.

It is only by knowing how little life has in store for us that we
are able to look on the bright side and avoid disappointment.
—Ellen Glasgow

The facts are to blame, my friend. We are all
imprisoned by facts: I was born, I exist.
—Luigi Pirandello

Intuition? Bosh! Women, in fact, are the supreme realists of the race.
—H.L. Mencken

When you have duly arrayed your "facts" in logical order, lo,
it is like an oil-lamp that you have made, filled and trimmed,
but which sheds no light unless first you light it.
—Antoine Saint-Exupery

COURAGE

If you risk nothing, then you risk everything.
—Geena Davis

Risk! Risk anything! Care no more for the opinions
of others, for those voices. Do the hardest thing on
earth for you. Act for yourself. Face the truth.
—Katherine Mansfield

Courage is the thing. All goes if courage goes.
—J. M. Barrie

Without justice, courage is weak.
—BENJAMIN FRANKLIN

No one would have crossed the ocean if he could
have gotten off the ship in the storm.
—CHARLES F. KETTERING

Sometimes even to live is an act of courage.
—SENECA

It is easy to be brave from a safe distance.
—AESOP

Courage is resistance to fear, mastery of fear-not absences of fear. Except
a creature be part coward it is not a compliment to say it is brave.
—MARK TWAIN

That is at bottom the only courage demanded of us: to
have courage for the most strange, the most singular and
the most inexplicable that we may encounter.
—RAINER MARIA RILKE

One man with courage makes a majority.
—ANDREW JACKSON

It's very simple. There's only one requirement of any of us, and that
is to be courageous. Because courage, as you might know, defines all
other human behavior. And, I believe—because I've done a little of this
myself—pretending to be courageous is just as good as the real thing.
—DAVID LETTERMAN

Courage is like love; it must have hope for nourishment.
—NAPOLEON BONAPARTE

You can measure opportunity with the same yardstick
that measures the risk involved. They go together.
—EARL NIGHTINGALE

Valor is a gift. Those having it never know for sure whether they
have it till the test comes. And those having it in one test never
know for sure if they will have it when the next test comes.
—CARL SANDBURG

It is courage, courage, courage, that raises the
blood of life to crimson splendor.
—GEORGE BERNARD SHAW

This is courage in a man: to bear unflinchingly what heaven sends.
—EURIPIDES

Courage is not a virtue or value among other personal values
like love or fidelity. It is the foundation that underlies and
gives reality to all other virtues and personal values.
—ROLLO MAY

The paradox of courage is that a man must be a little
careless of his life even in order to keep it.
—G.K. CHESTERTON

Few are they who have never had a chance to achieve
happiness—and fewer those who have taken that chance.
—ANDRÉ MAUROIS

They are surely to be esteemed the bravest spirits who,
having the clearest sense of both the pains and pleasures
of life, do not on that account shrik from danger.
—THUCYDIDES

Perfect valour consists in doing without witnesses that
which we would be capable of doing before everyone.
—FRANCOIS DE LA ROCHEFOUCAULD

Courage is being scared to death—and saddling up anyway
—JOHN WAYNE

None but the brave deserves the fair.
—JOHN DRYDEN

Courage is a kind of salvation.
—PLATO

If one is forever cautious, can one remain a human being?
—ALEKSANDR SOLZHENITSYN

Courage does not always march to airs blown by a bugle; is
not always wrought out of the fabric ostentation wears.
—FRANCES RODMAN

Tough guys don't dance. You had better believe it.
—NORMAN MAILER

Everyone becomes brave when he observes one who despairs.
—FRIEDRICH NIETZSCHE

True courage is facing danger when you are afraid.
—L. FRANK BAUM

Because it's there.
—GEORGE LEIGH MALLORY, WHEN ASKED WHY HE WANTED TO CLIMB MOUNT
EVEREST

FEAR

The meaning I picked, the one that changed my
life: Overcome fear, behold wonder.
—RICHARD BACH

Fear is the father of courage and the mother of safety.
—HENRY H. TWEEDY

Fear is an emotion indispensable for survival.
—HANNAH ARENDT

A good scare is worth more to a man than good advice.
—EDGAR WATSON HOWE

"Don't Panic." It's the first helpful or intelligible
thing anybody's said to me all day.
—DOUGLAS ADAMS

Just as courage imperils life, fear protects it.
—LEONARDO DA VINCI

The more one worries, the older one gets; the
more one laughs, the younger one feels.
—Chinese proverb

Fear is sharp-sighted, and can see things under
ground, and much more in the skies.
—Miguel de Cervantes

I quit being afraid when my first venture
failed and the sky didn't fall down.
—Allen H. Neuharth

Courage is the resistance to fear, mastery of fear—not absence
of fear. Except a creature be part coward it is not a compliment
to say it is brave; it is merely a loose misapplication of the
word. Consider the flea!—incomparably the bravest of all
the creatures of God, if ignorance of fear were courage.
—Mark Twain

Fear is an instructor of great sagacity and the herald of all revolutions.
—Ralph Waldo Emerson

What we fear comes to pass more speedily than what we hope.
—Publilius Syrus

Any device whatever by which one frees himself
from the fear of others is a natural good.
—Epicurus

The only thing we have to fear is fear itself—nameless,
unreasoning, unjustified terror which paralyzes
needed efforts to convert retreat into advance.
—Franklin D. Roosevelt

Fear gives sudden instincts of skill.
—Samuel Taylor Coleridge

ADVERSITY

The man who most vividly realizes a difficulty
is the man most likely to overcome it.
—JOSEPH FARRELL

Well everybody in Casablanca has problems. Yours may work out.
—HUMPHREY BOGART

We'd like to avoid problems, because when we
have problems, we can have troubles.
—ARIZONA GOVERNOR WESLEY BOLIN

Many a man curses the rain that falls upon his head, and
knows not that it brings abundance to drive away hunger.
—SAINT BASIL

A good problem statement often includes: (a) what is
known, (b) what is unknown, and (c) what is sought.
—EDWARD HODNETT

A solved problem creates two new problems, and the best prescription
for happy living is not to solve any more problems than you have to.
—RUSSELL BAKER

A great man is one who seizes the vital issue in a complex
question, what we might call the jugular vein of the whole
organism, and spends his energies upon that.
—JOSEPH RICKABY

The only people without problems are those in cemeteries.
—ANTHONY ROBBINS

Only one feat is possible: not to have run away.
—DAG HAMMARSKJOLD

We must look for the opportunity in every difficulty, instead of being
paralyzed at the thought of the difficulty in every opportunity.
—WALTER E. COLE

No matter how big and tough a problem may be, get rid
of confusion by taking one little step towards solution. Do
something. Then try again. At the worst, so long as you don't do
it the same way twice, you will eventually use up all the wrong
ways of doing it and thus the next try will be the right one.
—George F. Nordenholt

Conquering any difficulty always gives one a secret joy, for it means
pushing back a boundary-line and adding to one's liberty.
—Henri Frederic Amiel

No man will succeed unless he is ready to face and overcome
difficulties and is prepared to assume responsibilities.
—William J.H. Boetcher

You often get a better hold upon a problem by going away from
it for a time and dismissing it from your mind altogether.
—Dr. Frank Crane

When you approach a problem, strip yourself of preconceived opinions
and prejudice, assemble and learn the facts of the situation, make the
decision which seems to you to be the most honest, and then stick to it.
—Chester Bowles

When a man points a finger at someone else, he sould
remember that four of his fingers are pointing to himself.
—Louis Nizer

Real difficulties can be overcome, it is only the
imaginary ones that are unconquerable.
—Theodore N. Vail

You can overcome anything if you don't bellyache.
—Bernard M. Baruch

It isn't that they can't see the solution, it's
that they can't see the problem.
—G.K. Chesterton

What is difficulty? Only a word indicating the degree of strength
requisite for accomplishing particular objects; a mere notice
of the necessity for exertion . . . a mere stimulus to men.
—SAMUEL WARREN

All work of man is as the swimmer's: a vast ocean threatens to
devour him; if he front it not bravely, it will keep its word.
—THOMAS CARLYLE

If we can really understand the problem, the answer will come
out of it, because the answer is not separate from the problem.
—JIDDU KRISHNAMURTI

You can surmount the obstacles in your path if you are determined,
courageous and hard-working. Never be fainthearted. Be
resolute, but never bitter. . . . Permit no one to dissuade you
from pursuing the goals you set for yourselves. Do not fear
to pioneer, to venture down new paths of endeavor.
—RALPH J. BUNCHE

The greater the difficulty, the more glory in surmounting it.
—EPICURUS

Half the unhappiness in life comes from people
being afraid to go straight at things.
—WILLIAM J. LOCK

There is no other solution to a man's problems but the
day's honest work, the day's honest decisions, the day's
generous utterance, and the day's good deed.
—CLARE BOOTHE LUCE

All problems become smaller if you don't dodge them, but confront them.
—WILLIAM F. HALSEY

He who never made a mistake never made a discovery.
—SAMUEL SMILES

To overcome difficulties is to experience the full delight of existence.
—ARTHUR SCHOPENHAUER

Life affords no higher pleasure than that of surmounting difficulties.
—Samuel Johnson

Having problems may not be so bad. We have a special
place for folks who have none—it's called a cemetery.
—Frank A. Clark

Success is to be measured not so much by the position that one has
reached in life as by the obstacles he has overcome trying to succeed.
—Booker T. Washington

Can it be that man is essentially a being who loves to conquer
difficulties, a creature whose function is to solve problems?
—Gorham Munson

A problem well stated is a problem half solved.
—Charles F. Kettering

The block of granite, which was an obstacle in the path of the
weak, becomes a stepping stone in the path of the strong.
—Thomas Carlyle

We only really face up to ourselves when we are afraid.
—Thomas Bernhard

Happiness is the overcoming of not unknown
obstacles toward a known goal.
—L. Ron Hubbard

The greatest and most important problems of life are all in a certain
sense insoluble. They can never be solved, but only outgrown.
—Carl Jung

Every problem contains the seeds of its own solution.
—Stanley Arnold

Any concern too small to be turned into a prayer
is too small to be made into a burden.
—Corrie ten Bloom

Life is the acceptance of responsibilities or their evasion; it
is a business of meeting obligations or avoiding them. To
every man the choice is continually being offered, and by the
manner of his choosing you may fairly measure him.
—BEN AMES WILLIAMS

Although the world is full of suffering, it is
full also of the overcoming of it.
—HELEN KELLER

The superior man makes the difficulty to be overcome
his first interest; success comes only later.
—CONFUCIUS

When I feel difficulty coming on, I switch to another book I'm writing.
When I get back to the problem, my unconscious has solved it.
—ISAAC ASIMOV

Difficulties exist to be surmounted.
—RALPH WALDO EMERSON

If there are obstacles, the shortest line between
two points may be the crooked line.
—BERTOLT BRECHT

It is not always by plugging away at a difficulty and sticking at it that
one overcomes it; but, rather, often by working on the one next to it.
Certain people and certain things require to be approached on an angle.
—ANDRE GIDE

The harder the conflict, the more glorious the triumph.
What we obtain too cheap, we esteem too lightly; 'tis
dearness only that gives everything it's value.
—THOMAS PAINE

When you can't solve the problem, manage it.
—DR. ROBERT H. SCHULLER

Look for a tough wedge for a tough log.
—PUBLILIUS SYRUS

The art of living lies less in eliminating our
troubles than in growing with them.
—Bernard M. Baruch

We must somehow get comfortable with the reality of
periodic failure. . . . Like a trip to the dentist, the thought
of occasional reverses may not make us tingle with joyful
anticipation, but then again, it's not the end of the world.
—Sam Collins

Forget mistakes. Forget failure. Forget everything except what
you're going to do now and do it. Today is your lucky day.
—Will Durant

He only is exempt from failures who makes no effort.
—Richard Whately

I don't know the key to success, but the key to
failure is trying to please everybody.
—Bill Cosby

Anyone who has never made a mistake has never tried anything new.
-Albert Einstein

A clever man commits no minor blunders.
—Johann von Goethe

The man who makes no mistakes does not usually make anything.
—Bishop W.C. Magee

The fellow who never makes a mistake takes
his order from one who does.
—Herbert B. Prochnow

Entrepreneurs average 3.8 failures before final success. What
sets the successful ones apart is their amazing persistence. There
are a lot of people out there with good and marketable ideas,
but pure entrepreneurial types almost never accept defeat.
—Lisa M. Amos

Only he who does nothing makes no mistakes.
—FRENCH PROVERB

Victory goes to the player who makes the next-to-last mistake.
—SAVIELLY GRIGORIEVITCH TARTAKOWER

In all science, error precedes the truth, and it
is better it should go first than last.
—HUGH WALPOLE

Virtually nothing comes out right the first time. Failures,
repeated failures, are finger posts on the road to achievement.
The only time you don't want to fail is the last time you
try something. . . . One fails forward toward success.
—CHARLES F. KETTERING

He that has much to do will do something wrong.
—SAMUEL JOHNSON

They say President Wilson has blundered. Perhaps he
has, but I notice he usually blunders forward.
—THOMAS A. EDISON

All men are liable to error; and most men are . . . by
passion or interest, under temptation to it.
—JOHN LOCKE

No man ever progressed to greatness and
goodness but through great mistakes.
—FREDERICK W. ROBERTSON

Life is a series of relapses and recoveries.
—GEORGE ADE

The credit belongs to the man who is actually in the arena; whose
face is marred by dust and sweat and blood; who strives valiantly;
who errs and comes short again and again; who knows the great
enthusiasms, the great devotions, and spends himself in a worthy
cause; who, at the best, knows in the end the triumph of high
achievement; and who, at the worst, if he fails, at least fails

while daring greatly, so that his place shall never be with those
cold and timid souls who know neither victory nor defeat.
—THEODORE ROOSEVELT

Don't let a kick in the ass stop you. It's how
you cope that says what you are.
—GEORGE CUKOR

To err is human, to forgive divine.
—ALEXANDER POPE

Do not be afraid of mistakes, providing you
do not make the same one twice.
—ELEANOR ROOSEVELT

Success is going from failure to failure without loss of enthusiasm.
—SIR WINSTON CHURCHILL

Life is not life unless you make mistakes.
—JOAN COLLINS

What is to be got at to make the air sweet, the ground good under the
feet, can only be got at by failure, trial, again and again and again failure.
—SHERWOOD ANDERSON

Accept that all of us can be hurt, that all of us can—and surely
will at times—fail. Other vulnerabilities, like being embarrassed
or risking love, can be terrifying, too. I think we should follow
a simple rule: if we can take the worst, take the risk.
—DR. JOYCE BROTHERS

Any man can make mistakes, but only an idiot persists in his error.
—CICERO

He who has never failed somewhere, that man cannot be great.
—HERMAN MELVILLE

The only man who makes no mistakes is the
man who never does anything.
—ELEANOR ROOSEVELT

War is a series of catastrophes that results in victory.
—Georges Clemenceau

The greatest mistake you can make in life is to be
continually fearing you will make one.
—Elbert Hubbard

I made a mistake today, I made a mistake yesterday. I
think it's ... very important to ignore the negative.
—Jerry Rubin

He who is shipwrecked twice is foolish to blame the sea.
—Publilius Syrus

The errors of great men are venerable because they
are more fruitful than the truths of little men.
—Friedrich Nietzsche

A man finds he has been wrong at every stage of his career, only to
deduce the astonishing conclusion that he is at last entirely right.
—Robert Louis Stevenson

The progress of rivers to the ocean is not so rapid as that of man to error.
—Voltaire

If all else fails, immortality can always be assured by spectacular error.
—John Kenneth Galbraith

Never confuse a single defeat with a final defeat.
—F. Scott Fitzgerald

Learn from others' mistakes. We don't have the
time to make them all ourselves.
—Eleanor Roosevelt

He that's cheated twice by the same man is
an accomplice with the cheater.
—Thomas Fuller

And what if I did run my ship aground; oh, still it was splendid to sail it!
—Henrik Ibsen

The biggest quality in successful people I think is an impatience with negative thinking.... How many opportunities come along? If you wait for the right one, that's wrong, because it may never be right, and what have you got to lose? Even if it's a disaster, you've tried, you've learned something, you've had an adventure. And that doesn't mean you can't do it again.
—EDWARD MCCABE

I think and think for months, for years. Ninety-nine times the conclusion is false. The hundredth time I am right.
—ALBERT EINSTEIN

You can beat the Bear once, but never the same way twice.
—JOHN MCKAY

Mistakes are part of life; you can't avoid them. All you can hope is that they won't be too expensive and that you don't make the same mistake twice.
—LEE IACOCCA

In the game of life it's a good idea to have a few early losses, which relieves you of the pressure of trying to maintain an undefeated season.
—BILL VAUGHAN

We learn courageous action by going forward whenever fear urges us back. A little boy was asked how he learned to skate. "By getting up every time I fell down," he answered.
—DAVID SEABURY

If you would not have affliction visit you twice, listen at once to what it teaches.
—JAMES BURGH

Any man whose errors take ten years to correct is quite a man.
—J. ROBERT OPPENHEIMER, SPEAKING OF ALBERT EINSTEIN

He who is shipwrecked the second time cannot lay the blame on Neptune.
—ENGLISH PROVERB

Whenever people agree with me, I always feel I must be wrong.
—OSCAR WILDE

One loss is good for the soul. Too many losses are not good for the coach.
—KNUTE ROCKNE

There is something distinguished about even his failures;
they sink not trivially, but with a certain air of majesty,
like a great ship, its flags flying, full of holes.
—GEORGE JEAN NATHAN

Sometimes a noble failure serves the world as
faithfully as a distinguished success.
—DOWDEN

The road to wisdom? Well, it's plain and simple to express:
Err, and err, and err again. But less, and less, and less.
—PIET HEIN

The best brewer sometimes makes bad beer.
—GERMAN PROVERB

Who would not rather flounder in the fight than
not have known the glory of the fray?
—RICHARD HOVEY

You must have long-range goals to keep you from
being frustrated by short-range failures.
—CHARLES C. NOBLE

A good marksman may miss.
—THOMAS FULLER

A man must learn to forgive himself.
—ARTHUR DAVISON FICKE

The greatest general is he who makes the fewest mistakes.
—NAPOLEON BONAPARTE

To stumble twice against the same stone is a proverbial disgrace.
—CICERO

I would prefer even to fail with honor than win by cheating.
—SOPHOCLES

When we can begin to take our failures non-seriously,
it means we are ceasing to be afraid of them. It is of
immense importance to learn to laugh at ourselves.
—KATHERINE MANSFIELD

To make no mistake is not in the power of man; but from their errors
and mistakes the wise and good learn wisdom for the future.
—PLUTARCH

If you're gonna be a failure, at least be one at something you enjoy.
—SYLVESTER STALLONE

I don't accept defeat as final. Only death is final—
and even then I hope for a reprieve.
—PHIL GRAMM

If at first you don't succeed, failure may be your style.
—QUENTIN CRISP

Man errs as long as he struggles.
—JOHANN VON GOETHE

If I lose, I'll walk away and never feel bad. . . . Because
I did all I could, there was nothing more to do.
—JOE FRAZIER

Failure really isn't terrible if you can say to yourself, hey, I know
I'm gonna be successful at what I want to do someday. Failure
doesn't become a big hangup then because it's only temporary. If
failure is absolute, then it would be a disaster, but as long as it's
only temporary you can just go and achieve almost anything.
—JERRY DELLA FEMINA

Failure is an event, never a person.
—WILLIAM D. BROWN

In this world there are only two tragedies. One is not
getting what one wants, and the other is getting it.
—OSCAR WILDE

Men's best successes come after their disappointments.
—HENRY WARD BEECHER

Failure is not sweet, but it need not be bitter.
—Anon

Losses are comparative, imagination only makes them of any moment.
—Blaise Pascal

Flops are a part of life's menu, and I've never been
a girl to miss out on any of the courses.
—Rosalind Russell

He is always right who suspects that he makes mistakes.
—Spanish proverb

Fool me once, shame on you; fool me twice, shame on me.
—Chinese proverb

Experience was of no ethical value. It was merely
the name men gave to their mistaked.
—Oscar Wilde

There is nothing wrong with making mistakes.
Just don't respond with encores.
—Anon

All of us failed to match our dreams of perfection.
—William Faulkner

You may have a fresh start any moment you choose, for this thing
that we call "failure" is not the falling down, but the staying down.
—Mary Pickford

There is no such thing as failure. There are only results.
—Anthony Robbins

Every man's got to figure to get beat sometime.
—Joe Louis

Failure is delay, but not defeat. It is a temporary
detour, not a dead-end street.
—William Arthur Ward

The probability that we may fail in the struggle ought not to deter us from the support of a cause we believe to be just.
—ABRAHAM LINCOLN

There are times in everyone's life when something constructive is born out of adversity ... when things seem so bad that you've got to grab your fate by the shoulders and shake it.
—ANON

Trouble brings experience, and experience brings wisdom.
—ANON

Some minds seem almost to create themselves, springing up under every disadvantage and working their solitary but irresistible way through a thousand obstacles.
—WASHINGTON IRVING

In my youth, poverty enriched me, but now I can afford wealth.
—MARC CHAGALL

When a man is pushed, tormented, defeated, he has a chance to learn something; he has been put on his wits ... he has gained facts, learned his ignorance, is cured of the insanity of conceit, has got moderation and real skill.
—RALPH WALDO EMERSON

Our real blessings often appear to us in the shape of pains, losses and disappointments; but let us have patience, and we soon shall see them in their proper figures.
—JOSEPH ADDISON

Strong people are made by opposition, like kites that go up against the wind.
—FRANK HARRIS

Adversity is like the period of the rain ... cold, comfortless, unfriendly to man and to animal; yet from that season have their birth the flower, the fruit, the date, the rose and the pomegranate.
—SIR WALTER SCOTT

Every calamity is a spur and valuable hint.
—RALPH WALDO EMERSON

The man who doesn't read good books has no
advantage over the man who can't read them.
—MARK TWAIN

There are three modes of bearing the ills of life: by
indifference, by philosophy, and by religion.
—CHARLES CALEB COLTON

It is often better to have a great deal of harm happen to
one than a little; a great deal may rouse you to remove
what a little will only accustom you to endure.
—GRENVILLE KLEISER

Adversity is the trial of principle. Without it a man
hardly knows whether he is honest or not.
—HENRY FIELDING

Opposition inflames the enthusiast, never converts him.
—J.C.F. VON SCHILLER

Trust yourself. You know more than you think you do.
—BENJAMIN SPOCK

Disappointment is the nurse of wisdom.
—SIR BAYLE ROCHE

When things come to the worse, they generally mend.
—SUSANNA MOODIE

Trouble is the thing that strong men grow by. Met in the right
way, it is a sure-fire means of putting iron into the victim's will
and making him a tougher man to down forever after.
—H. BERTRAM LEWIS

Forget the times of your distress, but never forget what they taught you.
—HERBERT GASSER

The same reason makes a man a religious enthusiast
that makes a man an enthusiast in any other way: an
uncomfortable mind in an uncomfortable body.
—WILLIAM HAZLITT

There is only one thing in the world worse than being talked about, and that is not being talked about.
—OSCAR WILDE

It is often hard to distinguish between the hard knocks in life and those of opportunity.
—FREDERICK PHILLIPS

Emergencies have always been necessary to progress. It was darkness which produced the lamp. It was fog that produced the compass. It was hunger that drove us to exploration. And it took a depression to teach us the real value of a job.
—VICTOR HUGO

From a fallen tree, make kindling.
—SPANISH PROVERB

I'm very grateful that I was too poor to get to art school until I was 21....I was old enough when I got there to know how to get something out of it.
—HENRY MOORE

You'll never find a better sparring partner than adversity.
—WALT SCHMIDT

Of all the advantages which come to any young man ... poverty is the greatest.
—JOSIAH G. HOLLAND

A problem is a chance for you to do your best.
—DUKE ELLINGTON

I think the years I have spent in prison have been the most formative and important in my life because of the discipline, the sensations, but chiefly the opportunity to think clearly, to try to understand things.
—JAWAHARLAL NEHRU

Men habitually use only a small part of the powers which they possess and which they might use under appropriate circumstances.
—WILLIAM JAMES

Difficulties are meant to rouse, not discourage. The
human spirit is to grow strong by conflict.
—WILLIAM ELLERY CHANNING

Adversity leads us to think properly of our
state, and so is most beneficial to us.
—SAMUEL JOHNSON

Fire is the test of gold, adversity of strong men.
—MARCUS ANNAEUS SENECA

I have always been pushed by the negative.... The apparent failure of a
play sends me back to my typewriter that very night, before the reviews
are out. I am more compelled to get back to work than if I had a success.
—TENNESSEE WILLIAMS

Treasure the memories of past misfortunes;
they constitute our bank of fortitude.
—ERIC HOFFER

My luck was my father not striking oil ... we'd have
been rich. I'd never have set out for Hollywood with my
camera, and I'd have had a lot less interesting life.
—KING VIDOR

To turn an obstacle to one's advantage is a great step towards victory.
—FRENCH PROVERB

I was lucky I wasn't a better boxer, or that's
what I'd be now—a punchy ex-pug.
—BOB HOPE

Adversity causes some men to break, others to break records.
—WILLIAM A. WARD

To be thrown upon one's own resources is to be cast into the very
lap of fortune, for our faculties then undergo a development and
display an energy of which they were previously unsusceptible.
—BENJAMIN FRANKLIN

Difficulties are things that show what men are.
—EPICTETUS

The most valuable gift I ever received was ... the gift of insecurity ... my father left us. My mother's love might not have prepared me for life the way my father's departure did. He forced us out on the road, where we had to earn our bread.
—LILLIAN GISH

Victories that are cheap are cheap. Those only are worth having which come as the result of hard fighting.
—HENRY WARD BEECHER

The fiery trials through which we pass will light us down in honor or dishonor to the last generation.
—ABRAHAM LINCOLN

You can learn little from victory. You can learn everything from defeat.
—CHRISTY MATHEWSON

Pain is the root of knowledge.
—SIMONE WEIL

Many men owe the grandeur of their lives to their tremendous difficulties.
—CHARLES HADDON SPURGEON

He that wrestles with us strengthens our nerves and sharpens our skills. Our antagonist is our helper.
—EDMUND BURKE

Discontent is the first step in the progress of a man or a nation.
—OSCAR WILDE

A woman is like a tea bag: you never know her strength until you drop her in hot water.
—NANCY REAGAN

To understand everything makes one tolerant.
—MADAME DE STAEL

As there is no worldly gain without some loss, so there is no worldly loss without some gain.... Set the allowance against the loss, and thou shalt find no loss great.
—FRANCIS QUARLES

He that can't endure the bad will not live to see the good.
—Yiddish proverb

If we survive danger, it steels our courage more than anything else.
—Reinhold Niebuhr

A smooth sea never made a skillful mariner.
—English proverb

All things excellent are as difficult as they are rare.
—Baruch Spinoza

A clay pot sitting in the sun will always be a clay pot. It has to go
through the white heat of the furnace to become porcelain.
—Mildred W. Struven

It is the north wind that lashes men into Vikings; it is the soft,
luscious south wind which lulls them to lotus dreams.
—Ouida

In adversity, remember to keep an even mind.
—Horace

Sleep, riches and health, to be truly enjoyed, must be interrupted.
—Jean Paul Fichter

Flowers grow out of dark moments.
—Corita Kent

I have lived long enough to be battered by the realities
of life, and not too long to be downed by them.
—John Mason Brown

When I was very young, I tried selling used cars. It didn't last
long. I guess that was my good luck too, that I didn't show more
promise at it, or I might have been an automobile dealer.
—King Vidor

He knows not his own strength who hath not met adversity.
—Samuel Johnson

I have always grown from my problems and challenges, from the things that don't work out. That's when I've really learned.
—CAROL BURNETT

When the going gets tough, the tough get going.
—FRANK LEAHY

No man better knows what good is than he who has endured evil.
—ANON

To really enjoy the better things in life, one must first have experienced the things they are better than.
—OSCAR HOMOLKA

There is not enough darkness in all the world to put out the light of even one small candle.
—ROBERT ALDEN

Calamity is the test of integrity.
—SAMUEL RICHARDSON

You learn nothing from your success except to think too much of yourself. It is from failure that all growth comes, provided you can recognize it, admit it, learn from it, rise above it and then try again.
—DEE HOCK

Americans are like a rich father who wishes he knew how to give his sons the hardships that made him rich.
—ROBERT FROST

Who hath not known ill fortune, never knew himself, or his own virtue.
—MALLETT

Adversity comes with instruction in its hand.
—ANON

It's not that easy bein' green.
—KERMIT THE FROG

Best to have failure happen early. [It] wakes up the phoenix bird in you.
—ANNE BAXTER

Procrastination is the thief of time.
—Edward Young

I walk firmer and more secure up hill than down.
—Michel de Montaigne

Life can be real tough ... you can either learn from your
problems, or keep repeating them over and over.
—Marie Osmond

Times of stress and difficulty are seasons of opportunity
when the seeds of progress are sown.
—Thomas F. Woodlock

Restlessness is discontent, and discontent
is the first necessity of progress.
—Thomas A. Edison

In order to change, we must be sick and tired of being sick and tired.
—Anon

Even if misfortune is only good for bringing a fool to his senses,
it would still be just to deem it good for something.
—Jean de La Fontaine

Never does a man know the force that is in him till some
mighty affection or grief has humanized the soul.
—Frederick W. Robertson

Adversity is a severe instructor. ... He that wrestles with us strengthens
our nerves and sharpens our skill. Our antagonist is our helper.
—Edmund Burke

Adversity is, to me at least, a tonic and a bracer.
—Sir Walter Scott

By becoming more unhappy, we sometimes learn how to be less so.
—Madame Swetchine

To conquer without risk is to triumph without glory.
—Pierre Corneille

If you will call your troubles experiences, and remember
that every experience develops some latent force
within you, you will grow vigorous and happy, however
adverse your circumstances may seem to be.
—JOHN R. MILLER

Adversity has the effect of eliciting talents, which, in
prosperous circumstances, would have lain dormant.
—HORACE

Problems are the price of progress. Don't bring me anything but trouble.
—CHARLES F. KETTERING

No problem is so big or so complicated that it can't be run away from.
—CHARLES M. SCHULZ (PEANUTS)

Our trials are tests; our sorrows pave the way for
a fuller life when we have earned it.
—JEROME P. FLEISHMAN

When I have listened to my mistakes, I have grown.
—HUGH PRATHER

If there were no tribulation, there would be no rest; if
there were no winter, there would be no summer.
—SAINT JOHN CHRYSOSTOM

Difficulties should act as a tonic. They should spur us to greater exertion.
—B.C. FORBES

Prosperity is a great teacher; adversity is a greater. Possession
pampers the mind; privation trains and strengthens it.
—WILLIAM HAZLITT

Unless a man has been kicked around a little, you can't
really depend upon him to amount to anything.
—WILLIAM FEATHER

Challenges make you discover things about yourself that
you never really knew. They're what make the instrument
stretch, what make you go beyond the norm.
—CICELY TYSON

Wisdom comes by disillusionment.
—GEORGE SANTAYANA

We only really face up to ourselves when we are afraid.
—THOMAS BERNHARD

Those things that hurt, instruct.
—BENJAMIN FRANKLIN

The gem cannot be polished without friction,
nor man perfected without trials.
—CONFUCIUS

Let us not be needlessly bitter: certain failures are sometimes fruitful.
—E.M. CIORAN

Things have got to be wrong in order that they may be deplored.
—WHITNEY GRISWOLD

There is nothing the body suffers which the soul may not profit by.
—GEORGE MEREDITH

No man can lose what he never had.
—IZAAK WALTON

Mistakes are often the best teachers.
—JAMES A. FROUDE

Bad times have a scientific value. These are
occasions a good learner would not miss.
—RALPH WALDO EMERSON

People wish to be settled; only as far as they are
unsettled is there any hope for them.
—RALPH WALDO EMERSON

The same wind that extinguishes a light can set a brazier on fire.
—PIERRE DE BEAUMARCHAIS

Anything other than death is a minor injury.
—BILL MUNCEY

You have learned something. That always feels
at first as if you had lost something.
—George Bernard Shaw

There is no education like adversity.
—Benjamin Disraeli

When it is dark enough, you can see the stars.
—Charles A. Beard

All sorts of spiritual gifts come through privations, if they are accepted.
—Janet Erskine Stuart

It is grief that develops the powers of the mind.
—Marcel Proust

From the discontent of man, the world's best progress springs.
—Ella Wheeler Wilcox

There is in the worst of fortune the best of chances for a happy change.
—Euripides

A certain amount of opposition is a great help to a man; it is what
he wants and must have to be good for anything. Hardship and
opposition are the native soil of manhood and self-reliance.
—John Neal

Necessity is often the spur to genius.
—Honore de Balzac

When written in Chinese, the word "crisis" is composed of two
characters. One represents danger, and the other represents opportunity.
—John F. Kennedy

To conquer without risk is to triumph without glory.
—Pierre Corneille

Victory is sweetest when you've known defeat.
—Malcolm Forbes

Diseases can be our spiritual flat tires—disruptions in
our lives that seem to be disasters at the time, but end
by redirecting our lives in a meaningful way.
—Bernie S. Siegel, M.D.

Sweet are the uses of adversity.
—William Shakespeare

Adversity is another way to measure the greatness of individuals.
I never had a crisis that didn't make me stronger.
—Lou Holtz

The difficulties and struggles of today are but the price we must
pay for the accomplishments and victories of tomorrow.
—William J.H. Boetcker

God will not look you over for medals, degrees or diplomas, but for scars.
—Anon

In the depth of winter, I finally learned that there
was in me an invincible summer.
—Albert Camus

The greater the obstacle, the more glory in overcoming it.
—Moliere

There could be no honor in a sure success, but much
might be wrested from a sure defeat.
—T.E. Lawrence (Lawrence of Arabia)

Failure is, in a sense, the highway to success, inasmuch as
every discovery of what is false leads us to seek earnestly
after what is true, and very fresh experience points out some
form of error which we shall afterward carefully avoid.
—John Keats

Necessity is the mother of "taking chances."
—Mark Twain

Necessity makes even the timid brave.
—Sallust

It is the surmounting of difficulties that makes heroes.
—KOSSUTH

If you want to see the sun shine, you have to weather the storm.
—FRANK LANE

He that has never suffered extreme adversity knows
not the full extent of his own depravation.
—CHARLES CALEB COLTON

A man is insensible to the relish of prosperity till he has tasted adversity.
—SA'DI

If your house is on fire, warm yourself by it.
—SPANISH PROVERB

Failure in itself is success at something.
—ANON

It is from the level of calamities ... that we
learn impressive and useful lessons.
—WILLIAM MAKEPEACE THACKERAY

Never complain about your troubles; they are
responsible for more than half of your income.
—ROBERT R. UPDEGRAFF

Strength does not come from winning. Your struggles
develop your strengths. When you go through hardships
and decide not to surrender, that is strength.
—ARNOLD SCHWARZENEGGER

In order to have great happiness, you have to have great pain and
unhappiness—otherwise how would you know when you're happy?
—LESLIE CARON

Every experience, however bitter, has its lesson, and to focus one's
attention on the lesson helps one overcome the bitterness.
—EDWARD HOWARD GRIGGS

Adam and Eve had many advantages, but the principal
one was, that they escaped teething.
—Mark Twain

I didn't know I'd have to be torn down before I could be built up.
—Anon

Misfortunes tell us what fortune is.
—Thomas Fuller

It is not in the still calm of life, or the repose of a pacific station, that
great characters are formed.... Great necessities call out great virtues.
—Abigail Adams

The ultimate measure of a man is not where he stands
in moments of comfort and convenience, but where he
stands at times of challenge and controversy.
—Martin Luther King, Jr.

If you will call your troubles experiences, and remember
that every experience develops some latent force
within you, you will grow vigorous and happy, however
adverse your circumstances may seem to be.
—J.R. Miller

Faced with crisis, the man of character falls back on himself.
He imposes his own stamp on action, takes responsibility for
it, makes it his own.... Difficulty attracts the man of character
because it is in embracing it that he realizes himself.
—Charles De Gaulle

Who has never tasted what is bitter does not know what is sweet.
—German proverb

A good scare is worth more to a man than good advice.
—Edgar Watson Howe

Do not free a camel of the burden of his hump; you
may be freeing him from being a camel.
—G.K. Chesterton

RESPONDING AND REACTING

What life means to us is determined not so much by what life
brings to us as by the attitude we bring to life; not so much by
what happens to us as by our reaction to what happens.
—LEWIS L. DUNNINGTON

Results? Why, man, I have gotten a lot of results. I know
several thousand things that won't work.
—THOMAS A. EDISON

I'll not listen to reason.... Reason always means
what someone else has got to say.
—ELIZABETH GASKELL

When fate hands you a lemon, make lemonade.
—DALE CARNEGIE

Turn your stumbling blocks into stepping stones.
—ANON

Total absence of humor renders life impossible.
—COLETTE

A wise man turns chance into good fortune.
—THOMAS FULLER

Too much of a good thing can be wonderful.
—MAE WEST

Wise men ne'er sit and wail their loss, but cheerily
seek how to redress their harms.
—WILLIAM SHAKESPEARE

A sharp tongue is the only edged tool that
grows keener with constant use.
—WASHINGTON IRVING

He who, having lost one ideal, refuses to give his heart and soul to another and nobler, is like a man who declines to build a house on rock because the wind and rain ruined his house on the sand.
—Constance Naden

Acceptance of what has happened is the first step to overcoming the consequences of any misfortune.
—William James

The winds and waves are always on the side of the ablest navigators.
—Edward Gibbon

Any man who has had the job I've had and didn't have a sense of humor wouldn't still be here.
—Harry S Truman

The only way to get rid of a temptation is to yield to it.
—Oscar Wilde

Oh, a trouble's a ton, or a trouble's an ounce,
Or a trouble is what you make it,
And it isn't the fact that you're hurt that counts,
But only how you take it.
—Edmund Vance Cooke

The prizes go to those who meet emergencies successfully. And the way to meet emergencies is to do each daily task the best we can.
—William Feather

There are no accidents so unlucky from which clever people are not able to reap some advantage, and none so lucky that the foolish are not able to turn them to their own disadvantage.
—Francois de La Rochefoucauld

Humor is a means of obtaining pleasure in spite of the distressing effects that interface with it.
—Sigmund Freud

I love the man that can smile in trouble, that can gather strength from distress, and grow brave by reflection.
—Thomas Paine

Anyone can hold the helm when the sea is calm.
—Publilius Syrus

Happiness is not the absence of conflict, but the ability to cope with it.
—Anon

We must never despair; our situation has been compromising
before, and it has changed for the better; so I trust it will
again. If difficulties arise, we must put forth new exertion
and proportion our efforts to the exigencies of the times.
—George Washington

Things turn out best for people who make the
best of the way things turn out.
—Anon

We are troubled on every side, yet not distressed;
we are perplexed, but not in despair.
—2 Cor. 4:8

Never despair, but if you do, work on in despair.
—Edmund Burke

Fortune does not change men; it unmasks them.
—Madame Necker

What the caterpillar calls a tragedy, the Master calls a butterfly.
—Richard Bach

A sense of humor can help you overlook the
unattractive, tolerate the unpleasant, cope with the
unexpected, and smile through the unbearable.
—Moshe Waldoks

The tragedy is not that things are broken. The
tragedy is that they are not mended again.
—Anon

Trouble is the thing that strong men grow by. Met in the right
way, it is a sure-fire means of putting iron into the victim's will
and making him a tougher man to down forever after.
—H. Bertram Lewis

True contentment is the power of getting of
any situation all that there is in it.
—G.K. Chesterton

Losses are comparative, only imagination makes them of any moment.
—Blaise Pascal

Good people are good because they've come to wisdom through failure.
—William Saroyan

Mishaps are like knives that either serve us or cut us
as we grasp them by the blade or the handle.
—James Russell Lowell

Concern should drive us into action, not into a depression.
—Karen Horney

When the rock is hard, we get harder than the rock. When
the job is tough, we get tougher than the job.
—George Cullum, Sr.

The longer we dwell on our misfortunes, the
greater is their power to harm us.
—Voltaire

When the going gets tough, the tough get going.
—Frank Leahy

A man has no more character than he can command in a time of crisis.
—Ralph W. Sockman

If I had no sense of humor, I should long ago have committed suicide.
—Mahatma Gandhi

I have seen boys on my baseball team go into slumps and
never come out of them, and I have seen others snap right
out and come back better than ever. I guess more players lick
themselves than are ever licked by an opposing team. The first
thing any man has to know is how to handle himself.
—Connie Mack

Noble souls, through dust and heat, rise from
disaster and defeat the stronger.
—HENRY WADSWORTH LONGFELLOW

An error is simply a failure to adjust immediately
from a preconception to an actuality.
—JOHN CAGE

I never blame myself when I'm not hitting. I just blame the bat,
and if it keeps up, I change bats. After all, if I know it isn't my
fault that I'm not hitting, how can I get mad at myself?
—YOGI BERRA

We must make the best of those ills which cannot be avoided.
—ALEXANDER HAMILTON

Humor is the healthy way of feeling "distance" between
one's self and the problem, a way of standing off and
looking at one's problems with perspective.
—ROLLO MAY

Life is a grindstone, and whether it grinds a man down or
polishes him up depends on the stuff he's made of.
—JOSH BILLINGS

One cannot get through life without pain. . . . What we can
do is choose how to use the pain life presents to us.
—BERNIE S. SIEGEL, M.D.

To a brave man, good and bad luck are like his
right and left hand. He uses both.
—SAINT CATHERINE OF SIENA

Any man can shoot a gun, and with practice he can draw fast and
shoot accurately, but that makes no difference. What counts is
how you stand up when somebody is shooting back at you.
—LOUIS L'AMOUR

The great difference between one person and another
is how he takes hold and uses his first chance, and
how he takes his fall if it scored against him.
—THOMAS HUGHES

Experience is not what happens to you; it is what
you do with what happens to you.
—Aldous Huxley

Riches, like glory or health, have no more beauty or pleasure
than their possessor is pleased to lend them.
—Michel de Montaigne

Better by far you should forget and smile than
that you should remember and be sad.
—Christina Rossetti

On the occasion of every accident that befalls you . . . inquire
what power you have for turning it to use.
—Epictetus

It is arrogance to expect that life will always be music. . . . Harmony,
like a following breeze at sea, is the exception. In a world where
most things wind up broken or lost, our lot is to tack and tune.
—Harvey Oxenhorn

Let no feeling of discouragement prey upon you,
and in the end you are sure to succeed.
—Abraham Lincoln

Consider how much more you often suffer from your anger and grief
than from those very things for which you are angry and grieved.
—Marcus Aurelius

A sense of humor judges one's actions and the actions of
others from a wider reference . . . it pardons shortcomings;
it consoles failure. It recommends moderation.
—Thornton Wilder

Optimism and humor are the grease and glue of life. Without
both of them we would never have survived our captivity.
—Philip Butler, Vietnam POW

We can either change the complexities of life . . . or develop
ways that enable us to cope more effectively.
—Herbert Benson

Trouble has no necessary connection with discouragement; discouragement has a germ of its own, as different from trouble as arthritis is different from a stiff joint.
—F. Scott Fitzgerald

Always take an emergency leisurely.
—Chinese proverb

Humor is my sword and my shield. It protects me. You can open a door with humor and drive a truck right through.
—Alan Simpson

A person without a sense of humor is like a wagon without springs, jolted by every pebble in the road.
—Henry Ward Beecher

There are two ways of meeting difficulties. You alter the difficulties or you alter yourself to meet them.
—Phyllis Bottome

When we accept tough jobs as a challenge and wade into them with joy and enthusiasm, miracles can happen.
—Arland Gilbert

When I read about the evils of drinking, I gave up reading.
—Henny Youngman

Humor is an attitude. It's a way of looking at life and of telling others how you feel about what's happening around you.
—Gene Perret

Keep strong if possible; in any case, keep cool.
—Sir Basil Liddell Hart

Our mistakes won't irreparably damage our lives unless we let them.
—James E. Sweaney

Humor is the instinct for taking pain playfully.
—Max Eastman

Don't curse the darkness—light a candle.
—Chinese proverb

The difficulties of life are intended to make us better, not bitter.
—Anon

I'm not happy, I'm cheerful. There's a difference. A
happy woman has no cares at all. A cheerful woman
has cares but has learned how to deal with them.
—Beverly Sills

I make the most of all that comes and the least of all that goes.
—Sara Teasdale

Humor is an affirmation of dignity, a declaration of
man's superiority to all that befalls him.
—Roman Gary

All that is necessary is to accept the unacceptable, do
without the indispensable, and bear the unbearable.
—Kathleen Norris

So long as I am acting from duty and conviction, I am indifferent to
taunts and jeers. I think they will probably do me more good than harm.
—Winston Churchill

If you have to be in a soap opera, try not to get the worst role.
—Boy George

Your living is determined not so much by what life brings to you
as by the attitude you bring to life; not so much by what happens
to you as by the way your mind looks at what happens.
—John Homer Miller

What counts in making a happy marriage is not so much how
compatible you are, but how you deal with incompatibility.
—George Levinger

Let us not be needlessly bitter: certain failures are sometimes fruitful.
—E.M. Cioran

The most important thing in life is not to capitalize on your gains. Any fool can do that. The really important thing is to profit from your losses.
—WILLIAM BOLITHO

You are beaten to earth? Well, well, what's that?
Come up with a smiling face,
It's nothing against you to fall down flat
But to lie there—that's a disgrace.
—EDMUND VANCE COOKE

To be happy, drop the words "if only" and
substitute instead the words "next time."
—SMILEY BLANTON, M.D.

Were it not for my little jokes, I could not bear the burdens of this office.
—ABRAHAM LINCOLN

Whatever evil befalls us, we ought to ask ourselves . . . how
we can turn it into good. So shall we take occasion, from
one bitter root, to raise perhaps many flowers.
—LEIGH HUNT

Groan and forget it.
—JESSAMYN WEST

What—me worry?
HARVEY KURTZMAN'S WORDS FOR ALFRED E. NEUMAN

TRYING DAYS

The race is not to the swift, nor the battle to the strong.
—ECCL. 9:11

Adopt the pace of nature, her secret is patience.
—RALPH WALDO EMERSON

Did you ever get the feeling that the world was a
tuxedo and you were a pair of brown shoes?
—GEORGE GOBEL

A critic is a man who knows the way but can't drive the car.
—Kenneth Tynan

There are good days and there are bad days, and this is one of them.
—Lawrence Welk

The trouble with unemployment is that the minute
you wake up in the morning you're on the job.
—Slappy White

No great thing is created suddenly, any more than a bunch of grapes
or a fig. If you tell me that you desire a fig, I answer you that there
must be time. Let it first blossom, then bear fruit, then ripen.
—Epictetus

I often refer to Abraham Lincoln who said "When I do good I feel
good. When I do bad I feel bad. And that is my religion." I think we all
have a little voice inside us that will guide us. It may be God, I don't
know. But I think that if we shut out all the noise and clutter from
our lives and listen to that voice, it will tell us the right thing to do.
—Christopher Reeve

And he shall reign a goodly king
And sway his hand o'er every clime
With peace writ on his signet ring,
Who bides his time.
—James Whitcomb Riley

Who longest waits most surely wins.
—Helen Hunt Jackson

Have patience with all things, but chiefly have patience with yourself.
Do not lose courage in considering your own imperfections, but
instantly set about remedying them—every day begin the task anew.
—Saint Francis de Sales

Time deals gently only with those who take it gently.
—Anatole France

All human wisdom is summed up in two words: wait and hope.
—Alexandre Dumas

That's the advantage of having lived sixty-five years. You
don't feel the need to be impatient any longer.
—THORNTON WILDER

The secret of patience . . . to do something else in the meantime.
—ANON

He that can have patience can have what what he will.
—BENJAMIN FRANKLIN

Patience is a bitter plant, but it has sweet fruit.
—GERMAN PROVERB

It takes time to succeed because success is merely the
natural reward of taking time to do anything well.
—JOSEPH ROSS

Genius is eternal patience.
—MICHELANGELO

Patience and fortitude conquer all things.
—RALPH WALDO EMERSON

I generally avoid temptation unless I can't resist it.
—MAE WEST

Hold on; hold fast; hold out. Patience is genius.
—GEORGES DE BUFFON

Everything comes if a man will only wait.
—BENJAMIN DISRAELI

Patience is a bitter plant, but it has sweet fruit.
—GERMAN PROVERB

It takes time to succeed because success is merely the
natural reward of taking time to do anything well.
—JOSEPH ROSS

Serene I fold my hands and wait.
—JOHN BURROUGHS

Your three best doctors are faith, time, and patience.
—From a fortune cookie

When someone said, "I really can't come to your
party Mrs. Parker. I can't bear fools."
Parker replied, "That's strange; your mother could."
—Dorothy Parker

Everything comes to him who hustles while he waits.
—Thomas A. Edison

Wisely and slow. They stumble that run fast.
—William Shakespeare

All things come round to him who will but wait.
—Henry Wadsworth Longfellow

Be not afraid of growing slowly, be afraid only of standing still.
—Chinese proverb

Genius is nothing but a greater aptitude for patience.
—Benjamin Franklin

Cheer up—the worst is yet to come.
—Mark Twain

V. The Road To Success

ACTION

Many persons of high intelligence have notoriously poor judgement.
—SYDNEY J. HARRIS

We don't have enough time to premeditate all our actions.
—VAUVENARGUES

Decide on what you think is right, and stick to it.
—GEORGE ELIOT

Action will remove the doubt that theory cannot solve.
—TEHYI HSIEH

Only the action that is moved by love for the good at hand
has the hope of being responsible and generous.
—WENDELL BERRY

Action should culminate in wisdom.
—BHAGAVAD GITA

A man can only be judged by his actions, and not
by his good intentions or his beliefs.
—PAUL NEWMAN

In case of doubt, decide in favor of what is correct.
—KARL KRAUS

The test of any man lies in action.
—PINDAR

Life is the only art that we are required to practice without preparation, and without being allowed the preliminary trials, the failures and botches, that are essential for the training of a mere beginner.
—LEWIS MUMFORD

People who know how to act are never preachers.
—RALPH WALDO EMERSON

A decision is an action you must take when you have information so incomplete that the answer does not suggest itself.
—ARTHUR RADFORD

Every year, if not every day, we have to wager our salvation upon some prophecy based upon imperfect knowledge.
—OLIVER WENDELL HOLMES, JR.

When one bases his life on principle, 99 percent of his decisions are already made.
—ANON

Not all of your decisions will be correct. None of us is perfect. But if you get into the habit of making decisions, experience will develop your judgment to a point where more and more of your decisions will be right. After all, it is better to be right 51 percent of the time and get something done, than it is to get nothing done because you fear to reach a decision.
—H.W. ANDREWS

Human foresight often leaves its proudest possessor only a choice of evils.
—CHARLES CALEB COLTON

One's mind has a way of making itself up in the background, and it suddenly becomes clear what one means to do.
—ARTHUR CHRISTOPHER BENSON

Continually one faces the horrible matter of making decisions. The solution ... is, as far as possible, to avoid conscious rational decisions and choices; simply to do what you find yourself doing; to float in the great current of life with as little friction as possible; to allow things to settle themselves, as indeed they do with the most infallible certainty.
—CHRISTOPHER MORLEY

I learn by going where I have to go.
—THEODORE ROETHKE

Faith . . . acts promptly and boldly on the occasion, on slender evidence.
—JOHN HENRY CARDINAL NEWMAN

Pick battles big enough to matter, small enough to win.
—JONATHAN KOZEL

We don't have enough time to premeditate all our actions.
—VAUVENARGUES

I think we should follow a simple rule: if we
can take the worst, take the risk.
—DR. JOYCE BROTHERS

When making a decision of minor importance, I have always found
it advantageous to consider all the pros and cons. In vital matters,
however, such as the choice of a mate or a profession, the decision
should come from the unconscious, from somewhere within
ourselves. In the important decisions of personal life, we should
be governed, I think, by the deep inner needs of our nature.
—SIGMUND FREUD

There is no data on the future.
—LAUREL CUTLER

What I emphasize is for people to make choices based not on
fear, but on what really gives them a sense of fulfillment.
—PAULINE ROSE CHANCE

Every year, if not every day, we have to wager our salvation
upon some prophecy based upon imperfect knowledge.
—OLIVER WENDELL HOLMES, JR.

Each man must for himself alone decide what is right and what
is wrong, which course is patriotic and which isn't. You cannot
shirk this and be a man. To decide against your conviction is
to be an unqualified and inexcusable traitor, both to yourself
and to your country, let men label you as they may.
—MARK TWAIN

It's all right to hesitate if you then go ahead.
—BERTOLT BRECHT

Wisdom consists in being able to distinguish among
dangers and make a choice of the least harmful.
—NICCOLO MACHIAVELLI

Life is like playing a violin in public and learning
the instrument as one goes on.
—SAMUEL BUTLER

We don't have enough time to premeditate all our actions.
—VAUVENARGUES

To dispose a soul to action we must upset its equilibrium.
—ERIC HOFFER

We lose the fear of making decisions, great and small,
as we realize that should our choice prove wrong we
can, if we will, learn from the experience.
—BILL W.

The most important fact about Spaceship Earth:
an instruction book didn't come with it.
—R. BUCKMINSTER FULLER

How far would Moses have gone if he had taken a poll in Egypt?
—HARRY S TRUMAN

The Pilgrims didn't have any experience when they
landed here. Hell, if experience was that important,
we'd never have anybody walking on the moon.
—DOUG RADER

Lust and force are the source of all our actions; lust
causes voluntary actions, force involuntary ones.
—BLAISE PASCAL

Act quickly, think slowly.
—GREEK PROVERB

The best we can do is size up the chances, calculate the risks involved, estimate our ability to deal with them, and then make our plans with confidence.
—HENRY FORD

The tendency of modern science is to reduce proof to absurdity by continually reducing absurdity to proof.
—SAMUEL BUTLER

In the three years I played ball, we won six, lost seventeen and tied two. Some statistician . . . calculated that we won 75 percent of the games we didn't lose.
—ROGER M. BLOUGH

On action alone be thy interest,
Never on its fruits.
Let not the fruits of action be thy motive,
Nor be thy attachment to inaction.
—BHAGAVAD GITA

COMMITMENT

Happy are those who dream dreams and are ready to pay the price to make them come true.
—L.J. CARDINAL SUENENS

It is by losing himself in the objective, in inquiry, creation, and craft, that a man becomes something.
—PAUL GOODMAN

The secret of living is to find a pivot, the pivot of a concept on which you can make your stand.
—LUIGI PIRANDELLO

Nothing is so common as unsuccessful men with talent. They lack only determination.
—CHARLES SWINDOLL

The will to conquer is the first condition of victory.
—MARSHAL FERDINAND FOCH

The moment one definitely commits oneself, the Providence moves, too. All sorts of things occur to help that would never otherwise have occurred. A stream of events issues from the decision, raising unforeseen incidents and meetings and material assistance, which no man could have dreamt would have come his way.
—W.H. MURRAY

If a man hasn't discovered something that
he will die for, he isn't fit to live.
—MARTIN LUTHER KING, JR.

One advantage of marriage, it seems to me, is that when you
fall out of love with him, or he falls out of love with you, it
keeps you together until you maybe fall in love again.
—JUDITH VIORST

One's lifework, I have learned, grows with the working and
the living. Do it as if your life depended on it, and first thing
you know, you'll have made a life out of it. A good life, too.
—THERESA HELBURN

If you don't stand for something, you'll fall for anything.
—MICHAEL EVANS

It is fatal to enter any war without the will to win it.
—GENERAL DOUGLAS MACARTHUR

Men, like snails, lose their usefulness when they
lose direction and begin to bend.
—WALTER SAVAGE LANDOR

The only place you can win a football game is on the
field. The only place you can lose it is in your heart.
—DARRELL ROYAL

You can't try to do things; you simply must do them.
—RAY BRADBURY

I don't care a damn for your loyal service when you think I am
right; when I really want it most is when you think I am wrong.
—GENERAL SIR JOHN MONASH

Moderation in war is imbecility.
—ADMIRAL JOHN FISHER

Firmness of purpose is one of the most necessary sinews of
character, and one of the best instruments of success. Without
it, genius wastes its efforts in a maze of inconsistencies.
—LORD CHESTERFIELD

Your own resolution to success is more
important than any other one thing.
—ABRAHAM LINCOLN

Unless you can find some sort of loyalty, you cannot
find unity and peace in your active living.
—JOSIAH ROYCE

I am seeking, I am striving, I am in it with all my heart.
—VINCENT VAN GOGH

Nothing is difficult to those who have the will.
—MOTTO OF THE DUTCH POETS' SOCIETY

Now I am steel-set: I follow the call to the clear
radiance and glow of the heights.
—HENRIK IBSEN

You don't know what pressure is until you play
for $5 with only $2 in your pocket.
—LEE TREVINO

Sometimes success is due less to ability than zeal. The winner
is he who gives himself to his work body and soul.
—CHARLES BUXTON

There is no strong performance without a
little fanaticism in the performer.
—RALPH WALDO EMERSON

The fixed determination to have acquired the warrior soul, to
either conquer or perish with honor, is the secret of victory.
—GENERAL GEORGE S. PATTON

Our future and our fate lie in our wills more than in our
hands, for our hands are but the instruments of our wills.
—B.C. Forbes

If you deny yourself commitment, what can you do with your life?
—Harvey Fierstein

Poverty is uncomfortable, as I can testify: but nine times out
of ten the best thing that can happen to a young man is to be
tossed overboard and compelled to sink or swim for himself.
—James A. Garfield

Either do not attempt at all, or go through with it.
—Ovid

To say yes, you have to sweat and roll up your sleeves
and plunge both hands into life up to the elbows. It is
easy to say no, even if saying no means death.
—Jean Anouilh

If you don't make a total commitment to whatever you're doing, then
you start looking to bail out the first time the boat starts leaking. It's
tough enough getting that boat to shore with everybody rowing, let
alone when a guy stands up and starts putting his life jacket on.
—Lou Holtz

So will I go in unto the king . . . and if I perish, I perish.
—Est. 4:16

When you have decided what you believe, what you feel must
be done, have the courage to stand alone and be counted.
—Eleanor Roosevelt

What one has, one ought to use; and whatever he
does, he should do with all his might.
—Cicero

Love me, please, I love you; I can bear to be your friend.
So ask of me anything . . . I am not a tentative person.
Whatever I do, I give up my whole self to it.
—Edna Saint Vincent Millay

The worth of every conviction consists precisely in
the steadfastness with which it is held.
—Jane Adams

What distinguishes the majority of men from the few
is their ability to act accordingly to their beliefs.
—Henry Miller

A belief which does not spring from a conviction
in the emotions is no belief at all.
—Evelyn Scott

Even now we can draw back. But once we cross that
little bridge, we must settle things by the sword.
—Julius Caesar, to his troops as they prepared to cross the Rubicon River

Perform without fail what you resolve.
—Benjamin Franklin

He that rides his hobby gently must always give
way to him that rides his hobby hard.
—Ralph Waldo Emerson

To have no loyalty is to have no dignity, and in the end, no manhood.
—Peter Taylor Forsyth

We can do whatever we wish to do provided our wish is strong
enough. But the tremendous effort needed—one doesn't always
want to make it—does one? . . . But what else can be done?
What's the alternative? What do you want most to do? That's
what I have to keep asking myself, in the face of difficulties.
—Katherine Mansfield

I am in earnest; I will not equivocate; I will not excuse; I
will not retreat a single inch; and I will be heard.
—William Lloyd Garrison

Winners are men who have dedicated their whole lives to winning.
—Woody Hayes

You can be an ordinary athlete by getting away with less than your best. But if you want to be a great, you have to give it all you've got—your everything.
—Duke P. Kahanamoku

If you start to take Vienna, take Vienna.
—Napoleon Bonaparte

Anytime you play golf for whatever you've got, that's pressure. I'd like to see H.L. Hunt go out there and play for $3 billion.
—Lee Trevino

There is a point at which everything becomes simple and there is no longer any question of choice, because all you have staked will be lost if you look back. Life's point of no return.
—Dag Hammarskjold

Wars may be fought with weapons, but they are won by men. It is the spirit of the men who follow, and of the man who leads, that gains the victory.
—General George S. Patton

It was my tongue that swore; my heart is unsworn.
—Euripides

Nothing can resist a will which will stake even existence upon its fulfillment.
—Benjamin Disraeli

If you rest, you rust.
—Helen Hayes

My face is set, my gait is fast, my goal is Heaven, my road is narrow, my way is rough, my companions are few, my guide is reliable, my mission is clear. I cannot be bought, compromised, detoured, lured away, turned back, diluted, or delayed. I will not flinch in the face of sacrifice, hesitate in the presence of adversity, negotiate . . . at the table of the enemy, ponder at the pool of popularity, or meander in a maze of mediocrity. I won't give up, shut up, let up, or slow up.
—Robert Moorehead

The height of your accomplishments will
equal the depth of your convictions.
—WILLIAM F. SCOLAVINO

Great minds have purposes, others have wishes.
—WASHINGTON IRVING

Morale is the greatest single factor in successful wars.
—DWIGHT D. EISENHOWER

Nothing of worthy or weight can be achieved with half a
mind, with a faint heart, and with a lame endeavor.
—ISAAC BARROW

Whether you are really right or not doesn't
matter, it's the belief that counts.
—ROBERTSON DAVIES

He did it with all his heart, and prospered.
—2 CHR. 31:21

The person who makes a success of living is the one who sees his
goal steadily and aims for it unswervingly. That is dedication.
—CECIL B. DEMILLE

I bend but do not break.
—JEAN DE LA FONTAINE

Strength is a matter of the made-up mind.
—JOHN BEECHER

You can't just sit there and wait for people to give you that golden
dream, you've got to get out there and make it happen for yourself.
—DIANA ROSS

Put your heart, mind, intellect and soul even to your
smallest acts. This is the secret of success.
—SWAMI SIVANANDA

The dedicated life is the life worth living.
—ANNIE DILLARD

There is always a way—if you're committed.
—Anthony Robbins

You're only here for a short visit. Don't hurry. Don't worry.
And be sure to smell the flowers along the way.
—Walter Hagen

Many a man has walked up to the opportunity for which he has
long been preparing himself, looked it full in the face, and then
begun to get cold feet ... when it comes to betting on yourself and
your power to do the thing you know you must do or write yourself
down a failure, you're a chicken-livered coward if you hesitate.
—B.C. Forbes

You will go most safely by the middle way.
—Ovid

If ants are such busy workers, how come they
find time to go to all the picnics?
—Marie Dressler

I don't want people who want to dance, I want people who have to dance.
—George Balanchine

Theirs is not to reason why, theirs is but to do or die.
—Alfred, Lord Tennyson

If you don't wake up with something in your stomach every day that
makes you think, "I want to make this movie," it'll never get made.
—Sherry Lansing

He turns not back who is bound to a star.
—Leonardo da Vinci

ADVICE

Example moves the world more than doctrine.
—Henry Miller

I have a simple philosophy. Fill what's empty, empty
what's full, and scratch where it itches.
—Alice Roosevelt Longworth

When in doubt, win the trick.
—Edmond Hoyle

I'll tell you what my daddy told me after my first trial. I thought
I was just great. I asked him, "How did I do?" He paused and said,
"You've got to guard against speaking more clearly than you think."
—Howard H. Baker, Jr.

The test of a vocation is the love of the drudgery it involves.
—Logan Pearsall Smith

A doctor can bury his mistakes but an architect
can only advise his client to plant vines.
—Frank Lloyd Wright

To have no set purpose in one's life is harlotry of the will.
—Stephen McKenna

I always pass on good advice. It is the only thing to
do with it. It is never any use to oneself.
—Oscar Wilde

No man can produce great things who is not
thoroughly sincere in dealing with himself.
—James Russell Lowell

There is just one life for each of us: our own.
—Euripides

The world is filled with people who are anxious
to function in an advisory capacity!
— Charlie Brown (Charles Schulz)

Integrity simply means a willingness not to violate one's identity.
—Erich Fromm

No one so thoroughly appreciaes the value of
constructive criticism as the one who's giving it.
—Hal Chadwick

A first rate soup is better than a second rate painting.
—Abraham Maslow

We are frequently asked what is the ideal number for
a dinner party. Estimates vary. . . . We are reminded of
the response made to this question by a . . . nineteenth-
century gourmet: "Myself and the headwaiter."
—Irma S. Rombauer, *The Joy of Cooking*

Fortune knocks but once, but misfortune has much more patience.
—Laurence J. Peter

Skills vary with the man. We must . . . strive by that which is born in us.
—Pindar

Thrust ivrybody—but cut th' ca-ards.
—Finley Peter Dunne

If any one asks me for good advice, I say I will give it, but
only on condition that you promise me not to take it.
—Johann Wolfgang von Goethe

Don't accept rides from strange men, and remember
that all men are strange as hell.
—Robin Morgan

Only he who keeps his eye fixed on the far
horizon will find his right road.
—Dag Hammarskjold

If you drink, don't drive. Don't even putt.
—Dean Martin

If you don't like the heat, get out of the kitchen.
—Harry Vaughan

Nobody is so miserable as he who longs to be
somebody other than the person he is.
—Angelo Patri

Don't compromise yourself. You are all you've got.
—Janis Joplin

It seems a shame, when so many things we'd like to do are
sinful, that it should also be wrong to do nothing.
—Frank Clark

We may fail of our happiness, strive we ever so bravely;
but we are less likely to fail if we measure with
judgment our chances and our capabilities.
—Agnes Repplier

Somehow we learn who we really are and then live with that decision.
—Eleanor Roosevelt

If it ain't broke, don't fix it.
—Bert Lance

The greatest thing in the world is to know how to be one's own self.
—Michel de Montaigne

Be careful whose advice you buy, but, be
patient with those who supply it.
—Mary Schmich

Nothing is good for everyone, but only relatively to some people.
—André Gide

Never practice two vices at once.
—Tallulah Bankhead

The self is not something that one finds. It is something one creates.
—Thomas Szasz

I think it much better that ... every man paddle his own canoe.
—Frederick Marryat

Starting out to make money is the greatest mistake in
life. Do what you feel you have a flair for doing, and if
you are good enough at it, the money will come.
—GREER GARSON

Nothing is so infectious as example.
—FRANCOIS DE LA ROCHEFOUCAULD

Stay off the gobbledygook language. It only fouls people up. For
the Lord's sake, be short and say what you're talking about.
—MAURY MAVERICK IN A MEMO SENT TO GOVERNMENT EMPLOYEES

Our whole life is an attempt to discover when our spontaneity
is whimsical, sentimental irresponsibility and when it is a
valid expression of our deepest desires and values.
—HELEN MERRELL LYND

Never play cards with a man called Doc. Never eat
at a place called Mom's. Never sleep with a woman
whose troubles are greater than your own.
—NELSON ALGREN

Be what you are. This is the first step toward
becoming better than you are.
—JULIUS CHARLES HARE

I believe there's an inner power that makes winners or losers. And the
winners are the ones who really listen to the truth of their hearts.
—SYLVESTER STALLONE

The most important thing to do if you find
yourselve in a hole is to stop digging.
—WARREN BUFFETT

Are you doing the kind of work you were built for, so that you can expect
to be able to do very large amounts of that kind and thrive under it?
Or are you doing a kind of which you can do comparatively little?
—B.C. FORBES

Always listen to experts. They'll tell you what
can't be done, and why. Then do it.
—ROBERT A. HEINLEIN

You have to deal with the fact that your life is your life.
—ALEX HAILEY

This is the chief thing: be not perturbed, for all things
are according to the nature of the universal.
—MARCUS AURELIUS

There's no right way of writing. There's only your way.
—MILTON LOMASK

If you want to make peace, you don't talk to
your friends. You talk to your enemies.
—MOSHE DAYAN

Why not be oneself? That is the whole secret of a successful
appearance. If one is a greyhound, why try to look like a Pekingese?
—EDITH SITWELL

All is disgust when one leaves his own nature
and does things that misfit it.
—SOPHOCLES

To aim at the best and to remain essentially
ourselves is one and the same thing.
—JANET ERSKINE STUART

To be what we are, and to become what we are
capable of becoming, is the only end of life.
—ROBERT LOUIS STEVENSON

Brutes find out where their talents lie; a bear will not attempt to fly.
—JONATHAN SWIFT

Be not imitator; freshly act thy part;
Through this world be thou an independent ranger;
Better is the faith that springeth from thy heart
Than a better faith belonging to a stranger.
—PERSIAN PROVERB

Of all the paths a man could strike into, there is, at any
given moment, a best path . . . a thing which, here and now,
it were of all things wisest for him to do . . . to find this
path, and walk in it, is the one thing needful for him.
—THOMAS CARLYLE

No matter how ill we may be, nor how low we may have fallen,
we should not change identity with any other person.
—SAMUEL BUTLER

Personality, too, is destiny.
—ERIK ERIKSON

With begging and scrambling we find very little, but with
being true to ourselves we find a great deal more.
—RABINDRANATH TAGORE

Success based on anything but internal fulfillment is bound to be empty.
—DR. MARTHA FRIEDMAN

Reality is that which when you stop believing in it, it doesn't go away.
—PHILIP K. DICK

What's important is finding out what works for you.
—HENRY MOORE

Concentrate your energies, your thoughts and your capital. . . . The
wise man puts all his eggs in one basket and watches the basket.
—ANDREW CARNEGIE

This above all: to thine own self be true.
—WILLIAM SHAKESPEARE

Live as you will wish to have lived when you are dying.
—CHRISTIAN FURCHTEGOTT GELLERT

Choose always the way that seems the best, however rough it
may be; custom will soon render it easy and agreeable.
—PYTHAGORAS

Let the world know you as you are, not as you think you
should be, because sooner or later, if you are posing, you
will forget the pose, and then where are you?
—FANNY BRICE

The greatest achievement of the human spirit is to live up to
one's opportunities and make the most of one's resources.
—VAUVENARGUES

What's a joy to the one is a nightmare to the other.
—BERTOLT BRECHT

Let them know a real man, who lives as he was meant to live.
—MARCUS AURELIUS

Any path is only a path, and there is no affront, to oneself or to
others, in dropping it if that is what your heart tells you.
—CARLOS CASTANEDA

Until you know that life is interesting, and find
it so, you haven't found your soul.
—GEOFFREY FISHER

Education should be the process of helping
everyone to discover his uniqueness.
—LEO BUSCAGLIA

People are ridiculous only when they try or
seem to be that which they are not.
—GIACOMO LEOPARDI

In my clinical experience, the greatest block to a person's development is
his having to take on a way of life which is not rooted in his own powers.
—ROLLO MAY

There is always a certain peace in being what one is, in being
that completely. The condemned man has that joy.
—UGO BETTI

Virtue is insufficient temptation.
—GEORGE BERNARD SHAW

We can't all be heroes, because someone has to
sit on the curb and clap as they go by.
—Will Rogers

The most exhausting thing in life is being insincere.
—Anne Morrow Lindbergh

I wrote because I had to. I couldn't stop. There wasn't anything
else I could do. If no one ever bought anything, anything I
ever did, I'd still be writing. It's beyond a compulsion.
—Tennessee Williams

To be nobody-but-yourself—in a world which is doing its best, night
and day, to make you everybody else—means to fight the hardest
battle which any human being can fight; and never stop fighting.
—E.E. cummings

Nature magically suits a man to his fortunes, by
making them the fruit of his character.
—Ralph Waldo Emerson

The highest courage is to dare to appear to be what one is.
—John Lancaster Spalding

Whenever it is possible, a boy should choose some occupation
which he should do even if he did not need the money.
—William Lyon Phelps

I have the true feeling of myself only when I am unbearably unhappy.
—Franz Kafka

I'd rather be a lamppost in Chicago than a millionaire in any other city.
—William A. Hulbert

Whatever you are by nature, keep to it; never desert your own line
of talent. Be what nature intended you for, and you will succeed; be
anything else and you will be ten thousand times worse than nothing.
—Sydney Smith

Remember always that you have not only the right to be
an individual, you have an obligation to be one.
—Eleanor Roosevelt

Everybody undertakes what he sees another successful
in, whether he has the aptitude for it or not.
—Johann von Goethe

I will not cut my conscience to fit this year's fashions.
—Lillian Hellman

There are as many ways to live and grow as there are people.
Our own ways are the only ways that should matter to us.
—Evelyn Mandel

Ya gotta do what ya gotta do.
—Sylvester Stallone

I searched through rebellion, drugs, diets, mysticism, religions,
intellectualism and much more, only to begin to find ... that
truth is basically simple—and feels good, clean and right.
—Chick Corea

Seek out that particular mental attitude which makes
you feel most deeply and vitally alive, along with which
comes the inner voice which says, "This is the real me,"
and when you have found that attitude, follow it.
—William James

It is the chiefest point of happiness that a man is willing to be what he is.
—Erasmus

'Tis a gift to be simple, 'tis a gift to be free.
'Tis a gift to come round to where we ought to be.
And when we find a place that feels just right,
We will be in the valley of love and delight.
—Appalachian folk song

What's a man's first duty? The answer is brief: To be himself.
—Henrik Ibsen

To feel that one has a place in life solves half the problem of contentment.
—George E. Woodberry

It is not a dreamlike state, but the somehow insulated state, that
a great musician achieves in a great performance. He's aware of

where he is and what he's doing, but his mind is on the playing of his instrument with an internal sense of *rightness*—it is not merely mechanical, it is not only spiritual; it is something of both, on a different plane and a more remote one.
—ARNOLD PALMER

I look at ordinary people in their suits, them with no scars, and I'm different. I don't fit with them. I'm where everybody's got scar tissue on their eyes and got noses like saddles. I go to conventions of old fighters like me and I see the scar tissue and all them flat noses and it's beautiful. . . . They talk like me, like they got rocks in their throats. Beautiful!
—WILLIE PASTRANO

If all misfortunes were laid in one common heap whence everyone must take an equal portion, most people would be contented to take their own and depart.
—SOCRATES

I have the feeling when I write poetry that I'm doing what I'm supposed to do. You don't think about whether you're going to get money or fame, you just do it.
—DORIS LUND

If Heaven made him, earth can find some use for him.
—CHINESE PROVERB

You might as well fall flat on your face as lean over too far backward.
—JAMES THURBER

Everyone has a right to his own course of action.
—MOLIERE

Resolve to be thyself . . . he who finds himself loses his misery!
—MATTHEW ARNOLD

We may fail of our happiness, strive we ever so bravely; but we are less likely to fail if we measure with judgment our chances and our capabilities.
—AGNES REPPLIER

Each citizen should play his part in the community
according to his individual gifts.
—PLATO

Men are created different; they lose their social freedom and their
individual autonomy in seeking to become like each other.
—DAVID RIESMAN

It is possible to be different and still be all right.
—ANNE WILSON SCHAEF

The search for a new personality is futile; what is fruitful is the
human interest the old personality can take in new activities.
—CESARE PAVESE

To find out what one is fitted to do, and to secure an
opportunity to do it, is the key to happiness.
—JOHN DEWEY

Do you know that disease and death must need to overtake
us, no matter what we are doing? ... What do you wish to be
doing when it overtakes you? ... If you have anything better to
be doing when you are so overtaken, get to work on that.
—EPICTETUS

To be what we are, and to become what we are
capable of becoming, is the only end of life.
—ROBERT LOUIS STEVENSON

Brutes find out where their talents lie; a bear will not attempt to fly.
—JONATHAN SWIFT

No man can produce great things who is not
thoroughly sincere in dealing with himself.
—JAMES RUSSELL LOWELL

All I would tell people is to hold on to what was individual about
themselves, not to allow their ambition for success to cause them to try
to imitate the success of others. You've got to find in on your own terms.
—HARRISON FORD

God requires a faithful fulfillment of the merest
trifle given us to do, rather than the most ardent
aspiration to things to which we are not called.
—Saint Francis de Sales

Learn what you are, and be such.
—Pindar

Talk low, talk slow, and don't say too much.
—John Wayne

Choose a subject equal to your abilities; think carefully what your
shoulders may refuse, and what they are capable of bearing.
—Horace

We would have to settle for the elegant goal of becoming ourselves.
—William Stryon

Mountains should be climbed with as little effort as possible and
without desire. The reality of your own nature should determine the
speed. If you become restless, speed up. If you become winded, slow
down. You climb the mountain in an equilibrium between restlessness
and exhaustion. Then, when you're no longer thinking ahead, each
footstep isn't just a means to an end, but a unique event in itself.
—Robert M. Pirsig

If you have to support yourself, you had bloody well better
find some way that is going to be interesting.
—Katharine Hepburn

If a man has a talent and cannot use it, he has failed. If he has a talent
and uses only half of it, he has partly failed. If he has a talent and
learns somehow to use the whole of it, he has gloriously succeeded,
and won a satisfaction and a triumph few men ever know.
—Thomas Wolfe

A man can do only what he can do. But if he does that each
day he can sleep at night and do it again the next day.
—Albert Schweitzer

The great law of culture: Let each become all
that he was created capable of being.
—THOMAS CARLYLE

We do not write as we want but as we can.
—W. SOMERSET MAUGHAM

Those who love a cause are those who love the life
which has to be led in order to serve it.
—SIMONE WEIL

It is the soul's duty to be loyal to its own desires.
—REBECCA WEST

For me, writing is the only thing that passes the three tests of
metier: (1) when I'm doing it, I don't feel that I should be doing
something else instead; (2) it produces a sense of accomplishment
and, once in a while, pride; and (3) it's frightening.
—GLORIA STEINEM

What does reason demand of a man? A very easy
thing—to live in accord with his own nature.
—MARCUS ANNAEUS SENECA

It is better to be hated for what you are than loved for what you are not.
—ANDRÉ GIDE

[A] rose is a rose is a rose.
—GERTRUDE STEIN

Happiness, that grand mistress of the ceremonies in
the dance of life, impels us through all its mazes and
meanderings, but leads none of us by the same route.
—CHARLES CALEB COLTON

Each of us has some unique capability waiting for realization. Every
person is valuable in his own existence, for himself alone ... each
of us can bring to fruition these innate, God-given abilities.
—GEORGE H. BENDER

I write lustily and humorously. It isn't calculated; it's the way I
think. I've invented a writing style that expresses who I am.
—Erica Jong

The moment that any life, however good, stifles
you, you may be sure it isn't your real life.
—Arthur Christopher Benson

Starting out to make money is the greatest mistake in
life. Do what you feel you have a flair for doing, and if
you are good enough at it, the money will come.
—Greer Garson

All life is the struggle, the effort to be itself.
—José Ortega y Gasset

Everything keeps its best nature only by being put to its best use.
—Phillips Brooks

You must be holy in the way God asks you to be holy.
God does not ask you to be a Trappist monk or a hermit.
He wills that you sanctify your everyday life.
—Saint Vincent Pallotti

Do not wish to be anything but what you are.
—Saint Francis de Sales

It is only when I am doing my work that I feel
truly alive. It is like having sex.
—Federico Fellini

When I was young, I said to God, "God, tell me the mystery of the
universe." But God answered, "That knowledge is reserved for me
alone." So I said, "God, tell me the mystery of the peanut." Then God
said, "Well George, that's more nearly your size." And he told me.
—George Washington Carver

All of us attain the greatest success and happiness possible in
this life whenever we use our native capacities to their fullest
extent.... And every life must be chalked up at least a partial failure
when it does not succeed in reaching its inherent destiny.
—Smiley M. Blanton

We don't see many fat men walking on stilts.
—BUD MILLER

I was raised to sense what someone wanted me to be
and be that kind of person. It took me a long time not
to judge myself through someone else's eyes.
—SALLY FIELD

A happy life is one which is in accordance with its own nature.
—MARCUS ANNAEUS SENECA

People are always neglecting something they can
do in trying to do something they can't do.
—EDGAR WATSON HOWE

There is only one success—to be able to spend your life in your own way.
—CHRISTOPHER MORLEY

The same man cannot be skilled in everything;
each has his special excellence.
—EURIPIDES

There is always a certain peace in being what
one is, in being that completely.
—UGO BETTI

Ask yourself the secret of your success. Listen
to your answer, and practice it.
—RICHARD BACH

Never desert your own line of talent. Be what nature
intended you for, and you will succeed.
—SYDNEY SMITH

Our concern must be to live while we're alive ... to release our inner
selves from the spiritual death that comes with living behind a facade
designed to conform to external definitions of who and what we are.
—ELIZABETH KÜBLER-ROSS

Every man must get to heaven his own way.
—FREDERICK THE GREAT

If a man has a talent and cannot use it, he has failed. If he has a talent and uses only half of it, he has partly failed. If he has a talent and learns somehow to use the whole of it, he has gloriously succeeded, and won a satisfaction and a triumph few men ever know.
—THOMAS WOLFE

I'd rather be a failure at something I enjoy than a success at something I hate.
—GEORGE BURNS

Every human being is intended to have a character of his own; to be what no others are, and to do what no other can do.
—WILLIAM ELLERY CHANNING

Nature arms each man with some faculty which enables him to do easily some feat impossible to any other.
—RALPH WALDO EMERSON

Bloom where you are planted.
—ANON

Learn the lines and don't bump into the furniture.
—NOEL COWARD

Don't bother just to be better than your contemporaries or predecessors. Try to be better than yourself.
—WILLIAM FAULKNER

The fun of being alive is realizing you have a talent and you can use it every day so it grows stronger.... And if you're in an atmosphere where this talent is appreciated instead of just tolerated, why, it's just as good as sex.
—LOU CENTLIVRE

There are as many ways to live and grow as there are people. Our own ways are the only ways that should matter to us.
—EVELYN MANDEL

In efforts to soar above our nature, we invariably fall below it.
—EDGAR ALLAN POE

It requires a certain kind of mind to see beauty in a hamburger
bun. Yet, is it any more unusual to find grace in the texture and
softly curved silhouette of a bun than to reflect lovingly on ... the
arrangement of textures and colors in a butterfly's wing?
—RAY KROC

The question "Who ought to be boss" is like asking "Who ought to
be tenor in the quartet?" Obviously, the man who can sing tenor.
—HENRY FORD

Abasement, degradation is simply the manner of life of the
man who has refused to be what it is his duty to be.
—JOSÉ ORTEGA Y GASSET

Every person is responsible for all the good within
the scope of his abilities, and for no more.
—GAIL HAMILTON

Always do right. This will gratify some people & astonish the rest.
—MARK TWAIN

The white light streams down to be broken up by those
human prisms into all the colors of the rainbow. Take
your own color in the pattern and be just that.
—CHARLES R. BROWN

Freedom and constraint are two aspects of the same necessity,
the necessity of being the man you are, and not another.
You are free to be that man, but not free to be another.
—ANTOINE DE SAINT-EXUPERY

The great enemy of clear language is insincerity. When
there is a gap between one's real and one's declared aims,
one turns, as it were, instinctively to long words and
exhausted idioms, like a cuttlefish squirting out ink.
—GEORGE ORWELL

When men are rightfully occupied, then their amusement grows
out of their work as the color petals out of a fruitful garden.
—JOHN RUSKIN

Me, I'm just a hack. I'm just a schlepper. I just do what I can do.
—BETTE MIDLER

Don't take anyone else's definition of success as
your own. (This is easier said than done.)
—JACQUELINE BRISKIN

The high prize of life, the crowning fortune of a man, is to be born with
a bias to some pursuit which finds him in employment and happiness.
—RALPH WALDO EMERSON

Misfortunes occur only when a man is false.... Events,
circumstances, etc., have their origin in ourselves.
They spring from seeds which we have sown.
—HENRY DAVID THOREAU

The only success worth one's powder was success in the
line of one's idiosyncrasy ... what was talent but the art
of being completely whatever one happened to be?
—HENRY JAMES

One can never consent to creep when one feels an impulse to soar.
—HELEN KELLER

My mother said to me, "If you become a soldier, you'll be a
general, if you become a monk you'll end up as the pope."
Instead, I became a painter and wound up as Picasso.
—PABLO PICASSO

A man like Verdi must write like Verdi.
—VERDI

Different men seek after happiness in different ways and by different
means, and so make for themselves different modes of life.
—ARISTOTLE

All men have happiness as their object: there is no exception. However
different the means they employ, they aim at the same end.
—BLAISE PASCAL

The deepest personal defeat suffered by human beings
is constituted by the difference between what one was
capable of becoming, and what one has in fact become.
—ASHLEY MONTAGU

Every true man, sir, who is a little above the level of the beasts and
plants, lives so as to give a meaning and a value to his own life.
—LUIGI PIRANDELLO

A musician must make music, an artist must paint, a poet must write,
if he to be at peace with himself. What a man can be, he must be.
—ABRAHAM MASLOW

A man must be obedient to the promptings of his innermost heart.
—ROBERTSON DAVIES

We only do well the things we like doing.
—COLETTE

Man is not born to solve the problems of the universe, but to find
out what he has to do . . . within the limits of his comprehension.
—JOHANN VON GOETHE

Take short views, hope for the best and trust in God.
—SYDNEY SMITH

Skills vary with the man. We must . . . strive by that which is born in us.
—PINDAR

The weakest among us has a gift, however seemingly trivial, which is
peculiar to him and which worthily used will be a gift also to his race.
—JOHN RUSKIN

One cannot both feast and become rich.
—ASHANTI PROVERB

We succeed in enterprises which demand the positive qualities we
possess, but we excel in those which can also make use of our defects.
—ALEXIS DE TOCQUEVILLE

It is necessary to the happiness of man that
he be mentally faithful to himself.
—Thomas Paine

No amount of study or learning will make a man a
leader unless he has the natural qualities of one.
—Sir Archibald Wavell

CHANGE

One must be thrust out of a finished cycle in life, and that leap is the
most difficult to make—to part with one's faith, one's love, when
one would prefer to renew the faith and recreate the passion.
—Anaïs Nin

You cannot step twice into the same river, for
other waters are continually flowing in.
—Heraclitus

Change is the law of life. And those who look only to the
past or the present are certain to misse the future.
—John F. Kennedy

The mill wheel turns, it turns forever, though
what is uppermost remains not so.
—Bertolt Brecht

To change skins, evolve into new cycles, I feel one has to learn
to discard. If one changes internally, one should not continue to
live with the same objects. They reflect one's mind and psyche
of yesterday. I throw away what has no dynamic, living use.
—Anaïs Nin

The more things change, the more they remain the same.
—Alphonse Karr

Nature's mighty law is change.
—Robert Burns

One change always leaves the way open for the establishment of others.
—Niccolo Machiavelli

The hearts of great men can be changed.
—Homer

It is a mark of many famous people that they
cannot part with their brightest hour.
—Lillian Hellman

Since changes are going on anyway, the great thing is to learn enough
about them so that we will be able to lay hold of them and turn them in
the direction of our desires. Conditions and events are neither to be fled
from nor passively acquiesced in; they are to be utilized and directed.
—John Dewey

Keep your mind open to change all the time. Welcome
it. Court it. It is only by examining and reexamining
your opinions and ideas that you can progress.
—Dale Carnegie

There is danger in reckless change; but greater
danger in blind conservatism.
—Henry George

When one door of happiness closes, another opens;
but often we look so long at the closed door that we do
not see the one which has been opened for us.
—Helen Keller

The old order changeth yielding place to new,
and God fulfills himself in many ways.
—Alfred, Lord Tennyson

Everybody thinks of changing humanity and
nobody thinks of changing himself.
—Leo Tolstoy

Today changes must come fast; and we must adjust our mental habits,
so that we can accept comfortably the idea of stopping one thing and
beginning another overnight.... We must assume that there is probably

a better way to do almost everything. We must stop assuming that a thing which has never been done before probably cannot be done at all.
—Donald M. Nelson

Everything in life that we really accept undergoes a change.
—Katherine Mansfield

We are restless because of incessant change, but we would be frightened if change were stopped.
—Lyman Lloyd Bryson

We must therefore take account of this changeable nature of things and of human institutions, and prepare for them with enlightened foresight.
—Pope Pius XI

It's a bad plan that can't be changed.
—Publilius Syrus

Change is the price of survival.
—Winston Churchill

All changes, even the most longed for, have their melancholy, for what we leave behind us is a part of ourselves; we must die to one life before we can enter into another.
—Anatole France

Never doubt that a small group of committed people can change the world: Indeed it is the only thing that ever has.
—Margaret Mead

Change means the unknown.
—Eleanor Roosevelt

To remain young one must change. The perpetual campus hero is not a young man but an old boy.
—Alexander Chase

The moment of change is the only poem.
—Adrienne Rich

As we learn we always change, and so our perception. This changed
perception then becomes a new Teacher inside each of us.
—HYEMEYOHSTS STORM

Nothing is permanent but change.
—HERACLITUS

Such is the state of life that none are happy but by the
anticipation of change. The change itself is nothing. When
we have made it, the next wish is to change again.
—SAMUEL JOHNSON

He that has energy enough to root out a vice should
go further, and try to plant a virtue in its place.
—CHARLES CALEB COLTON

A man's fortune must first be changed from within.
—CHINESE PROVERB

All is change; all yields its place and goes.
—EURIPIDES

Change is what people fear most.
—FYODOR DOSTOYEVSKY

GREATNESS

But be not afraid of greatness. Some are born great, some achieve
greatness, and some have greatness thrust upon 'em.
—WILLIAM SHAKESPEARE

Greatness is a road leading towards the unknown.
—CHARLES DE GAULLE

Nothing is more simple than greatness;
indeed, to be simple is to be great.
—RALPH WALDO EMERSON

Great and good are seldom the same man.
—THOMAS FULLER

There are countless ways of attaining greatness, but any road to reaching
one's maximum potential must be built on a bedrock of respect for the
individual, a commitment to excellence, and a rejection of mediocrity.
—ROBERT LEROY (BUCK) RODGERS

No one ever achieved greatness by playing it safe.
—HARRY GRAY

Greater is he who acts from love than he who acts from fear
—SIMEON BEN ELEAZAR

Neither genius, fame, nor love show the greatness
of the soul. Only kindness can do that.
—JEAN BAPTISTE HENRI LACORDAIRE

Greatness and goodness are not means, but ends.
—SAMUEL TAYLOR COLERIDGE

Great men have all been formed either before
academies or independent of them.
—VOLTAIRE

Greatness lies not in being strong, but in the right use of strength.
—HENRY WARD BEECHER

Few great men could pass Personnel.
—PAUL GOODMAN

No really great man ever thought himself so.
—WILLIAM HAZLITT

He is greatest who is most often in men's good thoughts.
—SAMUEL BUTLER

Great men are but life-sized. Most of them, indeed, are rather short.
—MAX BEERBOHM

Nothing great in the world has ever been accomplished without passion.
—FRIEDRICH HEBBEL

Responsibility is the price of greatness.
—WINSTON CHURCHILL

I've always had a sneaking fondness for Martin Van Buren.
He wrote his autobiography, you know, and never once
mentioned his wife. Now that's what I call a man's man.
—CLEVELAND AMORY

No man is truly great who is great only in his lifetime.
The test of greatness is the page of history.
—WILLIAM HAZLITT

We must not measure greatness from the mansion
down, but from the manger up.
—JESSE JACKSON

The loftiest towers rise from the ground.
—CHINESE PROVERB

It's not what you take but what you leave behind that defines greatness.
—EDWARD GARDNER

Suffering becomes beautiful when anyone bears great calamities with
cheerfulness, not through insensibility but through greatness of mind.
—ARISTOTLE

No great thing is created suddenly.
—EPICTETUS

Great things are not done by impulse, but by a
series of small things brought together.
—VINCENT VAN GOGH

If any man seeks for greatness, let him forget greatness
and ask for truth, and he will find both.
—HORACE MANN

No man was ever great by imitation.
—Samuel Johnson

Man's greatness lies in his power of thought.
—Blaise Pascal

INSTINCTS

Trust your hunches. They're usually based on facts
filed away just below the conscious level.
—Dr. Joyce Brothers

The shrewd guess, the fertile hypothesis, the
courageous leap to a tentative conclusion—these are
the most valuable coin of the thinker at work.
—Jerome S. Bruner

A mind all logic is like a knife all blade. It
makes the hand bleed that uses it.
—Rabindranath Tagore

If you do not express your own original ideas, if you do not
listen to your own being, you will have betrayed yourself.
—Rollo May

We are not permitted to choose the frame of our
destiny. But what we put into it is ours.
—Dag Hammarskjold

Well-bred instinct meets reason halfway.
—George Santayana

I feel there are two people inside me—me and my
intuition. If I go against her, she'll screw me every time,
and if I follow her, we get along quite nicely.
—Kim Basinger

One of the reasons why so few of us ever act, instead of react, is because we are continually stifling our deepest impulses.
—HENRY MILLER

I follow my heart, for I can trust it.
—J.C.F. VON SCHILLER

The thinker philosophizes as the lover loves. Even were the consequences not only useless but harmful, he must obey his impulse.
—WILLIAM JAMES

Ideas pull the trigger, but instinct loads the gun.
—DON MARQUIS

We each need to let our intuition guide us, and then be willing to follow that guidance directly and fearlessly.
—SHAKTI GAWAIN

Weaseling out of things is important to learn. It's what separates us from the animals ... except the weasel.
—HOMER SIMPSON (MATT GROENING)

Instinct is untaught ability.
—BAIN

A true history of human events would show that a far larger proportion of our acts are the results of sudden impulses and accident than of that reason of which we so much boast.
—PETER COOPER

I write out of instinct.
—JEROME WEIDMAN

It is only by following your deepest instinct that you can lead a rich life.
—KATHARINE BUTLER HATHAWAY

We shall keep our horizon perfectly, absolutely, crystallinely open, ready every day for the scouring gales of impulse.
—JOHN MISTLETOE

All our reasoning ends in surrender to feeling.
—Blaise Pascal

Most of us have far more courage than we ever dreamed we possessed.
—Dale Carnegie

Heroism, the Caucasian mountaineers say, is
endurance for one moment more.
—George Kennan

Every time a resolve or fine glow of feeling evaporates without
bearing fruit, it is worse than a chance lost; it works to hinder
future emotions from taking the normal path of discharge.
—William James

Intuition ... appears to be the extrasensory perception of reality.
—Dr. Alexis Carrel

Hundreds of people can talk for one who can think, but
thousands can think for one who can see. To see clearly
is poetry, prophecy, and religion—all in one.
—John Ruskin

The truth of a thing is the feel of it, not the think of it.
—Stanley Kubrick

No one ever gets very far unless he accomplishes
the impossible at least once a day.
—Elbert Hubbard

Intuition is a spiritual faculty and does not
explain, but simply points the way.
—Florence Scovel Shinn

Visionary people are visionary partly because of
the very great many things they don't see.
—Berkeley Rice

If you let your fear of consequence prevent you from following
your deepest instinct, your life will be safe, expedient, and thin.
—Katharine Butler Hathaway

Instinct is the nose of the mind.
—Madame De Girardin

We are so clothed in rationalization and dissemblance that we can
recognize but dimly the deep primal impulses that motivate us.
—James Ramsey Ullman

A great mind is one that can forget or look beyond itself.
—William Hazlitt

Many a man gets weary of clamping down on his rough
impulses, which if given occasional release would encourage
the living of life with salt in it, in place of dust.
—Henry S. Haskins

To be faithful to your instincts and the impulses that carry
you in the direction of the excellence you most desire
and value . . . surely that is to lead the noble life.
—George E. Woodberry

Vision is the art of seeing things invisible.
—Jonathan Swift

Instinct is intelligence incapable of self-consciousness.
—John Sterling

By learning to contact, listen to, and act on our intuition,
we can directly connect to the higher power of the
universe and allow it to become our guiding force.
—Shakti Gawain

Impulse without reason is not enough, and reason
without impulse is a poor makeshift.
—William James

Reason, ruling alone, is a force confining; and passion,
unattended, is a flame that burns to its own destruction.
—Kahlil Gibran

To be great is to be misunderstood.
—Ralph Waldo Emerson

Common sense is instinct. Enough of it is genius.
—George Bernard Shaw

Good instincts usually tell you what to do long
before your head has figured it out.
—Michael Burke

The heart has reasons which reason cannot understand.
—Blaise Pascal

A rock pile ceases to be a rock pile the moment a single man
contemplates it, bearing within him the image of a cathedral.
—Antoine de Saint-Exupery

A trembling in the bones may carry a more convincing testimony
than the dry, documented deductions of the brain.
—Llewelyn Powers

The mind can assert anything, and pretend it has proved it.
My beliefs I test on my body, on my intuitional consciousness,
and when I get a response there, then I accept.
—D.H. Lawrence

The passion to get ahead is sometimes born
of the fear lest we be left behind.
—Eric Hoffer

It is wisdom to believe the heart.
—George Santayana

Man becomes man only by his intelligence,
but he is man only by his heart.
—Henri Frederic Amiel

To live is like to love: all reason is against it,
and all healthy instinct is for it.
—Samuel Butler

All I can do is act according to my deepest instinct, and be whatever I must be—crazy or ribald or sad or compassionate or loving or indifferent. That is all anybody can do.
—Katharine Butler Hathaway

Everyone was searching for a formula for survival ... and the only formula that worked was no formula. Instinct ... that's all you had to go on.
—Carolyn Kenmore

But are not this struggle and even the mistakes one may make better, and do they not develop us more, than if we kept systematically away from emotions?
—Vincent van Gogh

It is our business to go as we are impelled.
—D.H. Lawrence

I go by instinct. ... I don't worry about experience.
—Barbra Streisand

Life is not governed by will or intention. Life is a question of nerves, and fibers, and slowly built-up cells in which thought hides itself, and passion has its dreams.
—Oscar Wilde

People who lean on logic and philosophy and rational exposition end by starving the best part of the mind.
—William Butler Yeats

We should chiefly depend not upon that department of the soul which is most superficial and fallible (our reason), but upon that department that is deep and sure, which is instinct.
—Charles Sanders Peirce

The intellect is always fooled by the heart.
—Francois de La Rochefoucauld

Unconsciousness, spontaneity, instinct ... hold us to the earth and dictate the relatively good and useful.
—Henri Frederic Amiel

Every time I've done something that doesn't feel
right, it's ended up not being right.
—Mario Cuomo

Just be what you are and speak from your
guts and heart—it's all a man has.
—Hubert H. Humphrey

Some of the finest moral intuitions come to quite humble
people. The visiting of lofty ideas doesn't depend on
formal schooling. Think of those Galilean peasants.
—Alfred North Whitehead

We do not wish ardently for what we desire only through reason.
—Francois de La Rochefoucauld

There are no rules. Just follow your heart.
—Robin Williams

None of us can estimate what we do when we do it from instinct.
—Luigi Pirandello

Spend time every day listening to what your muse is trying to tell you.
—Saint Bartholomew

Statistics are no substitute for judgement.
—Henry Clay

Inspiration does not come like a bolt, nor is it kinetic energy
striving, but it comes to us slowly and quietly and all the time.
—Brenda Euland

I do not believe that the deeper problems of living can ever be
answered by the process of thought. I believe that life itself
teaches us either patience with regard to them, or reveals
to us possible solutions when our hearts are pressed close
against duties and sorrows and experiences of all kinds.
—Hamilton Wright Mabie

Life is one long struggle between conclusions based on abstract ways of conceiving cases, and opposite conclusions prompted by our instinctive perception of them.
—WILLIAM JAMES

Imagination is more important than knowledge.
—ALBERT EINSTEIN

Some other faculty than the intellect is necessary for the apprehension of reality.
—HENRI BERGSON

When love is not madness, it is not love.
—PEDRO CALDERON DE LA BARCA

Man is a passion which brings a will into play, which works an intelligence.
—HENRI FREDERIC AMIEL

You have first an instinct, then an opinion, then a knowledge, as the plant has root, bud and fruit. Trust the instinct to the end, though you can render no reason.
—RALPH WALDO EMERSON

Every time you don't follow your inner guidance, you feel a loss of energy, loss of power, a sense of spiritual deadness.
—SHAKTI GAWAIN

Modern man's besetting temptation is to sacrifice his direct perceptions and spontaneous feelings to his reasoned reflections; to prefer in all circumstances the verdict of his intellect to that of his immediate intuitions.
—ALDOUS HUXLEY

Command by instinct is swifter, subtler, deeper, more accurate, more in touch with reality than command by conscious mind. The discovery takes one's breath away.
—MICHAEL NOVAK

When a man begins to reason, he ceases to feel.
—FRENCH PROVERB

Truth made you a traitor as it often does in a time of scoundrels.
—LILLIAN HELLMAN

Cherish your emotions and never undervalue them.
—ROBERT HENRI

Nothing reaches the intellect before making its appearance in the senses.
—LATIN PROVERB

Decisions, particularly important ones, have always made me sleepy,
perhaps because I know that I will have to make them by instinct, and
thinking things out is only what other people tell me I should do.
—LILLIAN HELLMAN

It is the heart always that sees, before the head can see.
—THOMAS CARLYLE

Falling in love is one of the activities forbidden that
tiresome person, the consistently reasonable man.
—SIR ARTHUR EDDINGTON

I make all my decisions on intuition. I throw a spear into
the darkness. That is intuition. Then I must send an army
into the darkness to find the spear. That is intellect.
—INGMAR BERGMAN

Trust your own instinct. Your mistakes might as well
be your own, instead of someone else's.
—BILLY WILDER

The struggle to learn to listen to and respect our own intuitive,
inner promptings is the greatest challenge of all.
—HERB GOLDBERG

Calculation never made a hero.
—JOHN HENRY CARDINAL NEWMAN

Our real duty is always found running in the
direction of our worthiest desires.
—RANDOLPH BOURNE

What you intuitively desire, that is possible to you.
—D.H. Lawrence

It is the heart which experiences God, not the reason.
—Blaise Pascal

A goose flies by a chart which the Royal
Geographical Society could not improve.
—Oliver Wendell Holmes, Jr.

Call no man foe, but never love a stranger.
—Stella Benson

Every human being has, like Socrates, an attendant spirit;
and wise are they who obey its signals. If it does not always
tell us what to do, it always cautions us what not to do.
—Lydia M. Child

Passion and prejudice govern the world, only under the name of reason.
—John Wesley

Intuition is given only to him who has undergone
long preparation to receive it.
—Louis Pasteur

The great man is the one who does not lose his child's heart.
—Mencius

It is only with the heart that one can see rightly;
what is essential is invisible to the eye.
—Antoine de Saint-Exupery

Instinct guides the animal better than the man. In the animal it
is pure, in man it is led astray by his reason and intelligence.
—Denis Diderot

Pure logic is the ruin of the spirit.
—Antoine de Saint-Exupery

Don't be so humble—you're not that great.
—Golda Meir to Moshe Sayan

POWER

Power is the great aphrodesiac.
—HENRY KISSINGER

You should have joy, or you shall have power,
said God; you shall not have both.
—RALPH WALDO EMERSON

An honest man can feel no pleasure in the exercise
of power over his fellow citizens.
—THOMAS JEFFERSON

For the mighty even to give way is grace.
—AESCHYLUS

Power doesn't have to show off. Power is confident, self-
assuring, self-starting and self-stopping, self-warming,
and self justifying. When you have it, you know it.
—RALPH ELLISON

The sole advantage of power is that you can do more good.
—BALTASAR GRACIAN

Power can corrupt, but absolute power is absolutely delightful.
—ANON

True power and true politeness are above vanity.
—VOLTAIRE

The strongest is never strong enough to be always the master,
unless he transforms strength into right, and obedience into duty.
—HENRI ROUSSEAU

Unlimited power is apt to corrupt the minds of those who possess it.
—WILLIAM PITT, EARL OF CHATHAM

Every high degree of power always involves a corresponding
degree of freedom from good and evil.
—FRIEDRICH NIETZSCHE

Power and riches never want advocates.
—SAMUEL RICHARDSON

There is a homely adage which runs: "Speak softly
and carry a big stick; you will go far."
—THEODORE ROOSEVELT

Information is not power. If information were power, then
librarians would be the most powerful people on the planet.
—BRUCE STERLING

We have it in our power to begin the world over again.
—THOMAS PAINE

The hand that rocks the cradle rules the world.
—WILLIAM ROSS WALLACE

Might is right.
—PROVERB

To know the pains of power, we must go to those who have it; to
know its pleasures, we must go to those who are seeking it.
—CHARLES CALEB COLTON

Great power contitutes its own argument, and it never has much trouble
drumming up friends, applause, sympathetic exegesis, and a band.
—LEWIS LAPHAM

The only prize much cared for by the powerful is power. The
prize of the general is not a bigger tent, but command.
—OLIVER WENDELL HOLMES, JR.

The property of power is to protect.
—BLAISE PASCAL

The problem of power is how to achieve its responsible use
rather than its irresponsible and indulgent use—of how to get
men of power to live *for the public rather than off the public.*
—ROBERT F. KENNEDY

You only have power over people as long as you don't take *everything* away from them. But when you've robbed a man of *everything* he's no longer in your power—he's free again.
—Alexander I. Solzhenitsyn

God is usually on the side of big squadrons against little ones.
—Roger De Bussy-Rabutin

GOALS

All animals except man know that the ultimate goal of life is to enjoy it.
—Samuel Butler

Why should I deem myself to be a chisel, when I could be the artist?
—J.C.F. von Schiller

Happy the man who knows his duties!
—Christian Furchtegott Gellert

I seek the utmost pleasure and the least pain.
—Plautus

There are two things to aim at in life: first, to get what you want, and after that to enjoy it. Only the wisest of mankind achieve the second.
—Logan Pearsall Smith

If you would hit the mark, you must aim a little above it;
every arrow that flies feels the attraction of earth.
—Henry Wadsworth Longfellow

Let us live, while we are alive!
—Johann von Goethe

Enjoyment is not a goal, it is a feeling that
accompanies important ongoing activity.
—Paul Goodman

Life is about enjoying yourself and having a good time.
—CHER

All men seek one goal: success or happiness.
—ARISTOTLE

I believe half the unhappiness in life comes from
people being afraid to go straight at things.
—WILLIAM J. LOCKE

She's the kind of girl who climbed the ladder of success, wrong by wrong.
—MAE WEST

For my part, I travel not to go anywhere, but to go. I
travel for travel's sake. The great affair is to move.
—ROBERT LOUIS STEVENSON

Pleasure is the only thing to live for. Nothing ages like happiness.
—OSCAR WILDE

But man is not made for defeat. A man can be destroyed but not defeated.
—ERNEST HEMINGWAY

Never mind your happiness; do your duty.
—WILL DURANT

Man's reach should exceed his grasp, or what's a heaven for?
—ROBERT BROWNING

I never took a position we were going to be a good ball club. I
took the position we were going to be a *winning* ball club.
—RED AUERBACH

Before you begin a thing, remind yourself that difficulties and
delays quite impossible to foresee are ahead. . . . You can only
see one thing clearly and that is your goal. Form a mental
vision of that and cling to it through thick and thin.
—KATHLEEN NORRIS

Life exists for the love of music or beautiful things.
—G.K. CHESTERTON

Use your health, even to the point of wearing it out. That is what it
is for. Spend all you have before you die; do not outlive yourself.
—George Bernard Shaw

When you reach for the stars, you may not quite get one,
but you won't come up with a handful of mud, either.
—Leo Burnett

Unless in one thing or another we are straining toward
perfection, we have forfeited our manhood.
—Stephen McKenna

Happiness is the overcoming of not unknown
obstacles toward a known goal.
—L. Ron Hubbard

Aim at heaven and you get earth thrown in;
aim at earth and you get neither.
—C.S. Lewis

We are all in the gutter, but some of us are looking at the stars.
—Oscar Wilde

Happiness is essentially a state of going somewhere, wholeheartedly,
one—directionally, without regret or reservation.
—William H. Sheldon

The man who succeeds above his fellows is the one who
early in life discerns his object and toward that object
habitually directs his powers. Even genius itself is but
fine observation strengthened by fixity of purpose.
—Edward Bulwer-Lytton

There is only one meaning of life: the act of living itself.
—Erich Fromm

Whatever course you have chosen for yourself, it will not be a chore
but an adventure if you bring to it a sense of the glory of striving,
if your sights are set far above the merely secure and mediocre.
—David Sarnoff

Aim at perfection in everything, though in most things it is unattainable. However they who aim at it, and persevere, will come much nearer to it than those whose laziness and despondency make them give it up as unattainable.
—Lord Chesterfield

A man's happiness: to do the things proper to man.
—Marcus Aurelius

The main obligation is to amuse yourself.
—S.J. Perelman

One may miss the mark by aiming too high, as too low.
—Thomas Fuller

Happiness is not the end of life; character is.
—Henry Ward Beecher

The only true happiness comes from squandering ourselves for a purpose.
—William Cowper

Shoot for the moon. Even if you miss it, you will land among the stars.
—Les Brown

Aim at the sun, and you may not reach it; but your arrow will fly far higher than if aimed at an object on a level with yourself.
—J. Hawes

Once you say you're going to settle for second, that's what happens to you.
—John F. Kennedy

I take it as a prime cause of the present confusion of society that it is too sickly and too doubtful to use pleasure as a test of value.
—Rebecca West

Life's objective is life itself.
—Johann von Goethe

We aim above the mark to hit the mark. Every act
hath some falsehood or exaggeration in it.
—Ralph Waldo Emerson

Life is a petty thing unless it is moved by the
indomitable urge to extend its boundaries.
—José Ortega y Gasset

This is true joy of life—being used for a purpose that is recognized
by yourself as a mighty one . . . instead of being a feverish,
selfish little clod of ailments and grievances, complaining that
the world will not devote itself to making you happy.
—George Bernard Shaw

Since we must all die sooner or later, let us enjoy life while we can!
—Otoma no Tabito

Never undertake anything for which you wouldn't
have the courage to ask the blessings of heaven.
—Georg Christoph Lichtenberg

The tragedy of life doesn't lie in not reaching your goal. The
tragedy lies in having no goal to reach. It isn't a calamity to
die with dreams unfulfilled, but it is a calamity not to dream.
It is not disgrace to reach the stars, but it is a disgrace to have
no stars to reach for. Not failure, but low aim, is a sin.
—Benjamin Mays

I take it that what all men are really after is some
form of, perhaps only some formula of, peace.
—James Conrad

If one advances confidently in the direction of his dreams,
and endeavors to live the life which he has imagined, he will
meet with a success unexpected in common hours.
—Henry David Thoreau

The goal of all civilization, all religious thought, and all that
sort of thing is simply to have a good time. But man gets
so solemn over the process that he forgets the end.
—Don Marquis

Too low they build, who build beneath the stars.
—EDWARD YOUNG

He who never sacrificed a present to a future good, or a personal to a general one, can speak of happiness only as the blind speak of color.
—HORACE MANN

Reach high, for stars lie hidden in your soul. Dream deep, for every dream precedes the goal.
—PAMELA VAULL STARR

The business of life is to enjoy oneself; everything else is a mockery.
—NORMAN DOUGLAS

Life is an end in itself, and the only question as to whether it is worth living is whether you have had enough of it.
—OLIVER WENDELL HOLMES, JR.

What our deepest self craves is not mere enjoyment, but some supreme purpose that will enlist all our powers and give unity and direction to our life.
—HENRY J. GOLDING

The happiest excitement in life is to be convinced that one is fighting for all one is worth on behalf of some clearly seen and deeply felt good.
—RUTH BENEDICT

The one thing worth living for is to keep one's soul pure.
—MARCUS AURELIUS

Having a goal is a state of happiness.
—E.J. BARTEK

A person can grow only as much as his horizon allows.
—JOHN POWELL

A goal is a dream with a deadline.
—NAPOLEON HILL

The proper function of man is to live—not to exist.
—JACK LONDON

The very first condition of lasting happiness is that a life should
be full of purpose, aiming at something outside self.
—Hugh Black

Life has . . . taught me not to expect success to be the inevitable
result of my endeavors. She taught me to seek sustenance
from the endeavor itself, but to leave the result to God.
—Alan Paton

Far away in the sunshine are my highest inspirations. I
many not reach them, but I can look up and see the beauty,
believe in them and try to follow where they lead.
—Louisa May Alcott

Happiness is the natural flower of duty.
—Phillips Brooks

The secret of living is to find . . . the pivot of a concept
on which you can make your stand.
—Luigi Pirandello

Much pleasure and little grief is every man's desire.
—Spanish proverb

Happiness lies in the joy of achievement and the thrill of creative effort.
—Franklin Delano Roosevelt

Man can only receive what he sees himself receiving.
—Florence Scovel Shinn

I think the purpose of life is to be useful, to be responsible, to be
honorable, to be compassionate. It is, after all, to matter: to count, to
stand for something, to have made some difference that you lived at all.
—Leo C. Rosten

Human happiness and moral duty are inseparably connected.
—George Washington

When we . . . devote ourselves to the strict and unsparing
performance of duty, then happiness comes of itself.
—Wilhelm von Humboldt

The great business of life is to be, to do, to do without, and to depart.
—JOHN MORLEY

The only true happiness comes from
squandering ourselves for a purpose.
—JOHN MASON BROWN

Seek happiness for its own sake, and you will not find it; seek for duty,
and happiness will follow, as the shadow comes with the sunshine.
—TYRON EDWARDS

There is more to life than just existing and having a pleasant time.
—J.C.F. VON SCHILLER

True happiness, we are told, consists in getting out of one's
self, but the point is not only to get out; you must stay out,
and to stay out, you must have some absorbing errand.
—HENRY JAMES

Diplomacy is to do and say the nastiest thing in the nicest way.
—ISAAC GOLDBERG

The man who fails because he aims astray, or because
he does not aim at all, is to be found everywhere.
—FRANK SWINNERTON

A man's worth is no greater than the worth of his ambitions.
—MARCUS AURELIUS

The only ones among you who will be really happy are
those who will have sought and found how to serve.
—ALBERT SCHWEITZER

The greatest use of life is to spend it for something that will outlast it.
—WILLIAM JAMES

A determinate purpose of life, and steady adhesion to it through
all disadvantages, are indispensable conditions of success.
—WILLIAM M. PUNSHON

The secret of success is constancy to purpose.
—BENJAMIN FRANKLIN

If you break 100, watch your golf. If you break
eighty, watch your business.
—WALTER WINCHELL

Great is the road I climb, but ... the garland offered
by an easier effort is not worth the gathering.
—PROPERTIUS

I am searching for that which every man seeks—peace and rest.
—DANTE ALIGHIERI

The full-grown modern human being ... is conscious of touching
the highest pinnacle of fulfillment ... when he is consumed in
the service of an idea, in the conquest of the goal pursued.
—R. BRIFFAULT

The true object of human life is play.
—G.K. CHESTERTON

SUCCESS

Vacillating people seldom succeed. They seldom win the solid respect of
their fellows. Successful men and women are very careful in reaching
decisions, and very persistent and determined in action thereafter.
—L.G. ELLIOTT

Many of the most successful men I have known have never grown
up. They have retained bubbling-over boyishness. They have
relished wit, they have indulged in humor. They have not allowed
"dignity" to depress them into moroseness. Youthfulness of spirit is
the twin brother of optimism, and optimism is the stuff of which
American business success is fashioned. Resist growing up!
—B.C. FORBES

I'd rather be a failure at something I love than
a success at something I hate.
—GEORGE BURNS

We would accomplish many more things if we
did not think of them as impossible.
—C. Malesherbez

We are at our very best, and we are happiest, when we are fully engaged
in work we enjoy on the journey toward the goal we've established
for ourselves. It gives meaning to our time off and comfort to our
sleep. It makes everything else in life so wonderful, so worthwhile.
—Earl Nightingale

The penalty of success is to be bored by people who used to snub you.
—Nancy Astor

Morale is the greatest single factor in successful wars.
—Dwight D. Eisenhower

Without ambition one starts nothing. Without work one finishes
nothing. The prize will not be sent to you. As to methods there may
be a million and then some, but the principles are few. The man who
grasps principles can successfully select his own methods. The man
who tries methods, ignoring principles, is sure to have trouble.
—Ralph Waldo Emerson

The true perfection of man lies, not in what man has, but in what man is.
—Oscar Wilde

I've been polite and I've always shown up. Somebody
asked me if I had any advice for young people
entering the business. I said: "Yeah, show up."
—Tom T. Hall

Social success is the infinite capacity for being bored.
—Anon

Someone's always saying, "It's not whether you win or
lose," but if you feel that way, you're as good as dead.
—James Caan

The toughest thing about success is that you've
got to keep on being a success.
—Irving Berlin

A successful man is he who receives a great deal from his fellow men, usually incomparably more than corresponds to his service to them. The value of a man, however, should be seen in what he gives, and not in what he is able to receive.
—ALBERT EINSTEIN

No matter how much a man can do, no matter how engaging his personality may be, he will not advance far in business if he cannot work through others.
—JOHN CRAIG

The way to rise is to obey and please.
—BEN JOHNSON

The ability to form friendships, to make people believe in you and trust you is one of the few absolutely fundamental qualities of success. Selling, buying, negotiating are so much smoother and easier when the parties enjoy each other's confidence. The young man who can make friends quickly will find that he will glide, instead of stumble, through life.
—JOHN J. MCGUIRK

To burn always with this hard, gemlike flame, to maintain this ecstasy, is success in life.
—WALTER PATER

Success is to be measured not so much by the position that one has reached in life as by the obstacles which he has overcome.
—BOOKER T. WASHINGTON

Sometimes success is due less to ability than to zeal.
—CHARLES BUXTON

Thirteen virtues necessary for true success: temperance, silence, order, resolution, frugality, industry, sincerity, justice, moderation, cleanliness, tranquility, chastity, and humility.
—BENJAMIN FRANKLIN

Skill is fine, and genius is splendid, but the right contacts are more valuable than either.
—SIR ARCHIBALD MCINDOE

Success has always been easy to measure. It is the distance
between one's origins and one's final achievement.
—Michael Korda

Success follows doing what you want to do.
There is no other way to be successful.
—Malcolm Forbes

Success to me is having ten honeydew melons
and eating only the top half of each one.
—Barbra Streisand

To bring one's self to a frame of mind and to the proper
energy to accomplish things that require plain hard work
continuously is the one big battle that everyone has. When
this battle is won for all time, then everything is easy.
—Thomas A. Buckner

There is a passion for perfection which you rarely see fully developed; but
you may note this fact, that in successful lives it is never wholly lacking.
—Bliss Carman

A wise man will make more opportunities than he finds.
—Francis Bacon

Whatever your grade or position, if you know how and
when to speak, and when to remain silent, your chances
of real success are proportionately increased.
—Ralph C. Smedley

There are no secrets to success. It is the result of
preparation, hard work, learning from failure.
—General Colin L. Powell

Enthusiasm for one's goal lessens the
disagreeableness of working toward it.
—Thomas Eakins

I have fought a good fight, I have finished my course, I have kept the faith.
—2 Tm. 4:7

Always bear in mind that your own resolution to success
is more important than any other one thing.
—Abraham Lincoln

You should invest in a business that even a fool
can run, because someday a fool will.
—Warren Buffet

Faith that the thing can be done is essential to any great achievement.
—Thomas N. Carruther

We succeed in enterprises which demand the positive qualities we
possess, but we excel in those which can also make use of our defects.
—Alexis de Tocqueville

I cannot give you the formula for success, but I can give you
the formula for failure, which is—try to please everybody.
—Herbert Bayard Swope

Many people have the ambition to succeed; they may even
have a special aptitude for their job. And yet they do not
move ahead. Why? Perhaps they think that since they can
master the job, there is no need to master themselves.
—John Stevenson

A first rate soup is better than a second rate painting.
—Abraham Maslow

If, after all, men cannot always make history have a meaning,
they can always act so that their own lives have one.
—Albert Camus

Find a need and fill it.
—Ruth Stafford Peale

If you have the will to win, you have achieved half your
success; if you don't, you have achieved half your failure.
—David V.A. Ambrose

Four steps to achievement: plan purposefully, prepare
prayerfully, proceed positively, pursue persistently.
—William A. Ward

We can accomplish almost anything within our
ability if we but think that we can!
—GEORGE MATTHEW ADAMS

Optimism is essential to achievement and it is also the
foundation of courage and of true progress.
—NICHOLAS MURRAY BUTLER

There is only one success—to be able to spend your life in your own way.
—CHRISTOPHER MORLEY

The real difference between men is energy.
—THOMAS FULLER

Success is living up to your potential. That's all. Wake up with a
smile and go after life. . . . Live it, enjoy it, taste it, smell it, feel it.
—JOE KAPP

How can they say my life is not a success? Have I not for more
than sixty years got enough to eat and escaped being eaten?
—LOGAN PEARSALL SMITH

Success, which is something so simple in the end, is made
up of thousands of things, we never fully know what.
—RAINER MARIA RILKE

No man will succeed unless he is ready to face and overcome
difficulties and prepared to assume responsibilities.
—WILLIAM J.H. BOETCKER

The world belongs to the energetic.
—RALPH WALDO EMERSON

The art of dealing with people is the foremost secret of successful
men. A man's success in handling people is the very yardstick
by which the outcome of his whole life's work is measured.
—PAUL C. PACKE

The wise man puts all his eggs in one basket and watches the basket.
—ANDREW CARNEGIE

No bird soars too high, if he soars with his own wings.
—WILLIAM BLAKE

The conditions of conquest are always easy. We have but to toil
awhile, endure awhile, believe always, and never turn back.
—MARCUS ANNAEUS SENECA

The real secret of success is enthusiasm. Yes, more than
enthusiasm, I would say excitement. I like to see men get excited.
When they get excited, they make a success of their lives.
—WALTER CHRYSLER

Every man is the architect of his own fortune.
—SALLUST

Success is blocked by concentrating on it and planning for
it.... Success is shy—it won't come out while you're watching.
—TENNESSEE WILLIAMS

The successful person is the individual who forms the habit
of doing what the failing person doesn't like to do.
—DONALD RIGGS

Put your heart, mind, intellect and soul even to your
smallest acts. This is the secret of success.
—SWAMI SIVANANDA

Flaming enthusiasm, backed up by horse sense and persistence,
is the quality that most frequently makes for success.
—DALE CARNEGIE

Life is a succession of moments. To live each one is to succeed.
—CORITA KENT

Do it big or stay in bed.
—LARRY KELLY

A man can do only what he can do. But if he does that each
day he can sleep at night and do it again the next day.
—ALBERT SCHWEITZER

The very first step towards success in any
occupation is to become interested in it.
—Sir William Osler

It takes time to succeed because success is merely the
natural reward for taking time to do anything well.
—Joseph Ross

The will to conquer is the first condition of victory.
—Marshal Ferdinand Foch

Three outstanding qualities make for success: judgement,
industry, health. And the greatest of these is judgement.
—William Maxwell Aitken, Lord Beaverbrook

It is fatal to enter any war without the will to win it.
—General Douglas MacArthur

It is impossible to win the great prizes of life without running risks.
—Theodore Roosevelt

Every man is enthusiastic at times. One man has enthusiasm for
thirty minutes, another man has it for thirty days. But it is the
man who has it for thirty years who makes a success in life.
—Edward B. Butler

Success has nothing to do with what you gain in life or
accomplish for yourself. It's what you do for others.
—Danny Thomas

Nature magically suits a man to his fortunes, by
making them the fruit of his character.
—Ralph Waldo Emerson

Mighty rivers can easily be leaped at their source.
—Publilius Syrus

Our business in life is not to get ahead of others but to get ahead
of ourselves—to break our own records, to outstrip our yesterdays
by our today, to do our work with more force than ever before.
—Steward B. Johnson

I'd rather be a lamppost in Chicago than a millionaire in any other city.
—WILLIAM A. HULBERT

The brave man carves out his fortune, and every
man is the sum of his own works.
—MIGUEL DE CERVANTES

We may fail of our happiness, strive we ever so bravely,
but we are less likely to fail if we measure with
judgement our chances and our capabilities.
—AGNES REPPLIER

The man who will use his skill and constructive imagination
to see how much he can give for a dollar, instead of how
little he can give for a dollar, is bound to succeed.
—HENRY FORD

No one reaches a high position without daring.
—PUBLILIUS SYRUS

Nothing arouses ambition so much in the heart
as the trumpet-clang of another's fame.
—BALTASAR GRACIAN

I studied the lives of great men and famous women; and I
found that the men and women who got to the top were
those who did the jobs they had in hand, with everything
they had of energy and enthusiasm and hard work.
—HARRY S TRUMAN

On earth we have nothing to do with success or
results, but only with being true to God, and for God.
Defeat in doing right is nevertheless victory.
—FREDERICK W. ROBERTSON

Nature gave men two ends—one to sit on, and one to
think with. Ever since then man's success or failure
has been dependent on the one he used most.
—GEORGE R. KIRKPATRICK

Who never climbed high never fell low.
—THOMAS FULLER

Man is still responsible.... His success lies not with the stars, but with himself. He must carry on the fight of self-correction and discipline.
—FRANK CURTIS WILLIAMS

Great deeds are usually wrought at great risks.
—HERODOTUS

My success is measured by my willingness to keep trying.
—ANON

If you limit your actions in life to things that nobody can possibly find fault with, you will not do much.
—CHARLES LUTWIDGE DODGSON

Starting out to make money is the greatest mistake in life. Do what you feel you have a flair for doing, and if you are good enough at it, the money will come.
—GREER GARSON

Under normal periods, any man's success hinges about five percent on what others do for him and 95 percent on what he does.
—JAMES A. WORSHAM

The reward of a thing well done is to have done it.
—RALPH WALDO EMERSON

Be wise;
Soar not too high to fall;
But stoop to rise.
—PHILIP MASSINGER

We can't all be heroes because someone has to sit on the curb and clap as they go by.
—WILL ROGERS

Success is peace of mind, which is a direct result of knowing you did your best to become the best that you are capable of becoming.
—JOHN WOODEN

The men who have done big things are those who
were not afraid to attempt big things, who were not
afraid to risk failure in order to gain success.
—B.C. Forbes

Success is that old ABC—Ability, Breaks and Courage.
—Charles Luckman

Don't be afraid to take a big step if one is indicated.
You can't cross a chasm in two small jumps.
—David Lloyd George

If the risk-reward ratio is right, you can make big money buying trouble.
—Anon

Only those who dare to fail greatly can ever achieve greatly.
—Robert F. Kennedy

Whatever you are by nature, keep to it; never desert your own line
of talent. Be what nature intended you for, and you will succeed; be
anything else and you will be ten thousand times worse than nothing.
—Sydney Smith

The heights by great men reached and kept
Were not attained by sudden flight,
But they, while their companions slept,
Were toiling upward in the night.
—Henry Wadsworth Longfellow

Success is getting what you want; happiness is wanting what you get.
—Anon

What is the recipe for successful achievement? To my mind
there are just four essential ingredients: Choose a career
you love. . . . Give it the best there is in you. . . . Seize your
opportunities. . . . And be a member of the team.
—Benjamin F. Fairless

Nothing ventured, nothing gained.
—Anon

Nothing great was ever achieved without enthusiasm.
—Ralph Waldo Emerson

Hindsight is always twenty-twenty.
—Billy Wilder

Cadillacs are down at the end of the bat.
—Ralph Kiner, when asked why he didn't choke up and hit for average

Destiny is not a matter of chance, it is a matter of choice; it is
not a thing to be waited for, it is a thing to be achieved.
—William J. Bryan

The most important single ingredient in the formula of
success is knowing how to get along with people.
—Theodore Roosevelt

The method of the enterprising is to plan with
audacity and execute with vigor.
—Christian Bovee

What isn't tried won't work.
—Claude McDonald

If you want to succeed, you must make your own opportunities as you go.
—John B. Gough

The man who has done his level best, and who is
conscious that he has done his best, is a success, even
though the world may write him down a failure.
—B.C. Forbes

You have reached the pinnacle of success as soon as you
become uninterested in money, compliments, or publicity.
—Thomas Wolfe

He that is overcautious will accomplish little.
—J.C.F. von Schiller

Self-trust is the first secret of success.
—Ralph Waldo Emerson

Thou shalt ever joy at eventide if thou spend the day fruitfully.
—Thomas A Kempis

The secret of every man who has ever been successful lies in the fact that he formed the bait of doing those things that failures don't like to do.
—A. Jackson King

The measure of an enthusiasm must be taken between interesting events. It is between bites that the lukewarm angler loses heart.
—Edwin Way Teale

Who dares nothing, need hope for nothing.
—J.C.F. von Schiller

Ask yourself the secret of *your* success. Listen to your answer, and practice it.
—Richard Bach

You can't catch trout with dry breeches.
—Spanish proverb

The secret of success in life is for a man to be ready for his opportunity when it comes.
—Benjamin Disraeli

He has achieved success who has lived well, laughed often, and loved much; who has enjoyed the trust of pure women, the respect of intelligent men and the love of little children; who has filled his niche and accomplished his task; who has left the world better than he found it, whether by an improved poppy, a perfect poem, or a rescued soul; who has never lacked appreciation of earth's beauty or failed to express it; who has always looked for the best in others and and given them the best he had; whose life was an inspiration; whose memory is a benediction.
—Bessie A. Stanley

The ambitious climbs high and perilous stairs and never cares how to come down; the desire of rising hath swallowed up his fear of a fall.
—Thomas Adams

What a man accomplishes in a day depends upon the way in
which he approaches his tasks. When we accept tough jobs
as a challenge to our ability and wade into them with joy
and enthusiasm, miracles can happen. When we do our work
with a dynamic conquering spirit, we get things done.
—ARLAND GILBERT

Don't take anyone else's definition of success as
your own. (This is easier said than done.)
—JACQUELINE BRISKIN

Always aim for achievement, and forget about success.
—HELEN HAYES

When you feel how depressingly slowly you climb,
it's well to remember that Things Take Time.
—PIET HEIN

Progress always involves risks. You can't steal
second base and keep your foot on first.
—FREDERICK B. WILCOX

The people who get on in this world are the people who get up and look
for the circumstances they want, and, if they can't find them, make them.
—GEORGE BERNARD SHAW

Pray that success will not come any faster than you are able to endure it.
—ELBERT HUBBARD

To live only for some future goal is shallow. It's the sides
of the mountain that sustain life, not the top.
—ROBERT M. PIRSIG

If a man has a talent and cannot use it, he has failed. If he has a talent
and uses only half of it, he has partly failed. If he has a talent and
learns somehow to use the whole of it, he has gloriously succeeded,
and won a satisfaction and a triumph few men ever know.
—THOMAS WOLFE

I don't think about risks much. I just do what I
want to do. If you gotta go, you gotta go.
—MISS LILLIAN CARTER

To be ambitious for wealth, and yet always expecting to be poor; to be always doubting your ability to get what you long for, is like trying to reach east by traveling west. There is no philosophy which will help man to succeed when he is always doubting his ability to do so, and thus attracting failure. No matter how hard you work for success, if your thought is saturated with the fear of failure, it will kill your efforts, neutralize your endeavors and make success impossible.
—CHARLES BAUDOUIN

The method of the enterprising is to plan with audacity and execute with vigor.
—CHRISTIAN BOVEE

All great reforms require one to dare a lot to win a little.
—WILLIAM L. O'NEILL

If you have a good name, if you are right more often than you are wrong, if your children respect you, if your grandchildren are glad to see you, if your friends can count on you and you can count on them in time of trouble, if you can face your God and say "I have done my best," then you are a success.
—ANN LANDERS

To get profit without risk, experience without danger and reward without work is as impossible as it is to live without being born.
—A.P. GOUTHEY

The key to success isn't much good until one discovers the right lock to insert it in.
—TEHYI HSIEH

It takes twenty years to make an overnight success.
—EDDIE CANTOR

A man can succeed at almost anything for which he has unlimited enthusiasm.
—CHARLES M. SCHWAB

Success means we go to sleep at night knowing that our talents and abilities were used in a way that served others.
—MARIANNE WILLIAMSON

If you're not happy every morning when you get up, leave
for work, or start to work at home, if you're not enthusiastic
about doing that, you're not going to be successful.
—DONALD M. KENDALL

A double-minded man is unstable in all his ways.... A
determinate purpose in life and a steady adhesion to it through
all disadvantages are indispensable conditions of success.
—WILLIAM M. PUNSHION

Behold the turtle. He makes progress only when he sticks his neck out.
—JAMES BRYANT CONANT

Clothes make the man. Naked people have little or no influence in society.
—MARK TWAIN

A minute's success pays the failure of years.
—ROBERT BROWNING

You can't expect to hit the jackpot if you don't
put a few nickels in the machine.
—FLIP WILSON

If you've had a good time playing the game,
you're a winner even if you lose.
—MALCOLM FORBES

Success is a journey, not a destination.
—BEN SWEETLAND

In the midst of winter, I finallly learned that
there was in me an invincible summer.
—ALBERT CAMUS

With method and logic one can accomplish anything.
—AGATHA CHRISTIE

Despite the success cult, men are most deeply moved not
by the reaching of the goal, but by the grandness of effort
involved in getting there—or failing to get there.
—MAX LERNER

The reward of a thing well done is to have done it.
—Ralph Waldo Emerson

Every noble acquisition is attended with its risks; he who fears
to encounter the one must not expect to obtain the other.
—Pietro Metastasio

Some men succeed by what they know; some by
what they do; and a few by what they are.
—Elbert Hubbard

The ability to convert ideas to things is the secret of outward success.
—Henry Ward Beecher

Success only breeds a new goal.
—Bette Davis

Success is due less to ability than to zeal.
—Charles Buxton

A strong passion for any object will ensure success, for
the desire of the end will point out the means.
—William Hazlitt

The ability to concentrate and to use your time well is everything if you
want to succeed in business—or almost anywhere else, for that matter.
—Lee Iacocca

Before you can win a game, you have to not lose it.
—Chuck Noll

Your best shot at happiness, self-worth and personal
satisfaction—the things that constitute real success—is not
in earning as much as you can but in performing as well
as you can something that you consider worthwhile.
—William Raspberry

ENTHUSIASM

What is man but his passion?
—Robert Penn Warren

If we resist our passions, it is more from their
weakness than from our strength.
—Francois de La Rochefoucauld

Creativity is a natural extension of our enthusiasm.
—Earl Nightingale

I long to accomplish a great and noble task, but it is my chief duty
to acomplish humble tasks as though they were great and noble.
—Helen Keller

The real difference between men is energy.
—Thomas Fuller

Nothing is so contagious as enthusiasm; it moves stones,
it charms brutes. Enthusiasm is the genius of sincerity,
and truth accomplishes no victories without it.
—Edward Bulwer-Lytton

You can't sweep other people off their feet, if
you can't be swept off your own.
—Clarence Day

Zest is the secret of all beauty. There is no
beauty that is attractive without zest.
—Christian Dior

Our passions are ourselves.
—Anatole France

The longer I live, the more certain I am that enthusiasm
is the little recognized key to success.
—Frederick Williamson

Don't Sell the Steak—Sell the Sizzle!
—Elmer Wheeler

Life is enthusiasm, zest.
—Sir Lawrence Oliver

Exuberance is beauty.
—William Blake

Every man without passions has within him no
principle of action, nor motive to act.
—Claude Helvetius

What counts is not necessarily the size of the dog in
the fight, but the size of the fight in the dog.
—Dwight D. Eisenhower

The great man is he who does not lose his childlike heart.
—Mencius

Enthusiasm is the most important thing in life.
—Tennessee Williams

Passion, though a bad regulator, is a powerful spring.
—Ralph Waldo Emerson

Enthusiasm can only be aroused by two things: first, an ideal
which takes the imagination by storm, and second, a definite,
intelligible plan for carrying that ideal into practice.
—Arnold Toynbee

If you aren't fired with enthusiasm, you will be fired with enthusiasm.
—Vince Lombardi

The world belongs to the energetic.
—Ralph Waldo Emerson

The only thing that keeps a man going is energy.
And what is energy but liking life?
—Louis Auchincloss

Let us go singing as far as we go; the road will be less tedious.
—Virgil

Enthusiasm is life.
—Paul Scofield

The will to conquer is the first condition of victory.
—Marshal Ferdinand Foch

Man never rises to great truths without enthusiasm.
—Vauvenargues

A man can succeed at almost anything for
which he has unlimited enthusiasm.
—Charles M. Schwab

And whatsoever ye do, do it heartily.
—Col. 3:23

You will do foolish things, but do them with enthusiasm.
—Colette

We would accomplish many more things if we
did not think of them as impossible.
—C. Malesherbez

Most great men and women are not perfectly rounded in
their personalities, but are instead people whose one driving
enthusiasm is so great it makes their faults seem insignificant.
—Charles A. Cerami

Without passion man is a mere latent force and possibility, like the flint
which awaits the shock of the iron before it can give forth its spark.
—Henri Frederic Amiel

Enthusiasm signifies God in us.
—Madame de Stael

Whatever you attempt, go at it with spirit. Put some in!
—David Starr Jordan

Give me a man who sings at his work.
—Thomas Carlyle

The real secret of success is enthusiasm. Yes, more than
enthusiasm, I would say excitement. I like to see men get excited.
When they get excited they make a success of their lives.
—WALTER CHRYSLER

Every man is enthusiastic at times. One man has enthusiasm for
thirty minutes, another man has it for thirty days. But it is the
man who has it for thirty years who makes a success in life.
—EDWARD B. BUTLER

Sometimes success is due less to ability than to zeal.
—CHARLES BUXTON

All passions exaggerate; it is because they do that they are passions.
—NICOLAS DE CHAMFORT

People who never get carried away should be.
—MALCOLM FORBES

Only passions, great passions, can elevate the soul to great things.
—DENIS DIDEROT

There is nothing greater than enthusiasm.
—HENRY MOORE

Flaming enthusiasm, backed up by horse sense and persistence,
is the quality that most frequently makes for success.
—DALE CARNEGIE

Enthusiasm is the most beautiful word on earth.
—CHRISTIAN MORGENSTERN

The passions are the only orators which always persuade.
—FRANCOIS DE LA ROCHEFOUCAULD

Vitality! That's the pursuit of life, isn't it?
—KATHARINE HEPBURN

If you're not happy every morning when you get up, leave
for work, or start to work at home—if you're not enthusiastic
about doing that, you're not going to be successful.
—DONALD M. KENDALL

Wars may be fought with weapons, but they are won by men. It is the
spirit of men who follow and of the man who leads that gains the victory.
—GENERAL GEORGE S. PATTON

The measure of an enthusiasm must be taken between interesting
events. It is between bites that the lukewarm angler loses heart.
—EDWIN WAY TEALE

Energy will do anything that can be done in this world.
—JOHANN VON GOETHE

What a man knows only through feeling can be
explained only through enthusiasm.
—JOSEPH JOUBERT

To bring one's self to a frame of mind and to the proper
energy to accomplish things that require plain hard work
continuously is the one big battle that everyone has. When
this battle is won for all time, then everything is easy.
—THOMAS A. BUCKNER

What hunger is in relation to food, zest is in relation to life.
—BERTRAND RUSSELL

Nothing great in the world has been accomplished without passion.
—GEORGE HEGEL

It is energy, the central element of which is will, that produces the
miracles of enthusiasm in all ages. It is the mainspring of what is
called force of character and the sustaining power of all great action.
—SAMUEL SMILES

Energy and persistence conquer all things.
—BENJAMIN FRANKLIN

Always bear in mind that your own resolution to success
is more important than any other one thing.
—ABRAHAM LINCOLN

What a man accomplishes in a day depends upon the way in
which he approaches his tasks. When we accept tough jobs
as a challenge to our ability and wade into them with joy
and enthusiasm, miracles can happen. When we do our work
with a dynamic, conquering spirit, we get things done.
—ARLAND GILBERT

Faith that the thing can be done is essential to any great achievement.
—THOMAS N. CARRUTHER

Vigor is contagious, and whatever makes us either think or feel
strongly adds to our power and enlarges our field of action.
—RALPH WALDO EMERSON

No one keeps up his enthusiasm automatically. Enthusiasm
must be nourished with new actions, new aspirations, new
efforts, new vision. Compete with yourself; set your teeth and
dive into the job of breaking your own record. It is one's own
fault if his enthusiasm is gone; he has failed to feed it.
—PAPYRUS

If you have the will to win, you have achieved half your
success; if you don't, you have achieved half your failure.
—DAVID V.A. AMBROSE

In things pertaining to enthusiasm, no man is sane who
does not know how to be insane on proper occasions.
—HENRY WARD BEECHER

We can accomplish almost anything within our
ability if we but think that we can!
—GEORGE MATTHEW ADAMS

Optimism is essential to achievement and it is also the
foundation of courage and of true progress.
—NICHOLAS MURRAY BUTLER

Whatever course you have chosen for yourself, it will not be a chore
but an adventure if you bring to it a sense of the glory of striving,
if your sights are set far above the merely secure and mediocre.
—DAVID SARNOFF

I prefer the errors of enthusiasm to the indifference of wisdom.
—ANATOLE FRANCE

Be still when you have nothing to say; when genuine passion
moves you, say what you've got to say, and say it *hot*.
—D.H. LAWRENCE

My enthusiasms . . . constitute my reserves, my
unexploited resources, perhaps my future.
—E.M. CIORAN

Let a man in a garret burn with enough intensity,
and he will set fire to the world.
—ANTOINE DE SAINT-EXUPERY

There is a passion for perfection which you rarely see fully
developed, but . . . in successful lives it is never wholly lacking.
—BLISS CARMAN

None are so old as those who have outlived enthusiasm.
—HENRY DAVID THOREAU

Years wrinkle the face, but to give up enthusiasm wrinkles the soul.
—WATTERSON LOWE

Earnestness and sincereness are synonymous.
—CORITA KENT

Morale is the greatest single factor in successful wars.
—DWIGHT D. EISENHOWER

Enthusiasm for one's goal to lessens the
disagreeableness of working toward it.
—THOMAS EAKINS

Success is due less to ability than to zeal.
—CHARLES BUXTON

The difference between one man and another
is not mere ability ... it is energy.
—THOMAS ARNOLD

Human nature, if it healthy, demands excitement; and if it does not
obtain its thrilling excitement in the right way, it will seek it in the
wrong. God never makes bloodless stoics; He makes no passionless saints.
—OSWALD CHAMBERS

The same reason makes a man a religious enthusiast
that makes a man an enthusiast in any other way ... an
uncomfortable mind in an uncomfortable body.
—WILLIAM HAZLITT

When his enthusiasm goes, he's through as a player.
—PETE ROSE

The first requisite of a good citizen in this Republic of ours is
that he shall be able and willing to pull his his weight.
—THEODORE ROOSEVELT

The method of the enterprising is to plan with
audacity and execute with vigor.
—CHRISTIAN BOVEE

Enthusiasm is nothing more or less than faith in action.
—HENRY CHESTER

A strong passion for any object will ensure success, for
the desire of the end will point out the means.
—WILLIAM HAZLITT

Winning isn't everything. *Wanting* to win is.
—CATFISH HUNTER

Enthusiasm moves the world.
—J. BALFOUR

No one grows old by living, only by losing interest in living.
—MARIE BEYNON RAY

Opposition inflames the enthusiast, never converts him.
—J.C.F. VON SCHILLER

Zeal will do more than knowledge.
—WILLIAM HAZLITT

Knowledge is power, but enthusiasm pulls the switch.
—IVERN BALL

All we need to make us really happy is
something to be enthusiastic about.
—CHARLES KINGSLEY

Wake up with a smile and go after life.... Live
it, enjoy it, taste it, smell it, feel it.
—JOE KNAPP

It is the greatest shot of adrenaline to be doing what you've wanted
to do so badly. You almost feel like you could fly without the plane.
—CHARLES LINDBERGH

Through zeal, knowledge is gotten; through
lack of zeal, knowledge is lost.
—BUDDA

Give the lady what she wants!
—MARSHALL FIELD

Be intensely in earnest. Enthusiasm invites enthusiasm.
—RUSSELL H. CONWELL

A man can be short and dumpy and getting bald
but if he has fire, women will like him.
—MAE WEST

He did it with all his heart, and prospered.
—2 CHR. 31:21

The great composer does not set to work because he is inspired,
but becomes inspired because he is working. Beethoven, Wagner,
Bach and Mozart settled down day after day to the job in hand
with as much regularity as an accountant settles down each day
to his figures. They didn't waste time waiting for inspiration.
—Ernest Newman

What one has, one ought to use; and whatever he
does, he should do with all his might.
—Cicero

Without enthusiasm there is no progress in the world.
—Woodrow Wilson

Reason alone is insufficient to make us enthusiastic in any matter.
—Francois de La Rochefoucauld

Energy, even like the Biblical grain of mustard-
seed, will move mountains.
—Hosea Ballou

I rate enthusiasm even above professional skill.
—Sir Edward Appleton

We are all experiments in enthusiasms, narrow and preordained.
—Kurt Vonnegut

Success is not the result of spontaneous combustion,
you must set yourself on fire first.
—Reggie Leach

He too serves a certain purpose who only stands and cheers.
—Henry Adams

Every production of genius must be the production of enthusiasm.
—Benjamin Disraeli

POSITIVE THOUGHTS, BELIEFS, AND ACTIONS

Each of us makes his own weather, determines the color of
the skies in the emotional universe which he inhabits.
—Fulton J. Sheen

All the beautiful sentiments in the world weigh
less than a single lovely action.
—James Russell Lowell

You cannot escape the results of your thoughts.... Whatever your
present environment may be, you will fall, remain or rise with
your thoughts, your vision, your ideal. You will become as small as
your controlling desire, as great as your dominant aspiration.
—James Lane Allen

We become just by performing just actions, temperate by performing
temperate actions, brave by performing brave actions.
—Aristotle

Attempt easy tasks as if they were difficult, and difficult as
if they were easy; in the one case that confidence may not
fall asleep, in the other that it may not be dismayed.
—Baltasar Gracian

Notable deeds are most estimable when hidden.
—Blaise Pascal

Man does not simply exist, but always decides what his
existence will be, what he will become in the next moment.
—Viktor Frankel

The bigger they are, the further they have to fall.
—Robert Fitzgerald

All seems infected that the infected spy, as all
looks yellow to the jaundiced eye.
—Alexander Pope

God will help you if you try, and you can if you think you can.
—Anna Delaney Peale

Joe Gillis: You used to be in silent pictures. You used to be big.
Norma Desmond: I *am* big. It's the pictures that got small.
—Billy Wilder (*Sunset Boulevard*)

Anything that is worth doing has been done frequently. Things
hitherto undone should be given, I suspect, a wide berth.
—Max Beerbohm

It takes but one positive thought when given a chance to survive
and thrive to overpower an entire army of negative thoughts.
—Robert H. Schuller

A cheerful face is nearly as good for an invalid as healthy weather.
—Benjamin Franklin

To expect defeat is nine-tenths of defeat itself.
—Francis Marion Crawford

Rosiness is not a worse windowpane than
gloomy gray when viewing the world.
—Grace Paley

You have to believe in happiness, or happiness never comes.
—Douglas Malloch

It's better to be looked over than overlooked.
—Mae West

Since the human body tends to move in the direction of its
expectations—plus or minus—it is important to know that
attitudes of confidence and determination are no less a part of
the treatment program than medical science and technology.
—Norman Cousins

They can because they think they can.
—Virgil

The greatest pleasure I know is to do a good action by
stealth, and to have it found out by accident.
—CHARLES LAMB

A human being fashions his consequences as surely as
he fashions his goods or his dwelling. Nothing that he
says, thinks or does is without consequences.
—NORMAN COUSINS

Think of only three things: your God, your family
and the Green Bay Packers—in that order.
—VINCE LOMBARDI, TO HIS TEAM

Eliminate the impossible. Then if nothing remains,
some part of the "impossible" was possible.
—ANTHONY BOUCHER

The world has a way of giving what is demanded of it. If you are
frightened and look for failure and poverty, you will get them, no matter
how hard you may try to succeed. Lack of faith in yourself, in what life
will do for you, cuts you off from the good things of the world. Expect
victory and you make victory. Nowhere is this truer than in business
life, where bravery and faith bring both material and spiritual rewards.
—PRESTON BRADLEY

It is the nature of man to rise to greatness if greatness is expected of him.
—JOHN STEINBECK

We exaggerate misfortune and happiness alike. We are
never either so wretched or so happy as we say we are.
—HONORE DE BALZAC

Positive thinking is the key to success in business, education,
pro football, anything that you can mention. I go out there
thinking that I am going to complete every pass.
—RON JAWORSKI

I've never been poor, only broke. Being poor is a frame
of mind. Being broke is a temporary situation.
—MIKE TODD

Optimist: A man who gets treed by a lion but enjoys the scenery.
—WALTER WINCHELL

What we see depends mainly on what we look for.
—JOHN LUBBOCK

The words "I am ..." are potent words; be careful what you hitch them to.
The thing you're claiming has a way of reaching back and claiming you.
—A.L. KITSELMAN

All that we are is the result of what we have thought. The
mind is everything. What we think, we become.
—BUDDHA

The world is a looking glass and gives back to every man the
reflection of his own face. Frown at it and it will in turn look sourly
upon you; laugh at it and with it, and it is a jolly, kind companion.
—WILLIAM MAKEPEACE THACKERAY

The happiness of your life depends upon the quality of
your thoughts ... take care that you entertain no notions
unsuitable to virtue and reasonable nature..
—MARCUS AURELIUS

My center is giving way, my right is in retreat:
situation excellent. I am attacking.
—MARSHAL FERDINAND FOCH

A great manager has a knack for making ballplayers think they are
better than they think they are. He forces you to have a good opinion
of yourself. He lets you know he believes in you. He makes you get
more out of yourself. And once you learn how good you really are,
you never settle for playing anything less than your very best.
—REGGIE JACKSON

What we love, we shall grow to resemble.
—BERNARD OF CLAIRVAUX

Immense power is acquired by assuring yourself in your
secret reveries that you were born to control affairs.
—ANDREW CARNEGIE

Man's real life is happy, chiefly because he is
ever expecting that it soon will be so.
—EDGAR ALLAN POE

If you are possessed by an idea, you find it
expressed everywhere, you even *smell* it.
—THOMAS MANN

Make your judgement trustworthy by trusting it.
—GRENVILLE KLEISER

I am happy and content because I think I am.
—ALAIN-RENE LESAGE

Great men are they who see that the spiritual is stronger
than any material force, that thoughts rule the world.
—RALPH WALDO EMERSON

Man is what he believes.
—ANTON CHEKHOV

Could we change our attitude, we should not only see life differently, but
life itself would come to be different. Life would undergo a change of
appearance because we ourselves had undergone a change in attitude.
—KATHERINE MANSFIELD

People only see what they are prepared to see.
—RALPH WALDO EMERSON

The more wary you are of danger, the more likely you are to meet it.
—JEAN DE LA FONTAINE

People, by and large, will relate to the image you project.
—CHYATEE

We create our fate every day ... most of the ills we suffer
from are directly traceable to our own behavior.
—HENRY MILLER

The quality of our expectations determines the quality of our action.
—ANDRÉ GODIN

A vacant mind invites dangerous inmates, as a deserted
mansion tempts wandering outcasts to enter and take
up their abode in its desolate apartments.
—Hilliard

If we are not responsible for the thoughts that pass our doors,
we are at least responsible for those we admit and entertain.
—Charles B. Newcomb

The greatest discovery of my generation is that man can
alter his life simply by altering his attitude of mind.
—William James

Our visions begin without desires.
—Audre Lorde

The mere apprehension of a coming evil has put
many into a situation of the utmost danger.
—Lucan

As a man thinketh, so is he, and as a man chooseth, so is he.
—Ralph Waldo Emerson

People are not going to love you unless you love them.
—Pat Carroll

They can because they think they can.
—Virgil

The unthankful heart ... discovers no mercies; but the thankful
heart ... will find, in every hour, some heavenly blessings.
—Henry Ward Beecher

Your imagination has much to do with your life. . . . It is for you
to decide how you want your imagination to serve you.
—Philip Conley

The confidence which we have in ourselves gives birth
to much of that which we have in others.
—Francois de La Rochefoucauld

Thoughts lead on to purposes; purposes go forth in action; actions form habits; habits decide character; and character fixes our destiny.
—TYRON EDWARDS

I have learned to use the word *impossible* with the greatest caution.
—WERNHER VON BRAUN

What one believes to be true either is true or becomes true within limits to be found experimentally and experimentally. These limits are beliefs to be transcended.
—JOHN LILLY

If you think it's difficult to meet new people, try picking up the wrong golf ball!
—JACK LEMMON

If I were to wish for anything, I should not wish for wealth and power, but for the passionate sense of the potential, for the eye which, ever young and ardent, sees the possible ... what wine is so sparkling, so fragrant, so intoxicating, as possibility!
—SØREN KIERKEGAARD

The way a man's mind runs is the way he is sure to go.
—HENRY B. WILSON

A man is literally what he thinks.
—JAMES LANE ALLEN

Optimism is the faith that leads to achievement. Nothing can be done without hope and confidence.
—HELEN KELLER

The mind is its own place, and in itself can make a heaven of hell, a hell of heaven.
—JOHN MILTON

We are what we believe we are.
—BENJAMIN N. CARDOZO

The happiest person is the person who thinks the most interesting thoughts.
—WILLIAM LYON PHELPS

Opportunities multiply as they are seized; they die when
neglected. Life is a long line of opportunities.
—JOHN WICKER

As you think, you travel, and as you love, you attract. You
are today where your thoughts have brought you; you
will be tomorrow where your thoughts take you.
—JAMES LANE ALLEN

Keep your thoughts right, for as you think, so are you. Therefore, think
only those things that will make the world better, and you unashamed.
—HENRY H. BUCKLEY

It isn't our position, but our disposition, that makes us happy.
—ANON

I couldn't hit a wall with a sixgun, but I can twirl one. It looks good.
—JOHN WAYNE

All that a man does outwardly is but the expression and
completion of his inward thought. To work effectively, he
must think clearly; to act nobly, he must think nobly.
—WILLIAM ELLERY CHANNING

The only way to make a man trustworthy is to trust him.
—HENRY L. STIMSON

The principle of life is that life responds by corresponding;
your life becomes the thing you have decided it shall be.
—RAYMOND CHARLES BARKER

A great obstacle to happiness is to expect too much happiness.
—BERNARD DE FONTENELLE

Our best friends and our worst enemies are our thoughts. A
thought can do us more good than a doctor or a banker or a
faithful friend. It can also do us more harm than a brick.
—DR. FRANK CRANE

Trust men and they will be true to you; treat them
greatly and they will show themselves great.
—RALPH WALDO EMERSON

There is in the worst of fortune the best of chances for a happy change.
—EURIPIDES

Happiness will never be any greater than the idea we have of it.
—MAURICE MAETERLINCK

Nothing can stop the man with the right mental
attitude from achieving his goal; nothing on earth can
help the man with the wrong mental attitude.
—W.W. ZIEGE

If you constantly think of illness, you eventually become ill;
if you believe yourself to be beautiful, you become so.
—SHAKTI GAWAIN

We think in generalities, but we live in detail.
—ALFRED NORTH WHITEHEAD

Anyone can have an off decade.
—LARRY COLE

This I conceive to be the chemical function of humor:
to change the character of our thought.
—LIN YUTANG

Illusory joy is often worth more than genuine sorrow.
—RENE DESCARTES

The most unhappy of all men is he who believes himself to be so.
—DAVID HUME

If you keep on saying things are going to be bad,
you have a good chance of being a prophet.
—ISAAC BASHEVIS SINGER

If you expect nothing, you're apt to be surprised. You'll get it.
—MALCOLM FORBES

When you look at the world in a narrow way, how narrow it seems!
When you look at it in a mean way, how mean it is! When you look

at it selfishly, how selfish it is! But when you look at it in a broad, generous, friendly spirit, what wonderful people you find in it.
—Horace Rutledge

If you would be powerful, pretend to be powerful.
—Horne Tooke

It is by sitting down to write every morning that he becomes a writer. Those who do not do this remain amateurs.
—Gerald Brenan

Our destiny changes with our thoughts; we shall become what we wish to become, do what we wish to do, when our habitual thoughts correspond with our desires.
—Orison Swett Marden

Live as if you like yourself, and it may happen.
—Marge Piercy

On the human chessboard, all moves are possible.
—Miriam Schiff

An optimist is a guy that has never had much experience.
—Don Marquis

Think positively and masterfully, with confidence and faith, and life becomes more secure, more fraught with action, richer in achievement and experience.
—Eddie Rickenbacker

I'm not overweight, I'm just nine inches too short.
—Shelley Winters

You gotta believe.
—Tug McGraw (during the NY Mets miracle year, 1973)

Great things are not something accidental, but must certainly be willed.
—Vincent van Gogh

Nothing befalls us that is not of the nature of ourselves. There comes no adventure but wears to our soul the shape of our everyday thoughts.
—Maurice Maeterlinck

I once told a graduation class that fame is Madonna; success is Helen Keller. Know the difference.
—Erma Bombeck

To the timid and hesitating everything is impossible because it seems so.
—Sir Walter Scott

Getting people to like you is merely the other side of liking them.
—Norman Vincent Peale

Every noble work is at first impossible.
—Thomas Carlyle

Life is a mirror and will reflect back to the thinker what he thinks into it.
—Ernest Holmes

I'm in a wonderful position: I'm unknown, I'm underrated, and there's nowhere to go but up.
—Pierre S. DuPont IV

There is a very real relationship, both quantitatively and qualitatively, between what you contribute and what you get out of this world.
—Oscar Hammerstein II

In the long run, the pessimist may be proved to be right, but the optimist has a better time on the trip.
—Daniel L. Reardon

The soul contains the event that shall befall it, for the event is only the actualization of its thoughts, and what we pray to ourselves for is always granted.
—Ralph Waldo Emerson

Never think any oldish thoughts. It's oldish thoughts that make a person old.
—James A. Farley

Sunshine is delicious, rain is refreshing, wind braces us
up, snow is exhilarating; there is really no such thing as
bad weather, only different kinds of good weather.
—John Ruskin

Misery is almost always the result of thinking.
—Joseph Joubert

The thing always happens that you really believe in;
and the belief in a thing makes it happen.
—Frank Lloyd Wright

The life each of us lives is the life within the limits
of our own thinking. To have life more abundant, we
must think in limitless terms of abundance.
—Thomas Dreier

Optimism is essential to achievement and is also the
foundation of courage and of true progress.
—Nicholas Murray Butler

Self-image sets the boundaries of individual accomplishment.
—Maxwell Maltz

It doesn't hurt to be optimistic. You can always cry later.
—Lucimar Santos de Lima

My strength is as the strength of ten, because my heart is pure.
—Alfred, Lord Tennyson

Whoever said nothing is impossible never tried to slam a revolving door.
—Robert Orben

Think like a man of action, act like a man of thought.
—Henri Bergson

Man is only miserable so far as he thinks himself so.
—Sannazare

You can promote your healing by your thinking.
—James E. Sweeney

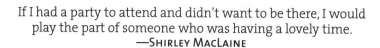

If I had a party to attend and didn't want to be there, I would
play the part of someone who was having a lovely time.
—SHIRLEY MACLAINE

There is no miraculous change that takes place in a boy that
makes him a man. He becomes a man by being a man.
—LOUIS L'AMOUR

All things are possible until they are proved impossible—
and even the impossible may only be so as of now.
—PEARL S. BUCK

Our belief at the beginning of a doubtful undertaking is the one
thing that ensures the successful outcome of our venture.
—WILLIAM JAMES

I am dying, but otherwise I am quite well.
—EDITH SITWELL, WHEN ASKED HOW SHE FELT

The quality of our expectations determines the quality of our actions.
—ANDRÉ GODIN

Our deeds determine us, as much as we determine our deeds.
—GEORGE ELIOT

Diplomacy is to do and say
The nastiest thing in the nicest way.
—ISAAC GOLDBERG

Man's rise or fall, success or failure, happiness or unhappiness depends
on his attitude . . . a man's attitude will create the situation he imagines.
—JAMES LANE ALLEN

A man is a method, a progressive arrangement;
a selecting principle, gathering his like unto him
wherever he goes. What you are comes to you.
—RALPH WALDO EMERSON

We choose our joys and sorrows long before we experience them.
—KAHLIL GIBRAN

Honor begets honor; trust begets trust; faith begets
faith; and hope is the mainspring of life.
—Henry L. Stimson

We must laugh before we are happy, for fear of
dying without having laughed at all.
—Jean de La Bruyere

Give to the world the best you have and the best will come back to you.
—Madeline Bridges

I believe that if you think about disaster, you will get it. Brood about
death and you hasten your demise. Think positively and masterfully
with confidence and faith, and life becomes more secure, more
fraught with action, richer in achievement and experience.
—Eddie Rickenbacker

Unhappiness indicates wrong thinking, just as
ill health indicates a bad regimen.
—Paul Bourge

The faultfinder will find faults even in paradise.
—Henry David Thoreau

If a man plants melons he will reap melons; if
he sows beans, he will reap beans.
—Chinese proverb

I can't say I was ever lost, but I was bewildered once for three days.
—Daniel Boone

If you would be loved, love and be lovable.
—Benjamin Franklin

What you think means more than anything else in your life.
—George Matthew Adams

The person who says it cannot be done should
not interrupt the person doing it.
—Chinese proverb

There is one possession I take with me from this place. Tonight when I stand before God ... I will stand again and proudly show Him that one pure possession. ... My enormous—panache.
—EDMOND ROSTAND

If one advances confidently in the direction of his dreams, and endeavors to live the life which he has imagined, he will meet with a success unexpected in common hours.
—HENRY DAVID THOREAU

Treat people as if they were what they should be, and you help them become what they are capable of becoming.
—JOHANN VON GOETHE

Think you can, think you can't; either way, you'll be right.
—HENRY FORD

Whatsoever a man soweth, that shall he also reap.
—GAL. 6:7

Being an optimist after you've got everything you want doesn't count.
—KIN HUBBARD

The world is a great mirror. It reflects back to you what you are. If you are loving, if you are friendly, if you are helpful, the world will prove loving and friendly and helpful to you. The world is what you are.
—THOMAS DREIER

Act so as to elicit the best in others and thereby in thyself.
—FELIX ADLER

If at first you don't succeed, try, try, and try again. Then give up. There's no use being a damned fool about it.
—W.C. FIELDS

No question is ever settled until it is settled right.
—ELLA WHEELER WILCOX

We become just by performing just actions, temperate by performing temperate actions, brave by performing brave actions.
—ARISTOTLE

Like begets like; honesty begets honesty; trust, trust; and so on.
—James F. Bell

Knock the "t" off the "can't."
—George Reeves

Whatever is worth doing at all is worth doing well.
—Lord Chesterfield

If we choose to be no more than clods of clay, then we shall
be used as clods of clay for braver feet to tread on.
—Marie Corelli

Children are likely to live up to what you believe of them.
—Lady Bird Johnson

Act as if it were impossible to fail.
—Dorothea Brande

Happiness does not depend on outward things,
but on the way we see them.
—Leo Tolstoy

Once you begin to believe there is help "out
there," you will know it to be true.
—Saint Bartholomew

Some folks think they are thinking when they
are only rearranging their prejudices.
—Anon

The young do not know enough to be prudent, and therefore they
attempt the impossible—and achieve it, generation after generation.
—Pearl S. Buck

If we live good lives, the times are also good.
As we are, such are the times.
—Saint Augustine

Failure is impossible.
—Susan B. Anthony

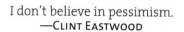

I don't believe in pessimism.
—Clint Eastwood

What we prepare for is what we shall get.
—William Graham Sumner

They couldn't kill an elephant at this distance.
—Gen. John Sedgwick, Union general, immediately prior to being killed
by Confederate fire in the Battle of Spottsylvania

A hero is an ordinary individual who finds the strength to
persevere and endure in spite of overwhelming obstacles.
—Christopher Reeve

I have found that if you love life, life will love you back.
—Arthur Rubinstein

Things are only impossible until they're not.
—Jean-Luc Picard

He was a "how" thinker, not an "if" thinker.
—Anon

I do not weep at the world—I am too busy sharpening my oyster knife.
—Zora Neale Hurston

The basic success orientation is having an optimistic attitude.
—John DePasquale

If you want your children to improve, let them overhear
the nice things you say about them to others.
—Haim Ginott

Act as if you were already happy, and that will tend to make you happy.
—Dale Carnegie

No man can think clearly when his fists are clenched.
—George Jean Nathan

We awaken in others the same attitude of mind we hold toward them.
—Elbert Hubbard

Our greatest glory is not in never falling, but in rising every time we fall.
—Confucius

The way in which we think of ourselves has
everything to do with how our world sees us.
—Arlene Raven

Believe that life is worth living, and your belief will help create that fact.
—William James

It is best to act with confidence, no matter how little right you have to it.
—Lillian Hellman

How things look on the outside of us depends
on how things are on the inside of us.
—Park Cousins

Optimism is an intellectual choice.
—Diana Schneider

People have a way of becoming what you encourage
them them to be—not what you nag them to be.
—S.N. Parker

It is good to act as if. It is even better to grow to
the point where it is no longer an act.
—Charles Caleb Colton

Hope is like a road in the country; there was never a road, but
when many people walk on it, the road comes into existence.
—Lin Yutang

How much shall I be changed, before I am changed!
—John Donnell

He who sows courtesy reaps friendship, and he
who plants kindness gathers love.
—Saint Basil

The wisdom of all ages and cultures emphasizes the tremendous
power our thoughts have over our character and circumstances.
—LIANE CORDES

Where much is expected from an individual, he may rise to
the level of events and make the dream come true.
—ELBERT HUBBARD

The only prison we need to escape from is the prison of our own minds.
—ANON

We must dare to think unthinkable thoughts.
—JAMES W. FULBRIGHT

We are made kind by being kind.
—ERIC HOFFER

I make the most of all that comes and the least of all that goes.
—SARA TEASDALE

Our minds can shape the way a thing will be because
we act according to our expectations.
—FEDERICO FELLINI

When in doubt, duck.
—MALCOLM FORBES

Be careful of your thoughts; they may become words at any moment.
—IRA GASSEN

Happiness is not a matter of events, it depends
upon the tides of the mind.
—ALICE MEYNELL

The Wright brothers flew right through the
smoke screen of impossibility.
—CHARLES FRANKLIN KETTERING

If you think it's going to rain, it will.
—CLINT EASTWOOD

A man's life is what his thoughts make it.
—MARCUS AURELIUS

If you want a quality, act as if you already had it.
—WILLIAM JAMES

There are more defects in temperament than in the mind.
—FRANCOIS DE LA ROCHEFOUCAULD

Man, being made reasonable, and so a thinking creature, there is nothing
more worthy of his being than the right direction and employment
of his thoughts; since upon this depends both his usefulness to the
public, and his own present and future benefit in all respects.
—WILLIAM PENN

Politeness is the art of choosing among one's real thoughts.
—ABEL STEVENS

Persistent prophecy is a familiar way of assuring the event.
—GEORGE R. GISSING

It seems to me probably that any one who has a series of intolerable
positions to put up with must have been responsible for them
to some extent . . . they have contributed to it by impatience
or intolerance, or brusqueness—or some provocation.
—ROBERT HUGH BENSON

If you've got it, flaunt it. If you do not, pretend.
—WALLY PHILLIPS

The more we do, the more we can do; the more
busy we are, the more leisure we have.
—WILLIAM HAZLITT

[Macbeth:] If we should fail?
[Lady Macbeth:] We fail! But screw your courage
to the sticking-place, and we'll not fail.
—WILLIAM SHAKESPEARE

I will say this about being an optimist: even when things
don't turn out well, you are certain they will get better.
—FRANK HUGHES

We have a problem. "Congratulations." But it's a tough
problem. "Then double congratulations."
—W. CLEMENT STONE

The biggest quality in successful people, I think, is an
impatience with negative thinking ... my feeling was,
even if it's as bad as I think it is, we'll make it work.
—EDWARD MCCABE

Optimism and humor are the grease and glue of life. Without
both of them we would never have survived our captivity.
—PHILIP BUTLER, VIETNAM POW

As is our confidence, so is our capacity.
—WILLIAM HAZLITT

The world is like a mirror; frown at it, and it
frowns at you. Smile and it smiles, too.
—HERBERT SAMUELS

Clear your mind of "can't."
—SAMUEL JOHNSON

Success produces success, just as money produces money.
—NICOLAS DE CHAMFORT

If you wish to live a life free from sorrow, think of what
is going to happen as if it had already happened.
—EPICTETUS

Thousands upon thousands are yearly brought into a state of
real poverty by their great anxiety not to be thought poor.
—WILLIAM COBBETT

The world has a way of giving what is demanded of it. If you are
frightened and look for failure and poverty, you will get them, no matter
how hard you may try to succeed. Lack of faith in yourself, in what life
will do for you, cuts you off from the good things of the world. Expect
victory and you make victory. Nowhere is this truer than in business that
is, where bravery and faith bring both material and spiritual rewards.
—PRESTON BRADLEY

The words "I am ..." are potent words; be careful what you hitch them to.
The thing you're claiming has a way of reaching back and claiming you.
—A.L. Kitselman

A pessimist looks at his glass and says it is half empty;
an optimist looks at it and says it is half full.
—The New York Times

There comes no adventure but wears to our soul
the shape of our everyday thoughts.
—Maurice Maeterlinck

In the end, the love you take is equal to the love you make.
—Song lyric, "The End," from Abbey Road Album, Paul McCartney

Our self-image, strongly held, essentially determines what we become.
—Maxwell Maltz

He is happy that knoweth not himself to be otherwise.
—Thomas Fuller

I learned really to practice mustard seed faith, and positive
thinking, and remarkable things happened.
—Sir John Walton

To find oneself jilted is a blow to one's pride. One must do one's best
to forget it and if one doesn't succeed, at least one must pretend to.
—Moliere

Women the most delicate get used to strange moral
situations. Eve probably regained her normal sweet
composure about a week after the Fall.
—Thomas Hardy

Miracles are instantaneous, they cannot be summoned,
but come of themselves, usually at unlikely moments
and to those who least expect them
—Katherine Ann Porter

What after all has maintained the human race on this old globe, despite all the calamities of nature and all the tragic failings of mankind, if not the faith in new possibilities and the courage to advocate them?
—JANE ADDAMS

However much we guard against it, we tend to shape ourselves in the image others have of us.
—ERIC HOFFER

It is easy enough to be pleasant, when life flows by like a song. But the man worthwhile is one who will smile, when everything goes dead wrong.
—ELLA WHEELER WILCOX

Men will get no more out of life than they put into it.
—WILLIAM J.H. BOETCKER

Events, circumstances, etc. have their origin in ourselves. They spring from seeds which we have sown.
—HENRY DAVID THOREAU

Blessings on your young courage, boy; that's the way to the stars.
—VIRGIL

Dream lofty dreams, and as you dream, so shall you become. Your vision is the promise of what you shall at last unveil.
—JOHN RUSKIN

If you act like you're rich, you'll get rich.
—ADNAN KOASHOGGI

Any man will usually get from other men just what he is expecting of them. If he is looking for friendship he will likely receive it. If his attitude is that of indifference, it will beget indifference. And if a man is looking for a fight, he will in all likelihood be accommodated in that.
—JOHN RICHELSEN

If you want to be a big company tomorrow, you have to start acting like one today.
—THOMAS WATSON

One should ... be able to see things as hopeless and
yet be determined to make them otherwise.
—F. Scott Fitzgerald

We are what we pretend to be, so we must be
careful about what we pretend to be.
—Kurt Vonnegut

Kindness gives birth to kindness.
—Sophocles

Better late than never.
—Proverb

Never think you've seen the last of anything.
—Eudora Welty

Progress ... is not an accident, but a necessity. Instead of
civilization being artificial, it is a part of nature.
—Herbert Spencer

To establish oneself in the world, one has to do
all one can to appear established.
—Francois de La Rochefoucauld

I dare you to be the strongest boy in this class.
—William H. Danforth's teacher

Comment is free, but facts are sacred.
—C.P. Scott

Whatever the ups and downs of detail within our limited
experience, the larger whole is primarily beautiful.
—Gregory Bateson

Skill to do comes of doing.
—Ralph Waldo Emerson

Fake feeling good.... You're going to have to learn to
fake cheerfulness. Believe it or not, eventually that effort
will pay off: you'll actually start feeling happier.
—JEAN BACH

Change your thoughts and you change your world.
—NORMAN VINCENT PEALE

Pessimism, when you get used to it, is just as agreeable as optimism.
—E. ARNOLD BENNETT

It is never too late to be what you might have been.
—GEORGE ELIOT

A positive attitude may not solve all your problems, but it
will annoy enough people to make it worth the effort.
—HERM ALBRIGHT

To believe in God is to yearn for His existence, and
furthermore, it is to act as if He did exist.
—MIGUEL DE UNAMUNO

To make the world a friendly place, one must show it a friendly face.
—JAMES WHITCOMB RILEY

Isn't it splendid to think of all the things there are to find out about?
It just makes me feel glad to be alive—it's such an interesting world.
—LUCY MONTGOMERY

So always look for the silver lining
And try to find the sunny side of life.
—P.G. WODEHOUSE

One of the things I learned the hard way was that it
doesn't pay to get discouraged. Keeping busy and making
optimism a way of life can restore faith in yourself
—LUCILLE BALL

Practice being excited.
—BILL FOSTER

Put your trust in God, my boys, and keep your powder dry.
—VALENTINE BLACKER

The best things come in small packages.
—PROVERB

MOTIVATION

The secret of discipline is motivation. When a man is
sufficiently motivated, discipline will take care of itself.
—SIR ALEXANDER PATERSON

Praise makes good men better and bad men worse.
—THOMAS FULLER

To have a grievance is to have a purpose in life.
—ERIC HOFFER

It is not enough to have a good mind. The main thing is to use it well.
—RENE DESCARTES

Somebody said that it couldn't be done,
But he with a chuckle replied
That maybe it couldn't, but he would be one
Who wouldn't say so till he'd tried.
—EDGAR A. GUEST

You'll never achieve 100 percent if 99 percent is okay.
—WILL SMITH

What is gamesmanship? ... "The Art of Winning Games Without
Actually Cheating" —that is my personal "working definition."
—STEPHEN POTTER

Pressure can burst a pipe, or pressure can make a diamond.
—ROBERT HORRY

Fortune favors the brave.
—Virgil

Everyone expects to go further than his father went; everyone
expects to be better than he was born and every generation has
one big impulse in its heart—to exceed all the other generations
of the past in all the things that make life worth living.
—William Allen White

We are all motivated by a keen desire for praise, and the
better a man is, the more he is inspired by glory.
—Cicero

Just about the only interruption we don't object to is applause.
—Sydney J. Harris

Chutzpah is that quality enshrined in a man who,
having killed his mother and father, throws himself on
the mercy of the court because he is an orphan.
—Leo Rosten

If Joan of Arc could turn the tide of an entire war before
her 18th birthday, you can get out of bed.
—E. Jean Carroll

Praise is always pleasing, let it come from
whom, or upon what account it will.
—Montaigne

It is the north wind that lashes men into Vikings; it is the soft,
luscious south wind which lulls them to lotus dreams.
—Ouida

Arriving at one goal is the starting point to another.
—John Dewey

Acting was a way out at first. A way out of not knowing what
to do, a way of focusing ambitions. And the ambition wasn't
for fame. The ambition was to do an interesting job.
—Harrison Ford

Praise, like gold and diamonds, owes its value only to its scarcity.
—Samuel Johnson

Any party which takes credit for the rain must not be
surprised its opponents blame it for the drought.
—Dwight Morrow

There's no praise to beat the sort you can put in your pocket.
—Moliere

Talent isn't enough. You need motivation—and persistence, too:
what Steinbeck called a blend of faith and arrogance. When
you're young, plain old poverty can be enough, along with an
insatiable hunger for recognition. You have to have that feeling
of "I'll show them." If you don't have it, don't become a writer.
—Leon Uris

If each of us were to confess his most secret desire, the one that inspires
all his plans, all his actions, he would say: "I want to be praised."
—E.M. Cioran

Now don't say you can't swear off drinking; it's
easy. I've done it a thousand times.
—W.C. Fields

Where the willingness is great, the difficulties cannot be great.
—Niccolo Machiavelli

It is the spur of ignorance, the consciousness of not
understanding, and the curiosity about that which
lies beyond that are essential to our progress.
—John Pierce

Action springs not from thought, but from a readiness for responsibility.
—Dietrich Bonhoeffer

I happened on the idea of fitting an engine to a bicycle simply
because I did not want to ride crowded trains and buses.
—Soichire Honda

Hardships, poverty and want are the best incentives,
and the best foundation, for the success of man.
—BRADFORD MERRILL

Your distress about life might mean you have been living for
the wrong reason, not that you have no reason for living.
—TOM O'CONNOR, PERSON WITH ARC

The applause of a single human being is of great consequence.
—SAMUEL JOHNSON

Anxiety and conscience are a powerful pair of dynamos. Between
them, they have ensured that I shall work hard, but they cannot
ensure that one shall work at anything worthwhile.
—ARNOLD J. TOYNBEE

Don't let other people tell you what you want.
—PAT RILEY

The world continues to offer glittering prizes to those
who have stout hearts and sharp swords.
—FREDERICK EDWIN SMITH, FIRST EARL OF BIRKENHEAD

Money and women. They're the two strongest things
in the world. There are things you do for a woman you
wouldn't do for anything else. Same with money.
—SATCHEL PAIGE

The greatest efforts of the race have always been traceable to the
love of praise, as the greatest catastrophes to the love of pleasure.
—JOHN RUSKIN

Every true man, sir, who is a little above the level of the beasts and
plants, lives so as to give a meaning and a value to his own life.
—LUIGI PIRANDELLO

To sink a six-foot putt with thirty million people
looking over your shoulder, convince yourself that, if
you miss it, you will be embarrassed and poor.
—JACK NICKLAUS

Football linemen are motivated by a more complicated, self-determining series of factors than the simple fear of humiliation in the public gaze, which is the emotion that galvanizes the backs and receivers.
—MERLIN OLSEN

We talk on principle, but we act on interest.
—WALTER SAVAGE LANDOR

One starts an action simply because one must do *something*.
—T.S. ELIOT

Discontent is the first step in progress. No one knows what is in him till he tries, and many would never try if they were not forced to.
—BASIL W. MATURIN

Some people are molded by their admirations, others by their hostilities.
—ELIZABETH BOWEN

I want to do it because I want to do it.
—AMELIA EARHART

Necessity is the mother of taking chances.
—MARK TWAIN

Take away the cause, and the effect ceases.
—MIGUEL DE CERVANTES

What you are must always displease you, if you would attain to that which you are not.
—SAINT AUGUSTINE

For every man there exists a bait which he cannot resist swallowing.
—FRIEDRICH NIETZSCHE

A loafer never works except when there is a fire; then he will carry out more furniture than anybody.
—EDGAR WATSON HOWE

We must each find our separate meaning in the persuasion of our days until we meet in the meaning of the world.
—CHRISTOPHER FRY

Every artist loves applause. The praise of his contemporaries
is th emost valuable part of his recompense.
—HENRI ROUSSEAU

Proper planning prevents poor performance.
—ANON

Fear, desire, hope still push us on toward the future.
—MICHEL DE MONTAIGNE

Interest speaks all sorts of tongues, and plays all
sorts of parts, even that of disinterestedness.
—FRANCOIS DE LA ROCHEFOUCAULD

We accept the verdict of the past until the need for change
cries out loudly enough to force upon us a choice between the
comforts of further inertia and the irksomeness of action.
—LOUIS L'AMOUR

All I want out of life is that when I walk down the street, folks
will say, "There goes the greatest hitter who ever lived."
—TED WILLIAMS

It seems to me we can never give up longing and wishing
while we are alive. There are certain things we feel to be
beautiful and good, and we must hunger for them.
—GEORGE ELIOT

One man with a dream, at pleasure,
Shall go forth and conquer a crown,
And three with a new song's measure,
Can trample an empire down.
—ARTHUR O'SHAUGHNESSY

There are only two stimulants to one's best efforts: the
fear of punishment, and the hope of reward.
—JOHN M. WILSON

Praise is the best diet for us, after all.
—SYDNEY SMITH

I never work better than when I am inspired by anger; when I am angry, I can write, pray, and preach well, for then my whole temperament is quickened, my understanding sharpened, and all mundane vexations and temptations depart.
—MARTIN LUTHER

I wish it, I command it. Let my *will* take the place of a reason.
—JUVENAL

Never let go of that fiery sadness called desire.
—PATTI SMITH

A man will fight harder for his interests than for his rights.
—NAPOLEON BONAPARTE

Great men undertake great things because they are great; fools, because they think them easy.
—VAUVENARGUES

I tried to treat them like me, and some of them weren't.
—COACH BILL RUSSELL, ON WHY HE HAD DIFFICULTY WITH SOME OF HIS PLAYERS

Urgent necessity prompts many to do things.
—MIGUEL DE CERVANTES

I am not sending messages with my feet. All I ever wanted was not to come up empty. I did it for the dough, and the old applause.
—FRED ASTAIRE

One must not lose desires. They are mighty stimulants to creativeness, to love and to long life.
—ALEXANDER A. BOGOMOLETZ

Men are more often bribed by their loyalties and ambitions than by money.
—ROBERT H. JACKSON

Discontent is the first step in the progress of a man or a nation.
—OSCAR WILDE

It is not merely cruelty that leads men to love war, it is excitement.
—HENRY WARD BEECHER

There's only one good reason to be a writer—we can't help it!
We'd all like to be successful, rich and famous, but if those are
our *goals*, we're off on the wrong foot.... I just wanted to earn
enough money so I could work at home on my writing.
—PHYLLIS WHITNEY

Applause is the spur of noble minds, the end and aim of weak ones.
—CHARLES CALEB COLTON

To be what we are, and to become what we are
capable of becoming, is the only end of life.
—BARUCH SPINOZA

Lust and force are the source of all our actions; lust
causes voluntary actions, force involuntary ones.
—BLAISE PASCAL

I can't concentrate on golf or bowling. Those bowling
pins aren't going to hurt me. I can concentrate in the
ring because someone is trying to kill me.
—CARMEN BASILIO

Drink and dance and laugh and lie,
Love, the reeling midnight through,
For tomorrow we shall die!
(But, alas, we never do.)
—DOROTHY PARKER

It is for the superfluous things of life that men sweat.
—MARCUS ANNAEUS SENECA

The moment somebody says to me, "This is very risky,"
is the moment it becomes attractive to me.
—KATE CAPSHAW

Always in a moment of extreme danger things can be done
which had previously been thought impossible.
—GENERAL ERWIN ROMMEL

Happiness is in the taste, and not in the things themselves; we are happy
from possessing what we like, not from possessing what others like.
—Francois de La Rochefoucauld

Yet we are the movers and shakers
Of the world for ever, it seems.
—Arthur O'Shaughnessy

When you get hungry enough, you find yourself
speaking Spanish pretty well.
—Josh Gibson, on playing baseball in Cuba

Wealth . . . and poverty: the one is the parent of luxury and indolence,
and the other of meanness and viciousness, and both of discontent.
—Plato

As long as I have a want, I have a reason for living. Satisfaction is death.
—George Bernard Shaw

I take it that what all men are really after is some
form of, perhaps only some formula of, peace.
—Joseph Conrad

Necessity, who is the mother of our invention.
—Plato

If you don't play to win, why keep score?
—Vernon Law

Winning isn't everything. *Wanting* to win is.
—Catfish Hunter

Human behavior flows from three main sources:
desire, emotion, and knowledge.
—Plato

Men's actions depend to a great extent upon fear. We do things either
because we enjoy doing them or because we are afraid not to do them.
—John F. Milburn

Love teaches even asses to dance.
—FRENCH PROVERB

You've got a life to live. It's short, at best. It's a wonderful
privilege and a terrific opportunity—and you've been equipped
for it. Use your equipment. Give it all you've got. Love your
neighbor—he's having just as much trouble as you are. Be
nice to him; be kind to him. Trust God. And work hard.
—NORMAN VINCENT PEALE

The technocratic imperative: "What can be done must be done."
—THEODORE ROSZAK

We all live with the objective of being happy; our
lives are all different, and yet the same.
—ANNE FRANK

OPPORTUNITY

I think luck is the sense to recognize an opportunity and
the ability to take advantage of it. Everyone has bad breaks,
but everyone also has opportunities. The man who can
smile at his breaks and grab his chances gets on.
—SAMUEL GOLDWYN

The impossible often has a kind of integrity
which the merely improbable lacks.
—DOUGLAS ADAMS

If you want a thing to be well done, you must do it yourself.
—HENRY WADSWORTH LONGFELLOW

It is less important to redistribute wealth than
it is to redistribute opportunity.
—ARTHUR VANDENBERG

In great affairs we ought to apply ourselves less to creating
chances than to profiting from those that are offered.
—FRANCOIS DE LA ROCHEFOUCAULD

What the student calls a tragedy, the master calls a butterfly.
—RICHARD BACH

You see things; and you say "Why?" But I dream
things that never were: and I say "Why not?"
—GEORGE BERNARD SHAW

Know thine opportunity.
—PITTACUS

Vigilance in watching opportunity; tact and daring in
seizing upon opportunity; force and persistence in crowding
opportunity to its utmost possible achievement—these are
the martial virtues which must command success.
—AUSTIN PHELPS

Words are only painted fire; a look is the fire itself.
—MARK TWAIN

Opportunity knocks at every man's door once. On some
men's door it hammers till it breaks down the door and
then it goes in and wakes him up if he's asleep, and ever
afterward it works for him as a night watchman.
—FINLEY PETER DUNNE

The opportunity that God sends does not wake up him who is asleep.
—SENEGALESE PROVERB

Great opportunities come to all, but many do not know they
have met them. The only preparation to take advantage of
them is simple fidelity to watch what each day brings.
—ALBERT E. DUNNING

The opportunities for enjoyment in your life are limitless. If you feel
you are not experiencing enough joy, you have only yourself to blame.
—DAVID E. BRESLER

Nothing is so often irretrievably missed as a daily opportunity.
—MARIE VON EBNER-ESCHENBACH

Opportunities do not come with their values stamped upon them.... To face every opportunity of life thoughtfully, and ask its meaning bravely and earnestly, is the only way to meet supreme opportunities when they come, whether open-faced or disguised.
—Maltbie D. Babcock

Unless a man has trained himself for his chance,
the chance will only make him ridiculous.
—William Matthews

Small opportunities are often the beginning of great enterprises.
—Demosthenes

Do not wait for ideal circumstances, nor for the
best opportunities; they will never come.
—Janet Erskine Stuart

[Don Quixote] thought that every windmill was a giant.... If
we never looked at things and wondered what they might be,
we'd all still be out there in the tall grass with the apes.
—James Goldman, They Might Be Giants

To avoid an occasion for our virtues is a worse degree of
failure than to push forward pluckily and make a fall.
—Robert Louis Stevenson

Our opportunities to do good are our talents.
—Cotton Mather

I was seldom able to see an opportunity until it had ceased to be one.
—Mark Twain

Opportunity is as scarce as oxygen; men fairly
breathe it and do not know it.
—Doc Sane

Men do with opportunities as children do at the seashore;
they fill their little hands with sand, and then let the
grains fall through, one by one, till all are gone.
—T. Jones

Man is not the sum of what he has already, but rather the sum of what he does not yet have, of what he could have.
—Jean-Paul Sartre

Opportunities multiply as they are seized; they die when neglected. Life is a long line of opportunities.
—John Wicker

Ability is of little account without opportunity.
—Napoleon Bonaparte

Opportunities are often things you haven't noticed the first time around.
—Catherine Deneuve

No great man ever complains of want of opportunity.
—Ralph Waldo Emerson

Next to knowing when to seize an opportunity, the most important thing in life is to know when to forgo an advantage.
—Benjamin Disraeli

To improve the golden moment of opportunity, and catch the good that is within our reach, is the great art of life.
—Samuel Johnson

How many opportunities present themselves to a man without his noticing them?
—Arab proverb

Remember that you ought to behave in life as your would at a banquet. As something is being passed around, it comes to you; stretch out your hand, take a portion of it politely. It passes on; do not detain it. Or it has not come to you yet; do not project your desire to meet it, but wait until it comes in front of you.
—Epictetus

Fortune helps the brave.
—Terence

The successful man is one who had the chance and took it.
—Roger Babson

The secret of success in life is for a man to be
ready for his opportunity when it come.
—Benjamin Disraeli

Opportunity is missed by most people because it
is dressed in overalls, and looks like work.
—Thomas A. Edison

If your ship doesn't come in, swim out to it.
—Jonathan Winters

Look what can happen in this country, they'd say. A girl lives in some out-
of-the-way town for nineteen years, so poor she can't afford a magazine,
and then she gets a scholarship to college and wins a prize here and a
prize there and ends up steering New York like her own private car.
—Sylvia Plath

Let us do something beautiful for God.
—Mother Teresa

The follies which a man regrets most in his life are those
which he didn't commit when he had the opportunity.
—Helen Rowland

It is often hard to distinguish between the hard
knocks in life and those of opportunity.
—Frederick Phillips

The important thing is this: to be able at any moment to
sacrifice what we are for what we could become.
—Charles Du Bos

We are told that talent creates its own opportunities.
But it sometimes seems that intense desire creates not
only its own opportunities, but its own talents.
—Eric Hoffer

A door that seems to stand open must be a man's size, or
it is not the door that Providence means for him.
—Henry Ward Beecher

If Fortune calls, offer him a seat.
—Yiddish proverb

It is not manly to turn one's back on fortune.
—Marcus Annaeus Seneca

Reality is that stuff which, no matter what
you believe, just won't go away.
—David Paktor

In dreams begin responsibility.
—William Butler Yeats

A ship in harbor is safe, but that is not what ships are built for.
—John A. Shedd

Look with favor upon a bold beginning.
—Virgil

While we stop to think, we often miss our opportunity.
—Publilius Syrus

So many worlds, so much to do,
So little done, such things to be.
—Alfred, Lord Tennyson

A wise man will make more opportunities than he finds.
—Francis Bacon

VI. Faith, Hope, Charity

BELIEF/GOD

To Be is to live with God.
—Ralph Waldo Emerson

God is no enemy to you. He asks no more than
that He hear you call Him "Friend."
—A Course in Miracles

Bidden or not bidden, God is present.
—Carl Jung

An act of God was defined as "something which
no reasonable man could have expected."
—A.P. Herbert

One person with a belief is equal to a force of
ninety-nine who have only interests.
—Peter Marshall

God delays, but doesn't forget.
—Spanish proverb

I believe that our Heavenly Father invented man
because he was disappointed in the monkey.
—Mark Twain

A man with God is always in the majority.
—John Knox

All who call on God in true faith, earnestly from the heart, will certainly
be heard, and will receive what they have asked and desired.
—MARTIN LUTHER

Yet, in the maddening maze of things,
And tossed by storm and flood,
To one fixed trust my spirit clings;
I know that God is good!
—JOHN GREENLEAF WHITTIER

I have never understood why it should be considered derogatory
to the Creator to suppose that He has a sense of humor.
—WILLIAM RALPH INGE

God is in the details.
—ABY WARBURG

"What do you think of God," the teacher asked. After a pause,
the young pupil replied, "He's not a think, he's a feel."
—PAUL FROST

Religion is to mysticism what popularization is to science.
—HENRI BERGSON

The God of many men is little more than their court
of appeal against the damnatory judgement passed
on their failures by the opinion of the world.
—WILLIAM JAMES

An honest God is the noblest work of man.
—ROBERT G. INGERSOLL

To them that ask, where have you seen the Gods, or how do you know for
certain there are Gods, that you are so devout in their worship? I answer:
Neither have I ever seen my own soul, and yet I respect and honor it.
—MARCUS AURELIUS

God Almighty first planted a garden; and, indeed,
it is the purest of human pleasures.
—FRANCIS BACON

Without the assistance of the Divine Being . . . I cannot
succeed. With that assistance, I cannot fail.
—ABRAHAM LINCOLN

God is clever, but not dishonest.
—ALBERT EINSTEIN

Then comes the insight that All is God. One still realizes that the world
is as it was, but it does not matter, it does not affect one's faith.
—ABRAHAM HESCHEL

Every law of matter or the body, supposed to govern man,
is rendered null and void by the law of life, God.
—MARY BAKER EDDY

Nothing hath separated us from God but our own will,
or rather our own will is our separation from God.
—WILLIAM LAW

I will not fear, for you are ever with me, and you
will never leave me to face my perils alone.
—THOMAS MERTON

God uses lust to impel men to marry, ambition to office, avarice
to earning, and fear to faith. God led me like an old blind goat.
—MARTIN LUTHER

God is incorporeal, divine, supreme, infinite. Mind,
Spirit, Soul, Principle, Life, Truth, Love.
—MARY BAKER EDDY

Talking about God is not at all the same thing as
experiencing God, or acting out God through our lives.
—PHILLIP HEWETT

In the faces of men and women I see God.
—WALT WHITMAN

Pardon, not wrath, is God's best attribute.
—BAYARD TAYLOR

The things which are impossible with men are possible with God.
—Lk. 18:27

A true love of God must begin with a delight in his holiness.
—Jonathan Edwards

What is there in man so worthy of honor and reverence
as this, that he is capable of contemplating something
higher than his own reason, more sublime than the whole
universe—that Spirit which alone is self-subsistent, from
which all truth proceeds, without which there is no truth?
—Friedrich Jacobi

God knows no distance.
—Charleszetta Waddles

Courage is not afraid to weep, and she is not afraid to pray,
even when she is not sure who she is praying to.
—J. Ruth Gendler

God is to me that creative Force, behind and in the
universe, who manifests Himself as energy, as life, as
order, as beauty, as thought, as conscience, as love.
—Henry Sloane Coffin

Gawd knows, and 'E won't split on a pal.
—Rudyard Kipling

Who fathoms the Eternal Thought?
Who talks of scheme and plan?
The Lord is God! He needeth not
The poor device of man.
—John Greenleaf Whittier

The person who has a firm trust in the Supreme Being is powerful
in his power, wise by his wisdom, happy by his happiness.
—Joseph Addison

I believe in the incomprehensibility of God.
—Honore de Balzac

Not only then has each man his individual relation to
God, but each man has his peculiar relation to God.
—George MacDonald

God is what man finds that is divine in himself. God is the
best way man can behave in the ordinary occasions of life,
and the farthest point to which man can stretch himself.
—Max Lerner

The deep emotional conviction of the presence of a
superior reasoning power, which is revealed in the
incomprehensible universe, forms my idea of God.
—Albert Einstein

God is love, but get it in writing.
—Gypsy Rose Lee

For the multitude of worldly friends profiteth not, nor may
strong helpers anything avail, nor wise counselors give profitable
counsel, nor the cunning of doctors give consolation, nor riches
deliver in time of need, nor a secret place to defend, if Thou, Lord,
do not assist, help, comfort, counsel, inform, and defend.
—Thomas a'Kempis

One unquestioned text we read,
All doubt beyond, all fear above;
Nor crackling pile nor cursing creed
Can burn or blot it: God is Love.
—Oliver Wendell Holmes

The experience of God, or in any case the
possibility of experiencing God, is innate.
—Alice Walker

How is it, Lord, that we are cowards in everything save in opposing Thee?
—Saint Teresa of Avila

Hunting God is a great adventure.
—Marie DeFloris

God speaks to all individuals through what
happens to them moment by moment.
—J.P. DeCaussade

I would rather walk with God in the dark than go alone in the light.
—Mary Gardiner Brainard

God has many names, though He is only one Being.
—Aristotle

Above all am I convinced of the need, irrevocable and inescapable,
of every human heart, for God. No matter how we try to escape,
to lose ourselves in restless seeking, we cannot separate ourselves
from our divine source. There is no substitute for God.
—A.J. Cronin

God is an unutterable sigh, planted in the depths of the soul.
—Jean Paul Richter

It's only by forgetting yourself that you draw near to God.
—Henry David Thoreau

Some people want to see God with their eyes as they see a cow,
and to love Him as they love their cow—for the milk and cheese
and profit it brings them. This is how it is with people who love
God for the sake of outward wealth or inward comfort.
—Meister Eckhart

Trust in the Lord with all thine heart, and lean not
unto thine own understanding. In all thy ways
acknowledge Him, and He shall direct thy paths.
—Prv. 3:5-6

Whoever falls from God's right hand
Is caught into His left.
—Edwin Markham

The God of many men is little more than their court
of appeal against the damnatory judgement passed
on their failures by the opinion of the world.
—William James

The kingdom of God is within you.
—Lk. 17:21

By learning to contact, listen to, and act on our intuition,
we can directly connect to the higher power of the
universe and allow it to become our guiding force.
—Shakti Gawain

To think you are separate from God is to remain
separate from your own being.
—D.M. Street

Gabriel: How about clenin' up de whole mess of 'em and
sta'tin' all over ag'in wid some new kind of animal?
God: An' admit I'm licked?
—Marc Connelly

Words are men's daughters, but God's sons are things.
—Samuel Madden

We have to believe in free will. We have no choice.
—Isaac Bashevis Singer

The person who has a firm trust in the Supreme Being is powerful
in his power, wise by his wisdom, happy by his happiness.
—Joseph Addison

God has not promised skies always blue,
flower-strewn pathways all our lives through;
God has not promised sun without rain,
joy without sorrow, peace without pain.
But God has promised strength for the day,
rest for the labor, light for the way,
Grace for the trials, help from above,
unfailing sympathy, undying love.
—Kristone

Let God love you through others and let God love others through you.
—D.M. Street

Your mind cannot possibly understand God. Your heart already knows.
Minds were designed for carrying out the orders of the heart.
—EMMANUEL

Courage is not afraid to weep, and she is not afraid to pray,
even when she is not sure who she is praying to.
—J. RUTH GENDLER

When we lose God, it is not God who is lost.
—ANON

Before me, even as behind, God is, and all is well.
—JOHN GREENLEAF WHITTIER

We may say of angling as Dr. Boteler said of strawberries: "Doubtless
God could have made a better berry, but doubtless God never did."
—IZAAK WALTON

There is but one ultimate Power. This Power is to each one what he is to it.
—ERNEST HOLMES

There are two people I must please—God and Garfield. I
must live with Garfield here, with God hereafter.
—JAMES A. GARFIELD

What we are is God's gift to us. What we become is our gift to God.
—ANON

God is like a mirror. The mirror never changes, but
everybody who looks at it sees something different.
—RABBI HAROLD KUSHNER

Every conjecture we can form with regard to the works
of God has as little probability as the conjectures of
a child with regard to the works of a man.
—THOMAS REID

Every morning I spend fifteen minutes filling my mind full
of God, and so there's no room left for worry thoughts.
—HOWARD CHANDLER CHRISTY

When a man takes one step toward God, God takes more steps
toward that man than there are sands in the worlds of time.
—THE WORK OF THE CHARIOT

The most beautiful of all emblems is that of God, whom Timaeus
of Locris describes under the image of "A circle whose centre
is everywhere and whose circumference is nowhere."
—VOLTAIRE

In God we trust.
— MOTTO THAT HAS APPEARED ON MOST ISSUES OF U.S. COINS SINCE ABOUT 1864

Man can believe the impossible, but man can
never believe the improbable.
—OSCAR WILDE

Walk boldly and wisely.... There is a hand above that will help you on.
—PHILIP JAMES BAILEY

Most of the time, God speaks in a whisper.
—JEAN GRASSO FITZPATRICK

We have grasped the mystery of the atom and
rejected the Sermon on the Mount.
—GENERAL OMAR N. BRADLEY

Any god who can invent hell is no candidate for the Salvation Army.
—JOSEPH CAMPBELL

Loving is half of believing.
—VICTOR HUGO

A myth is a religion in which no one any longer believes.
—JAMES K. FEIBLEMAN

Frisbeetarianism is the belief that when you die,
your soul goes up on the roof and gets stuck
—GEORGE CARLIN

HELPING OTHERS/CHARITY

To give and then not feel that one has given is
the very best of all ways of giving.
—MAX BEERBOHM

The truest help we can render an afflicted man is not
to take his burden from him, but to call out his best
energy, that he may be able to bear the burden.
—PHILLIPS BROOKS

If you haven't any charity in your heart, you
have the worst kind of heart trouble.
—BOB HOPE

There is no exercise better for the heart than
reaching down and lifting people up.
—JOHN ANDREW HOLMES

A little help is worth a great deal of pity.
—ANON

In this world we must help one another.
—JEAN DE LA FONTAINE

Goodness is the only investment that never fails.
—HENRY DAVID THOREAU

What we frankly give, forever is our own.
—JOHN CARTERET GRANVILLE

He that will not permit his wealth to do any good for others . . . cuts
himself off from the truest pleasure here and the highest happiness later.
—CHARLES CALEB COLTON

He who wants to do good knocks at the gate;
he who loves finds the gate open.
—RABINDRANATH TAGORE

An effort made for the happiness of others lifts us above ourselves.
—LYDIA M. CHILD

In faith and hope the world will disagree, but
all mankind's concern is charity.
—Alexander Pope

Happiness is the cheapest thing in the world
when we buy it for someone else.
—Paul Flemming

To feel sorry for the needy is not the mark of a Christian—to help them is.
—Frank A. Clark

If we could all hear one another's prayers, God
might be relieved of some of his burden.
—Ashleigh Brilliant

We cannot live only for ourselves. A thousand
fibers connect us with our fellow men.
—Herman Melville

Charity begins at home, but should not end there.
—Thomas Fuller

May the good God pardon all good men.
—Elizabeth Barrett Browning

Who is the happiest of men? He who values the merits of others,
and in their pleasure takes joy, even as though it were his own.
—Johann von Goethe

Do good even to the wicked; it is as well to
shut a dog's mouth with a crumb.
—Sa'di

For we must share, if we would keep, that blessing from above;
Ceasing to give, we cease to have; such is the law of love.
—Richard C. Trench

Whoever in trouble and sorrow needs your help, give it to him. Whoever
in anxiety or fear needs your friendship, give it to him. It isn't important
whether he likes you. It isn't important whether you approve of his
conduct. It isn't important what his creed or nationality may be.
—E.N. West

If you judge people, you have no time to love them.
—MOTHER TERESA

It is his nature, not his standing, that makes the good man.
—PUBLILIUS SYRUS

There is no real religious experience that
does not express itself in charity.
—C.H. DODD

Everyone needs help from everyone.
—BERTOLT BRECHT

Good people are good because they've come to wisdom through failure.
—WILLIAM SAROYAN

In the time we have it is surely our duty to do all the good
we can to all the people we can in all the ways we can.
—WILLIAM BARCLAY

You can get much further with a kind word and a
gun than you can with a kind word alone.
—AL CAPONE

Goodness is uneventful. It does not flash, it glows.
—DAVID GRAYSON

Every charitable act is a stepping stone toward heaven.
—HENRY WARD BEECHER

Find out how much God has given you and from it take
what you need; the remainder is needed by others.
—SAINT AUGUSTINE

Be charitable and indulgent to every one but thyself.
—JOSEPH JOUBERT

The good life, as I conceive it, is a happy life. I do not mean that if you are
good you will be happy; I mean that if you are happy you will be good.
—BERTRAND RUSSELL

How far that little candle throws his beams! So
shines a good deed in a naughty world.
—William Shakespeare

It is more blessed to give than to receive.
—Acts 20:35

'Tis not enough to help the feeble up, but to support him after.
—William Shakespeare

Goodness is easier to recognize than to define.
—W. H. Auden

He who lives only for himself is truly dead to others.
—Publilius Syrus

I know some good marriages—marriages where both
people are just trying to get through their days by
helping each other, being good to each other.
—Erica Jong

Living or dead, to a good man there can come no evil.
—Socrates

Presents, believe me, seduce both men and gods.
—Ovid

To devote a portion of one's leisure to doing something for
someone else is one of the highest forms of recreation.
—Gerald B. Fitzgerald

Time and money spent in helping men to do more
for themselves is far better than mere giving.
—Henry Ford

As the purse is emptied, the heart is filled.
—Victor Hugo

Surely great loving-kindness yet may go
With a little gift:
All's dear that comes from friends.
—THEOCRITUS

The entire sum of existence is the magic of
being needed by just one person.
—VI PUTNAM

They're only truly great who are truly good.
—GEORGE CHAPMAN

Philanthropy is almost the only virtue which is
sufficiently appreciated by mankind.
—HENRY DAVID THOREAU

People who won't help others in trouble "because they
got into trouble through their own fault" would probably
not throw a lifeline to a drowning man until they learned
whether he fell in through his own fault or not.
—SYDNEY J. HARRIS

The race of mankind would perish did they cease to aid each
other. We cannot exist without mutual help. All therefore that
need aid have a right to ask it from their fellow man; and no one
who has the power of granting can refuse it without guilt.
—SIR WALTER SCOTT

The place to improve the world is first in one's own heart and
head and hands, and then work outward from there.
—ROBERT M. PIRSIG

Everything that lives, lives not alone, nor for itself.
—WILLIAM BLAKE

A good man's pedigree is little hunted up.
—SPANISH PROVERB

In every part and corner of our life, to lose oneself is
to be a gainer; to forget oneself is to be happy.
—ROBERT LOUIS STEVENSON

Live for thy neighbor if thou wouldst live for thyself.
—Marcus Annaeus Seneca

He who is too busy doing good finds no time to be good.
—Rabindranath Tagore

Waste no more time arguing what a good man should be. Be one.
—Marcus Aurelius

A man of humanity is one who, in seeking to establish
himself, finds a foothold for others and who, desiring
attainment for himself, helps others to attain.
—Confucius

The true way to soften one's troubles is to solace those of others.
—Madame de Maintenon

Sharing what you have is more important than what you have.
—Albert M. Wells, Jr.

To make one good action succeed another, is the perfection of goodness.
—Ali Ibn-Abi-Talib

The most infectiously joyous men and women are those who
forget themselves in thinking about others and serving others.
—Robert J. McCracken

The small share of happiness attainable by man exists
only insofar as he is able to cease to think of himself.
—Theodor Reik

The entire population of the universe, with one
trifling exception, is composed of others.
—John Andrew Holmes

Anything done for another is done for oneself.
—Boniface VIII

Goodness thinks no ill
Where no ill seems
—John Milton

Charity looks at the need, not at the cause.
—GERMAN PROVERB

Help your brother's boat across, and your own will reach the shore.
—HINDU PROVERB

It is the individual who is not interested in his fellow men who has the greatest difficulties in life and provides the greatest injury to others. It is from among such individuals that all human failures spring.
—ALFRED ADLER

The greatest good you can do for another is not just to share your riches, but to reveal to him his own.
—BENJAMIN DISRAELI

That action is best which procures the greatest happiness for the greatest numbers.
—FRANCIS HUTCHESON

You must give some time to your fellow men. Even if it's a little thing, do something for others—something for which you get no pay but the privilege of doing it.
—ALBERT SCHWEITZER

God loveth a cheerful giver.
—2 COR. 9:7

A man is called selfish not for pursuing his own good, but for neglecting his neighbor's.
—RICHARD WHATELY

There ain't nothing but one thing wrong with every one of us, and that's selfishness.
—WILL ROGERS

There are as many opinions as there are people.
—TERENCE

Good men are the stars, the planets of the ages wherein they live, and illustrate the times.
—BEN JONSON

Altruism has always been one of biology's deep mysteries. Why should any animal, off on its own, specified and labeled by all sorts of signals as its individual self, choose to give up its life in aid of someone else?
—LEWIS THOMAS

HOPE

Hope sees the invisible, feels the intangible and achieves the impossible.
—ANON

In the face of uncertainty, there is nothing wrong with hope.
—O. CARL SIMONTON

All human wisdom is summed up in two words—wait and hope.
—ALEXANDRE DUMAS

While there's life, there's hope.
—PROVERB

There's a hope for every woe, and a balm for every pain.
—ROBERT GITFILLAN

I steer my bark with hope in my heart, leaving fear astern.
—THOMAS JEFFERSON

There is nothing that fear or hope does not make men believe.
—VAUVENARGUES

Think of the hopes that lie before you.
Not the waste that lies behind;
Think of the treasures you have gathered.
Not the ones you failed to find;
Think of the service you may render.
Not of serving self alone;
Think of the happiness of others.
And in this you'll find your own!
—ROBERT E. FARLEY

Hope is a light diet, but very stimulating.
—Honore de Balzac

Hope! Of all the ills that men endure, the only cheap and universal cure.
—Abraham Cowley

Hope is some extraordinary spiritual grace that God
gives us to control our fears, not to oust them.
—Vincent NcNabb

Hold your head high, stick your chest out. You can make it. It gets
dark sometimes but morning comes. . . . Keep hope alive.
—Jesse Jackson

Hope is the word which God has written on the brow of every man.
—Victor Hugo

In all pleasure hope is a considerable part.
—Samuel Johnson

He who does not hope to win has already lost.
—José Joaquin Olmedo

Hope is the only bee that makes honey without flowers.
—Robert G. Ingersoll

Even the cry from the depths is an affirmation: why
cry if there is no hint of hope of hearing?
—Martin Marty

None are completely wretched but those who are
without hope, and few are reduced so low as that.
—William Hazlitt

Hope is one of the principal springs that keep mankind in motion.
—Thomas Fuller

Hope and patience are two sovereign remedies for all, the
surest reposals, the softest cushions to lean on in adversity.
—Robert Burton

Lord save us all from ... a hope tree that has lost
the faculty of putting out blossoms.
—Mark Twain

Everybody lives for something better to come.
—Anon

Hope is the parent of faith.
—C.A. Bartol

Just as dumb creatures are snared by food, human beings
would not be caught unless they had a nibble of hope.
—Petronius

If winter comes, can spring be far behind?
—Percy Bysshe Shelley

If it were not for hopes, the heart would break.
—Thomas Fuller

There is no hope unmingled with fear, and no fear unmingled with hope.
—Baruch Spinoza

They sailed. They sailed. Then spoke the mate:
"This mad sea shows its teeth tonight
He curls his lip, he lies in wait,
With lifted teeth, as if to bite!
Brave admiral, say but one good word:
What shall we do when hope is gone?"
The words leapt like a leaping sword: "Sail on! sail on! and on!"
—Joaquin Miller

And thou shalt be secure because there is hope.
—Jb. 11:18

The important thing is not that we can live on hope
alone, but that life is not worth living without it.
—Harvey Milk

Hope is desire and expectation rolled into one.
—Ambrose Bierce

A leader is a dealer in hope.
—Napoleon Bonaparte

Forgiving means to pardon the unpardonable,
Faith means believing the unbelievable,
And hoping means to hope when things are hopeless.
—G.K. Chesterton

If we were logical, the future would be bleak indeed. But
we are more than logical. We are human beings, and we
have faith, and we have hope, and we can work.
—Jacques Cousteau

Hope is one of those things in life you cannot do without.
—LeRoy Douglas

The hopeful man sees success where others see failure,
sunshine where others see shadows and storm.
—Orison Swett Marden

Our greatest good, and what we least can spare, is hope.
—John Armstrong

Now the God of hope fills you with all joy and peace
in believing, that ye may abound in hope.
—Rom. 15:13

Hope is faith holding out its hand in the dark.
—George Iles

The gift we can offer others is so simple a thing as hope.
—Daniel Berrigan

Hope, like the gleaming taper's light,
adorns and cheers our way;
And still, as darker grows the night,
emits a lighter ray.
—Oliver Goldsmith

Hope is a very unruly emotion.
—Gloria Steinem

Hope is the second soul of the unhappy.
—Johann von Goethe

It has never been, and never will be, easy work! But the road that
is built in hope is more pleasant to the traveler than the road built
in despair, even though they both lead to the same destination.
—Marian Zimmer Bradley

Ten thousand men possess ten thousand hopes.
—Euripides

Hope is the thing with feathers that perches in the soul and
sings the tune without words and never stops at all.
—Emily Dickinson

Hope is the first thing to take some sort of action.
—John Armstrong

It's never too late—in fiction or in life—to revise.
—Nancy Thayer

Hope is brightest when it dawns from fears.
—Sir Walter Scott

It is the around-the-corner brand of hope that prompts people
to action, while the distant hope acts as an opiate.
—Eric Hoffer

Hope is a risk that must be run.
—Georges Bernanos

Hope has as many lives as a cat or a king.
—Henry Wadsworth Longfellow

We want to create hope for the person ... we
must give hope, always hope.
—Mother Teresa, on AIDS

Hope is like a road in the country; there was never a road, but
when many people walk on it, the road comes into existence.
—Lin Yutang

Hope is the anchor of the soul, the stimulus to
action, and the incentive to achievement.
—ANON

Hope is the feeling we have that the feeling we have is not permanent.
—MIGNON MCLAUGHLIN

Hope is a vigorous principle . . . it sets the head and heart
to work, and animates a man to do his utmost.
—JEREMY COLLIER

Oh, what a valiant faculty is hope.
—MICHEL DE MONTAIGNE

Hope, that star of life's tremulous ocean.
—PAUL MOON JAMES

They say a person needs just three things to be truly happy in this
world. Someone to love, something to do, and something to hope for.
—TOM BODETT

Hope is patience with the lamp lit.
—TERTULLIAN

Extreme hopes are born of extreme misery.
—BERTRAND RUSSELL

Hope is the positive mode of awaiting the future.
—EMIL BRUNNER

Hope springs eternal in the human breast:
Man never Is, but always To be blest.
—ALEXANDER POPE

Hope is itself a species of happiness, and, perhaps,
the chief happiness which this world affords.
—SAMUEL JOHNSON

While there's life, there's hope.
—TERENCE

When you're depressed, the whole body is depressed, and it translates to the cellular level. The first objective is to get your energy up, and you can do it through play. It's one of the most powerful ways of breaking up hopelessness and bringing energy into the situation.
—O. Carl Simonton

There is no medicine like hope, no incentive so great, and no tonic so powerful as expectation of something tomorrow.
—Orison Swett Marden

True hope is swift and flies with swallow's wings;
Kings it makes Gods, and meaner creatures kings.
—William Shakespeare

Every area of trouble gives out a ray of hope, and the one unchangeable certainty is that nothing is certain or unchangeable.
—John F. Kennedy

Great hopes make great men.
—Thomas Fuller

Hope is a satisfaction unto itself, and need not be fulfilled to be appreciated.
—Dr. Fred O. Henker

Hope is not the conviction that something will turn out well but the certainty that something makes sense, regardless of how it turns out.
—Vaclav Havel

Hope is putting faith to work when doubting would be easier.
—Anon

Honor begets honor, trust begets trust, faith begets faith, and hope is the mainspring of life.
—Henry L. Stimson

Hope is an adventure, a going forward, a confident search for a rewarding life.
—Dr. Karl Menninger

Hope is the belief, more or less strong, that joy will
come; desire is the wish it may come.
—Sydney Smith

"Wait'll next year!" is the favorite cry of baseball fans,
football fans, hockey fans, and gardeners.
—Robert Orben

At first we hope too much; later on, not enough.
—Joseph Roux

Hope is the power of being cheerful in circumstances
which we know to be desperate.
—G.K. Chesterton

The miserable have no medicine but hope.
—William Shakespeare

Patience is the art of hoping.
—Vauvenargues

Have hope. Though clouds environs now,
And gladness hides her face in scorn,
Put thou the shadow from thy brow—
No night but hath its morn.
—J.C.F. von Schiller

In time of trouble avert not thy face from hope, for
the soft marrow abideth in the hard bone.
—Hafez

We should not let our fears hold us back from pursuing our hopes.
—John F. Kennedy

Hope and patience are two sovereign remedies for all, the
surest reposals, the softest cushions to lean on in adversity.
—Robert Burton

Without hope men are only half alive. With
hope they dream and think and work.
—Charles Sawyer

In the night of death, hope sees a star, and listening
love can hear the rustle of a wing.
—ROBERT G. INGERSOLL

The wind was cold off the mountains and I was a naked man
with enemies behind me, and nothing before me but hope.
—LOUIS L'AMOUR

Take hope from the heart of man and you make him a beast of prey.
—OUIDA

Hope arouses, as nothing else can arouse, a passion for the possible.
—WILLIAM SLOAN COFFIN, JR.

To hope is to enjoy.
—JACQUES DELILLE

Hope is the last thing to abandon the unhappy.
—ANON

Things which you do not hope happen more
frequently than things which you do hope.
—PLAUTUS

Hope works in these ways: it looks for the good in people instead
of harping on the worst; it discovers what can be done instead
of grumbling about what cannot; it regards problems, large or
small, as opportunities; it pushes ahead when it would be easy
to quit; it "lights the candle" instead of "cursing the darkness."
—ANON

There is no Hope without Fear, and no Fear without Hope.
—BARUCH SPINOZA

They who dream by day are cognizant of many things
which escape those who dream only by night.
—EDGAR ALLAN POE

Hope for the best and prepare for the worst.
—PROVERB

In the factory, we make cosmetics; in the store we sell hope.
—CHARLES H. REVSON

Man needs, for his happiness, not only the enjoyment of
this or that, but hope and enterprise and change.
—BERTRAND RUSSELL

RELIGION/PRAYER

I pray on the principle that wine knocks the cork out of a bottle.
There is an inward fermentation, and there must be a vent.
—HENRY WARD BEECHER

Bear up the hands that hang down, by faith and prayer;
support the tottering knees. Storm the throne of grace
and persevere therein, and mercy will come down.
—JOHN WESLEY

The value of consistent prayer is not that He will
hear us, but that we will hear Him.
—WILLIAM McGILL

We, one and all of us, have an instinct to pray; and this
fact constitutes an invitation from God to pray.
—CHARLES SANDERS PEIRCE

We may as well not pray at all as offer our prayers in a lifeless manner.
—WILLIAM S. PLUMER

And whatever ye shall ask in my name, that will I do.
—1 JN. 14:13

Pray, always pray; when sickness wastes thy frame,
Prayer brings the healing power of Jesus' name.
—A.B. SIMPSON

True religion . . . is giving and finding one's happiness
by bringing happiness into the lives of others.
—WILLIAM J.H. BOETCKER

When we go to our meeting with God, we should go like a patient to his doctor, first to be thoroughly examined and afterwards to be treated for our ailment. Then something will happen when you pray.
—O. HALLESBY

Trouble and perplexity drive me to prayer and prayer drives away perplexity and trouble.
—PHILIPP MELANCHTHON

Let your requests be made known unto God.
—PHIL. 4:6

You can't pray a lie.
—MARK TWAIN

We cannot talk to God strongly when we have not lived for God strongly. The closet cannot be made holy to God when the life has not been holy to God.
—E.M. BOUNDS

Religion is for people who are afraid of hell, and spirituality is for people who have been in hell.
—LIZA MINNELLI

In Fellowship; alone
To God, with Faith, draw near,
Approach His Courts, besiege His Throne
With all the power of Prayer.
—CHARLES WESLEY

Prayer crowns God with the honor and glory due to His name, and God crowns prayer with assurance and comfort. The most praying souls are the most assured souls.
—THOMAS B. BROOKS

Rejoice always, pray constantly, and in all circumstances give thanks.
—THE DESERT FATHERS

We must wrestle earnestly in prayer, like men contending with a deadly enemy for life.
—J.C. RYLE

Let prayer be the key of the morning and the bolt at night.
—Philip Henry

Don't try to reach God with your understanding; that
is impossible. Reach him in love; that is possible.
—Carlo Carretto

Cold prayers shall never have any warm answers.
—Thomas B. Brooks

We have to pray with our eyes on God, not on the difficulties.
—Oswald Chambers

Let me burn out for God ... prayer is the great
thing. Oh, that I may be a man of prayer!
—Henry Martyn

O thou, by whom we come to God,
The Life, the Truth, the Way,
The path of prayer Thyself hast trod—
Lord teach us how to pray.
—James Montgomery

You don't have to be dowdy to be a Christian.
—Tammy Faye Bakker Messner

We can do nothing without prayer. All things can be
done by importunate prayer. It surmounts or removes
all obstacles, overcomes every resisting force and gains
its ends in the face of invincible hindrances.
—E.M. Bounds

We read of preaching the Word out of season, but we do not
read of praying out of season, for that is never out of season.
—Matthew Henry

The right way to pray, then, is any way that
allows us to communicate with God.
—Colleen Townsend Evans

A sensible thanksgiving for mercies received is a mighty prayer
in the Spirit of God. It prevails with Him unspeakably.
—John Bunyan

Pray if thou canst with hope, but ever pray, though hope be weak or
sick with long delay; pray in the darkness if there be no light; and if for
any wish thou dare not pray, then pray to God to cast that wish away.
—Anon

Grant us grace, Almighty Father, so to pray as to deserve to be heard.
—Jane Austen

Without prayer I should have been a lunatic long ago.
—Mahatma Gandhi

Time spent on the knees in prayer will do more to remedy
heart strain and nerve worry than anything else.
—George David Stewart

Prayer is of transcendent importance. Prayer is the mightiest
agent to advance God's work. Praying hearts and hands only
can do God's work. Prayer succeeds when all else fails.
—E.M. Bounds

He that will learn to pray, let him to sea.
—George Herbert

Spread out your petition before God, and then say, "Thy
will, not mine, be done." The sweetest lesson I have learned
in God's school is to let the Lord choose for me.
—Dwight L. Moody

Do I want to pray or only to think about my human problems? Do I
want to pray or simply kneel there contemplating my sorrow? Do I
want to direct my prayer toward God or let it direct itself towards me?
—Hubert Van Zeller

There must be fired affections before our prayers will go up.
—William Jenkyn

When we go to our meeting with God, we should go like a patient
to his doctor, first to be thoroughly examined and afterwards to be
treated for our ailment. Then something will happen when you pray.
—O. HALLESBY

We can never know God as it is our privilege to know Him by brief
repetitions that are requests for personal favors, and nothing more.
—E.M. BOUNDS

Search me, O God, and know my heart: try me, and know my
thoughts: and see if there be any wicked way in me.
—Ps. 139:23-24

God tells us to burden him with whatever burdens us.
—ANON

The influence of prayer on the human human mind and body . . . can
be measured in terms of increased physical buoyancy, greater
intellectual vigor, moral stamina, and a deeper understanding
of the realities underlying human relationships.
—DR. ALEXIS CARREL

When our will wholeheartedly enters into the
prayer of Christ, then we pray correctly.
—DIETRICH BONHOEFFER

Religion is no more possible without prayer than poetry
without language or music without atmosphere.
—JAMES MARTINEAU

Religion . . . is a man's total rection upon life.
—WILLIAM JAMES

Teach us to pray that we may cause
The enemy to flee,
That we his evil power may bind,
His prisoners to free.
—WATCHMAN NEE

All the prayers in the Scripture you will find to be reasoning
with God, not a multitude of words heaped together.
—STEPHEN CHARNOCK

He prayeth well, who loveth well
Both man and bird and beast.
He prayeth best, who loveth best
All things both great and small;
For the dear God who loveth us,
He made and loveth all.
—SAMUEL TAYLOR COLERIDGE

Prayer is not an old woman's idle amusement. Properly understood
and applied, it is the most potent instrument of action.
—MAHATMA GANDHI

How those holy men of old could storm the battlements above!
When there was no way to look but up, they lifted up their eyes
to God who made the hills, with unshakable confidence.
—HERBERT LOCKYER

No matter what may be the test,
God will take care of you;
Lean, weary one, upon His breast,
God will take care of you.
—C.D. MARTIN

They who have steeped their soul in prayer
can every anguish calmly bear.
—RICHARD M. MILNES

From silly devotions and from sourfaced saints, good Lord, deliver us.
—SAINT TERESA OF AVILA

By prayer we couple the powers of heaven to our helplessness, the
powers which can capture strongholds and make the impossible possible.
—O. HALLESBY

He who has learned to pray has learned the
greatest secret of a holy and a happy life.
—WILLIAM LAW

Today any successful and competent businessman will employ
the latest and best-tested methods in production, distribution,
and administration, and many are discovering that one of
the greatest of all efficiency methods is prayer power.
—NORMAN VINCENT PEALE

He who ceases to pray ceases to prosper.
—Sir William Gurney Benham

The goal of prayer is the ear of God, a goal that can only be reached
by patient and continued and continuous waiting upon Him,
pouring out our heart to Him and permitting Him to speak to us.
Only by so doing can we expect to know Him, and as we come to
know Him better we shall spend more time in His presence and
find that presence a constant and ever-increasing delight.
—E.M. Bounds

Prayer should be the means by which I, at all times, receive all that I
need, and, for this reason, be my daily refuge, my daily consolation,
my daily joy, my source of rich and inexhaustible joy in life.
—Saint John Chrysostom

It is the will of our heavenly Father that we should come to Him
freely and confidently and make known our desires to Him, just as
we would have our children come freely and of their own accord
and speak to us about the things they would like to have.
—O. Hallesby

No heart thrives without much secret converse with God
and nothing will make amends for the want of it.
—John Berridge

Our Father, let the spirit of gratitude so prevail in our
hearts that we may manifest thy Spirit in our lives.
—W.B. Slack

Productive prayer requires earnestness, not eloquence.
—Anon

Tomorrow I plan to work, work, from early until late. In fact I have
so much to do that I shall spend the first three hours in prayer.
—Martin Luther

Do not have as your motive the desire to be known as a praying
man. Get an inner chamber in which to pray where no one knows
you are praying, shut the door, and talk to God in secret.
—Oswald Chambers

I have never made but one prayer to God, a very short one: "O Lorde, make my enemies ridiculous." And God granted it.
—Voltaire

To pray is nothing more involved than to open the door, giving Jesus access to our needs and permitting Him to exercise His own power in dealing with them.
—O. Hallesby

It is not so true that "prayer changes things" as that prayer changes me and I change things. God has so constituted things that prayer on the basis of Redemption alters the way in which a man looks at things. Prayer is not a question of altering things externally, but of working wonders in a man's disposition.
—Oswald Chambers

To have a curable illness and to leave it untreated except for prayer is like sticking your hand in a fire and asking God to remove the flame.
—Sandra L. Douglas

I care not what black spiritual crisis we may come through or what delightful spiritual Canaan we may enter, no blessing of the Christian life becomes continually possessed unless we are men and women of regular, daily, unhurried, secret lingerings in prayer.
—J. Sidlow Baxter

Prayer is an end to isolation. It is living our daily life with someone; with him who alone can deliver us from solitude.
—Georges Lefevre

The effectual, fervent prayer of a righteous man availeth much.
—Jas. 5:16

Prayer requires more of the heart than of the tongue.
—Adam Clarke

The entire day receives order and discipline when it acquires unity. This unity must be sought and found in morning prayer. The morning prayer determines the day.
—Dietrich Bonhoeffer

The first purpose of prayer is to know God.
—CHARLES L. ALLEN

Don't pray to escape trouble. Don't pray to be comfortable
in your emotions. Pray to do the will of God in every
situation. Nothing else is worth praying for.
—SAMUEL M. SHOEMAKER

The fewer the words, the better the prayer.
—MARTIN LUTHER

Look, as a painted man is no man, and as painted
fire is no fire, so a cold prayer is no prayer.
—THOMAS B. BROOKS

In the war upon the powers of darkness, prayer is the primary and
mightiest weapon, both in aggressive war upon them and their
works; in the deliverance of men from their power; and against
them as a hierarchy of powers opposed to Christ and His Church.
—JESSIE PENN-LEWIS

Pray for whatsoever you will. In the name of Jesus you
have permission, not only to stand in the presence of
God, but also to pray for everything you need.
—O. HALLESBY

Seven days without prayer makes one weak.
—ALLEN E. BARTLETT

If you are swept off your feet, it's time to get on your knees.
—FRED BECK

Constant prayer quickly straightens out our thoughts.
—THE DESERT FATHERS

Those who always pray are necessary to those who never pray.
—VICTOR HUGO

Prayer covers the whole of man's life. There is no thought, feeling,
yearning, or desire, however low, trifling, or vulgar we may deem it,
which, if it affects our real interest or happiness, we may not lay before

God and be sure of sympathy. His nature is such that our often coming does not tire him. The whole burden of the whole life of every man may be rolled on to God and not weary him, though it has wearied the man.
—HENRY WARD BEECHER

It is by no haphazard chance that in every age men have risen early to pray. The first thing that marks decline in spiritual life is our relationship to the early morning.
—OSWALD CHAMBERS

Lord, you know how busy I must be this day. If I forget You, do not You forget me.
—JACOB ASTLEY

Productive prayer requires earnestness, not eloquence.
—ANON

Do not work so hard for Christ that you have no strength to pray, for prayer requires strength.
—J. HUDSON TAYLOR

Confess your faults one to another, and pray one for another, that ye may be healed. The effectual, fervent prayer of a righteous man availeth much.
—JAS. 5:16

Prayer does not change God, but it changes him who prays.
—SØREN KIERKEGAARD

We look upon prayer as a means of getting things for ourselves, but the biblical purpose of prayer is that we may get to know God Himself.
—OSWALD CHAMBERS

All who have walked with God have viewed prayer as the main business of their lives.
—DELMA JACKSON

In the morning, prayer is the key that opens to us the treasures of God's mercies and blessings; in the evening, it is the key that shuts us up under His protection and safeguard.
—ANON

Prayer may not change things for you, but it
for sure changes you for things.
—Samuel M. Shoemaker

Even if no command to pray had existed, our very
weakness would have suggested it.
—Francois de Fenelon

Evening, and morning, and at noon, will I pray.
—Ps. 55:17

The purpose of prayer is to reveal the presence of God
equally present, all the time, in every condition.
—Oswald Chambers

Though smooth be the heartless prayer, no ear in heaven will mind it;
And the finest phrase falls dead, if there is no feeling behind it.
—Ella Wheeler Wilcox

By prayer, the ability is secured to feel the law of love, to speak according
to the law of love, and to do everything in harmony with the law of love.
—E.M. Bounds

If you can't pray as you want to, pray as you
can. God knows what you mean.
—Vance Havner

Our immediate temptation will be to ask for specific
solutions to specific problems, and for the ability to help
other people as we have already thought they should be
helped. In that case, we are asking God to do it our way.
—Bill W.

As impossible as it is for us to take a breath in the morning large enough
to last us until noon, so impossible is it to pray in the morning in such a
way as to last us until noon. Let your prayers ascend to Him constantly,
audibly or silently, as circumstances throughout the day permit.
—O. Hallesby

An agnostic found himself in trouble, and a friend suggested he pray. "How can I pray when I do not know whether or not there is a God?" he asked. "If you are lost in the forest," his friend replied, "you do not wait until you find someone before shouting for help."
—DAN PLIES

Prayer is not eloquence, but earnestness; not the definition of helplessness, but the feeling of it; not figures of speech, but earnestness of soul.
—HANNAH MORE

Sometimes we think we are too busy to pray. That is a great mistake, for praying is a saving of time.
—CHARLES HADDON SPURGEON

To God your every Want
In instant Prayer display,
Pray always; Pray, and never faint;
Pray, without ceasing, Pray.
—CHARLES WESELY

Of all things, guard against neglecting God in the secret place of prayer.
—WILLIAM WILBERFORCE

O Lord, forgive what I have been, sanctify what I am, and order what I shall be.
—ANON

A day without prayer is a boast against God.
—OWEN CARR

Short prayers pierceth Heaven.
—THE CLOUD OF UNKNOWING

Prayer is the great engine to overthrow and rout my spiritual enemies, the great means to procure the graces of which I stand in hourly need.
—JOHN NEWTON

Men would pray better if they lived better. They would get more from God if they lived more obedient and well-pleasing to God.
—E.M. BOUNDS

If you have ever prayed in the dawn you will ask yourself why
you were so foolish as not to do it always: it is difficult to get into
communion with God in the midst of the hurly-burly of the day.
—Oswald Chambers

True religion . . . is giving and finding one's happiness
by bringing happiness into the lives of others.
—William J.H. Boetcker

The more praying there is in the world, the better the world
will be; the mightier the forces against evil everywhere.
—E.M. Bounds

Don't pray when it rains if you don't pray when the sun shines.
—Satchel Paige

The Christian will find his parentheses for prayer
even in the busiest hours of life.
—Richard Cecil

Ask, and it shall be given you; seek, and ye shall find;
knock, and it shall be opened unto you.
—Mt. 7:7

God is in heaven, and thou upon earth: therefore let thy words be few.
—Eccl. 5:2

In prayer the lips ne'er act the winning part, without
the sweet concurrence of the heart.
—Robert Herrick

Pray, always pray; beneath sins heaviest load,
Prayer claims the blood from Jesus' side that flowed.
Pray, always pray; though weary, faint, and lone,
Prayer nestles by the Father's sheltering throne.
—A.B. Simpson

You need not cry very loud; He is nearer to us than we think.
—Brother Lawrence

Pray without ceasing. In everything give thanks.
—1 Th. 5:17

Spread out your petition before God, and then say, "Thy will, not mine, be done." The sweetest lesson I have learned in God's school is to let the Lord choose for me.
—DWIGHT L. MOODY

When I am weak, then am I strong.
—2 COR. 12:10

The main lesson about prayer is just this: Do it! Do it! Do it! You want to be taught to pray? My answer is: pray.
—JOHN LAIDLAW

Teach us to pray often, that we may pray oftener.
—JEREMY TAYLOR

God may turn his ears from prattling prayers, or preaching prayers, but never from penitent, believing prayers.
—WILLIAM S. PLUMER

Time spent in prayer is never wasted.
—FRANCOIS DE FENELON

Prayer time must be kept up as duly as meal-time.
—MATTHEW HENRY

But thou, when thou prayest, enter into thy room, and when thou hast shut thy door, pray to thy Father who is in secret; and thy Father who seeth in secret, shall reward thee openly.
—MT. 6:6

I did this night promise my wife never to go to bed without calling upon God, upon my knees, in prayer.
—SAMUEL PEPYS

Private place and plenty of time are the life of prayer.
—E.M. BOUNDS

The whole meaning of prayer is that we may know God.
—OSWALD CHAMBERS

The clue is not to ask in a miserly way—the
key is to ask in a grand manner.
—ANN WIGMORE

Abiding fully means praying much.
—ANDREW MURRAY

Fear of trouble, present and future, often blinds us to the numerous small
blessings we enjoy, silencing our prayers of praise and thanksgiving.
—ANON

He prays best who does not know that he is praying.
—SAINT ANTHONY OF PADUA

Prayer is not eloquence, but earnestness; not the
definition of helplessness, but the feeling of it; not
figures of speech, but earnestness of soul.
—HANNAH MORE

The less I pray, the harder it gets; the more I pray, the better it goes.
—MARTIN LUTHER

One night alone in prayer might make us new men, changed from
poverty of soul to spiritual wealth, from trembling to triumphing.
—CHARLES HADDON SPURGEON

If we rely on the Holy Spirit, we shall find that our prayers
become more and more inarticulate; and when they are
inarticulate, reverence grows deeper and deeper.
—OSWALD CHAMBERS

He who cannot pray when the sun is shining will not
know how to pray when the clouds come.
—ANON

If our petitions are in accordance with His will, and if we seek
His glory in the asking, the answers will come in ways that will
astonish us and fill our hearts with songs of thanksgiving.
—J.K. MACLEAN

We must lay before him what is in us, not what ought to be in us.
—C.S. LEWIS

Ask in faith.
—Jas. 1:6

If you're caught on a golf course during a storm and are afraid
of lightning, hold up a 1-iron. Not even God can hit a 1-iron.
—Lee Trevino

Faith, and hope, and patience and all the strong, beautiful, vital
forces of piety are withered and dead in a prayerless life. The life
of the individual believer, his personal salvation, and personal
Christian graces have their being, bloom, and fruitage in prayer.
—E.M. Bounds

The cry of a young raven is nothing but the natural cry of a creature, but
your cry, if it be sincere, is the result of a work of grace in your heart.
—Charles Haddon Spurgeon

Prayer should be the key of the day and the lock of the night.
—Thomas Fuller

He prayeth well, who loveth well
Both man and bird and beast.
He prayeth best, who loveth best
All things both great and small;
For the dear God who loveth us,
He made and loveth all.
—Samuel Taylor Coleridge

Prayer, to the patriarchs and prophets, was more than the recital of well-
known and well-worn phrases—it was the outpouring of the heart.
—Herbert Lockyer

God prefers bad verses recited with a pure heart to
the finest verses chanted by the wicked.
—Voltaire

Every time we pray our horizon is altered, our attitude
to things is altered, not sometimes but every time, and
the amazing thing is that we don't pray more.
—Oswald Chambers

O Lord, you know what is best for me. Let this or that be done, as you please. Give what you will, how much you will, and when you will.
—THOMAS A'KEMPIS

God hears no more than the heart speaks; and if the heart be dumb, God will certainly be dumb.
—THOMAS B. BROOKS

When you pray, rather let your heart be without words than your words without heart.
—JOHN BUNYAN

Now I am past all comforts here, but prayer.
—WILLIAM SHAKESPEARE

There come times when I have nothing more to tell God. If I were to continue to pray in words, I would have to repeat what I have already said. At such such times it is wonderful to say to God, "May I be in Thy presence, Lord? I have nothing more to say to Thee, but I do love to be in Thy presence."
—O. HALLESBY

You are coming to a King,
Large petitions with you bring
For his grace and power are such
None can ever ask too much.
—JOHN NEWTON

When praying for healing, ask great things of God and expect great things from God. But let us seek for that healing that really matters, the healing of the heart, enabling us to trust God simply, face God honestly, and live triumphantly.
—ARLO F. NEWELL

It is convenient that there be gods, and, as it is convenient, let us believe that there are.
—OVID

Of all things, guard against neglecting God in the secret place of prayer.
—WILLIAM WILBERFORCE

To stand on one leg and prove God's existence is a very different thing from going down on one's knees and thanking him.
—SØREN KIERKEGAARD

We had not even prayed rightly. We had always said, "Grant me my wishes" instead of "Thy will be done."
—TWELVE STEPS AND TWELVE TRADITIONS

God's ear lies close to the believer's lip.
—ANON

They tell about a fifteen-year-old boy in an orphans' home who had an incurable stutter. One Sunday the minister was detained and the boy volunteered to say the prayer in his stead. He did it perfectly, too, without a single stutter. Later he explained, "I don't stutter when I talk to God. He loves me."
—BENNETT CERF

Begin to realize more and more that prayer is the most important thing you do. You can use your time to no better advantage than to pray whenever you have an opportunity to do so, either alone or with others; while at work, while at rest, or while walking down the street. Anywhere!
—O. HALLESBY

Temptations which accompany the working day will be conquered on the basis of the morning breakthrough to God. Decisions, demanded by work, become easier and simpler where they are made not in the fear of men, but only in the sight of God. He wants to give us today the power which we need for our work.
—DIETRICH BONHOEFFER

No one is a firmer believer in the power of prayer than the devil; not that he practices it, but he suffers from it.
—GUY H. KING

Whether we like it or not, asking is the rule of the Kingdom.
—CHARLES HADDON SPURGEON

The simple heart that freely asks in love, obtains.
—JOHN GREENLEAF WHITTIER

Prayer is a kind of calling home every day. And there can come to you a serenity, a feeling of at-homeness in God's universe, a peace that the world can neither give nor disturb, a fresh courage, a new insight, a holy boldness that you'll never, never get any other way.
—EARL G. HUNT, JR.

Private place and plenty of time are the life of prayer.
—E.M. BOUNDS

Nowhere can we get to know the holiness of God, and come under His influence and power, except in the inner chamber. It has been well said: "No man can expect to make progress in holiness who is not often and long alone with God."
—ANDREW MURRAY

All who have walked with God have viewed prayer as the main business of their lives.
—DELMA JACKSON

The minds of people are so cluttered up with every-day living these days that they don't, or won't, take time out for a little prayer—for mental cleansing, just as they take a bath for physical, outer cleansing. Both are necessary.
—JO ANN CARLSON

I have to hurry all day to get time to pray.
—MARTIN LUTHER

There is no need to get to a place of prayer; pray wherever you are.
—OSWALD CHAMBERS

When we succeed in truly thanking God, we feel good at heart. The reason is that we have been created to give glory to God, now and forevermore. And every time we do so, we feel that we are in harmony with His plans and purposes for our lives. Then we are truly in our element. That is why it is so blessed.
—O. HALLESBY

What is the life of a Christian but a life of prayer!
—DAVID BROWN

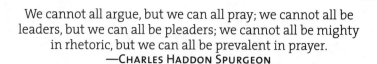

We cannot all argue, but we can all pray; we cannot all be
leaders, but we can all be pleaders; we cannot all be mighty
in rhetoric, but we can all be prevalent in prayer.
—CHARLES HADDON SPURGEON

Helplessness becomes prayer the moment that you go to Jesus and speak
candidly and confidently with him about your needs. This is to believe.
—O. HALLESBY

Heaven is never deaf but when man's heart is dumb.
—FRANCIS QUARLES

Prayer is a serious thing. We may be taken at our words.
—DWIGHT L. MOODY

In prayer it is better to have a heart without
words than words without a heart.
—JOHN BUNYAN

God eagerly awaits the chance to bless the person
whose heart is turned toward Him.
—ANON

If we are willing to spend hours on end to learn to play the piano,
operate a computer, or fly an airplane, it is sheer nonsense for us to
imagine that we can learn the high art of getting guidance through
communion with the Lord without being willing to set aside time for it.
—PAUL REES

The effectual, fervent prayer of a righteous man availeth much.
—JAS. 5:16

Prayer should be short, without giving God Almighty reasons why
He should grant this or that; He knows best what is good for us.
—JOHN SELDEN

For food, for raiment, for life and opportunity, for sun and rain,
for water and the portage trails, we give you thanks, O Lord.
—A PRAYER FROM THE NORTH WOODS

Do not have as your motive the desire to be known as a praying man. Get an inner chamber in which to pray where no one knows you are praying, shut the door, and talk to God in secret.
—OSWALD CHAMBERS

What is the life of a Christian but a life of prayer!
—DAVID BROWN

It is good for us to keep some account of our prayers,
that we may not unsay them in our practice.
—MATTHEW HENRY

To avail yourself of His certain wisdom, ask of Him whatever questions you have. But do not entreat Him, for that will never be necessary.
—HUGH PRATHER

Every chain that spirits wear crumbles in the breadth of prayer.
—JOHN GREENLEAF WHITTIER

I feel it is far better to begin with God, to see His face first, to get my soul near Him before it is near another. In general it is best to have at least one hour alone with God before engaging in anything else.
—E.M. BOUNDS

All those football coaches who hold dressing-room prayers before a game should be forced to attend church once a week.
—DUFFY DAUGHERTY

Prayer is not merely an occasional impulse to which we respond when we are in trouble: prayer is a life attitude.
—WALTER A. MUELLER

We pray pious blether, our will is not in it, and then we say God does not answer; we never asked Him for anything. Asking means that our wills are in what we ask.
—OSWALD CHAMBERS

When you cannot pray as you would, pray as you can.
—EDWARD M. GOULBURN

A man's state before God may always be measured by his prayers.
—J.C. RYLE

Every time you pray, if your prayer is sincere, there will be
new feeling and new meaning in it which will give you fresh
courage, and you will understand that prayer is an education.
—FYODOR DOSTOYEVSKY

God tells us to burden him with whatever burdens us.
—ANON

Ask the gods nothing excessive.
—AESCHYLUS

Ordinarily when a man in difficulty turns to prayer, he
has already tried every other means of escape.
—AUSTIN O'MALLEY

Without the incense of heartfelt prayer, even
the greatest of cathedrals is dead.
—ANON

We ought to act with God in the greatest simplicity, speak to Him
frankly and plainly, and implore His assistance in our affairs.
—BROTHER LAWRENCE

Certain thoughts are prayers. There are moments when,
whatever be the attitude of the body, the soul is on its knees.
—VICTOR HUGO

The best prayers have often more groans than words.
—JOHN BUNYAN

Prayer is not asking. It is a longing of the soul.
—MAHATMA GANDHI

He offered a prayer so deeply devout that he seemed
kneeling and praying at the bottom of the sea.
—HERMAN MELVILLE

Thou who has given so much to me, give one thing more: a grateful heart.
—GEORGE HERBERT

Let us come before His presence with thanksgiving.
—Ps. 95:2

It is impossible to conduct your life as a disciple
without definite times of secret prayer.
—Oswald Chambers

Though we cannot by our prayers give God any information,
yet we must by our prayers give him honor.
—Matthew Henry

When prayer is a struggle, do not worry about the prayers
that you cannot pray. You yourself are a prayer to God at
that moment. All that is within you cries out to Him. And
He hears all the pleas that your suffering soul and body are
making to Him with groanings which cannot be uttered.
—O. Hallesby

The man who says his prayers in the evening is a captain
posting his sentries. After that, he can sleep.
—Charles Baudelaire

Pray for one another.
—Jas. 5:16

When at night you cannot sleep, talk to the
Shepherd and stop counting sheep.
—Anon

Let me burn out for God ... prayer is the great
thing. Oh, that I may be a man of prayer!
—Henry Martyn

A little lifting of the heart suffices; a little remembrance
of God, one act of inward worship are prayers which,
however short, are nevertheless acceptable to God.
—Brother Lawrence

God bless all those that I love; God bless all those that
love me; God bless all those that love those that I love
and all those that love those that love me.
—A New England Sampler

The only way to pray is to pray, and the way to pray well is to pray much.
—ANON

I have been driven many times to my knees by the overwhelming
conviction that I had nowhere else to go. My own wisdom
and that of all about me seemed insufficient for the day.
—ABRAHAM LINCOLN

From silly devotions and from sourfaced saints, good Lord, deliver us.
—SAINT TERESA OF AVILA

If the only prayer you say in your whole life is
"Thank you," that would suffice.
—MEISTER ECKHART

God never denied that soul anything that went as far as heaven to ask it.
—JOHN TRAPP

It has been well said that almost the only scoffers at
prayer are those who never tried it enough.
—TWELVE STEPS AND TWELVE TRADITIONS

Prayer is not only asking, it is an attitude of heart that
produces an atmosphere in which asking is perfectly natural,
and Jesus says, "every one that asketh receiveth."
—OSWALD CHAMBERS

God can pick sense out of a confused prayer.
—RICHARD SIBBES

Sincerity is the prime requisite in every approach to the
God who . . . hates all hypocrisy, falsehood, and deceit.
—GEOFFREY B. WILSON

Our prayers must mean something to us if
they are to mean anything to God.
—MALTBIE D. BABCOCK

He who prays for his neighbors will be heard for himself.
—TALMUD

Let us thank God heartily as often as we pray that we have
His Spirit in us to teach us to pray. Thanksgiving will draw our
hearts out to God and keep us engaged with Him; it will take our
attention from ourselves and give the Spirit room in our hearts.
—Andrew Murray

Get into the habit of dealing with God about everything. Unless
in the first waking moment of the day you learn to fling the door
wide back and let God in, you will work on a wrong level all day;
but swing the door wide open and pray to your Father in secret, and
every public thing will be stamped with the presence of God.
—Oswald Chambers

Prayers not felt by us are seldom heard by God.
—Philip Henry

Prayer must never be answered; if it is, it ceases to
be a prayer, and becomes a correspondence.
—Oscar Wilde

Prayer in the sense of petition, asking for things, is a small part of it;
confession and penitence are its threshold, adoration its sanctuary,
the presence and vision and enjoyment of God its bread and wine.
—C.S. Lewis

Prayer begins where human capacity ends.
—Marian Anderson

Intercessory prayer for one who is sinning prevails. God says so!
The will of the man prayed for does not come into question at all,
he is connected with God by prayer, and prayer on the basis of the
Redemption sets the connection working and God gives life.
—Oswald Chambers

Religion is love; in no case is it logic.
—Beatrice Potter Webb

Our prayers must spring from the indigenous soil of our own
personal confrontation with the Spirit of God in our lives.
—Malcolm Boyd

The Lord's Prayer may be committed to memory
quickly, but it is slowly learnt by heart.
—FREDERICK DENISON MAURICE

When you enter your secret chamber, take plenty of time before
you begin to speak. Let quietude wield its influence upon you. Let
the fact that you are alone assert itself. Give your soul time to get
released from the many outward things. Give God time to play
the prelude to prayer for the benefit of your distracted soul.
—O. HALLESBY

In the war upon the powers of darkness, prayer is the primary and
mightiest weapon, both in aggressive war upon them and their
works; in the deliverance of men from their power; and against
them as a hierarchy of powers opposed to Christ and His Church.
—JESSIE PENN-LEWIS

Prayer at its best is the expression of the total life, for all things
else being equal, our prayers are only as powerful as our lives.
—A.W. TOZER

Prayer is not artful monologue
Of voice uplifted from the son;
It is Love's tender dialogue
Between the soul and God.
—JOHN RICHARD MORELAND

No one who has had a unique experience with
prayer has a right to withhold it from others.
—SOONG MEL-LING

Many words do not a good prayer make; what counts is the heartfelt
desire to commune with God, and the faith to back it up.
—ANON

You need not cry very loud; He is nearer to us than we think.
—BROTHER LAWRENCE

There is neither encouragement nor room in Bible religion
for feeble desires, listless efforts, lazy attitudes; all must be
strenuous, urgent, ardent. Flamed desires, impassioned,

unwearied insistence delight heaven. God would have His children incorrigibly in earnest and persistently bold in their efforts. Heaven is too busy to listen to half-hearted prayers or to respond to pop-calls. Our whole being must be in our praying.
—E.M. Bounds

FORGIVENESS/ACCEPTANCE

I bear no grudges. I have a mind that retains nothing.
—Bette Midler

The real world is not easy to live in. It is rough; it is slippery. Without the most clear-eyed adjustments we fall and get crushed.
—Clarence Day

Let us forget and forgive injuries.
—Miguel de Cervantes

The resistance to the unpleasant situation is the root of suffering.
—Ram Dass and Paul Gorman

To understand is to forgive, even oneself.
—Alexander Chase

It is very easy to forgive others their mistakes; it takes more grit and gumption to forgive them for having witnessed our own.
—Jessamyn West

Forgiveness is the power that enlivens relationships. Forgiveness keeps life moving forward, creates harmony and makes you spiritually strong.
—Maoshing Ni, M.D.

Life's under no obligation to give us what we expect.
—Margaret Mitchell

People are lucky and unlucky ... according to the ratio between what they get and what they have been led to expect.
—Samuel Butler

Always forgive your enemies—but never forget their names.
—ROBERT F. KENNEDY

Nobody ever forgets where he buried a hatchet.
—KIN HUBBARD

If you haven't forgiven yourself something, how can you forgive others?
—DOLORES HUERTA

When we see ourselves in a situation which must be endured and gone through, it is best to meet it with firmness, and accommodate everything to it in the best way practicable. This lessens the evil, while fretting and fuming only increase your own torments.
—THOMAS JEFFERSON

There are two ways of meeting difficulties: you alter the difficulties, or you alter yourself to meet them.
—PHYLLIS BOTTOME

The individual who is best prepared for any occupation is the one . . . able to adapt himself to any situation.
—MORTIMER SMITH

The greatest evil which fortune can inflict on men is to endow them with small talents and great ambitions.
—VAUVENARGUES

He that cannot forgive others breaks the bridge over which he must pass himself; for every man has need to be forgiven.
—THOMAS FULLER

He who cannot do what he wants must make do with what he can.
—TERENCE

Buddha's doctrine: Man suffers because of his craving to possess and keep forever things which are essentially impermanent . . . this frustration of the desire to possess is the immediate cause of suffering.
—ALAN WATTS

The stupid neither forgive nor forget; the naive forgive and forget; the wise forgive, but do not forget.
—THOMAS SZASZ

Act so that you use humanity, as much in your own
person as in the person of every other, always at the
same time as end and never merely as means.
—Immanuel Kant

One cannot get through life without pain.... What we can
do is choose how to use the pain life presents to us.
—Bernie S. Siegel, M.D.

If you hate a person, you hate something in him that is part of yourself.
—Herman Hesse

One forgives to the degree that one loves.
—Francois de La Rochefoucauld

Not the power to remember, but its very opposite, the power
to forget, is a necessary condition for our existence.
—Sholem Asch

I don't hold no grudges more'n five years.
—William Kennedy

Humanity is never so beautiful as when praying
for forgiveness, or else forgiving another.
—Jean Paul Richter

Forgiveness is the giving, and so the receiving, of life.
—George Macdonald

Love is an act of endless forgiveness, a tender
look which becomes a habit.
—Peter Ustinov

Forgiveness is all-powerful. Forgiveness heals all ills.
—Catherine Ponder

How unhappy is he who cannot forgive himself.
—Publilius Syrus

The point . . . is to dwell upon the brightest parts in every prospect,
to call off the thoughts when turning upon disagreeable objects,
and strive to be pleased with the present circumstances.
—ABRAHAM TUCKER

I make the most of all that comes and the least of all that goes.
—SARA TEASDALE

We may fail of our happiness, strive we ever so bravely;
but we are less likely to fail if we measure with
judgment our chances and our capabilities.
—AGNES REPPLIER

Abandon your animosities and make your sons Americans!
—ROBERT E. LEE

Good is not good, where better is expected.
—THOMAS FULLER

The best thing we can do is to make wherever we're
lost look as much like home as we can.
—CHRISTOPHER FRY

Anger dwells only in the bosom of fools.
—ALBERT EINSTEIN

It is right it should be so,
Man was made for joy and woe;
And when this we rightly know,
Through the world we safely go.
—WILLIAM BLAKE

All that is necessary is to accept the impossible, do
without the indispensable, and bear the intolerable.
—KATHLEEN NORRIS

Forgiveness is the answer to the child's dream of a miracle by which
what is broken is made whole again, what is soiled is again made clean.
—DAG HAMMARSKJOLD

Into each life some rain must fall, some days must be dark and dreary.
—HENRY WADSWORTH LONGFELLOW

One is as one is, and the love that can't
encompass both is a poor sort of love.
—MARYA MANNES

The practice of forgiveness is our most important
contribution to the healing of the world.
—MARIANNE WILLIAMSON

The greatest and most important problems in life are all in a certain
sense insoluble. They can never be solved, but only outgrown.
—CARL JUNG

Forgiveness is the highest and most difficult of all moral lessons.
—JOSEPH JACOBS

Forgiveness is the remission of sins. For it is by this that what
has been lost, and was found, is saved from being lost again.
—SAINT AUGUSTINE

Life is 10 percent what you make it, and 90 percent how you take it.
—IRVING BERLIN

Adapt yourself to the things among which your lot has
been cast and love sincerely the fellow creatures with
whom destiny has ordained that you shall live.
—MARCUS AURELIUS

Forgive all who have offended you, not for them, but for yourself.
—HARRIET UTS NELSON

I have looked on a lot of women with lust. I've committed adultery in
my heart many times. God recognizes I will do this and forgives me.
—JIMMY CARTER

Those who are free of resentful thoughts surely find peace.
—BUDDHA

Who except the gods can live without any pain?
—AESCHYLUS

We must make the best of those ills which cannot be avoided.
—ALEXANDER HAMILTON

Many promising reconciliations have broken down
because while both parties came prepared to forgive,
neither party came prepared to be forgiven.
—CHARLES WILLIAM

Today I forgive all those who have ever offended me.
I give my love to all thirsty hearts, both to those who
love me and to those who do not love me.
—PARAMAHANSA YOGANANDA

How shall I love the sin, yet keep the sense,
And love the offender, yet detest the offence?
—ALEXANDER POPE

Free man is by necessity insecure; thinking man by necessity uncertain.
—ERICH FROMM

Forgiveness means letting go of the past.
—GERALD JAMPOLSKY

I find that it is not the circumstances in which we are placed, but
the spirit in which we face them, that constitutes our comfort.
—ELIZABETH T. KING

Maturity is achieved when a person accepts life as full of tension.
—JOSHUA L. LIEBMAN

What has always made a hell on earth has been
that man has tried to make it his heaven.
—FRIEDRICH HOLDERLIN

The happy and efficient people in this world are those
who accept trouble as a normal detail of human life
and resolve to capitalize it when it comes along.
—H. BERTRAM LEWIS

We win half the battle when we make up our minds to
take the world as we find it, including the thorns.
—ORISON S. MARDEN

If one has to submit, it is wasteful not to do
so with the best grace possible.
—SIR WINSTON CHURCHILL

To forgive is the highest, most beautiful form of love. In
return, you will receive untold peace and happiness.
—ROBERT MULLER

Life is an adventure in forgiveness.
—NORMAN COUSINS

Life has no smooth road for any of us; and in the bracing atmosphere
of a high aim the very roughness stimulates the climber to steadier
steps 'til the legend, "over steep ways to the stars," fulfills self.
—WILLIAM C. DOANE

The real world is not easy to live in. It is rough; it is slippery. Without
the most clear-eyed adjustments we fall and get crushed.
—CLARENCE DAY

Make a virtue of necessity.
—GEOFFREY CHAUCER

Forgiveness is the final form of love.
—REINHOLD NIEBUHR

What you can't get out of, get into wholeheartedly.
—MIGNON MCLAUGHLIN

To be wronged is nothing unless you continue to remember it.
—CONFUCIUS

Unhappiness is best defined as the difference
between our talents and our expectations.
—DR. EDWARD DE BONO

Forgiveness is man's deepest need and highest achievement.
—HORACE BUSHNELL

Always forgive your enemies; nothing annoys them so much.
—OSCAR WILDE

All that is necessary is to accept the impossible, do
without the indispensable, and bear the intolerable.
—KATHLEEN NORRIS

Once a woman has forgiven a man, she must
not reheat his sins for breakfast.
—MARLENE DIETRICH

Forgiving those who hurt us is the key to personal peace.
—G. WEATHERLY

The reasonable man adapts himself to the world; the unreasonable
one persists in trying to adapt the world to himself.
—GEORGE BERNARD SHAW

God will forgive me, that is His business.
—HEINRICH HEINE

The moment an individual can accept and forgive himself, even a
little, is the moment in which he becomes to some degree lovable.
—EUGENE KENNEDY

There is no armor against fate; death lays his icy hands on kings.
—JAMES SHIRLEY

We do not write as we want, but as we can.
—W. SOMERSET MAUGHAM

No man can have society upon his own terms.
—RALPH WALDO EMERSON

It is a common observation that those who dwell continually
upon their expectations are apt to become oblivious
to the requirements of their actual situation.
—CHARLES SANDERS PEIRCE

Into each life some rain must fall, some days must be dark and dreary.
—HENRY WADSWORTH LONGFELLOW

Flow with whatever may happen and let your mind be free. Stay centered by accepting whatever you are doing. This is the ultimate.
—CHUANG-TZU

I can pardon everybody's mistakes except my own.
—MARCUS CATO THE ELDER

The fragrance of the violet sheds on the heel that has crushed it.
—MARK TWAIN

Trouble will come soon enough, and when he does come receive him as pleasantly as possible ... the more amiably you greet him, the sooner he will go away.
—ARTEMUS WARD

When you have got an elephant by the hind legs and he is trying to run away, it is best to let him run.
—ABRAHAM LINCOLN

Life is not always what one wants it to be, but to make the best of it, as it is, is the only way of being happy.
—JENNIE JEROME CHURCHILL

If you bear the cross unwillingly, you make it a burden, and load yourself more heavily; but you must bear it.
—THOMAS A'KEMPIS

I forgive myself for having believed for so long that ... I was never good enough to have, get, be what I wanted.
—CEANNE DEROHAN

Those who can't forget are worse off than those who can't remember.
—ANON

The ideal man bears the accidents of life with dignity and grace, making the best of circumstances.
—ARISTOTLE

No traveler e'er reached that blest abode who found not thorns and briers in his road.
—WILLIAM COWPER

He is happy whose circumstances suit his temper; but he is more
excellent who can suit his temper to any circumstances.
—DAVID HUME

Anger is a killing thing: it kills the man who angers, for each rage leaves
him less than he had been before—it takes something from him.
—LOUIS L'AMOUR

I can have peace of mind only when I forgive rather than judge.
—GERALD JAMPOLSKY

Hate is a prolonged form of suicide.
—DOUGLAS V. STEERE

You have to take it as it happens, but you should try to
make it happen the way you want to take it.
—OLD GERMAN PROVERB

They may not deserve forgiveness, but I do.
—ANON

Forgiveness is the noblest vengeance.
—H.G. BOHN

It is very easy to forgive others their mistakes; it takes more grit
and gumption to forgive them for having witnessed your own.
—JESSAMYN WEST

There is no easy path leading out of life, and few
are the easy ones that lie within it.
—WALTER SAVAGE LANDOR

Know all and you will pardon all.
—THOMAS A'KEMPIS

Arrange whatever pieces come your way.
—VIRGINIA WOOLF

In the face of an obstacle which is impossible
to overcome, stubbornness is stupid.
—SIMONE DE BEAUVOIR

Without forgiveness life is governed ... by an
endless cycle of resentment and retaliation.
—ROBERT ASSAGLIOLI

Never deny a diagnosis, but do deny the
negative verdict that may go with it.
—NORMAN COUSINS

We must like what we have when we don't have what we like.
—ROGER DE BUSSY-RABUTIN

All I can do is play the game the way the cards fall.
—JAMES A. MICHENER

There is no good in arguing with the inevitable. The only argument
available with an east wind is to put on your overcoat.
—JAMES RUSSELL LOWELL

To understand is to forgive, even oneself.
—ALEXANDER CHASE

Resentments are burdens we don't need to carry.
—ANON

There is no man in this world without some manner of
tribulation or anguish, though he be king or pope.
—THOMAS A'KEMPIS

If you aspire to the highest place, it is no disgrace to
stop at the second, or even the third, place.
—CICERO

One of the signs of maturity is a healthy respect for reality—a
respect that manifests itself in the level of one's aspirations and
in the accuracy of one's assessment of the difficulties which
separate the facts of today from the bright hopes of tomorrow.
—ROBERT H. DAVIES

The forgiving state of mind is a magnetic power for attracting good.
—CATHERINE PONDER

There are no conditions to which a man cannot become accustomed.
—LEO TOLSTOY

One learns to adapt to the land in which one lives.
—LOUIS L'AMOUR

Real life is, to most men ... a perpetual compromise
between the ideal and the possible.
—BERTRAND RUSSELL

Only the brave know how to forgive. . . . A coward
never forgave; it is not in his nature.
—LAURENCE STERNE

When we accept tough jobs as a challenge to our ability and wade
into them with joy and enthusiasm, miracles can happen.
—ARLAND GILBERT

To carry a grudge is like being stung to death by one bee.
—WILLIAM H. WALTON

Nobody has things just as he would like them. The thing
to do is to make a success with what material I have. It is a
sheer waste of time and soul power to imagine what I would
do if things were different. They are not different.
—DR. FRANK CRANE

Holding on to anger is like grasping a hot coal with the intent of
throwing it at someone else; you are the one who gets burned.
—BUDDHA

There is no easy path leading out of life, and few
are the easy ones that lie within it.
—WALTER SAVAGE LANDOR

The chief pang of most trials is not so much the actual
suffering itself as our own spirit of resistance to it.
—JEAN NICHOLAS GROU

The weak can never forgive. Forgiveness is the attribute of the strong.
—MAHATMA GHANDI

The art of life lies in a constant readjustment to our surroundings.
—Okakura Kakuzo

Anger is a short madness.
—Horace

Good breeding consists in concealing how much we think of
ourselves and how little we think of the other person.
—Mark Twain

Acceptance is not submission; it is acknowledgement of the facts
of a situation. Then deciding what you're going to do about it.
—Kathleen Casey Theisen

The survival of the fittest is the ageless law of nature, but the fittest are
rarely the strong. The fittest are those endowed with the qualifications
for adaptation, the ability to accept the inevitable and conform to the
unavoidable, to harmonize with existing or changing conditions.
—Dave E. Smalley

Maturity is achieved when a person accepts life as full of tension.
—Joshua L. Liebman

There is no cure for birth or death save to enjoy the interval.
—George Santayana

Man is the only animal that laughs and weeps; for he is
the only animal that is struck with the difference between
what things are and what they might have been.
—William Hazlitt

It is right it should be so,
Man was made for joy and woe;
And when this we rightly know,
Through the world we safely go.
—William Blake

To exist is to adapt, and if one could not adapt, one
died and made room for those who could.
—Louis L'Amour

Forgiveness is the key to action and freedom.
—HANNAH ARENDT

Her breasts and arms ached with the beauty of her own forgiveness.
—MERIDEL LE SUEUR

Dream of your brother's kindnesses instead of dwelling in
your dreams on his mistakes. Select his thoughtfulness to
dream about instead of counting up the hurts he gave.
—*A COURSE IN MIRACLES*

To expect life to be tailored to our specifications is to invite frustration.
—ANON

Any man can seek revenge; it takes a king or prince to grant a pardon.
—ARTHUR J. REHRAT

Free man is by necessity insecure; thinking man by necessity uncertain.
—ERICH FROMM

Judge not, that ye be not judged.
—MT. 7:1

It is almost more important how a person takes his fate than what it is.
—WILHELM VON HUMBOLDT

Don't be sad, don't be angry, if life deceives you! Submit to
your grief; your time for joy will come, believe me.
—ALEKSANDR PUSHKIN

Man adapts himself to everything, to the best and the worst.
—JOSÉ ORTEGA Y GASSET

The secret of forgiving everything is to understand nothing.
—GEORGE BERNARD SHAW

We must accept finite disappointment, but
we must never lose infinite hope.
—MARTIN LUTHER KING, JR.

To be angry about trifles is mean and childish; to rage and be
furious is brutish; and to maintain perpetual wrath is akin to
the practice and temper of devils; but to prevent and suppress
rising resentment is wise and glorious, is manly and divine.
—Isaac Watts

The happy and efficient people in this world are those
who accept trouble as a normal detail of human life
and resolve to capitalize it when it comes along.
—H. Bertram Lewis

Who except the gods can live without any pain?
—Aeschylus

It is easier to stay out than to get out.
—Mark Twain

Happy the man who early learns the wide chasm
that lies between his wishes and his powers.
—Johann von Goethe

Revenge could steal a man's life until there
was nothing left but emptiness.
—Louis L' Amour

Nothing you write, if you hope to be any good,
will ever come out as you first hoped.
—Lillian Hellman

The trouble with most people is that they think with their
hopes or fears or wishes rather than with their minds.
—Will Durant

People, people who need people
Are the luckiest people in the world.
—Bob Merrill

The ineffible joy of forgiving and being forgiven forms an
ecstasy that might well arouse the envy of the gods.
—Elbert Hubbard

Teach me to feel another's woe,
To hide the fault I see;
That mercy I to others show,
That mercy show to me.
—ALEXANDER POPE

FAITH

Faith enables persons to be persons because it lets God be God.
—CARTER LINDBERG

Faith is hidden household capital.
—JOHANN WOLFGANGE VON GOETHE

I am living on hope and faith ... a pretty good
diet when the mind will receive them.
—EDWIN ARLINGTON ROBINSON

If life is a comedy to him who thinks, and a tragedy to
him who feels, it is a victory to him who believes.
—ANON

Faith ... acts promptly and boldly on the occasion, on slender evidence.
—JOHN HENRY CARDINAL NEWMAN

What's up is faith, what's down is heresy.
—ALFRED, LORD TENNYSON

Faith assuages, guides, restores.
—ARTHUR RIMBAUD

Faith is believing what you know ain't so.
—MARK TWAIN

Faith is the soul riding at anchor.
—JOSH BILLINGS

Your faith is what you believe, not what you know.
—JOHN LANCASTER SPALDING

It is faith, and not reason, which impels men to action. . . . Intelligence
is content to point out the road, but never drives us along it.
—DR. ALEXIS CARREL

Faith can move mountains.
—PROVERB

'Tis not the dying for a faith that's so hard, Master Harry—every man
of every nation has done that—'tis the living up to it that is difficult.
—WILLIAM MAKEPEACE THACKERAY

Faith is not something to grasp, it is a state to grow into.
—MAHATMA GANDHI

Faith is the response of our spirits to beckonings of the eternal.
—GEORGE A. BUTTRICK

The principle part of faith is patience.
—GEORGE MACDONALD

Faith is primarily a process of identification; the process by which the
individual ceases to be himself and becomes part of something eternal.
—ERIC HOFFER

Man makes holy what he believes, as he makes beautiful what he loves.
—ERNEST RENAN

The person who has a firm trust in the Supreme Being is powerful
in His power, wise by His widsom, happy by His happiness.
—JOSEPH ADDISON

Faith is a theological virtue that inclines the mind, under
the influence of the will and grace, to yield firm assent to
revealed truths, because of the authority of God.
—ADOLPHE TANQUERAY

Faith is God's work within us.
—SAINT THOMAS AQUINAS

Faith is the substance of things hoped for,
the evidence of things not seen.
—Heb. 11:1

Faith is the sturdiest, the most manly of the virtues. It lies
behind our pluckiest . . . strivings. It is the virtue of the
storm, just as happiness is the virtue of the sunshine.
—Ruth Benedict

Faith is a gift of God.
—Blaise Pascal

Life without faith in something is too narrow a space in which to live.
—George Lancaster Spalding

A believer, a mind whose faith is consciousness, is never disturbed
because other persons do not yet see the fact which he sees.
—Ralph Waldo Emerson

Can a faith that does nothing be called sincere?
—Jean Racine

Faith:
Tendrils of our lives stretching outward for support,
Helping us grow upward to produce a design
Worthy of the Creator.
—Evelyn Anderson

The great act of faith is when a man decides that he is not God.
—Oliver Wendell Holmes

Faith is the final triumph over incongruity, the final
assertion of the meaningfulness of existence.
—Reinhold Niebuhr

Faith is an outward and visible sign of an inward and spiritual grace.
—Book of Common Prayer

Faith sees the invisible, believes the incredible
and receives the impossible.
—Anon

The primary cause of unhappiness in the world today is . . . lack of faith.
—CARL JUNG

Faith without works is dead.
—JAS. 2:26

Faith is the capacity of the soul to perceive the
abiding . . . the invisible in the visible.
—LEO BAECK

Faith is the little night-light that burns in a sick-room;
as long as it is there, the obscurity is not complete,
we turn towards it and await the daylight.
—ABBÉ HENRI HUVELIN

Faith is spiritualized imagination.
—HENRY WARD BEECHER

Faith is loyalty to some inspired teacher, some spiritual hero.
—THOMAS CARLYLE

Faith. You can do very little with it, but you can do nothing without it.
—SAMUEL BUTLER

The will of God will not take you where the grace of God cannot keep you.
—ANON

I would rather live in a world where my life is surrounded by mystery
than live in a world so small that my mind could comprehend it.
—HENRY EMERSON FOSDICK

It is the heart which experiences God, and not the reason.
—BLAISE PASCAL

Let us train our minds to desire what the situation demands.
—MARCUS ANNAEUS SENECA

No faith is our own that we have not arduously won.
—HAVELOCK ELLIS

Faith is hidden household capital.
—Johann von Goethe

Seek not to understand that thou mayest believe,
but believe that thou mayest understand.
—Saint Augustine

I believe in the sun even if it isn't shining. I believe in love even
when I am alone. I believe in God even when He is silent.
—World War II refugee

Perfect courage is to do unwitnessed what we should
be capable of doing before all the world.
—Francois de la Rochefoucauld

To me, faith means not worrying.
—John Dewey

Living is a form of not being sure, not knowing what next,
or how. The moment you know how, you begin to die a
little. The artist never entirely knows. We guess. We may
be wrong, but we take leap after leap in the dark.
—Agnes de Mille

Faith is the summit of the Torah.
—Solomon Ibn Gabirol

Some like to understand what they believe in. Others
like to believe in what they understand.
—Stanislaus

Reason is our soul's left hand, Faith her right. By this we reach divinity.
—John Donne

It is as absurd to argue men, as to torture them, into believing.
—John Henry Cardinal Newman

Loving is half of believing.
—Victor Hugo

A faith that sets bounds to itself, that will believe so much
and no more, that will trust so far and no further, is none.
—Julius Charles Hare

Faith is ... knowing with your heart.
—N. Richard Nash

Faith is a kind of betting, or speculation.
—Samuel Butler

Faith is an encounter in which God takes and keeps the initiative.
—Eugene Joly

Faith is an assent of the mind and a consent of the
heart, consisting mainly of belief and trust.
—E.T. Hiscox

Faith doesn't wait until it understands; in that case it wouldn't be faith.
—Vance Havner

Faith is the continuation of reason.
—William Adams

As your faith is strengthened you will find that there is no longer the
need to have a sense of control, that things will flow as they will, and
that you will flow with them, to your great delight and benefit.
—Emmanuel

Reason's voice and God's, Nature's and Duty's, never are at odds.
—John Greenleaf Whittier

Faith is a practical attitude of the will.
—John MacMurray

Without risk, faith is an impossibility.
—Søren Kierkegaard

Peter Marshall: What should you do if you're going 55
miles per hour and your tires suddenly blow out?
Paul Lynde: Honk if you believe in Jesus.
—Hollywood Squares

All the scholastic scaffolding falls, as a ruined
edifice, before a single word: faith.
—Napoleon Bonaparte

Faith is a gift of God which man can neither give nor take
away by promise of rewards, or menaces of torture.
—Thomas Hobbes

Faith is a certitude without proofs . . . a sentiment, for it is a
hope; it is an instinct, for it precedes all outward instruction.
—Henry Frederic Amiel

Faith declares what the senses do not see, but
not the contrary of what they see.
—Blaise Pascal

A person consists of his faith. Whatever is his faith, even so is he.
—Hindu proverb

Faith is kind of like jumping out of an airplane at ten thousand
feet. If God doesn't catch you, you splatter. But how do you know
whether or not He is going to catch you unless you jump out?
—Ann Kiemel

Only the person who has faith in himself is able to be faithful to others.
—Erich Fromm

Faith is one of the forces by which men live, and
the total absence of it means collapse.
—William James

He does not believe who does not live according to his belief.
—Thomas Fuller

Through the dark and stormy night
Faith beholds a feeble light
Up the blackness streaking;
Knowing God's own time is best,
In a patient hope I rest
For the full day-breaking!
—John Greenleaf Whittier

Faith is an act of self-consecration, in which the will, the
intellect, and the affections all have their place.
—WILLIAM RALPH INGE

The only faith that wears well and holds its color in all
weather is that which is woven of conviction.
—JAMES RUSSELL LOWELL

There is one inevitable criterion of judgment touching religious
faith . . . Can you reduce it to practice? If not, have none of it.
—HOSEA BALLOU

For the believer, there is no question; for the
non-believer, there is no answer.
—ANON

All effort is in the last analysis sustained by faith that it is worth making.
—ORDWAY TWEED

Faith, to my mind, is a stiffening process, a sort of mental starch.
—E.M. FORSTER

Faith is nothing but obedience and piety.
—BARUCH SPINOZA

Don't lose faith in humanity: think of all the people in the United
States who have never played you a single nasty trick.
—ELBERT HUBBARD

Faith is a sounder guide than reason. Reason can
go only so far, but faith has no limits.
—BLAISE PASCAL

Fear imprisons, faith liberates; fear paralyzes, faith empowers;
fear disheartens, faith encourages; fear sickens, faith
heals; fear makes useless, faith makes serviceable.
—HARRY EMERSON FOSDICK

Faith is the only known cure for fear.
—LENA K. SADLER

Faith consists, not in ignorance, but in knowledge, and
that, not only of God, but also of the divine will.
—John Calvin

You're not free until you've been made captive by supreme belief.
—Marianne Moore

Faith may be relied upon to produce sustained action
and, more rarely, sustained contemplation.
—Aldous Huxley

Ride the horse in the direction that it's going.
—Werner Ehrhard

Deep faith eliminates fear.
—Lech Walesa

If it wasn't for faith, there would be no living in this
world; we couldn't even eat hash with any safety.
—Josh Billings

Faith is that which is woven of conviction and set
with the sharp mordant of experience.
—James Russell Lowell

Faith is the daring of the soul to go farther than it can see.
—William Newton Clark

Let us move on, and step out boldly, though it be into
the night, and we can scarcely see the way. A Higher
Intelligence than the mortal sees the road before us.
—Charles B. Newcomb

To disbelieve is easy; to scoff is simple; to have faith is harder.
—Louis L'Amour

The way to see by Faith is to shut the eye of Reason.
—Benjamin Franklin

You do build in darkness if you have faith. When the light returns
you have made of yourself a fortress which is impregnable
to certain kinds of trouble; you may even find yourself
needed and sought by others as a beacon in their dark.
—Olga Rosmanith

An oak and a reed were arguing about their strength.
When a strong wind came up, the reed avoided being
uprooted by bending and leaning with the gusts of wind.
But the oak stood firm and was torn up by the roots.
—Aesop

Faith in our associates is part of our faith in God.
—Charles Horton Cooley

Faith is the art of holding on to things your reason has
once accepted, in spite of your changing moods.
—C.S. Lewis

Our faith triumphant o'er our fears.
—Henry Wadsworth Longfellow

Faith is love taking the form of aspiration.
—William Ellery Channing

Because you cannot see him, God is everywhere.
—Yasunari Kawabata

The historic glory of America lies in the fact that it is the one nation that
was founded like a church. That is, it was founded on a faith that was not
merely summed up after it had exited, but was defined before it existed.
—G.K. Chesterton

We must have infinite faith in each other.
—Henry David Thoreau

To win true peace, a man needs to feel himself directed, pardoned
and sustained by a supreme power, to feel himself in the right
road, at the point where God would have him be—in order with
God and the universe. This faith gives strength and calm.
—Henri Frederic Amiel

Faith is a living and unshakable confidence, a belief in the grace of God so assured that a man would die a thousand deaths for its sake.
—MARTIN LUTHER

All I have seen teaches me to trust the Creator for all I have not seen.
—RALPH WALDO EMERSON

Far graver is it to corrupt the faith that is the life of the soul than to counterfeit the money that sustains temporal life.
—SAINT THOMAS AQUINAS

Faith is nothing else than trust in the divine mercy promised in Christ.
—PHILIPP MELANCHTHON

Faith is to believe what we do not see; the reward of this faith is to see what we believe.
—SAINT AUGUSTINE

Faith is believing when it is beyond the power of reason to believe.
—VOLTAIRE

It is by faith that poetry, as well as devotion, soars above this dull earth; that imagination breaks through its clouds, breathes a purer air, and lives in a softer light.
—HENRY GILES

Faith is the soul's adventure.
—WILLIAM BRIDGES

Faith, as an intellectual state, is self-reliance.
—OLIVER WENDELL HOLMES,

Faith has to do with things that are not seen, and hope with things that are not in hand.
—SAINT THOMAS AQUINAS

We walk by faith, not by sight.
—2 COR. 5:7

The opposite of having faith is having self-pity.
—OG GUINNESS

Every tomorrow has two handles. We can take hold of it
by the handle of anxiety, or by the handle of faith.
—Anon

Faith is an attitude of the person. It means you are
prepared to stake yourself on something being so.
—Arthur M. Ramsey

In Israel, in order to be a realist, you must believe in miracles.
—David Ben-Gurion

Faith is not merely hope, and it must be more than
belief; faith is a knowing of the heart.
—Floyd and M. Elaine Flake

Be thou faithful unto death.
—Rev. 2:10

Faith is the divine evidence whereby the spiritual
man discerneth God, and the things of God.
—John Wesley

Religious faith, indeed, relates to that which is above us,
but it must arise from that which is within us.
—Josiah Royce

The disease with which the human mind now labors is want of faith.
—Ralph Waldo Emerson

Faith is verification by the heart; confession
by the tongue; action by the limbs.
—Anon

So often we have a kind of vague, wistful longing that the promises
of Jesus should be true. The only way really to enter into them is to
believe them with the clutching intensity of a drowning man.
—William Barclay

You do build in darkness if you have faith. When the light returns
you have made of yourself a fortress which is impregnable

to certain kinds of trouble; you may even find yourself
needed and sought by others as a beacon in their dark.
—Olga Rosmanith

Faith is the function of the heart.
—Mahatma Gandhi

Strike from mankind the principle of faith, and men
would have no more history than a flock of sheep.
—Edward Bulwer-Lytton

Faith is believing what we cannot prove.
—Alfred, Lord Tennyson

Fear knocked at the door. Faith answered. And lo, no one was there.
—Anon

Faith is the result of the act of the will, following
upon a conviction that to believe is a duty.
—John Henry Cardinal Newman

We are twice armed if we fight with faith.
—Plato

Faith is a total attitude of the self.
—John Macquarrie

Faith is to believe what you do not yet see; the reward
for this faith is to see what you believe.
—Saint Augustine

Faith is like radar that sees through the fog—the reality of
things at a distance that the human eye cannot see.
—Corrie Ten Boom

Don't worry about what you don't have if you do have faith.
—Rick Warren

It is by faith that poetry, as well as devotion, soars above
this dull earth; that imagination breaks through its clouds,
breathes a purer air, and lives in a softer light.
—HENRY GILES

Faith makes the discords of the present the harmonies of the future.
—ROBERT COLLYER

Faith may be defined briefly as an illogical belief
in the occurrence of the improbable.
—H.L. MENCKEN

He who has no faith in others shall find no faith in them.
—LAO-TZU

Religious faith, indeed, relates to that which is above us,
but it must arise from that which is within us.
—JOSIAH ROYCE

Faith in oneself . . . is the best and safest course.
—MICHELANGELO

Faith is much better than belief. Belief is when
someone else does the thinking.
—R. BUCKMINSTER FULLER

I never went to bed in my life and I never ate a meal in my
life without saying a prayer. I know my prayers have been
answered thousands of times, and I know that I never said a
prayer in my life without something good coming of it.
—JACK DEMPSEY

We cannot hand our faith to one another. . . . Even
in the Middle Ages, when faith was theoretically
uniform, it was always practically individual.
—JOHN JAY CHAPMAN

Some things have to be believed to be seen.
—RALPH HODGSON

I stopped believing in Santa Clause when I was six. Mother took me to see him in a department store and he asked me for my autograph.
—SHIRLEY TEMPLE BLACK

KINDNESS

We have fought this fight as long, and as well, as we know how. We have been defeated. There is now but one course to pursue. We must accept the situation.
—ROBERT E. LEE

Three things in human life are important: The first is to be kind. The second is to be kind. And the third is to be kind.
—HENRY JAMES

Nature, to be commanded, must be obeyed.
—FRANCIS BACON

Give, if thou can, an alms; if not, a sweet and gentle word.
—ROBERT HERRICK

Wherever there is a human being there is a chance for a kindness.
—SENECA

I wonder why it is that we are not all kinder to each other.... How much the world needs it! How easily it is done!
—HENRY DRUMMOND

A helping word to one in trouble is often like a switch on a railroad track ... an inch between wreck and smooth, rolling prosperity.
—HENRY WARD BEECHER

The world has cares enough to plague us; but he who meditates on others' woes shall, in that meditation, lose his own.
—CUMBERLAND

Consideration for the lives of others and the laws of
humanity, even when one is struggling for one's life and in
the greatest stress, does not go wholly unrewarded.
—Winston Churchill

A man wrapped up in himself makes a very small bundle.
—Benjamin Franklin

Today I bent the truth to be kind, and I have no regret, for I
am far surer of what is kind that I am of what is true.
—Robert Brault

A kind word can warm three winter months.
—Japanese proverb

There is no such thing as pure pleasure; some
anxiety always goes with it.
—Ovid

Give what you have. To someone else it may
be better than you dare to think.
—Henry Wadsworth Longfellow

We must learn to accept life and to accept ourselves ... with
a shrug and a smile ... because it's all we've got.
—Harvey Mindess

He who sees a need and waits to be asked for
help is as unkind as if he had refused it.
—Dante Alighieri

We cannot change anything unless we accept it.
Condemnation does not liberate, it oppresses.
—Carl Jung

Our worth is determined by the good deeds we do,
rather than by the fine emotions we feel.
—Elias L. Magoon

Wood may remain ten years in the water, but
it will never become a crocodile.
—Congolese proverb

I hate the giving of the hand unless the whole man accompanies it.
—Ralph Waldo Emerson

It takes wisdom and discernment to minister to people
in need. We must look beyond the apparent and
seek to meet the needs of the whole person.
—Richard C. Chewning

Our very first problem is to accept our present circumstances as they
are, ourselves as we are, and the people about us as they are. This
is to adopt a realistic humility without which no genuine advance
can even begin.... Provided we strenuously avoid turning these
realistic surveys of the facts of life into unrealistic alibis for apathy
or defeatism, they can be the sure foundation upon which increased
emotional health and therefore spiritual progress can be built.
—As Bill Sees It

No life is so hard that you can't make it easier by the way you take it.
—Ellen Glasgow

He who attempts to resist the wave is swept
away, but he who bends before it abides.
—Leviticus

Wherever there is a human being, there is an opportunity for a kindness.
—Marcus Annaeus Seneca

If we had no regard for others' feelings or fortune, we
would grow cold and indifferent to life itself.
—George Matthew Adams

You can never expect too much of yourself in the
matter of giving yourself to others.
—Theodore C. Speers

Isn't it better to have men be ungrateful,
than to miss a chance to do good?
—Denis Diderot

Knowing sorrow well, I learn to succor the distressed.
—Virgil

Kindness, I've discovered, is everything in life.
—Isaac Bashevis Singer

What wisdom can you find that is greater than kindness?
—Jean-Jacques Rousseau

Be kind, for everyone you meet is fighting a hard battle.
—Philo

If you have not often felt the joy of doing a kind act, you
have neglected much, and most of all yourself.
—A. Neilen

We are made kind by being kind.
—Eric Hoffer

Goodwill is the mightiest practical force in the universe.
—Charles F. Dole

A word of kindness is seldom spoken in vain, while witty sayings
are as easily lost as the pearls slipping from a broken string.
—George Prentice

Simply give others a bit of yourself; a thoughtful act, a helpful
idea, a word of appreciation, a lift over a rough spot, a sense
of understanding, a timely suggestion. You take something
out of your mind, garnished in kindness out of your heart,
and put it into the other fellow's mind and heart.
—Charles H. Burr

Do not inflict your will. Just give love. The soul will take
that love and put it where it can best be used.
—Emmanuel

Live and let live is not enough; live and help live is not too much.
—Orison Swett Marden

Without kindness, there can be no true joy.
—Thomas Carlyle

Compassion is the basis of all morality.
—Arthur Schopenhauer

What we call reality is an agreement that people
have arrived at to make life more livable.
—Louise Nevelson

Much misconstruction and bitterness are spared to him
who thinks naturally upon what he owes to others, rather
than on what he ought to expect from them.
—Elizabeth de Meulan Guizot

An act of goodness is of itself an act of happiness.
—Maurice Maeterlinck

Happiness ... is achieved only by making others happy.
—Stuart Cloete

Pity costs nothing and ain't worth nothing.
—Josh Billings

When you make your peace with authority, you become authority.
—Jim Morrison

... My mother used to say to me, "In this world, Elwood"—she always
called me Elwood—she'd say, "In this world, Elwood, you must be oh, so
smart or oh, so pleasant." For years I was smart. I recommend pleasant.
—Mary Chase (*Harvey*)

Often we can help each other most by leaving each other alone;
at other times we need the hand-grasp and the word of cheer.
—Elbert Hubbard

Happiness ... consists in giving, and in serving others.
—Henry Drummond

Anything in life that we don't accept will simply make
trouble for us until we make peace with it.
—Shakti Gawain

That best portion of a good man's life, his little, nameless,
umremembered, acts of kindness and of love.
—William Wordsworth

There's no use in doing a kindness if you do it a day too late.
—Charles Kingsley

You give but little when you give of your possessions. It
is when you give of yourself that you truly give.
—Kahlil Gibran

Unless we give part of ourselves away, unless we can live
with other people and understand them and help them, we
are missing the most essential part of our own lives.
—Harold Taylor

One of the many lessons that one learns in prison is that
things are what they are and will be what they will be.
—Oscar Wilde

Ours must be the first age whose great goal, on a
nonmaterial plane, is not fulfillment but adjustment.
—Louis Kronenberger

The healthy and strong individual is the one who asks for help when
he needs it. Whether he's got an abscess on his knee, or in his soul.
—Rona Barrett

You cannot imagine the kindness I've received
at the hands of perfect strangers.
—W. Somerset Maugham

There is nothing in life but refraining from hurting
others, and comforting those that are sad.
—Olive Schreiner

Success has nothing to do with what you gain in life or
accomplish for yourself. It's what you do for others.
—Danny Thomas

The great soul surrenders itself to fate.
—Marcus Annaeus Seneca

Two thirds of help is to give courage.
—IRISH PROVERB

The only gift is a portion of thyself.
—RALPH WALDO EMERSON

Kindness is in our power, even when fondness is not.
—SAMUEL JOHNSON

To give pleasure to a single heart by a single kind act is
better than a thousand head-bowings in prayer.
—SA'DI

If you cast away one cross, you will certainly
find another, and perhaps a heavier.
—THOMAS A'KEMPIS

Better to expose ourselves to ingratitude than
fail in assisting the unfortunate.
—DU COEUR

Kindness is the language which the deaf can hear and the blind can see.
—MARK TWAIN

The unknown is what it is. And to be frightened of it is
what sends everybody scurrying around chasing dreams,
illusions, wars, peace, love, hate, all that. Unknown is what
it is. Accept that it's unknown, and it's plain sailing.
—JOHN LENNON

It is not necessarily those lands which are the most fertile or
most favored in climate that seem to me the happiest, but those
in which a long struggle of adaptation between man and his
environment has brought out the best qualities of both.
—T.S. ELIOT

A kind word is like a Spring day.
—RUSSIAN PROVERB

Kindness in words creates confidence. Kindness in thinking
creates profoundness. Kindness in giving creates love.
—LAO-TZU

The beauty of the soul shines out when a man bears with composure one heavy mischance after another, not because he does not feel them, but because he is a man of high and heroic temper.
—ARISTOTLE

If you want a place in the sun, you've got to put up with a few blisters.
—ABIGAIL VAN BUREN

I never yet met a man that I didn't like.
—WILL ROGERS

What must be shall be; and that which is a necessity to him that struggles, is little more than choice to him that is willing.
—MARCUS ANNAEUS SENECA

Only a life lived for others is a life worth while.
—ALBERT EINSTEIN

Better to accept whatever happens.
—HORACE

Keep doing what you're doing and you'll keep getting what you're getting.
—ANON

Like the body that is made up of different limbs and organs, all mortal creatures exist depending upon one another.
—HINDU PROVERB

Almost any event will put on a new face when received with cheerful acceptance.
—HENRY S. HASKINS

Be brave enough to accept the help of others.
—MELBA COLGROVE, HAROLD H. BLOOMFIELD, PETER MCWILLIAMS,
HOW TO SURVIVE THE LOSS OF A LOVE

No man is more cheated than the selfish man.
—HENRY WARD BEECHER

The grass must bend when the wind blows across it.
—Confucius

He is rich who hath enough to be charitable.
—Sir Thomas Browne

Let a man accept his destiny. No pity and no tears.
—Euripides

One's first step in wisdom is to question everything;
one's last is to come to terms with everything.
—Georg Christoph Lichtenberg

Things turn out best for people who make the
best of the way things turn out.
—Anon

As the soft yield of water cleaves obstinate stone,
So to yield with life solves the insolvable:
To yield, I have learned, is to come back again.
—Lao-tzu

Every new adjustment is a crisis in self-esteem.
—Eric Hoffer

Sow good services; sweet remembrances will grow from them.
—Madame de Stael

There is only one way to happiness, and that is to cease worrying
about things which are beyond the power of our will.
—Epictetus

Everything in life that we really accept undergoes a change.
So suffering must become love. That is the mystery.
—Katherine Mansfield

Acceptance of what has happened is the first step to
overcoming the consequence of any misfortune.
—William James

Goodwill ... is an immeasurable and tremendous
energy, the atomic energy of the spirit.
—Eleanor B. Stock

True freedom lies in the realization and calm acceptance of
the fact that there may very well be no perfect answer.
—Allen Reid McGinnis

The golden rule is of no use whatsoever unless
you realize that it is your move.
—Dr. Frank Crane

Goodwill to others ... helps build you up. It is good for your body.
It makes your blood purer, your muscles stronger, and your whole
form more symmetrical in shape. It is the real elixir of life.
—Prentice Mulford

Pleasure is a reciprocal; no one feels it who does not at the
same time give it. To be pleased, one must please.
—Lord Chesterfield

Happiness comes from within a man, from
some curious adjustment to life.
—Hugh Walpole

Do things for others and you'll find your self-
consciousness evaporating like morning dew.
—Dale Carnegie

I have accepted all and I am free. The inner chains
are broken, as well as those outside.
—C.F. Ramuz

Life is not always what one wants it to be, but to make the
best of it, as it is, is the only way of being happy.
—Jennie Jerome Churchill

What boundary ever set limits to the service of mankind?
—Claudian

You cannot do a kindness too soon, for you never
know how soon it will be too late.
—Ralph Waldo Emerson

When one's own problems are unsolvable and all best efforts are
frustrated, it is lifesaving to listen to other people's problems.
—Suzanne Massie

Peace of mind is that mental condition in
which you have accepted the worst.
—Lin Yutang

If I can stop one heart from breaking, I shall not live in vain.
—Emily Dickinson

When I decided to go into politics I weighed the costs. I would
get criticism. But I went ahead. So when virulent criticism
came I wasn't surprised. I was better able to handle it.
—Herbert Hoover

There is one thing that matters—to set a chime of words
tinkling in the minds of a few fastidious people.
—Logan Pearsall Smith

I will not meddle with that which I cannot mend.
—Thomas Fuller

The habit of being uniformly considerate toward
others will bring increased happiness to you.
—Grenville Kleiser

It is enough that I am of value to somebody today.
—Hugh Prather

Doing good is the only certainly happy action of a man's life.
—Sir Philip Sidney

Wise sayings often fall on barren ground, but
a kind word is never thrown away.
—Sir Arthur Helps

Part of the happiness of life consists not in fighting battles, but
in avoiding them. A masterly retreat is in itself a victory.
—Norman Vincent Peale

We make a living by what we get, but we make a life by what we give.
—Norman MacEwan

There is no greater loan than a sympathetic ear.
—Frank Tyger

Every job has drudgery.... The first secret of happiness
is the recognition of this fundamental fact.
—M.C. McIntosh

Happy he who learns to bear what he cannot change!
—J.C.F. von Schiller

When you cease to make a contribution, you begin to die.
—Eleanor Roosevelt

Contentment, and indeed usefulness, comes as the infallible
result of great acceptances, great humilities—of not trying
to conform to some dramatized version of ourselves.
—David Grayson

I not only bow to the inevitable, I am fortified by it.
—Thornton Wilder

Acceptance is the truest kinship with humanity.
—G.K. Chesterton

Better bend than break.
—Scottish proverb

If you are wise, live as you can; if you cannot, live as you would.
—Baltasar Gracian

Wisdom never kicks at the iron walls it can't bring down.
—Olive Schreiner

In about the same degree as you are helpful, you will be happy.
—KARL REILAND

He who does not live in some degree for others, hardly lives for himself.
—MICHEL DE MONTAIGNE

The secret of success is to be in harmony with existence, to be always
calm . . . to let each wave of life wash us a little farther up the shore.
—CYRIL CONNOLLY

One completely overcomes only what one assimilates.
—ANDRÉ GIDE

Accept that all of us can be hurt, that all of us can—and surely
will at times—fail. Other vulnerabilities, like being embarrassed
or risking love, can be terrifying too. I think we should follow
a simple rule: if we can take the worst, take the risk.
—DR. JOYCE BROTHERS

He who has calmly reconciled his life to
fate . . . can look fortune in the face.
—BOETHIUS

Happiness is a function of accepting what is.
—WERNER ERHARD

We cannot hold a torch to light another's path
without brightening our own.
—BEN SWEETLAND

The best portion of a good man's life, his little
nameless, unremembered acts of kindness.
—WILLIAM WORDSWORTH

Those who aim at great deeds must also suffer greatly.
—PLUTARCH

What it is forbidden to be put right becomes lighter by acceptance.
—HORACE

No rose without a thorn.
—FRENCH PROVERB

There is no happiness in having or in getting, but only in giving.
—HENRY DRUMMOND

No matter how much you feed a wolf, he will always return to the forest.
—RUSSIAN PROVERB

The greatest happiness in the world is to make others happy.
—LUTHER BURBANK

We cannot change anything unless we accept it.
—CARL JUNG

I wash everything on the gentle cycle. It's much more humane.
—ERMA BOMBECK

Adapt or perish, now as ever, is nature's inexorable imperative.
—H.G. WELLS

The most exquisite pleasure is giving pleasure to others.
—JEAN DE LA BRUYERE

The fragrance of what you give away stays with you.
—EARL ALLEN

Kindness is the ability to love people more than they deserve.
—ANON

For this is wisdom: to live, to take what fate, or the Gods, may give.
—LAURENCE HOPE

Man is a pliant animal, a being who gets accustomed to anything.
—FYODOR DOSTOYEVSKY

VII. Love Ever After

ADMIRATION

To love is to admire with the heart; to admire is to love with the mind.
—THEOPHILE GAUTIER

The love of family and the admiration of friends is much
more important than wealth and privilege.
—CHARLES KURALT

We admire people to the extent that we cannot explain what
they do, and the word "admire" then means "marvel at."
—B.F. SKINNER

A lady's imagination is very rapid; it jumps from admiration
to love, from love to matrimony in a moment.
—DARCY IN *PRIDE AND PREJUDICE*, BY JANE AUSTEN

[Boswell] ... insisted that admiration was more pleasing
than judgment, as love is more pleasing than friendship. The
feeling of friendship is like that of being comfortably filled with
roast beef; love like being enlivened with champagne.
JOHNSON. "No, Sir; admiration and love are like being intoxicated
with champagne; judgment and friendship like being enlivened."
— SAMUEL JOHNSON

Do Not Trifle with Love.
—ALFRED DE MUSSET

Admiration, *n.* Our polite recognition of
another's resemblance to ourselves.
—AMBROSE BIERCE

It is better in some respects to be admired by those with whom you live, than to be loved by them. And this is not on account of any gratification of vanity, but because admiration is so much more tolerant than love.
—Sir Arthur Helps

Fools admire, but men of sense approve.
—Alexander Pope

Won't say I hate you—but my admiration for you is under control.
—Fred Allen

If you can't say anything good about someone, sit right here by me.
—Alice Roosevelt Longworth

Always we like those who admire us, but we do not always like those whom we admire.
—Francois de La Rochefoucauld

AFFECTION

Happiness comes more from loving than being loved; and often when our affection seems wounded it is only our vanity bleeding. To love, and to be hurt often, and to love again—this is the brave and happy life.
—J.E. Buchrose

Most people would rather get than give affection.
—Aristotle

A mixture of admiration and pity is one of the surest recipes for affection.
—Andre Maurois

Kissing your hand may make you feel very, very good, but a diamond and sapphire bracelet lasts forever.
—Anita Loos (*Gentlemen Prefer Blondes*)

Talk not of wasted affection, affection never was wasted, If it enrich not the heart of another, its waters returning

Back to their springs, like the rain shall fill them full of refreshment;
That which the fountain sends forth returns again to the fountain
—HENRY WADSWORTH LONGFELLOW

A kiss on the hand may be quite Continental,
but diamonds are a girl's best friend.
—LEO ROBIN

Affection is responsible for nine-tenths of whatever
solid and durable happiness there is in our lives.
—C.S. LEWIS

Affection is created by habit, community of interests, convenience and
the desire of companionship. It is a comfort rather than an exhilaration.
—W. SOMERSET MAUGHAM

In nine cases out of ten, a woman had better
show more affection than she feels.
—JANE AUSTEN

Human nature is so constructed that it gives affection
most readily to those who seem least to demand it.
—BERTRAND RUSSELL

Affection can withstand very severe storms of vigor,
but not a long polar frost of indifference.
—SIR WALTER SCOTT

HEART

You change your life by changing your heart.
—MAX LUCADO

All the knowledge I possess everyone else can
acquire, but my heart is all my own.
—JOHANN WOLFGANG VON GOETHE

My heart is a lonely hunter that hunts on a lonely hill.
—WILLIAM SHARP

Whatever makes an impression on the heart seems lovely in the eye.
—Sa'di

The head does not know how to play the part of the heart for long.
—Francois de La Rochefoucauld

Here are fruits, flowers, leaves and branches, And
here is my heart which beats only for you.
—Paul Verlaine

Let my heart be wise.
It is the gods' best gift.
—Euripides

The heart has reasons which reason knows nothing of.
—Blaise Pascal

Whatever comes from the brain carries the hue of the
place it came from, and whatever comes from the heart
carries the heat and color of its birthplace.
—Oliver Wendell Holmes, Sr.

The heart wants what it wants. There's no logic.
—Woody Allen

The head does not know how to play the part of the heart for long.
—Francois de La Rochefoucauld

Where the heart lies, let the brain lie also.
—Robert Browning

What the heart gives away is never gone....
It is kept in the hearts of others.
—Robin St. John

The greatest happiness in life is the conviction that we are
loved—loved for ourselves, or rather, loved in spite of ourselves.
—Victor Hugo

Unlearn'd, he knew no schoolman's subtle art, No
language, but the language of the heart.
—ALEXANDER POPE

True love is the only heart disease that is best left to "run on"—the only
affection of the heart for which there is no help, and none desired.
—MARK TWAIN

To love and be loved is to feel the sun from both sides.
—DAVID VISCOTT

The best and most beautiful things in the world cannot be
seen or even touched—they must be felt with the heart.
—HELEN KELLER

Faint heart never won fair lady.
—WILLIAM CAMDEN

True love comes quietly, without banners or flashing
lights. If you hear bells, get your ears checked.
—ERICH SEGAL

A heart is not judged by how much you love; but
by how much you are loved by others.
—NOEL LANGLEY, FLORENCE RYERSON AND EDGAR ALLAN WOOLF,
THE WIZARD OF OZ

The human heart is like a ship on a stormy sea driven about
by winds blowing from all four corners of heaven.
—MARTIN LUTHER

You gotta have heart
All you really need is heart.
—JERRY ROSS

"Real isn't how you are made," said the Skin Horse. "It's a thing that
happens to you. When a child loves you for a long, long time, not
just to play with, but REALLY loves you, then you become Real."
—MARGERY WILLIAMS, THE VELVETEEN RABBIT

We have hearts within,
Warm, live, improvident, indecent hearts.
—Elizabeth Barrett Browning

In a full heart there is room for everything, and in
an empty heart there is room for nothing.
—Antonio Porchia

The heart has such an influence over the understanding
that it is worth while to engage it in our interest.
—Lord Chesterfield

The heart is forever inexperienced.
—Henry David Thoreau

LOVE

Love isn't a decision. It's a feeling. If we could decide who we
loved, it would be much simpler, but much less magical.
—Trey Parker and Matt Stone

There is only one happiness in life, to love and be loved.
—George Sand

All's fair in love and war.
—F.E. Smedley

Love is like playing checkers. You have to know which man to move.
—Jackie "Moms" Mabley

Love, and a cough, cannot be hid.
—George Herbert

One word frees us of all the weight and pain of life: That word is love.
—Sophocles

I have an inalienable constitutional and natural right
to love whom I may, to love as long or as short a period
as I can, to change that love every day if I please!
—Victoria Claflin Woodhull

It's no trick loving somebody at their best.
Love is loving them at their worst.
—Tom Stoppard

Gravitation cannot be held responsible for people falling in love.
—Albert Einstein

I have been missing the point. The point is not knowing another
person, or learning to love another person. The point it simply
this: how tender can we bear to be? What good manners can we
show as we welcome ourselves and others into our hearts?
—Rebecca Wells

The day will come when, after harnessing space, the
winds, the tides, gravitations, we shall harness for god the
energies of love. And, on that day, for the second time in the
history of the world, man will have discovered fire.
—Pierre Teilhard de Chardin

There is no love sincerer than the love of food.
—George Bernard Shaw

To love oneself is the beginning of a life-long romance.
—Oscar Wilde

I love her too, but our neuroses just don't match.
—Arthur Miller

The first symptom of true love in a young man is
timidity; in a young woman, it is boldness.
—Victor Hugo

To love for the sake of being loved is human, but
to love for the sake of loving is angelic.
—Alphonse de Lamartine

Love is life. All, everything that I understand, I understand only because I love. Everything is, everything exists, only because I love. Everything is united by it alone. Love is God, and to die means that I, a particle of love, shall return to the general and eternal source.
—LEO TOLSTOY

Will You Love Me in December as You Do in May?
—JAMES J. WALKER

What will survive of us is love.
—PHILIP LARKIN

Love is, above all, the gift of oneself.
—JEAN ANOUILH

Where both deliberated, the love is slight; who ever loved that loved not at first sight?
—CHRISTOPHER MARLOWE

Love, which is the essence of God, is not for levity, but for the total worth of man.
—RALPH WALDO EMERSON

The best proof of love is trust.
—DR. JOYCE BROTHERS

If music be the food of love, play on.
—WILLIAM SHAKESPEARE

Love lasts about seven years. That's how long it takes for the cells of the body to totally replace themselves.
—FRANCOISE SAGAN

There's always one who loves and one who lets himself be loved.
—W. SOMERSET MAUGHAM

Love means not ever having to say you're sorry.
—ERICH SEGAL

Love conquers all things: let us too give in to Love.
—VIRGIL

Absence makes the heart grow fonder.
—PROPERTIUS

Love's best friend is honesty.
—ANON

Harmony is pure love, for love is complete agreement.
—LOPE DE VEGA

It is best to love wisely, no doubt: but to love foolishly
is better than not to be able to love at all.
—WILLIAM MAKEPEACE THACKERAY

Passion makes the world go round. Love just makes it a safer place.
—ICE T

Love is an irresistible desire to be irresistibly desired.
—ROBERT FROST

This is the miracle that happens ever time to those who
really love; the more they give, the more they possess.
—RAINER MARIA RILKE

I find as I grow older that I love those most whom I loved first.
—THOMAS JEFFERSON

A cigarette that bears a lipstick's traces,
An airline ticket to romantic places,
And still my heart has wings:
These foolish things
Remind me of you.
—HOLT MARVELL

One of the best things about love is just recognizing
a man's step when he climbs the stairs.
—COLLETTE

O Jerry ... Don't let's ask for the moon! We have the stars!
—OLIVE HIGGINS PROUTY

Out of love you can speak with straight fury.
—Eudora Welty

Love is much nicer to be in that an automobile accident, a tight
girdle, a higher tax bracket, or a holding pattern over Philadelphia.
—Judith Viorst

Love is the most fun you can have without laughing.
—H.L. Mencken

For hate is not conquered by hate; hate is
conquered by love. This is a law eternal.
—Pali Tripitaka

Love will find a way.
—Thomas Deloney

Love Is a Many-Splendored Thing.
—Han Suyin

MARRIAGE

A happy marriage is a long conversation which always seems too short.
—André Maurois

There is nothing nobler or more admirable than when two
people who see eye to eye keep house as man and wife,
confounding their enemies and delighting their friends.
—Homer

Husbands are like fires, they go out when unattended.
—Zsa Zsa Gabor

Whoso findeth a wife findeth a good thing.
—Proverbs 18:22

To keep your marriage brimming,
With love in the loving cup,

Whenever you're wrong,
Admit it;
Whenever you're right,
Shut up.
—OGDEN NASH

All men make mistakes, but married men find out about them sooner.
—RED SKELTON

A happy home is one in which each spouse grants the possibility
that the other may be right, though neither believes it.
—DON FRASER

Men with pierced ears are better prepared for marriage—
they've experienced pain and bought jewelry.
—RITA RUDNER

There is no more lovely, friendly and charming relationship,
communion or company than a good marriage.
—MARTIN LUTHER

Marriage is not just spiritual communion and
passionate embraces; marriage is also three-meals-a-
day and remembering to take out the trash.
—DR. JOYCE BROTHERS

Marriage is a wonderful invention; but, then
again, so is a bicycle repair kit.
—BILLY CONNOLLY

The heart of marriage is memories.
—BILL COSBY

I never mind my wife having the last word. In
fact, I'm delighted when she gets to it.
—WALTER MATTHAU

The best way to find out about a man is to have lunch with his ex-wife.
—SHELLEY WINTERS

Choose a wife rather by your ear than your eye.
—THOMAS FULLER

Marriage ... is a damnably serious business, particularly around Boston.
—John P. Marquand

The critical period in matrimony is breakfast-time.
—Sir Alan Patrick Herbert

Marriages are made in heaven and consummated on earth.
—John Lyly

Mother told me a couple of years ago, "Sweetheart, settle down and marry a rich man." I said, "Mom, I am a rich man."
—Cher

The very fact that we make such a to-do over golden weddings indicates our amazement at human endurance. The celebration is more in the nature of a reward for stamina.
—Ilka Chase

No man is truly married until he understand every word his wife is NOT saying.
—Anon

An ideal wife is any woman who has an ideal husband.
—Booth Tarkington

Wedding is destiny, and hanging likewise.
—John Heywood

It was so cold I almost got married.
—Shelley Winters

Bachelor ... a man who never makes the same mistake once.
—Ed Wynn

Hear the mellow wedding bells, golden bells! What a world of happiness their harmony foretells!
—Edgar Allan Poe

A good marriage is that in which each appoints the other the guardian of his solitude.
—Rainer Maria Rilke

A husband is a man who two minutes after his head
Touches the pillow is snoring like an overload omnibus.
—OGDEN NASH

Marriage is not merely sharing the fettucini, but sharing the
burden of finding the fettucini restaurant in the first place
—CALVIN TRILLIN

Some people claim that marriage interferes with
romance. There's no doubt about it. Anytime you have
a romance, your wife is bound to interfere.
—GROUCHO MARX

A wife is the joy of a man's heart.
—TALMUD

It is a matter of life and death for married people to interrupt
each other's stories; for if they did not, they would burst.
—LOGAN PEARSALL SMITH

My definition of marriage ... it resembles a pair of shears, so joined
that they cannot be separated; often moving in opposite directions,
yet always punishing anyone who comes between them.
—SYDNEY SMITH

With children no longer the universally accepted reason for marriage,
marriages are going to have to exist on their own merits.
—ELEANOR HOLMES NORTON

When marrying, one should ask oneself this question: do you believe
that you will be able to converse well with this woman into your old age?
—FRIEDRICH NIETZSCHE

To marry a second time represents the triumph of hope over experience.
—DR. SAMUEL JOHNSON

When you are in love with someone you want to be near him all the
time, except when you are out buying things and charging them to him.
—MISS PIGGY (MUPPET)

It's just as hard ... staying happily married as it is doing movies.
—TOM HANKS

Early marriage, long love.
—GERMAN SAYING

Take my wife . . . please.
—HENNY YOUNGMAN

Marriage is . . . the union of hands and hearts.
—JEREMY TAYLOR

It takes a loose rein to keep a marriage tight.
—JOHN STEVENSON

Keep your eyes wide open before marriage, half shut afterwards.
—BENJAMIN FRANKLIN

God created man and, finding him not sufficiently alone, gave
him a companion to make him feel his solitude more keenly.
—PAUL VALERY

One reason people get divorced is that they run out of gift ideas.
—ROBERT BYRNE

Married men live longer than single men. But
married men are a lot more willing to die.
—JOHNNY CARSON

Bigamy is having one husband too many. Monogamy is the same.
—ERICA JONG

Marriage is popular because it combines the maximum
of temptation with the maximum of opportunity.
—GEORGE BERNARD SHAW

I believe a little incompatibility is the spice of life,
particularly if he has income and she is pattable.
—OGDEN NASH

When you see what some girls marry, you realize
how they must hate to work for a living.
—HELEN ROWLAND

The contract 'twixt Hannah, God and me,
Was not for one or twenty years, but for eternity.
—David Ross Locke as Petroleum V. Nasby

Fighting is essentially a masculine idea; a
woman's weapon is her tongue.
—Hermione Gingold

Sometimes I wonder if men and women really suit each other.
Perhaps they should live next door and just visit now and then.
—Katharine Hepburn

Man's best possession is a sympathetic wife.
—Euripides

A woman has got to love a bad man once or twice
in her life, to be thankful for a good one.
—Marjorie Rawlings

You can no more keep a martini in the refrigerator than
you can keep a kiss there. The proper union of gin and
vermouth is a great and sudden glory; it is one of the happiest
marriages on earth and one of the shortest-lived.
—Bernard De Voto

SEX

Sex is two plus two making five, rather than four. Sex is the
X ingredient that you can't define, and it's that X ingredient
between two people that make both a man and a woman
good in bed. It's all relative. There are no rules.
—Marty Feldman

Kissing is a means of getting two people so close together
that they can't see anything wrong with each other.
—René Yasenek

Sex appeal is 50% what you've got and 50% what people think you've got.
—Sophia Loren

Certainly nothing is unnatural that is not physically impossible.
—WILLIAM SHAKESPEARE

[Dancing is] a perpendicular expression of a horizontal desire.
—GEORGE BERNARD SHAW

I think making love is the best form of exercise.
—CARY GRANT

A kiss can be a comma, a question mark, or an exclamation
point. That's a basic spelling that every woman should know.
—MISTINGUETT [JEANNE BOURGEOIS]

You'll have to ask somebody older than me.
—EUBIE BLAKE, AGE 97, WHEN ASKED AT WHAT AGE DOES THE SEX DRIVE END

I do not know, I am only sixty-five.
—PAULINE METTERNICH, WHEN ASKED AT WHAT AGE A WOMAN'S SEXUAL URGES
CEASE

My own view, for what it's worth, is that sexuality is lovely, there cannot
be too much of it, it is self-limiting if it is satisfactory, and satisfaction
diminishes tension and clears the mind for attention and learning.
—PAUL GOODMAN

In the spring a young man's fancy lightly turns to thoughts of love.
—ALFRED, LORD TENNYSON

Why do they put the Gideon Bibles only in the bedrooms, where
it's usually too late, and not in the barroom downstairs?
—CHRISTOPHER MORLEY

Sex and golf are the two things you can enjoy
even if you're not good at them.
—KEVIN COSTNER

I love the idea of there being two sexes, don't you?
—JAMES THURBER (CARTOON CAPTION IN THE NEW YORKER)

Sex is one of the nine reasons for reincarnation.
The other eight are unimportant.
—HENRY MILLER

If I hold you any closer, I'll be in back of you.
—GROUCHO MARX IN *A DAY AT THE RACES*

Sex is nature's way of saying "Hi!"
—ANON

I'll have what she's having.
—WOMAN DINER IN *WHEN HARRY MET SALLY*

Sex is like money; only too much is enough.
—JOHN UPDIKE

The sexual embrace can only be compared with music and with prayer.
—HAVELOCK ELLIS

The other day we had a long discourse with [Lady Orkney] about
love; and she told us a saying . . . which I thought excellent, that,
"in men, desire begets love; and in women, love begets desire."
—JONATHAN SWIFT

People who throw kisses are hopelessly lazy.
—BOB HOPE

I kissed my first girl and smoked my first cigarette on the
same day. I haven't had time for tobacco since.
—ARTURO TOSCANINI

Bed is the poor man's opera.
—ITALIAN SAYING

Civilized people cannot fully satisfy their sexual instinct without love.
—BERTRAND RUSSELL

Anybody who believes that the way to a man's heart
is through his stomach flunked geography.
—ROBERT BYRNE

Sex is good, but not as good as fresh sweet corn.
—GARRISON KEILLOR

No act can be quite so intimate as the sexual embrace.
In its accomplishment, for all who have reached a
reasonably human degree of development, the communion
of bodies becomes the communion of souls.
—HAVELOCK ELLIS

If you can't be with the one you love,
Love the one you're with.
—STEPHEN STILLS

Venus favors the bold
—OVID

The only reason I would take up jogging is so that
I could hear heavy breathing again.
—ERMA BOMBECK

No sex, please—we're British!!!!!!
—ANTHONY MARRIOTT

Sex is a part of nature. I go along with nature.
—MARILYN MONROE

There are three possible parts to a date, of which at least two must
be offered: entertainment, food, and affection. It is customary to
begin a series of dates with a great deal of entertainment, a moderate
amount of food, and the merest suggestion of affection. As the
amount of affection increases, the entertainment can be reduced
proportionately. When the affection is the entertainment, we no longer
call it dating. Under no circumstances can the food be omitted.
— JUDITH MARTIN, *MISS MANNER'S GUIDE TO EXCRUCIATINGLY CORRECT
BEHAVIOUR*

Men wake up aroused in the morning. We can't help it. We just
wake up and we want you. And the women are thinking, "How
can he want me the way I look in the morning?" It's because we
can't see you. We have no blood anywhere near our optic nerve.
—ANDY ROONEY

Takes Two to Tango.
—AL HOFFMAN

Sex without love is as hollow and ridiculous as love without sex.
—HUNTER S. THOMPSON

Sex is the great amateur art. The professional, male or female, is
frowned on; he or she misses the whole point and spoils the show.
—DAVID CORT

He: Do you like Kipling?
She: I don't know, you naughty boy, I've never Kippled.
—DONALD MCGILL

Literature is mostly about having sex and not much about
having children. Life is the other way around.
—DAVID LODGE

I need sex for a clear complexion, but I'd rather do it for love.
—JOAN CRAWFORD

Sex: the thing that takes up the least amount of time
and causes the most amount of trouble.
—JOHN BARRYMORE

Making love? It's a communion with a woman. The bed is
the holy table. There I find passion—and purification.
—OMAR SHARIF

So we think of Marilyn who was every man's love affair with
America. Marilyn Monroe who was blonde and beautiful and
had a sweet little rinky-dink of a voice and all the cleanliness
of all the clean American backyards. She was our angel, the
sweet angel of sex, and the sugar of sex came up from her
like a resonance of sound in the clearest grain of a violin.
—NORMAN MAILER

[H]ow can we describe the most exalted experience of
our physical lives [sex] as it—jack, wrench, hubcap, and
nuts—we were describing the changing of a flat tire?
—JOHN CHEEVER

Chess, like love, like music, has the power to make men happy.
—Siegbert Tarrasch

Sure he was great, but don't forget that Ginger Rogers did
everything he did ... backwards and in high heels.
—Bob Thaves, on Fred Astaire

Familiarity breeds contempt—and children.
—Mark Twain

I have an idea that the phrase "weaker sex" was coined by some
woman to disarm the man she was preparing to overwhelm.
—Ogden Nash

I don't know whether it's normal or not, but sex has always
been something that I take seriously. I would put it higher
than tennis on my list of constructive things to do.
—Art Buchwald

Ah, Dubin, you meet a pretty girl on the road and are
braced to hop on a horse in pursuit of youth.
—Bernard Malamud

Sex is a conversation carried out by other means.
—Peter Ustinov

Kissing don't last: cookery do!
—George Meredith

MEN AND WOMEN

I'd much rather be a woman than a man. Women can cry, they can
wear cute clothes, and they're the first to be rescued off sinking ships.
—Gilda Radner

Here's to woman! Would that we could fall into
her arms without falling into her hands.
—Ambrose Bierce

Alas! The love of Women! It is known to be a lovely and a fearful thing.
—LORD BYRON

That's the nature of women, not to love when we love
them, and to love when we love them not.
—MIGUEL DE CERVANTES

In politics, if you want anything said, ask a man. If
you want anything done, ask a woman.
—MARGARET THATCHER

A study in *The Washington Post* says that women have better verbal
skills than men. I just want to say to the authors of that study: Duh.
—CONAN O'BRIEN

I . . . understand why the saints were rarely married women.
I am convinced it has nothing inherently to do, as I once
supposed, with chastity or children. It has to do primarily with
distractions. . . . Woman's normal occupations in general run
counter to creative life, or contemplative life or saintly life.
—ANNE MORROW LINDBERGH

A beautiful woman is a practical poet.
—RALPH WALDO EMERSON

In Sicily, women are more dangerous than shotguns.
—MARIO PUZO, *THE GODFATHER*

There is in every true woman's heart a spark of heavenly fire,
which lies dormant in the broad daylight of prosperity, but which
kindles up and beams and blazed in the dark hour of adversity.
—WASHINGTON IRVING

To be married to a good woman is to live with tender surprise.
—NORMAN MAILER

We don't love a woman for what she says, we
like what she says because we love her.
—ANDRE MAUROIS

The difficulty of course is that I like women. It
is only wives I am in trouble with.
—JOHN STEINBECK

A healthy male adult consumes each year one and a half
times his own weight in other people's patience.
—JOHN UPDIKE

God created man, but I could do better.
—ERMA BOMBECK

Men build bridges and throw railroads across deserts, and yet
they contend successfully that the job of sewing on a button is
beyond them. Accordingly, they don't have to sew buttons.
—HAYWOOD BROUN

A handsome man is not quite poor.
—SPANISH PROVERB

Women like silent men. They think they're listening.
—MARCEL ACHARD

I'm not denyin' the women are foolish: God
Almighty made 'em to match the men.
—GEORGE ELIOT

Men live by forgetting—women live on memories.
—T.S. ELIOT

She plucked from my lapel the invisible strand of lint (the
universal act of woman to proclaim ownership).
—O. HENRY

God created man and, finding him not sufficiently alone, gave
him a companion to make him feel his solitude more keenly.
—PAUL VALERY

Woman is man's confusion.
—VINCENT OF BEAUVAIS

COMMITMENT

We've been married for twenty-two years. And I have
learned a long time ago that the only two people who
count in any marriage are the two who are in it.
—HILLARY RODHAM CLINTON

Unless commitment is made, there are only
promises and hopes ... but no plans.
—PETER DRUCKER

Being deeply loved by someone gives you strength,
while loving someone deeply gives you courage.
—LAO TZU

Love is ... born with the pleasure of looking at each other,
it is fed with the necessity of seeing each other, it is
concluded with the impossibility of separation!
—JOSE MARTI

The need for devotion to something outside ourselves is even
more profound than the need for companionship. If we are
not to go to pieces or wither away, we all must have some
purpose in life; for not man can live for himself alone.
—ROSS PARMENTER

Love is how you stay alive, even after you are gone.
—MORRIE SCHWARTZ

Only do what your heart tells you.
—PRINCESS DIANA

[I will not] sulk about having no boyfriend, but develop inner
poise and authority and sense of self as woman of substance,
complete without boyfriend, as best way to obtain boyfriend.
—HELEN FIELDING (BRIDGET JONES'S DIARY)

If you want to get along, go along.
—SAM RAYBURN

The beauty of a strong, lasting commitment is often
best understood by a man incapable of it.
—Murray Kempton

'Tis strange what a man may do, and a woman yet think him an angel.
—William Makepeace Thackeray

Experience shows us that love does not consist in gazing at
each other but in looking together in the same direction.
—Antoine de Saint-Exupery

Stand by your man.
And tell the world you love him
Keep giving all the love you can.
—Tammy Wynette and Billy Sherrill

Behind every successful man there is a surprised woman.
—Maryon Pearson, former first lady of Canada

Acknowledgments

Without the help, support, and love of the following people, this book would not have come about.

First and foremost, my thanks go to Sheryl Stebbins, Random House publisher and lifelong friend, who knew I had another book in me. She worked her usual "stealth magic" in encouraging me to tackle this enormous project. Erie, PA should be most proud of its hometown girl (as am I!) with her illustrious publishing career! Also thank you to my Random House "Command Central," Patricia Dublin, Amy Bozek, Helena Santini, and Bistra Bogdanova, all whose talents and knowledge I was blessed to have assist me in assembling this vast volume of quotes. I am truly in their debt. I am also grateful to the many friends who suggested quotes or books of quotes when I was running low on resources. I could not have done this without them.

To special friend Darlene Loebig, who kept me on track by making sure I still kept my head clear with walks on the "DarKoBar Trail" with four-footed furry wonders, Kodie and Barney, I am most grateful. I cannot think of any activity more uplifting than spending time with you three!

Many thanks go to Diane Gloor and Roberta Eckman in the volunteer office of University of Pittsburgh Medical Center/Passavant Hospital and my fellow volunteers for maneuvering their schedules to cover for me while I worked on this book. I am most appreciative for their willingness to fill in my seat during my absence.

Special appreciation goes to my Bestest, Barb Wyllie. You are always there with so much love, hugs, encouraging words, or a nice, cool house in which to work when my air conditioner died in stifling

hot weather. God truly smiled the day we became friends and I thank Him every day for you.

And to my handsome husband, Tod, thank you for taking over my chores while I worked on this book. There is no greater love or sacrifice of a husband, allergic to grass, who will mow the lawn regardless, when his wife is busy with literary endeavors. Thank you so much for your love, support and still being my greatest cheerleader. You do not have to worry about being named after Lotus and Lily on the book jacket. You are always Number 1 with me!

Index

Elizabeth I, Queen, 16
Ellington, Duke, 105, 295
Elliot, Thelma, 47
Elliott, L.G., 376
Ellis, Havelock, 512, 553, 554
Ellison, Ralph, 366
Emerson, F.L., 148
Emerson, Ralph Waldo, 10, 14, 17, 25, 27, 29, 31, 33, 39, 41, 46, 50, 59, 61, 66, 79, 83, 96, 108, 111, 118, 124, 126, 134, 138, 141, 143, 148, 159, 171, 173, 174, 177, 179, 180, 189, 197, 200, 206, 207, 225, 227, 228, 234, 235, 237, 240, 245, 252, 267, 273, 274, 275, 279, 284, 293, 302, 315, 317, 320, 325, 327, 338, 346, 348, 353, 360, 363, 366, 372, 377, 381, 383, 385, 387, 392, 394, 398, 407, 408, 410, 413, 415, 426, 440, 443, 501, 511, 519, 520, 525, 529, 533, 544, 557
Emmanuel, 52, 80, 450, 514, 526
Engle, Paul, 139
English proverb, 114, 145, 218, 289, 298
English saying 4, 127
Ennius, Quintus, 87, 176
Ephron, Nora, 165
Epictetus, 6, 21, 90, 95, 100, 115, 138, 158, 202, 210, 253, 256, 296, 312, 316, 341, 355, 423, 440, 531
Epicurus, 35, 43, 100, 172, 178, 252, 257, 260, 279, 282
Erasmus, 72, 176, 205, 339
Erhard, Werner, 535
Erikson, Erik, 336
Erskine, John, 104
Ertz, Susan, 5
Esar, Evan, 149
Eskimo proverb, 207
Est. 4:16, 326
Estienne, Henri, 1
Estonian proverb, 251
Euland, Brenda, 362
Euripides, 16, 33, 127, 155, 161, 171, 175, 186, 253, 257, 266, 277, 303, 328, 331, 345, 353, 411, 463, 531, 540, 551

Evans, Colleen Townsend, 470
Evans, Michael, 324
Evans, Richard L., 253
Everage, Dame Edna (Barry Humphries), 60

Faber, Frederick W., 192
Fabre, Jean-Henri, 193
Fadiman, Clifton, 229
Fairless, Benjamin F., 386
Farley, James A., 413
Farley, Robert E., 459
Farmer, Frances, 188
Farrall, Joseph, 225
Farrell, Joseph, 8, 27, 280
Faulkner, William, 11, 120, 292, 346
Feather, William, 17, 21, 40, 143, 156, 176, 201, 301, 308
Feibleman, James K., 451
Feldman, Marty, 551
Fellini, Federico, 92, 142, 266, 344, 421
Fichter, Jean Paul, 298
Ficke, Arthur Davison, 290
Field, Marshall, 401
Field, Sally, 345
Fielding, Henry, 30, 294
Fields, W.C., 270, 417, 430
Fierstein, Harvey, 326
Filson, Floyd V., 86
Fine, Robert M., 15, 18
Finley, Charles O., 146
Finley, John H., 45
Firkins, Oscar W., 197
Fisher, Admiral John, 325
Fisher, Geoffrey, 337
Fisher, M.F.K., 38
Fiske, John, 51
FitzGerald, Edward, 239
Fitzgerald, F. Scott, 238, 271, 288, 313, 426
Fitzgerald, Gerald B., 455
Fitzgerald, Robert, 403
Fitzosborne, Thomas, 204, 258
Fitzpatrick, Jean Grasso, 451
Flake, Floyd and M. Elaine, 520
Flandrau, Charles Macomb, 24
Fleishman, Jerome P., 301
Flemming, Paul, 453

Flynn, Errol, 129
Foch, Marshal Ferdinand, 323, 383, 395, 406
Foley, Elizabeth, 178
Fontane, Theodore, 12
Fontey, Margaret, 75
Fonteyn, Margot, 149
Forbes, B.C., 81, 150, 153, 157, 198, 217, 301, 326, 330, 334, 376, 386, 387
Forbes, Malcolm, 79, 263, 303, 379, 391, 396, 411, 421
Ford, Harrison, 154, 341, 429
Ford, Henry, 31, 205, 323, 347, 384, 417, 455
Ford, Lena Guilbert, 228—229
Forster, E.M., 270, 517
Forsyth, Peter Taylor, 327
Fortune Cookie, 318
Fosdick, Harry Emerson, 70, 512, 516
Foster, Bill, 427
Foster, John, 33
France, Anatole, 119, 222, 316, 352, 393, 399
Francis, Arlene, 188
Francis of Assisi, Saint, 111
Francis de Sales, Saint, 7, 74, 172, 175, 316, 342, 344
Frank, Anne, 92, 210, 437
Frankel, Viktor, 215, 403
Franklin, Benjamin, 1, 7, 18, 38, 88, 89, 95, 120, 127, 137, 193, 209, 213, 238, 253, 257, 271, 276, 296, 302, 317, 318, 327, 376, 378, 397, 404, 416, 517, 524, 550
Franklin, Jon, 113
Fraser, Don, 547
Frazier, Joe, 291
Frederick, Robert E., 186
Frederick the Great, 345
Freedman, Ruth P., 74
French proverb, 75, 156, 162, 254, 262, 286, 296, 363, 437, 536
Freud, Clement, 3
Freud, Sigmund, 73, 308, 321
Friedman, Cynthia, 111
Friedman, Dr. Martha, 336
Frohman, Daniel, 177

Fromm, Erich, 87, 114, 331,
370, 499, 507, 515
Frost, Paul, 444
Frost, Robert, 177, 229, 299,
545
Froud, James A., 77, 302
Fry, Christopher, 58, 432,
497
Fulbright, James W., 421
Fulgham, Robert, 264, 272
Fulheim, Dorothy, 1
Fuller, R. Buckminster,
322, 522
Fuller, Thomas, 46, 55, 122,
134, 137, 162, 182, 185,
188, 193, 197, 252, 259,
262, 268, 288, 290, 306,
307, 354, 371, 381, 384,
393, 424, 428, 453, 460,
461, 465, 483, 495, 497,
515, 533, 547

Gable, Clark, 229
Gabor, Zsa Zsa, 546
Gabrielle, Sidonie, 105
Gaines, William, 246
Gal. 6:7, 417
Gal. 6:9, 158
Galbraith, John Kenneth,
288
Galen, 144
Gandhi, Mahatma, 219,
310, 471, 473, 489, 505,
510, 521
Garagiola, Joe, 25
Gardner, Ava, 236
Gardner, Edward, 355
Gardner, Herb, 21
Gardner, John W., 8
Gardner, Victor E., 258
Garfield, James A., 93, 326,
450
Garrison, William Lloyd,
327
Garson, Greer, 334, 344,
385
Gary, Roman, 314
Gaskell, Elizabeth, 227, 307
Gassen, Ira, 421
Gasser, Herbert, 294
Gates, Bill, 54
Gautier, Theophile, 537
Gawain, Shakti, 73, 357,
359, 363, 411, 449, 527
Gay, John, 87
Gayler, T.L., 13

Gellert, Christian
Furchtegott, 206, 336,
368
Gendler, J. Ruth, 446, 450
Gentry, Dave Tyson, 183
George, Boy, 314
George, Henry, 128, 351
German proverb, 49, 99,
117, 244, 290, 306, 317,
458
German saying, 550
Gerould, Katherine F., 110
Getty, J. Paul, 126
Gibbon, Edward, 91, 308
Gibbs, Willard, 117
Gibran, Kahlil, 9, 27, 47,
113, 123, 141, 194, 212, 235,
359, 415, 528
Gibson, Josh, 436
Gide, André, 8, 34, 38, 70,
121, 203, 222, 248, 249,
284, 333, 343, 535
Gielgud, Sir John, 84
George, David Lloyd, 386
Gilbert, Arland, 20, 148,
313, 389, 398, 505
Gilbert, W.S., 273
Giles, Henry, 519, 522
Gilman, Charlotte Perkins,
213
Gingold, Hermione, 551
Ginott, Haim, 419
Gish, Lillian, 2, 297
Gissing, George R., 71, 422
Gita, Bhagavad, 272, 319,
323
Gitfillan, Robert, 459
Glasgow, Ellen, 4, 275, 525
Glasow, Arnold H., 89, 112,
176, 197
Glinka, Mikhail, 102
Gobel, George, 315
Godin, André, 407, 415
Godwin, Gail, 177
Goethe, 234
Goldberg, Herb, 364
Goldberg, Isaac, 375, 415
Goldberg, James, 439
Golding, Henry J., 373
Goldsmith, Oliver, 71, 265,
462
Goldwyn, Samuel, 437
Gomez, Lefty, 119
Goodier, Alban, 15
Goodman, Paul, 210, 323,
354, 368, 552
Gordan, Ruth, 163

Gordy, Charles, 237
Gorky, Maxim, 129, 225, 257
Gorman, Paul, 494
Gottlieb, Annie, 196
Gough, John B., 99, 387
Goulburn, Edward M., 488
Gould, Glenn, 236
Goulding, Raymond H.,
146
Gouthey, A.P., 390
Gracian, Baltasar, 134, 138,
176, 184, 194, 252, 270,
366, 384, 403, 534
Graham, Katharine, 145
Graham, Martha, 242
Gramm, Phil, 291
Grant, Cary, 27, 114, 552
Grant, Ulysses S., 143
Granville, John Carteret,
452
Graves, Richard, 184
Gray, Harry, 354
Grayson, David, 70, 72, 74,
108, 184, 195, 259, 454,
534
Greek proverb, 162, 184,
221, 262, 322
Greeley, Horace, 6
Greene, Graham, 77, 97
Greene, Robert, 6
Greenfield, Jeff, 112
Gregory, Dick, 216
Greville, Fulke, 3
Gribble, Phillip, 37
Grieg, Edvard, 187
Griffin, Merv, 270
Griffith, Bill, 62
Griggs, Edward Howard,
305
Griswald, Whitney, 302
Groening, Matt, 357
Grou, Jean Nicholas, 505
Groult, Benoite, 169
Guest, Edgar A., 228, 428
Guicciardini, Francesco,
180
Guinness, Og, 519
Gunther, John, 202
Gurdjieff, Georges, 70
Gwenn, Edmund, 64

Haddow, Sir Henry, 24
Haeker, Theodore, 8
Hafez, 244, 466
Hagen, Walter, 330
Hagman, Larry, 49

Hailey, Alex, 71, 335
Hailey, Arthur, 269
Halberstam, David, 49
Hale, Edward Everett, 19, 77
Half, Robert, 148
Hall, Tom T., 377
Hallesby, O., 469, 472, 473, 474, 475, 476, 478, 484, 485, 486, 487, 490, 493
Halloway, Richard, 115, 207
Halsey, William F., 282
Hamilton, Alexander, 311, 499
Hamilton, Gail, 347
Hamilton, William, 130
Hammarskjold, Dag, 44, 196, 280, 328, 332, 356, 497
Hammer, Armand, 267
Hammerstien, Oscar II, 102, 413
Hanks, Tom, 549
Hannibal, 93
Hardy, Thomas, 271, 424
Hare, Julius Charles, 115, 183, 258, 334, 514
Hart, Moss, 55
Hart, Sir Basil Liddell, 313
Hartley, L.P., 7
Harriman, Edward Henry, 52
Harris, Frank, 293
Harris, Sydney J., 67, 164, 319, 429, 456
Harrison, George, 92
Haskins, Henry S., 359, 530
Hathaway, Katherine Butler, 357, 358, 361
Havel, Vaclav, 465
Havighurst, Robert J., 176
Havner, Vance, 478, 514
Hawes, J., 371
Hawley, Charles A., 73
Hay, John, 178, 193
Hayakawa, S.I., 64
Hayes, Helen, 328, 389
Hayes, Woody, 327,
Hazard, Robert, 211
Hazlitt, William, 10, 41, 59, 69, 77, 81, 113, 135, 178, 189, 193, 197, 238, 261, 294, 301, 354, 355, 359, 392, 400, 401, 422, 423, 460, 506
Heb. 11:1, 511
Heb. 13:5, 261

Hebbel, Friedrich, 355
Hedge, H.F., 91
Hegel, George, 397
Hein, Piet, 112, 290, 389
Heine, Heinrich, 102, 501
Heinleil, Robert A., 334
Helburn, Theresa, 324
Hellman, Lillian, 339, 351, 364, 420, 508
Helps, Sir Arthur, 533, 538
Helvetius, Claude-Adrien, 122, 394
Hemingway, Earnest, 113, 150, 369
Hendrix, Jimi, 101, 107
Henker, Dr. Fred O., 465
Henley, William Ernest, 84, 158
Henri, Robert, 207, 226, 364
Henry, Matthew, 250—251, 470, 481, 490
Henry, O., 252, 263, 558
Henry, Philip, 470, 492
Hepburn, Katharine, 95, 271, 342, 396, 551
Heraclitus, 350, 353
Herbert, A.P., 443
Herbert, George, 86, 103, 129, 471, 489, 542
Herbert, Sir Alan Patrick, 548
Herodotus, 88, 385
Herold, Don, 225, 237
Herrick, Robert, 480, 523
Hesburgh, Theodore, 170
Heschel, Abraham Joshua, 139, 253, 445
Hesiod, 169, 229
Hesse, Hermann, 59, 90, 136, 496
Hewett, Phillip, 13, 445
Heywood, John, 548
Hickson, W.E., 156
Hightower, Cullen, 135
Hill, James B., 267
Hill, Napoleon, 74, 157, 373
Hillel, 79, 126
Hilliard, 408
Hindu proverb, 458, 515, 530
Hirsch, Mary, 58
Hiscox, E.T., 514
Hitchcock, Alfred, 116, 268
Hobbes, Thomas, 515
Hobbs, John Oliver, 263
Hock, Dee, 299

Hodges, Leigh Mitchell, 45
Hodgson, Ralph, 522
Hodnett, Edward, 280
Hoffer, Eric, 42, 296, 322, 360, 421, 425, 428, 441, 463, 510, 526, 531
Hoffman, Abbie, 44
Hoffman, Al, 555
Hoffman, Eva, 57
Hofmann, Hans, 116
Holdcraft, L. Thomas, 108
Holderlin, Friedrich, 499
Holland, Josiah G., 100, 155, 295
Holler, William E., 154
Hollywood Squares, 232, 514
Holmes, Ernest, 413, 450
Holmes, John Andrew, 452, 457
Holmes, Oliver Wendell, 238, 239, 259, 275, 447, 511, 519, 540
Holmes, Oliver Wendell Jr., 19, 22, 72, 74, 121, 135, 150, 157, 175, 178, 186, 203, 226, 245, 320, 321, 365, 367, 373
Holt, Hamilton 140
Holtz, Lou, 304, 326
Homer, 180, 259, 351, 546
Homer Simpson, 357
Homolka, Oscar, 299
Honda, Soichire, 430
Hood, Thomas, 233
Hoover, Herbert, 112, 246, 533
Hope, Anthony, 60
Hope, Bob, 296, 452, 553
Hope, Laurence, 536
Hopkins, Jane Ellice, 237
Horace, 22, 23, 28, 38, 39, 58, 76, 137, 221, 245, 251, 298, 301, 342, 506, 530, 535
Horban, Donald, 259
Horney, Karen, , 243, 310
Horry, Robert, 428
Houghton, 22
Housman, A.E., 46
Hovey, Richard, 290
How To Survive The Loss of a Love, 530
Howard, Maureen, 61
Howe, Edgar Watson, 46, 99, 131, 176, 181, 182, 262, 278, 306, 345, 432

Hoyle, Edmond, 331
Hsieh, Tehyi, 319, 390
Hubbard, Elbert, 28, 40, 47,
    95, 117, 134, 162, 163, 190,
    194, 210, 228, 240, 250,
    288, 358, 389, 392, 419,
    421, 508, 516, 527
Hubbard, Kin, 126, 129, 165,
    259, 417, 495
Hubbard, L. Ron, 207, 283,
    370
Huerta, Delores, 495
Hughes, Frank, 422
Hughes, Thomas, 172, 311
Hugo, Victor, 48, 103, 217,
    295, 451, 455, 460, 476,
    489, 513, 540, 543
Hulbert, William A., 338,
    384
Hume, David, 411, 503
Hummell, Charles, 35
Humphrey, Hubert H.,
    362
Humphreys, Harry E. Jr.,
    174
Hunt, Earl G. Jr., 486
Hunt, Leigh, 315
Hunter, Catfish, 400, 436
Hurston, Zora Neale, 419
Hutcheson, Francis, 458
Huvelin, Abbeé Henri, 512
Huxley, Aldous, 92, 103,
    188, 248, 312, 363, 517

Iacocca, Lee, 25, 165, 166,
    289, 392
Ibn-Abi-Talib, Ali, 457
Ibn Gabirol, Soloman, 513
Ibsen, Henrik, 201, 288,
    325, 339
Ice T, 545
Iles, George, 462
Inge, William Ralph, 141,
    210, 214, 255, 444, 516
Ingersoll, Robert G., 38, 121,
    126, 227, 444, 460, 467
Irish proverb, 88, 143, 529
Iron, Mary Jean, 263
Irving, Washington, 293,
    307, 329, 557
Irwin, Ben, 26
Irwin, William A., 23
Isidore of Seville, 39
Italian saying, 553
Ivener, Goldie, 35
Izzard, Wes, 145

Jackson, Andrew, 276
Jackson, Delma, 477, 486
Jackson, Dr. Bill, 71
Jackson, Helen Hunt, 316
Jackson, Holbrook, 211
Jackson, Jesse, 45, 355, 460
Jackson, Mahalia, 105
Jackson, Reggie, 406
Jackson, Robert H., 434
Jacobi, Friedrich, 446
Jacobs, Joseph, 498
Jakes, John, 266
James, Henry, 200, 348,
    358, 375, 472, 523
James, Paul Moon, 464
James, William, 57, 80, 138,
    182, 196, 212, 295, 308,
    339, 357, 359, 363, 375,
    408, 415, 420, 422, 444,
    448, 515, 531
Jameson, Storm, 30, 42,
    118, 204
Jampolsky, Gerald, 499,
    503
Japanese proverb, 255, 524
Jas. 1:6, 483
Jas. 2:6
Jas. 5:16, 475, 487, 490
Jaworski, Ron, 405
Jayasi, Malik Muhammad,
    185
Jb. 11:18, 461
Jefferson, Charles E., 199
Jefferson, Thomas, 53, 136,
    139, 160, 203, 222, 243,
    251, 268, 366, 459, 495,
    545
Jenkyn, William, 471
Jennings, Gary, 19
Jepson, J.W., 86
Jerome, Jerome K., 121, 149,
    208
Jerrold, Douglas, 218
Jimenel, Juan Ramon, 23
1 Jn. 14:13, 468
1 Jn. 15:13, 174
Joel, Billy, 80
John Chrysostom, Saint,
    301, 474
John XXIII, Pope, 167
John, Viscount Morley of
    Blackburn, 27, 114, 250
Johnson, Ben, 15, 378, 458
Johnson, Howard E., 242
Johnson, Lady Bird, 418
Johnson, Lyndon B., 54
Johnson, Robert, 85

Johnson, Samuel, 30, 40,
    84, 101, 125, 127, 164, 186,
    187, 191, 191, 193, 196,
    211, 256, 283, 286, 296,
    298, 353, 356, 423, 430,
    431, 440, 460, 464, 529,
    537, 549
Johnson, Spencer, 122
Johnson, Steward B., 383
Johnston, Lynn, 5
Johnstone, Margaret B., 13
Joly, Eugene, 514
Jones, Charles, 188
Jones, T., 439
Jong, Erica, 163, 344, 455,
    550
Jonson, Ben, 118
Joplin, Janis, 333
Jordan, David Starr, 134,
    135, 395
Jordan, Sara M.D., 15
Joseph, Jenny, 4
Joubert, Joseph, 11, 92, 134,
    177, 209, 222, 245, 253,
    255, 397, 414, 454
Joyce, James, 37, 199
Jung, Carl, 66, 225, 283, 443,
    498, 512, 524, 536
Jusserano, Jules, 87
Juvenal 127, 434

Kafka, Franz, 67, 338
Kahanamoku, Duke P., 328
Kaiser, Henry J., 141, 248
Kakuzo, Okakura, 506
Kant, Immanuel, 136, 496
Kanteletar, The, 179
Kapp, Joe, 381
Karr, Alphonse, 250, 350
Kaufman, George S., 63
Kawabata, Yasunari, 518
Keats, John, 102, 103, 236,
    237, 304
Keillor, Garrison, 60, 262,
    554
Keller, Helen, 54, 77, 84, 85,
    108, 150, 174, 242, 284,
    348, 351, 393, 409, 541
Kelley, James, 56
Kelly, Larry, 382
Kemp, Jack, 143
Kempton, Murray, 560
Kendall, Donald M., 391,
    397
Kenmore, Carolyn, 361
Kennan, George, 358

Mays, Willie, 27, 160
McCabe, Edward, 289, 423
McCant, Jerry W., 108
McCarthy, Charlie, 140
McCarthy, Marthy, 220
McCartney, Paul, 424
McCracken, Robert J., 209, 457
McDonald, Claude, 387
McFee, William, 131, 270
McGill, Donald, 555
McGill, William, 468
McGinnis, Allen Reid, 532
McGinnis, Mack, 78
McGranahan, Norvin G., 65
McGraw, Tug, 17, 129, 412
McGuane, Thomas, 142, 266
McGuirk, John J., 378
McIndoe, Sir Archibald, 378
McIntosh, Joan, 212
McIntosh. M.C., 534
McKay, John, 289
McKenna, Stephen, 331, 370
McLaughlin, Mignon, 43, 182, 223, 464, 500
McLuhan, Marshall, 180
McNabb, Vincent, 460
McSorely, Joseph, 31
McWilliams, Peter, 272, 530
Mead, Margaret, 167, 352
Meir, Golda, 26, 235, 365
Melanchthon, Philipp, 469, 519
Melchart, Harold B., 8
Mel-Ling Soong, 493
Melville, Herman, 287, 453, 489
Menander, 97, 142
Mencius, 195, 365, 394
Mencken, H.L., 32, 63, 64, 134, 275, 522, 546
Mendelssohn, Moses, 27
Menninger, Dr. Karl, 78, 465
Mercier A.T., 152
Meredith, George, 117, 270, 302, 556
Merrill, Bob, 508
Merrill, Bradford, 431
Merton, Thomas, 86, 445
Messner, Tammy Faye Bakker, 470

Metastasio, Pietro, 392
Metternich, Pauline, 552
Meynell, Alice, , 216, 421
Michelangelo, 83, 239, 317, 522
Michener, James A., 504
Midler, Bette, 6, 348, 494
Milburn, John F., 436
Milk, Harvey, 461
Mill, John Stuart, 215, 217, 239, 258
Millay, Edna St. Vincent, 119, 326
Miller, Alice Duer, 186
Miller, Arthur, 543
Miller, Bud, 345
Miller, Henry, 106, 108, 150, 267, 327, 330, 357, 407, 553
Miller, Joaquin, 162, 461
Miller, John Homer, 314
Miller, John R., 301, 306
Milligan, Spike, 130
Millman, Dan, 259
Mills, C. Wright, 129
Milne, A.A., 135
Milnes, Richard M., 473
Milton, John, 84, 109, 198, 409, 457
Minab, Sandor, 26
Mindess, Harvey, 524
Minnelli, Liza, 469
Miro, Joan, 113
Miss Manner's Guide, 554
Miss Piggy, 549
Mistinguett, 552
Mistletoe, John, 357
Mitchell, Donald G., 51, 52, 54
Mitchell, Margaret, 88, 144, 494
Mitchell, S. Weir, 191
Mitford, Nancy, 170
Mizner, Wilson, 65, 190
Moliere, 57, 66, 181, 304, 340, 424, 430
Monash, General Sir John, 191, 324
Monson, Thomas S., 119
Moody, Dwight L., 487
Moore, George, 10, 228
Moore, Henry, 48, 270, 295, 336, 396
Moore, Marianne, 236, 517
Moorehead, Robert, 328
Monroe, Marilyn, 28, 126, 554

Montagu, Ashley, 349
Montagu, Lady Mary Wortley, 62
Montaigne, 168, 429
Montgomery, James, 5, 470
Montgomery, Lucy, 427
Mooddie, Susanna, 294
Moody, Dwight L., 471, 481
More, Hannah, 479, 482
More, Sir Thomas, 119
Moreland, John Richard, 493
Morely, Christopher, 123, 160
Morgan, Charles L., 220—221
Morgan, Marabel, 164
Morgan, Robin, 332
Morgenstern, Christian, 396
Morley, Christopher, 202, 320, 345, 381, 552
Morley, John, 76, 113, 375
Moroccan proverb, 181
Morris, George Pope, 141
Morrison, Jim, 527
Morrison, John A., 139
Morrow, Dwight, 430
Mortman, Doris, 79, 243
Moses, Grandma, 9
Moskin, J. Robert, 200
Mother Teresa, 34, 108, 115, 441, 454, 463
Motto on U.S. Coins, 451
Mt. 6:3, 50, 51
Mt. 6:6, 481
Mt. 7:1, 507
Mt. 7:7, 480
Mt. 10:22, 151
Mueller, Robert K.
Mueller, Walter A., 488
Muggeridge, Malcolm, 57
Muhammad, 130
Mulford, Prentice, 532
Mull, Martin, 165
Muller, Robert, 500
Mumford, Ethel Watts, 187
Mumford, Lewis, 320
Muncey, Bill, 302
Munson, Gorham, 283
Munthe, Axel, 75
Murdoch, Iris, 124
Murphy, Thomas P., 18
Murray, Andrew, 482, 486, 492
Murray, W.H., 324

Peirce, Charles Sanders, 361, 468, 501
Penn, William, 7, 184, 244, 422
Penn-Lewis, Jessie, 476, 493
Pepys, Samuel, 481
Perelman, S.J., 119, 371
Pericles, 5
Perignon, Dom, 218
Perret, Gene, 313
Perry, Gaylord, 86
Persian proverb, 195, 227, 266, 335
Persig, Robert M., 389
Peter, Laurence J., 147, 176, 332
Peterson, Tom, 74
Petit-Senn, J., 171, 252
Petronius, 128, 461
Phelps, Austin, 438
Phelps, William Lyon, 144, 217, 225, 255, 338, 409
Phil. 4:6, 469
Phil, Sidney J., 87
Phillips, Bum, 87, 90
Phillips, Frederick, 295, 441
Phillips, Wally, 422
Philo, 526
Picard, Jean-Luc, 419
Picasso, Pablo, 128, 188, 233, 348
Pickford, Mary, 47, 292
Pierce, John, 430
Piercy, Marge, 171, 247, 412
Pierro, Antonio, 1
Piggy, Miss, 549
Pike, James A., 78
Pindar, 50, 65, 67, 77, 129, 319, 332, 342, 349
Pinero, Arthur Wing, 51
Pirandello, Luigi, 204, 274, 275, 323, 349, 362, 374, 431
Pirsig, Robert M., 40, 90, 274, 342, 456
Pitkin, Walter B., 4
Pitt, William, 366
Pittacus of Mitylene, 24, 438
Pius XI, Pope, 352
Plante, Jacques, 141
Plath, Sylvia, 441
Plato, 12, 57, 64, 94, 104, 110, 133, 207, 277, 341, 436, 521
Plautus, , 181, 249, 368, 467

Plies, Dan, 479
Pliny, the Younger, 9, 227
Plumer, William S., 468, 482
Plutarch, 16, 23, 34, 182, 265, 291, 535
Po, Li, 264
Poe, Edgar Allan, 226, 236, 346, 407, 467, 548
Pollock, Channing, 82, 255
Polybius, 154, 157
Ponder, Catherine, 496, 504
Poole, Mary Pettibone, 56
Pope, Alexander, 113, 173, 232, 287, 403, 453, 464, 499, 509, 538, 541
Pope John XXIII, 167
Pope Pius XI, 352
Porchia, Antonio, 542
Porter, Cole, 56
Porter, Jane, 218
Porter, Katherine Ann, 424
Potter, Stephen, 428
Pound, Ezra, 239, 241
Powell, General Colin L., 379
Powell, John, 373
Powers, David Guy, 45
Powers, Llewelyn, 204, 360
Powers, Thomas, 122
Prather, Hugh, 42, 44, 78, 80, 302, 488, 533
Prayer From the North Woods, 487
Preistly, J.B., 45
Prentice, George, 526
Prentiss, Elizabeth, 147
Presley, Elvis, 102, 106, 123
Presnall, Lewis F., 159
Price, Vincent, 203
Prince, 220
Princess Diana, 132, 559
Priscian, 180
Prochnow, Herbert B., 285
Propertius, 376, 545
Proust, Marcel, 101, 303
Prouty, Olive Higgins, 545
Proverb, 167, 367, 426, 428, 459, 467, 510
Proverbs 14:21, 215
Proverbs 18:22, 546
Proverbs 30:8, 110
Prv. 3:5-6, 448
Prv. 27:17, 195
Ps. 55:17, 478
Ps. 90:12, 20

Ps. 95:2, 490
Ps. 104:23, 15
Ps. 111:10, 137
Ps. 139:23-24, 472
Punshon, William M., 375, 391
Purana, Garuda, 97
Purkiser, W.T., 256
Pushkin, Aleksandr, 507
Putnam, Vi, 221, 456
Puzo, Mario, 557
Pythagoras, 14, 336

Quarles, Francis, 197, 297, 487
Quincy, Josiah Jr., 122
Quisenberry, Dan, 53

Rabelais, Francois, 57
Rachmaninov, Sergei, 102
Racine, Jean, 511
Rader, Doug, 322
Radford, Arthur, 320
Radiguet, Raymond, 17
Radner, Gilda, 242, 556
Raleigh, Sir Walter, 74
Ram, N. Sri, 139
Ramsey, Arthur M., 520
Ramuz, C.F., 256, 532
Raspberry, William, 392
Rathbone, Josephine, 206
Raven, Arlene, 85, 420
Rawlings, Marjorie, 551
Ray, John, 137
Ray, Marie Beynon, 401
Ray, Sondra, 80
Rayburn, Sam, 559
Reagan, Nancy, 228, 297
Reagan, Ronald, 48, 149, 258
Reardon, Daniel L., 413
Rees, Paul, 487
Reeve, Christopher, 316, 419
Reeves, George, 418
Regnard, Jean Francois, 258
Rehrat, Arthur J., 507
Reid, Thomas, 450
Reik, Theodor, 201, 457
Reiland, Karl, 205, 535
Reiner, Carl, 66
Renan, Ernest, 510
Renard, Jules, 62, 127, 133, 249

Sarnoff, David, 272, 370, 399
Saroyen, William, 138, 161, 251, 310, 454
Sarton, May, 20, 78
Sartre, Jean-Paul, 440
Sasson, Remez, 271
Saunders, Allen, 263
Sawyer, Charles, 466
Sayers, Dorothy, 181
Saying, 227, 229
Scalpone, Al, 165
Schabacker, Ruth Ann, 246
Schaef, Anne Wilson, 341
Schell, Maria, 107
Schiff, Miriam, 412
Schmich, Mary, 168, 174, 333
Schmidt, Walt, 295
Schnabel, Arthur, 105
Schneider, Diana, 420
Schopenhauer, Arthur, 27, 29, 47, 82, 98, 282, 527
Schreiner, Olive, 168, 528, 534
Schuller, Dr. Robert H., 284, 404
Schulz, Charles M., 170, 217, 230, 301, 331
Schumann, Robert, 238
Schwab, Charles M., 390, 395
Schwartz, Morrie, 559
Schwarzenegger, Arnold, 305
Schweitzer, Albert, 220, 232, 342, 375, 382, 458
Scofield, Paul, 395
Scolavino, William F., 329
Scott, C.P., 426
Scott, Evelyn, 327
Scott, Sir Walter, 175, 177, 182, 293, 300, 413, 456, 463, 539
Scottish proverb, 181, 182, 534
Seabury, David, 289
Seale, Bobby, 5
Sedgwick, Gen. John, 419
Segal, Erich, 541, 544
Segall, Lee, 258
Selden, John, 487
Sellers, Peter, 230
Sendak, Maurice, 253
Seneca, Marcus Annaeus, 8, 22, 47, 68, 83, 87, 107, 125, 139, 191, 194, 246, 247, 251, 263, 264, 276, 296, 343, 345, 382, 435, 442, 457, 512, 525, 528, 530
Senegalese proverb, 438
Sennet, Mack, 56
Service, Robert W., 66, 153
Seton, Julia, 174
Setter, Maurice, 247
Seuss, Dr., 5
Sexton, Anne, 5
Shackelford, Ted, 114
Shakespeare, William, 1, 7, 15, 44, 48, 62, 69, 75, 76, 87, 99, 103, 140, 159, 163, 167, 168, 170, 179, 192, 253, 254, 261, 262, 263, 304, 307, 318, 336, 353, 422, 455, 465, 466, 484, 544, 552
Shankly, Bill, 261
Sharif, Omar, 555
Sharp, William, 539
Shaw, George Bernard, 10, 60, 63, 94, 99, 121, 153, 166, 171, 208, 220, 277, 303, 337, 360, 370, 372, 389, 436, 438, 501, 507, 543, 550, 552
Shedd, John A., 442
Sheen, Fulton J., 93, 96, 403
Sheerin, John B., 93
Sheldon, Charles M., 49
Sheldon, William H., 205, 370
Shelley, Percy Bysshe, 461
Shenstone, William, 260
Shepherd, Jean, 124
Sheridan, Richard, 104
Sherrill, Billy, 560
Shinn, Florence Scovel, 358, 374
Shirer, W.L., 216
Shirley, James, 501
Shoemaker, Samuel M., 476, 478
Shoffstal, Veronica, 50
Sibbes, Richard, 491
Sidey, Hugh, 59
Sidney, Sir Philip, 533
Siegel, Bernie S. M.D., 80, 304, 311, 496
Sills, Beverly, 161, 223, 314
Simon, Julian, 256
Simonton, O. Carl, 459, 465
Simpson, A.B., 468, 480
Simpson, Alan, 313
Simpson, Wallie, 132
Sinclair, Upton, 144
Singer, Isaac Bashevis, 411, 449, 526
Sitwell, Edith, 335, 415
Sivananda, Swami, 329, 382
Skelton, Philip, 204
Skelton, Red, 4, 547
Skinner, B.F., 537
Slack, W.B., 474
Slater, Philip, 162
Slick, Grace, 46
Small Change, 250
Smalley, Dave E., 506
Smedley, F.E., 542
Smedley, Ralph C., 379
Smeltzer, Ruth, 9
Smiles, Samuel, 151, 282, 397
Smith, Adam, 207
Smith, Alexander, 18, 173, 265
Smith, Ashley, 235
Smith, Edgar, 149
Smith, Frederick Edwin, 431
Smith, Jack, 26
Smith, Logan Pearsall, 144, 187, 219, 240, 247, 331, 368, 381, 533, 549
Smith, Mortimer, 495
Smith, Patti, 434
Smith, Roy L., 253, 258
Smith, Stan, 82
Smith, Stevie, 236
Smith, Sydney, 15, 40, 161, 246, 338, 345, 349, 386, 433, 466, 549
Smith, Will, 428
Snow, C.P., 210
Snyder, Gary, 261
Sockman, Ralph W.D.D., 12, 310
Socrates, 140, 192, 202, 255, 261, 340, 455
Sokoloff, Dr. Boris, 203
Solzhenitsyn, Aleksandr, 203, 277, 368
Sondheim, Stephen, 241
Sondreal, Palmer, 212
Soong Mel-Ling, 493
Sophocles, 14, 98, 145, 172, 175, 186, 188, 221, 223, 264, 270, 290, 335, 426, 542